D1422576

Building
Information
Modeling

Building Information Modeling

BIM in Current and Future Practice

Karen M. Kensek,
LEED BD+C, Assoc. AIA

Douglas Noble, FAIA, PhD

WILEY

Cover images: Courtesy of CO Architects; Los Angeles County Natural History Museum,
Otis Booth Pavilion
Cover design: C. Wallace

This book is printed on acid-free paper.

Library of Congress Cataloging-in-Publication data is available upon request.

ISBN 9781118766309 (cloth); 9781118766378 (ebk.); 9781118766613 (ebk.)

Printed in the United States of America

10 9 8 7 6 5 4 3 2

Contents

Foreword

BIM IN EDUCATION—TRANSFORMING THE PROFESSION

No one denies that architecture directly addresses crucially important realms, as we are reminded in discussions of sustainability, various forms of public health, and safety. It has a direct role in dealing with human comfort and well-being. It has huge impacts on energy, water and resource needs, and later with refuse. Yet here in the United States, only tertiary attention to the science and systematic development of knowledge in these domains is undertaken by schools of architecture. They rather tend to focus on the composition of form and space as the assemblers and composers of products and technologies. The technologies dealing with resources, energy, and most aspects of well-being generally have been picked up, developed, and applied by other professions, usually within engineering including structural, energy, acoustical, and other types of phenomena. As a result architecture has the primary responsibility for a declining range of issues and decisions within the construction industry. Explanation for this observable trend is liability and risk. Another may be the traditional size of firms offering architectural services. They do not have the scale needed to support this range of services, although consulting firms, often manned with architects, do offer these services. Is this a premonition for the development and use of BIM in architecture? Will it be outsourced to consultants, like CAD services have been, to satisfy contractual requirements? Is it a tool mainly for contractors?

University schools of architecture are the training ground for future architects. How is BIM being accepted in the universities? It was my hope and I think the hopes of other early developers of parametric modeling of buildings—the earlier, more general name of systems before the acronym BIM was conceived—that parametric modeling of buildings would provide the leverage to re-capture the issues dwindling from the profession's grasp. BIM was thought to facilitate and integrate assessment of functionality, performance, and increasing complexity to give architects better technology to integrate these new aspects into design with those already integrated regarding the more subjective social well-being and aesthetics. It was hoped that future architects would consider all these central issues within the field.

This book serves as an early milestone for examining the status of the BIM endeavor in the universities. From this viewpoint, it can also be used to assess other perspectives dealing with the interaction of social values and technology in design. It offers an implicit review of the relation of architecture to the new technological environment of modern society. With twenty-six chapters by a diverse set of mostly North American authors, the volume offers a good sense of current thinking in universities. To date, the potential uses and impacts of BIM have only been partially explored. What will be the external impacts of new technologies, —for example, having close to infinite computing power available everywhere, with integrated sensors increasingly leading toward smart buildings, and new smart materials, and tablet-based access? How is architecture likely to evolve technology-wise as we move through the twenty-first century?

There are several repeating themes in these chapters. One deals with BIM's ability to accelerate current design processes, through faster iteration cycles regarding structure, cost, lighting, air flows, costs, schedules, and other assessments, to realize close to real-time feedback. Faster design is not the end goal. By making such feedback quickly, the experiential and systematic development leading to better alternatives and integrating multiple evaluations leads to better design. Tracking the results, the client can see the value added through design, generating better value for the client. Multiple chapters discuss the expected richer set of services the BIM potentially offers building project clients/owner (Bernstein and Jezyk; Kalay, Schaumann, Hong, and Simeone; Trubiano; Goldman and Zarzycki).

Bernstein and Jezyk lay out the evolution path for BIM, based on these analysis/simulation cycles posed by other authors. They point out the changes in design process enabled by tightly coupled design and simulation/analysis, and the potential values and added benefits that can be offered by architecture when increasing dimensions of design are directly viewable and measurable. The question is posed whether the architecture schools will rise to incorporate these ranges of intellectual contribution.

One particular aspect received special attention regarding feedback: energy usage. The chapters by Hemsath, Sanguinetti et al., Yan, and Donn offer methods for integrating both the automatic generation of zonal energy models and feedback for interpreting the many multidimensional data results. A variety of design-supporting feedback options are proposed and prototyped. Energy considerations are not best unitized only at the level of the building; heat islands and energy recovery schemes from high-heat generating buildings suggest that neighborhoods and urban zones provide important unit of analysis and energy system designs. Some of the approaches are reviewed in the chapter by Baird, Ramesh, Johnstone, Lam.

Kalay et al. provides an important critique of current BIM models, regarding their limited ability to represent functional, behavior, comfort and other essential aspects of building space. Their critique suggests several paths for research and innovation. Akin's chapter lays out a different set of research and development areas, dealing with interoperability and further improving BIM's basic usability and facilitation of collaboration.

There seems to be broad recognition that architectural design will have an increasingly strong analytical base. There is a professional need to develop market differentiation to support these services. A variety of organizational structures (in-house departments, consultants) will support these knowledge areas.

Another theme is the benefits of customizing BIM tools for special problems, and to provide unique services. While custom design styles and materials is one path (Beorkrem), Burry lays out the need and context for metaBIM, where design innovation leads to the customization of the tool and the designs are co-developed more or less in parallel. The results are outlined in the astounding *Sala Creuer* above the nave of Sagrada Familia, now being constructed.

Embedding enhanced design expertise is another theme. Sheward and Eastman offer two examples of embedding design expertise into BIM environments: automated conceptual level layout of high-rise building cores and air-handling equipment in laboratory buildings to gain instant feedback of laboratory building layouts from this major energy perspective. The design firm CASE (chapter by Davis and Miller) examines different kinds of analytics applied to BIM models and develops "dashboard" types of feedback for use during design. These include analytics at the design project scale, regarding productivity, number of revisions, and other project data. They develop methods of workflow integration. Other firms are providing similar services. This is a step recognizing, like Integrated Project Delivery (IPD), that processes are crucial determinants in product success.

As a business, architecture provides a service that has been licensed since the early days of the last century. Predominantly composed of small partnerships, the AIA had until recently ethical covenants prohibiting financial involvement in projects, advertising, and delimited the services that could be offered. Only in the last 40 years have these culturally defined limitations been partially removed. Today, architecture has as its core service the production of a set of drawings, sufficient for civic governmental approval (code check) and for construction bidding on the project. The AIA contract forms provide variations on these roles for other forms of project delivery. Bid documents have always been incomplete, with major references to standards of practice, which have been accepted in construction law. BIM addresses many of these issues and in some areas challenges them. They all add to the complexity of fully integrating BIM into current practices. It forces recognition of the design intent level of modeling as distinguished from the means-and-methods level of fabrication models. There is growing recognition that the recognized collaboration benefits of BIM are also reducing the scope of value adding services at the fabrication level. Harfmann's chapter airs these concerns while also addressing the issue of one BIM versus many (also Johnson and Kensek).

BIM allows addressing new areas of focus. A primary objective of the architectural design is the design and composition of space. Spaces were only represented diagrammatically until recently. Hagan presents an insightful review of the explicit representation of space and the role of GSA in its development. BIM tools still do not facilitate the full modeling of a space with its surfaces fully apparent for review. Krishnamurti, Toulkeridou, and Biswas examine the development of topological structures for representing systems, including circulation systems, in IFC models.

Ahrens and Sprecher describe how the immense potential of sensor data might be used aesthetically as well as analytically to enhance building experience. They rightly point out the uncertainty associated with computational simulations.

Deamer provides a valuable perspective on the role of BIM managers within architectural offices, using information from BIM managers themselves. Her chapter offers advice on the nature of the work, its rewards, and frustrations. Gu, Singh, and London address BIM project and office management at the more operational level. Martens and Peter report on an important issue for the future: archival data and its maintenance.

Akin emphasizes the cognitive challenge required to address the new complex and detailed information required of full deployment of BIM technologies. I would also note, in addition to his insights, the great facilitation that 3D modeling provides as a more direct link to cognitive experience.

It is replacing the arcane notations embedded in traditional architectural drawings and the manual mapping and management costs of generating and maintaining 3D renderings. Other authors (Gu, Singh, and London; Clayton; Paranandi; Kam; Davis and Miller) provide their insights on the nature of BIM.

To summarize, this volume provides strong indications that the integrative and rich simulation capabilities offered by BIM are being adopted, further developed, and integrated into architectural education. The topics addressed in the volume offer strong agreement and support with the new capabilities emerging almost monthly, some based on work produced by the authors of this volume. We can expect to see integrated analysis/simulation tools foremost for energy, lighting, and comfort, but also for costs and various forms of human activity and emergencies. Architectural practice and the schools will be moving strongly into a data-rich design environment. It is apparent that BIM practice, although already different from earlier forms of CAD-based architectural practice, is certain to undergo additional changes that will continue to improve our ability to build sustainably and to build more effectively, creatively, and economically.

The demand for customization is already apparent in the BIM community; it is a growing need. Some firms are already selecting BIM platforms based on the need to be able to customize and extend the object classes, to better control parametric behavior, and to integrate different simulation/analysis tools. The tying into generative plug-ins and with performance application interfaces will become more visible priorities in offices that are interested in supporting new market capabilities and differentiation. Architecture has an exciting future.

This volume provides a good roadmap of where we are going, in the schools and in practice. Written by BIM leaders, the agenda defined here will depend on the leadership of the authors and their advocates in practice and university administration.

Chuck Eastman
Georgia Institute of Technology

Acknowledgments

ACCOLADES FOR CHAPTER AUTHORS

When the idea for this book was proposed, the chapter contributors were passionate and supportive. It was their enthusiasm, energy, and expertise that helped bring the proposal through to completion. Editing a book with a large number of authors requires tact, patience, and tenacity. Not having these skills, we would like to sincerely thank the writers for responding positively to our communications even when we were demanding immediate responses regardless of international and national time zones. We could not have completed this book without their support and deep knowledge of the field.

Many of the authors gathered to discuss draft chapters with one another in a face-to-face meeting held at the University of Southern California, School of Architecture, in Los Angeles in summer of 2013. By coming together we were able to discuss our ideas and hone them for this book. While the USC School of Architecture has supported our work for more than two decades, we must also thank the dozens of other universities and professional firms that supported each of the individual authors.

SINCERE APPRECIATION FOR OTHER THOUGHT LEADERS

Over the years, leading architecture, engineering, and construction firms have presented innovative work at the USC School of Architecture annual BIM symposia. We thank the firms for their participation, but more importantly for the inspiring work they are doing in pushing BIM as both a design and construction tool. Advances in the theory and practice of building information modeling are just as likely to come from the profession as from university research. The editors are grateful to those from the professionals who were able to take time from their primary work to provide insights into BIM innovations from practice.

There are even more thought leaders not in this book than those contained within. The advances in building information modeling have been accomplished by leading researchers in academia, architecture, and construction who advance the profession through the use of technology, and sophisticated clients who are demanding better ways of constructing and operating buildings. The ideas in this book represent more than the thoughts of the forty-three contributing authors. There are many others who have made important content suggestions. To keep the size of the book manageable, unfortunately many of the world's leading BIM authorities are not included as chapter contributors. Even though their work is not directly contained here, they deserve a standing ovation for their work and their leadership into the future.

Finally, we are colleagues at the same institution and have collaborated for more than a quarter of a century. This history has given us advantages as we worked together, bumped heads, and tried often to amicably edit this book together.

Karen would also like to thank her husband, Joe Pingree, for supporting her and her work.

Karen Kensek
Douglas Noble
University of Southern California

Introduction: On the Theory and Practice of BIM

Karen M. Kensek, LEED AP BD+C, Assoc. AIA

BUILDING INFORMATION MODELING

Building Information Modeling (BIM) is fundamentally transforming modes of design practice and standards of building design, delivery, and operation. BIM has matured from object-based parametric modeling developed by innovative software companies and university research programs into suites of software programs widely used in the architecture, engineering, and construction professions. BIM has gained rapid acceptance in architecture and engineering schools, the building design and delivery professions, the construction and manufacturing industries, and by building owners and managers.

BIM is not CAD. In some respects BIM is a natural progression in the evolution of computer-supported practice. However, much more so than CAD, BIM is revolutionizing the way the building partners practice and document their work, even changing the nature of the design process. While computer-aided design provided some tools to support new ways of working, CAD adoption was heavily based on direct substitution of existing practice modes. In the early years of CAD, debates raged about the potential detrimental impacts that CAD might have on design and practice. Early CAD was essentially divorced from building analysis, and CAD was frequently employed by a separate technical team within the firm. Sharing even basic CAD data was initially difficult, and the pace of CAD adoption in professional practice was slow. Architects could integrate CAD into the workflow without significantly improving the way consultants, clients, and contractors worked. The decision to adopt CAD usually involved discussions of drafting speed, ease of making updates, and the limited benefits that might accrue with enhanced accuracy. In later incarnations of CAD, three-dimensional computing added capabilities, including visualization and clash-detection.

BIM is landmark technology that dramatically alters the way participants work and interact, and opting-out is not a real choice. BIM is engaging design analytics in ways that allow architects to make far better performance-based decisions. As BIM tools allow for deeper comprehensiveness, the tools are better at revealing accidental conflict earlier in the process. BIM processes are giving each of the stakeholders new appreciation for the work of the other players in building design and delivery, and we are seeing increased potential for engagement of building owners, managers, and occupants in the process.

Although BIM is now widely adopted, the broader potentials for BIM implementation and process are not yet uniformly achieved, and the foundations for a truly analytical and comprehensive BIM are just starting to be built. Highly successful BIM will require new ways of design thinking and reasoning, and the BIM leaders in the profession and at the universities can provide important insights into current and next-generation BIM.

The 2008 publication of the *BIM Handbook* (Eastman et al.) provided powerful examples of BIM use "for owners, managers, designers, engineers, and contractors." That seminal book is a compilation of the state-of-art in BIM technology both for its thorough background examination of BIM (including chapters on BIM tools and parametric modeling, interoperability, and stakeholder specific information) and its case studies of ground-breaking implementations of BIM (including the El Camino Medical Office Building, the Beijing National Aquatics Center, and the San Francisco Federal Building). Since 2008, several additional excellent books have been written that focus on different aspects of BIM's potential use for sustainable design, construction, facilities management, building owners, and others.

Building Information Modeling: BIM in Current and Future Practice is not intended to duplicate the structure or content of the *BIM Handbook*, which was updated in 2011. This book assumes that the reader understands the fundamentals of building information modeling, is aware of the diversity of software tools that are available for implementation, and has observed case studies where BIM improved the design, construction, and delivery of notable buildings. This book stretches the boundaries of BIM and challenges the profession to examine its full potential by considering, for example, how BIM could support design thinking and reasoning, support simulation, and provide insights into the profession and the direction it is heading.

Continuing advances in BIM teaching, research, and practice are resulting in new tools and improved approaches to software integration and collaboration approaches. At the forefront of these advances, there are a few dozen individuals who have established themselves as global "BIM thought leaders" for academia and the professions. These are the people who are leading the transformation of the way professionals and students think about BIM integration. These individuals are challenging us to reconsider what building information modeling could become, to expand the ways BIM is used in practice, and to rethink the structure and content of the tools themselves. As the technology evolves, even more voices are contributing to the discussion.

This book contains an edited compilation of provocative essays providing a forum for many leadership voices in the marketplace of ideas about building information modeling in architecture. They provide clarity and direction for thinking about the current practice and the future directions of BIM, instigating commentary by foremost thinkers about both research about BIM and speculation into the future of BIM. The chapters cover a range of topics, from theoretical research that can inform future BIM performance-based design to commentary on current issues in BIM such as "single BIM" versus "multiple BIMs" and the role of materiality in the age of digital.

The twenty-six individual chapters can be read in any order as each is a self-contained node sharing overlapping ideas with other chapters. They are grouped together thematically in six sections with others that present both complementary and sometimes incompatible positions: Design Thinking and BIM, BIM Analytics, Comprehensive BIM, Reasoning with BIM, Professional BIM, and BIM Speculations.

DESIGN THINKING AND BIM

"Design Thinking and BIM" (Part 1, chapters 1 through 4) begins with a concise overview of BIM by Goldman and Zarzycki that sets the stage for the rest of the book. It describes attributes of BIM, including evaluation of visual information, parametric modeling (generative abilities and limitations), how analytic modeling can drive design, and the assertion that materiality should be part of a comprehensive BIM. In contrast, Akin approaches design thinking from a psychological approach, elaborating cognitive strategies for BIM. He observes that whereas software maximizes choices, "the designer tries to reduce variables that cause cognitive overload." That cognitive stress is mitigated by the correlation between specific tools that BIM provides and the historical shared architectural ontology, based on a taxonomy of concepts and relations among them. Considering BIM in this manner ties its abstract computational data structures and regulating lines to parallel ideas in architectural theory (Clayton).

The incorporation of design thinking into BIM is the premise of Sheward's and Eastman's proto-types for knowledge-based building information modeling. Their goal is to take the deep understanding of experts and incorporate them into tools that help designers at the early stages of design.

BIM ANALYTICS

In "BIM Analytics" (Part 2, chapters 5 through 12), several similar themes tie the chapters together, including the critical need for performance-based design driven by intelligent use of simulation software, the power of parametric modeling in support of analytics, and current inadequacies of software inter-operability. BIM plus analysis tools for simulation can help architects achieve sustainable design goals. This can happen at many different times during the design process and at varying levels of complexity. A "proto-BIM," a 3D model, can assist with shadow casting and wind studies. Conceptual whole build-ing energy modeling during the early design stages is easily achievable even with the somewhat limited interoperability that exists between software programs. And high performance design extends beyond energy concerns to other areas of efficiency and life-cycle modeling. Professionals and designers need to be aware of the issues that affect the use of BIM for simulation. Recently, applications have become available that "automatically" find optimal solutions for complex trade-off problems such as windows, heat gain, and savings from daylight harvesting. Although not yet integrated into BIM software, steps are being taken in that direction.

Important new research questions have been uncovered, and building simulation software needs to address important issues of complexity and computability for achieving current goals and new applica-tions in physical BIM and parametric BIM-based energy optimization (Yan). Bernstein and Jezyk bring both industry and academic expertise to exploring the ramifications of BIM 1.0 evolving to BIM 2.0

and the affordances this allows design empowerment and integration of technology in the practice of architecture. Energy modeling during conceptual design, sensitivity analysis of the parameters, and optimization are available now (Hemsath). This extends not only to individual buildings, but also to district energy systems, one example of BIM being used for urban energy information modeling (Baird et al.).

Dashboards are one mode that designers and owners have of understanding building performance. Collaboration between tool crafters and users is showcased in this "new theater" of design practice (Davis and Miller). In order to perform the energy calculations during the early stages of design, the building model needs to be broken into thermal zones, a subtle yet critical aspect of energy modeling (Sanguinetta, Paasiala, and Eastman). Yet one cannot overlook the role of the analyst in performance simulation, whether that is an architect or consultant, a student, or professional. The original dream of BIM is the integration of many different digital design decision support tools (Donn), but the user has to understand the real material aspects that describe the building in order to have the virtual model behave properly and give results that can be trusted.

The last chapter in this section straddles BIM Analytics and Comprehensive BIM. Whereas the previous authors demonstrated the use of BIM plus analytical modeling for predicting performance, Kensek categorizes the many types of BIM including the AIA Levels of Development (LOD), "BIM Light," and "BIM fragments," privileging those that allow for simulation. Chasms of interoperability lead to questions of the value of federated or comprehensive BIMs as potential solutions.

COMPREHENSIVE BIM

In what direction is the profession heading, and is it the correct way to go? Although BIM can be described as "a digital representation of a physical entity, whether existing in the physical world or intended to exist in the future; an integrated, structured database, informed by the building industry, and consisting of 3D parametric objects." It is fair to say that "BIM" is neither comprehensive nor singular in how it is currently being implemented. Understanding the theoretical issues of why this is so will provide deeper understanding into other practical questions such as: "Why did the contractor create his own model," "Will the client be able to use the BIM for building operations?" and "Are there other frameworks that are different from how we are currently categorizing BIM?" This chapter does not answer these specific questions, but it provides educated opinions concerning the nature of an all-inclusive BIM.

The chapter authors of "Comprehensive BIM" (Part 3, chapters 13 through 15) agree to the consequences of a "single" BIM versus "many" but differ as to resolutions. After a brief review of the history of BIM, Johnson delineates the limitations of a single model, a BIM unity, by exploring the implications it has on complexity, cognition, and culture. By a completely different rationale, Harfmann concludes that a single component-based BIM linked to manufacturer databases is valuable to the architect and contractor. His BIM is more nuanced than most, however, in that it allows for a digital model that is light on embedded information but requires externally linked information to real building components. This allows for improved design coordination and construction while inherently recognizing that building component geometry differs in meaning by those who rely on it. Gu, Singh, and London sidestep the entire issue and explore the establishment of BIM ecosystems and how products, processes, and people have to co-evolve for progress to continue. This is based on their understanding of the fundamental characteristics of BIM (representation, documentation and information, inbuilt intelligence and analysis, and collaboration and integration). Their result is a flowchart for a collaborative BIM decision framework.

REASONING WITH BIM

"Reasoning with BIM" (Part 4, chapters 16 through 19) covers a diverse set of topics of importance to the profession. Fabrication is probably the one most concrete. Our buildings are designed virtually. Yet they intended to be physically constructed and occupied. Computer numeric controlled (CNC) machines take the digital and create the real. But software can hamper or deaden the sensitivity of designers to the actual characteristics of the material.

Beorkrem argues that designers must not lose sight of materiality and the practical aspects of fabrication even when using computational tools to generate form. A bit more esoteric, the chapter by Krishnamurti, Toulkeridou, and Biswas formulates a method for data extraction from spatial topology. Building upon these ideas, a theoretical prototype is defined for using green building certification requirements with the extracted model for assessing the data and representing it in formats as required by the agencies.

How students reason and collaborate differs from professionals. But in both cases BIM can be used as a catalyst for encouraging creativity and collaboration. Social frameworks and computational workflows that include collaborative prototyping, crowd-sourcing, and knowledge capture and storage in the cloud can be created to assist with this (Paranandi).

Is it reasonable to use BIM for long-term projects? Martens and Peter have an ongoing, fifteen-year-long project of documenting destroyed synagogues. They discuss issues of virtual construction with a lens toward longevity of model information. Their experiences have practical benefit for office managers considering methods of keeping their data and drawings "alive" for expected renovations and retrofits in the future.

PROFESSIONAL BIM

"Professional BIM" (Part 5, chapters 20 through 23) is not a collection of practical case studies, although certainly those would have value. Instead, these chapters focus on broader concerns. For example, what is a successful BIM building and/or process? How can one determine if the architecture firm, compared with others, is taking full advantage of the BIM ecosystem? One evaluation process is described; its weighted metrics are based on planning, adoption, technology, and performance. Quantifying BIM performance allows firms and owners to assess their current level of BIM maturity and use that information to improve their own implementation of BIM (Kam).

Space is not only critical for defining architecture, but necessary for defining programmatic needs. It is a simple concept (e.g., what rooms are needed by the client; how big are they; who uses them?) and is linked to data that is critical, especially for owners in charge of a lot of real estate. Spatial BIM benefits the clients, owners, and facilities managers while providing for the needs of the occupants (Hagan). Going beyond spatial information, Trubiano asserts that "building information modeling affords the building industry an important opportunity for expanding the range, comprehensiveness, and critical dimension of how buildings are conceived, fabricated, and simulated. Not only is it capable of altering the architect's relationship with construction, it is equally adept at transforming the profession's engagement with architectural design and building operations."

BIM "is a systemic innovation in the AEC sector that impacts all aspects of the industry, beyond just the development and adoption of a specific technology." Deamer presents a compelling argument that BIM is not just about optimizing building design and construction, but instead it provides an opportunity to explore the processes of an office from the role of the BIM manager to reconceptualizing the entire firm organization.

BIM SPECULATIONS

The book ends with "BIM Speculations" (Part 6, chapters 24 through 26) and invites the reader to consider other modalities of building information modeling. Users are reexamined as a primary stakeholder in the building, but ones that are often ignored in simulations that attempt to predict the performance of the building (Kalay, Schaumann, Hong, Simeone). This is one hurdle that designers of high-performance buildings will eventually have to overcome as accusations are already being made that some buildings are not performing as the simulations foretold. Further research into the actions of the occupant need to be coupled with the software.

In addition, a more fully developed modeling system will also represent form, function, and use as part of the building components' definitions. Information modeling is proposed as the next iteration because the BIM is not just about the building as an artifact, but includes transdisciplinary knowledge unique to its context, program, and performance (Ahrens and Sprecher). Burry reports on how he and his team produced precise building information through a shared model that is beyond conventional BIM capability and in conclusion, provides fundamental points for the continuing development of BIM: metaBIM.

THEORETICAL FOUNDATIONS

It would be inaccurate to characterize building information modeling as a thoroughly new idea, or simply a product of industry software development dating from the earliest releases of programs that have become relatively mainstream in the architecture and construction industry today.

Instead, its pedigree stretches back to those first builders, architect-contractors, who envisioned for their clients something grander than a large house for ceremonial or religious purposes. This was a remarkable transition as it not only managed to create a new profession, a middle class of craftsmen, and cohort of workers, but sharply marked a divide between vernacular architecture where everyone had the common information and skills necessary to build their own homes, to "architecture" that employed specialists and arcane knowledge. The complex construction management projects called the pyramids, engineering feats of the aqueducts, the soaring edifices of cathedrals, and the earliest skyscrapers before the invention of computers—these also depended on "building information models." In each of these cases, the architect-contractor created a mental model, physical representations, and drawings to inform the client, develop the design, and communicate with the tradesmen and unskilled workers. The image this evokes is that of the master builder, pointing into the uncompleted vault of the cathedral and discussing details of design and construction with the stone cutter. It is not difficult to mentally transform that image to that of a project architect, squinting, with a tablet computer held to the sky, listening to the structural steel detailer describe how the complex joint is going to be achieved.

The virtual design model is a meta-version of the BIMs that have come before. Plans, sections, and elevations, critical tools to previous generations of architects, are mere queries to its 3D database. It can also produce the perspectives used by Renaissance builders and even physical models through 3D printing and CNC milling. It assists in the communication between the design, construction, and facilities management teams. It allows for collaboration, analysis, and scrutiny of the design process.

Yet, twenty years from now (or probably less), BIM will be labeled something completely different, include features yet unimagined, and run on computers that make ours seem as slow and limited as slide-rulers. The theoretical underpinnings, however, remain the same and are based on the earliest idea that architecture transcends the mundane and that designer-builders need tools to translate their mental models to their collaborators to achieve their visions.

Software Mentioned

The chapter authors in this book discussed many software programs. Many others are used in the profession that were not referred to. The book authors are software agnostic and do not specifically endorse the products mentioned. However, the names of these software programs are often trademarks of or copyrighted by their respective companies and are listed here in recognition of that. We apologize if any were inadvertently left off.

3DVIA Virtools

Aconex and Team Binder

Adobe Illustrator

Adobe Photoshop

Athena EcoCalculator

Autodesk 3ds Max

Autodesk 3ds Max Design

Autodesk AutoCAD

Autodesk BIM 360 Glue

Autodesk Dynamo Visual Programming for BIM

Autodesk Ecotect

Autodesk FormIt

Autodesk Green Building Studio

Autodesk Maya

Autodesk Navigation

Autodesk Navisworks

Autodesk Revit

Autodesk Revit Architecture

Autodesk Revit Structure

Autodesk Vasari

AutoDeSys form•Z

Bentley Architecture

Bentley GenerativeComponents

Bentley MicroStation

bimSCORE

BREEAM (rating system)

Building Design Advisor (BDA)

Building for Environmental and Economic Sustainability Tool (BEES)

CASE Design Iteration Dashboard

CASE Plastarc

CASE/Autodesk comparative energy instrument

CASE/Snohetta daylight instrument

CASE/SOM BIM Dashboard

CATT

Chameleon

Corel Draw

Corel PaintShop Pro

Dassault Systèmes CATIA

Dassault Systèmes SolidWorks

DAYSIM

DesignBuilder

DIVA

DOE 2.0

EnergyPlus (US DOE)

eQuest

ESP-r

ESRI ArcMap

ESRI ArcScene

ESRI CityEngine

Galapagos

Geco

Gehry Technologies Digital Project

Google Earth

Graphisoft ArchiCAD

Green Globes (rating system)

IES<VE>

KieranTimeberlake Research Group—Tally plugin

Kjenner of Manasc Isaac Architects, SU2DS Sketchup to Daysim exporter

LBNL Modelica Buildings

LEED (rating system)

Linux Operating System

Maxis, the Sims

McNeel & Associates Grasshopper

McNeel & Associates Rhino

Microsoft Excel

Microsoft Word

Microsoft Visual Studio

MIT Design Advisor

Mozilla Firefox

Multiplan

Nemetschek Vectorworks

NREL interface for EnergyPlus OpenStudio

NREL SuNREL

Odeon Room Acoustics Software

Onuma Planning System

Open Source light rendering software Radiance

Open IFC Tools

Protégé

PTC CADDS5

Radiance

Rahe Kraft SU2CATT exporter

Rahe Kraft SU2ODEON exporter

RUCAPS

Sketchpad

Solibri Model Checker

Thomas Bleicher's SU2RAD

Trelligence Inc. Affinity

Trimble Sketchup

TRNSY

PART 1

DESIGN THINKING AND BIM

CHAPTER 1

Smart Buildings/Smart(er) Designers: BIM and the Creative Design Process

Glenn Goldman, New Jersey Institute of Technology
Andrzej Zarzycki, New Jersey Institute of Technology

1.1 INTRODUCTION

Despite the myth of the heroic architect, popularized by Ayn Rand's novel *The Fountainhead*, whose Howard Roark–like designs spring entirely from personal inspiration, architects and engineers need information to design buildings. Few people today question the needs of the clients and/or users so at least a rough program of activity spaces is usually embedded within the design process if it doesn't precede the actual building design. But there is a lot more information that helps architects make decisions during the design process. While it may not be possible to know everything involved in the design and construction processes prior to the completion of a building, there are assumptions that having information is better than not having it, that informed decisions are better than uninformed ones, and that design is a knowledge-based activity. If one does not object to designing with information that includes maximizing building performance, budgeting, and material optimizations, then building information modeling (BIM), almost by definition, has the potential to improve the products and processes of architectural design.

Building information modeling provides the implied promise of integrating all types of needed data into one file or model (perhaps with separate but linked files with easy bilateral information transfer). While the fulfillment of that promise depends, in part, on both the pace of commercial software development and academic researchers, any current lack of a single integrated information model is not a reason to avoid the process. Furthermore, as long as there are competing products for use by architects, the features and ability to integrate different types of data are likely to vary. As architects are by nature and profession optimists, the type of integrated data and information in this discussion may not (always or currently) be ubiquitously available, but the information not available in the application of choice, may and probably will (or at least should) be part of and contained within any future development.

Tools are needed for form-making, simulation and analysis, and document production. Clearly these tools may be discrete, or they might be combined into one or more separate applications. A value of reducing the number of separate tools is to facilitate the ability to cyclically and iteratively move back and forth between tasks, especially between schematic design (of which form-making is a part) and analysis (which may rely on simulation). Note that none of these relationships assume an artificial intelligence or machine-determined decision-making process. While that may be possible at some point, its desirability is not assumed, and the purpose of using BIM in this case is to use the attributes of computational, information technology-enabled design to provide any member of the building design team with information helpful in making decisions. It is critical to understand, however, that success in the integration of BIM into the design and building delivery process relies, at least in part, on a combination of robust hardware and software.

Digital media in general, and building information modeling in particular, have the ability to inform the very beginning of the design process. The ability to associate data with geometry allows designers to begin to (1) integrate technical and performance criteria at early stages of design thinking while including advanced visualization capabilities and (2) algorithmically and/or iteratively test design implications. BIM starts redefining the way design ideas are generated by bridging formal creativity with design and technological innovation through a close integration of parametric generative tools, through the introduction of physically accurate digital materiality, and through intelligent database-enriched digital objects. Finally, BIM affords the architect (and client) an opportunity to include life-cycle assessment as part of the design process when considering alternatives. As design implementation in BIM becomes more tightly intertwined, there is the potential to combine multiple roles in the design process much in the way that "typists" have been replaced as authors write/type and compose with one tool. BIM also facilitates bridging across disciplinary boundaries.

It now remains to determine the kinds of tools that can facilitate creativity and innovative thinking within the design process. Creativity tools need to provide design feedback, help designers to gain new experiences, and allow for unexpected associations with pattern-breaking functionalities. They need to allow for inductive and lateral thinking, as well as to connect with broader expertise from other building delivery team partners.

Present BIM platforms have a legacy that derives from a combination of early CAD software and visualization applications—all of which are based on geometric logic. The software relies on shapes and forms to delineate architecture. Moreover, there is a proclivity to look at or define a building as a set of parts, components, or "families." As such, it promotes mainly visually driven design validation in an additive design process. The other component of the current BIM platform, the database, is usually implemented as an extension of geometry, an attribute of a model. It is rarely a part of a broader datascape that considers user behaviors, functional patterns, relationships between the cost and performance, simulation of energy use, or life-cycle analysis. In a design context BIM may be used to evaluate form, to look at generative abilities of parametric models, and as a tool to see how analysis can drive (or at least influence) the building delivery process.

1.2 EVALUATION OF VISUAL INFORMATION: FORM

The attributes of BIM software allow it to be used for schematic "uninformed" design—a designer can do everything he or she wanted to do with "dumb software" (i.e., applications restricted to geometric modeling) or pen and pencil by:

- "Turning off" associated attributes and designing with geometry (e.g., rectangular solids or surface models rather than walls)
- Visualizing with rendering and ignoring realistic lighting (e.g., shadows as if the sun rises in the north) or actual material attributes (even visual attributes).

BIM applications have progressed to the point where they may be effectively used to visualize form with materials by adding realistic finishes with reflectivity, texture, and color, thereby enabling the designer to judge based on visual criteria (in or out of context) (Figure 1.1).

It is possible in both BIM and non-BIM geometric visualization applications to parametricize components so that not all repetitive elements are one-off objects (e.g., provides the ability to change all or one window at a time when evaluating a façade based on visual criteria/composition). This ability facilitates smooth interaction in an iterative design process that is essential for any tool and saves time over the use

FIGURE 1.1   BIM models account for material properties, lighting levels, and furniture layouts. While providing a visual feedback to designers and clients, they also keep track of types and schedules for construction components, finishes, and furniture.

(Images courtesy of Mina J. Liba—left, and Peter Fritzky—right. Designed, modeled, and rendered with Autodesk Revit. Grayscale conversion and image processing with Adobe Photoshop and/or Corel PaintShop Pro)

FIGURE 1.2   Parametric variations of the column and space frame connection detail.
(Images by George Ricardo Miller. Designed, modeled, and rendered with Autodesk Revit. Grayscale conversion and image processing with Adobe Photoshop and/or Corel PaintShop Pro)

of traditional media, which effectively improves creative operations. For example, associative attributes of parametric models allow for autonomous resolution of the edge condition between various elements and are imperative in relieving designers from continuous verifications and modifications of design changes.

1.3 GENERATIVE ABILITIES OF PARAMETRIC MODELS

Parametric relationships offered by current BIM platforms facilitate generative processes by allowing design versioning while maintaining integrity of an overall assembly. Figure 1.2 shows a number of design variations of a column-to-space frame detail. Through parametrically defined interoperabilities within the connection, a design can morph between multiple states and at the same time preserve the logic of the construction detail. This is an important associative quality that distinguishes BIM from CAD models. However, while this approach provides an effective tool for design versioning and assembly resolution, it also lacks broader validation criteria such as performance, costs, and material usage that would provide designers with other than just visual feedback. This limitation is characteristic of most generative software applications that utilize algorithmic and geometric procedures without physics-based form-making mechanisms.

1.4 HOW LIGHTING, THERMAL, AND STRUCTURAL CONSIDERATIONS CAN DRIVE THE DESIGN

The ability to add technical information specific to components, context, and/or place can provide valuable information during the design process. The ability to apply this information during the design process does not require the elimination of traditional visual evaluation, but does imply that the designer should consider multiple criteria when making decisions. The following three lists on lighting, thermal performance, and structure provide some examples of data that can/should be added as part of a true building information model.

1. Lighting
   - Using exterior location data to test illumination inside a building when looking at the size of windows.
   - Adjusting design elements based on site data (e.g., exterior shading devices, interior light shelves).
   - Specifying luminaires and lamps and testing light distribution visually (interactively test against surface reflectivity and color; change lamps within luminaire; add, remove, modify reflectors).
   - Associating calculations for lumen levels on surfaces (Figure 1.3).
   - Providing life-cycle assessment of lighting.
2. Thermal performance
   - Modifying the wall construction to compare thermal performance, and other wall attributes: thickness, weight, space, details, finish options, cost, and more.
   - Interactive calculation of internal loads (large buildings) may be tied into engineering decisions that affect space allocation (e.g., lighting loads, HVAC equipment, heat sinks/cooling towers).
3. Structure
   - Modifying structural system at different levels (e.g., concrete vs. steel; size of structural bays/distance between columns) and visually seeing different implications (e.g., heavy vs. light).
   - Detailing parametric variation with visual results (note that this is the kind of work architects and designers did in traditional structures classes).

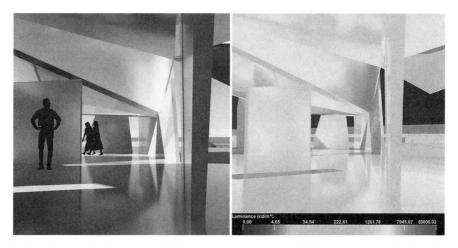

FIGURE 1.3   (Left) photorealistic image, (right) the same image with luminance mode showing the levels of surface illumination in candela per square meter (cd/m2).

(Images by Travis New. Designed, modeled in McNeel & Associates Rhino and rendered with Autodesk 3DS Max. Image composition and grayscale conversion and image processing with Adobe Photoshop and/or Corel PaintShop Pro)

An important feature of future BIM platforms would be to provide multiple modes of data visualization, both quantitative and qualitative, that can relate to diverse types of communications and user's needs. Decision making may be heavily influenced by way information is represented. Creativity and new ideas are often triggered by an unconventional look at the already known problem. Solutions emerge when various perspectives are considered.

1.5 LIMITATIONS OF CURRENT PARAMETRIC MODELS

A number of current BIM packages allow for establishing parametric relationships between various model components by feeding values from one object into another (Figure 1.4). However, they still function within limited scope without bi-directional feedback loops. Parameters are passed along established routes in a linear manner that reinforces the hierarchical and didactic design processes rather than providing opportunities for unexpected discoveries. With most of modeled components functioning as inert geometries and deprived "smart" behavior, they relay data "down the stream" rather than allow for a multidirectional dialog and interoperability. While they work effectively in producing outcomes based on initial assumptions (operands), they are incapable of reversing the reasoning sequence and using the outcomes as starting points to examine initial design assumptions.

The goal is a platform where members of the building delivery team could reexamine initial design decisions at any point in the process, including topics such as construction types, budgetary constraints, site placement, and/or program adjacencies, and substitute them with new priorities. This would facilitate the inquisitive "what if . . ." explorations with building performance data, carbon footprint, or material substitutions as design informing factors.

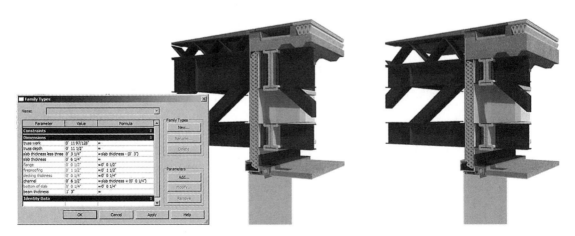

FIGURE 1.4   Parametric relationships are passed between various assembly components.
(Images by Alexander Merlucci, Nicholas Giuliano, and Aidan Migani. Designed, modeled, and rendered with Autodesk Revit. Grayscale conversion and image processing with Adobe Photoshop and/or Corel PaintShop Pro)

The bi-directional interoperability is particularly important when considering multiple, often competing, design criteria and the need to solve for the most optimal collective solution, not a single variable. Additionally, clients' priorities change and so do the site and marketplace conditions. Consequently, an effective computational design delivery platform needs to accommodate the volatility and uncertainty of the design process.

1.6 PHYSICS AND MATERIALITY

What other input will be critical for future BIM models to support the design process? In addition to associative quality of geometry and parametric relationships, the physics-based behaviors, materiality, and more intuitive user interface are among the most pressing needs for an effective computational design platform. The lack of materiality considerations hinders the creative process when considering current digital or analog design tools. With the ability to generate complex forms, designers sometimes operate within scaleless and etherlike environs that bear little resemblance to actual built designs. Materiality and physics-based behavior brings a scale and "bite" into otherwise abstracted forms. Emerging design BIM platforms need to consider physicality of the final product and be able to account for it in all design stages. This physical awareness needs to be both quantitatively expressed in units and costs and qualitatively contributing to a designer's intuitive understanding of performance and informing his/her tacit knowledge.

While materiality and physics-based behavior is critical, in understanding design implications, assembly and manufacturing processes as well as a broader impact on material usage and life-cycle analysis are equally important. Current tools allow designers to model more complex designs than those that can be effectively built or solved. When digital fabrication combined with NURBS surface modeling results in fabrication strategies that produce a significant amount of material waste, the issues of material usage optimization and zero-waste designs become critical. The project in Figure 1.5 investigates this condition by analyzing design methodologies for form-making and form-solving. Unfortunately,

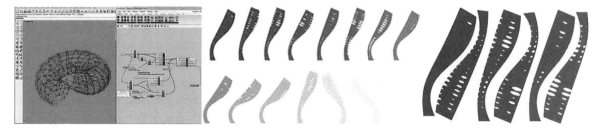

FIGURE 1.5 Initial form-finding exercises led to the discussions on material usage in fabrication and zero-waste strategies. Form-finding for pneumatic design with generative/algorithmic tools (right). Unrolled and fragmented surface of the pneumatic form (center). Finding complementary unrolled components to optimize material usage (left).

(Images by Gayatri Desai, Edward Perez, and Joseph Ribaudo. Designed and modeled with McNeel & Associates Rhino, Grasshopper, and Kangaroo. Graphic layout with Adobe Illustrator and/or Corel Draw. Grayscale conversion and image processing with Adobe Photoshop and/or Corel PaintShop Pro)

in this particular case, the zero-waste part of the project relied significantly on the analog try-and-see method to optimize material layouts. Computer tools provided limited value in addressing this important design consideration.

Future BIM platforms need to account for fabrication and manufacturing processes in order for designers to consider them in their design process. This is a particularly pressing issue since many current designers empowered by fabrication technologies expand the traditional definition of an architect into the maker (master builder) of architecture. This is evident is emerging innovative practices such as SHoP where architects assumed a broader role similar to what was historically considered a master builder. These new practices not only take responsibility for building design but also are aspects of fabrication and oversight of the overall construction delivery. Furthermore, their contribution toward a project goes beyond design intent and often involves industry research and technology/tool development. These practices are the next step in the evolution of the traditional integrated team delivery (ITD) project with much closer collaborations between thinkers and makers. As with the traditional ITD projects, the success of these emerging practices depends on the unified building information platform that guarantees a high level of integration and efficiencies due to the greater level of building delivery control. However, with such highly interconnected and finely tuned design-build pipelines, there is a question of system adaptability, and continuous creative evolution remains to be explored for best possible outcomes.

1.6.1 Solving for Multiple Criteria

Most simulation and optimization approaches such as genetic algorithms allow for a single variable optimization and usually solve for a local optimal solution rather than a global one affecting many variables. This limitation applies to both analog and digital design process where designers address a limited, and often narrow, number of variables without fully investigating all possible scenarios. Architectural design requires solving for multiple criteria based on a particular value judgment. Solving for multiple variables, developing higher-level evaluation mechanism, and going beyond genetic algorithms would provide more effective creative tools. Furthermore, the ability to adaptively reprioritize evaluation criteria during the lifespan of the project would provide a better fit with real-life situations.

1.6.2 Other Data Types

Parametric relationships should go beyond geometric properties and include other data types such as building performance or user behavior. These data types need to feed into form- and space-making while considering constructability, assemblies, and user experience. Whereas solar or lighting analyses are effective tools to inform a designer's thinking and are helpful in justifying a particular course of action, they often do little to quantify design in terms of the actual performance particularly from the multiple criteria perspective.

For example, the following question is not uncommon when designing a curtain wall. What are the benefits and drawbacks of a large glazed façade from the standpoint of solar gains, thermal losses, natural lighting, and possible condensation issues? While it is common for designers to latch on to a single criterion to justify their preferred design directions, an actual quantification of the competing design objectives would provide designers and clients with a broader understanding of their decisions and ultimately with better performing buildings. While the current state-of-the-practice assumes that all these are part of mental validation processes designers consider when designing a building, these processes are often based on intuitive thinking and unquantified experience rather than on sound and current data. This also limits clients' ability to understand a design decision process and shape it in an informed way.

1.6.3 Soft Constraints

While parametric definitions can be effective design aids in relating multiple assembly components, their binary state functionality (works or does not work) sets a serious limitation for design explorations. Designers experimenting with parametric systems may get overconstraint messages from BIM software when there is a conflict between various competing parameters. However, this does not provide constructive feedback that can help advance the design. What is needed is a soft constraint platform that communicates to the designer the degree to which the design is working. The qualitative message "you are 95 percent there" is more effective from the design process viewpoint than the mechanical response "overconstrained; it does not work."

The case study shown in Figure 1.6 demonstrates such functionality achieved with chipboard models of kinetic assemblies using scissor mechanisms. In this case, the physical material used for the

FIGURE 1.6 Materiality (digital and analog) provides valuable design feedback and facilitates problem solving.

(Images by Elvira Hoxha, Michael Middleton, and Travis Stracquadanio. Image composition and grayscale conversion and image processing with Adobe Photoshop and/or Corel PaintShop Pro)

mock-ups provided enough flexibility and strain to allow for the soft constraint functionality. Students were able to use interactions with physical models to understand kinetic movements of their designs and later bring them within a computational platform for further design explorations and resolutions. What was learned from this case study was that while physical interactions were helpful, materiality of a model was critical in providing the desired design feedback. Using acrylic glass or other rigid material would not provide the same results as chipboard models. This suggests that computational materiality employed in a similar manner could also be an effective response for soft constraint system.

1.7 DESIGN AND CONSTRUCTION 2.0

Analogous to Web 2.0 functionalities that utilize context-awareness, track user interactions and preferences, and incorporate crowd-sourcing, the future BIM platform may find it worthwhile to break away from a single data node mindset and become a part of a broad data-sharing network. This raises several questions:

- Can the experience of one designer contribute to the success of another one?
- Can data make the design process and design knowledge modular enough to be quantified, compared, and shared?
- What is required of the BIM platform to facilitate broader collaboration, knowledge transfer, and experience building?

Of course, this may posit a somewhat different business relationship between owner, architect/interior designer, contractor, and facilities management personnel as well as a redistribution of liability. Nevertheless, "turf wars" aside, there are opportunities that could be *technically* feasible that would benefit future designers. It is possible, for example, that the collection and (re)distribution of data (with appropriate identity protections) may create an entirely new area for employment. For example, some architects could specialize in development of fully integrated digital prototypes (virtual prefabs) that can be used as parametrically flexible design modules. These design assets could be reused by others and franchised as long as the digital building models would allow for easy and flexible parametric reconfigurations, thus leading to genetic standardization of architecture and formatting it into universalities that go beyond the traditional one-off designs. Additionally, this could lead toward considering designs as forms of intellectual property, not unlike the situation with tangible objects.

1.7.1 Context-Aware Data

With the exponential growth of datasets and design models, the question of filtering information, just-in-time, and just-in-place functionalities is critical. Having access to relevant information at the appropriate level of abstraction or detail would streamline design process and eliminate unnecessary trial-and-error attempts. While often criticized for the requirement of too-much-data-too-early in the design process, future BIM platforms could adapt its dataset into the level of the design resolution. While this is a representational rather than systematic issue, the initial data required by a BIM model would not have to be input by a designer, but it could be intelligently guessed based on the past or similar projects. The key consideration is how the data and knowledge developed on the past projects or by other designers could feed into new work.

Other aspects of context-aware data refer to associative qualities of BIMs that would develop lateral connections between various design components as well as the contextualization of design within a particular locality (environment, codes, process, and construction culture), culture (human factors), and types of users. Furthermore, with the "Internet of Things" on the horizon, the building information models need to include a persistent monitoring, data gathering, and connectivity with everyday objects.

One note, however: It must be acknowledged that there could be a danger in creating formulaic algorithmically derived design with information that would actually work against lateral thinking that leads to conceptual breakthroughs and innovation. To avoid this, designers must still be educated in and facile in the ability to manipulate all of the criteria traditionally associated with good design and architecture.

1.7.2 Beyond a Single Lifespan of the Project

Future building information models need to facilitate the extension of the dataset use beyond single project or a single designer. While there is a significant discussion about extending the use of BIM into early design stages and into the post-occupancy, these are not sufficient. Certainly, building information models can help in the management of facilities, maintenance, and operations especially when coupled with mobile technologies such as an augmented reality platform (Figure 1.7).

FIGURE 1.7 Augmented reality (AR) environments provide a location-awareness platform for combining data and video camera feeds to facilitate more effective construction and facility management.
(Image by Andrzej Zarzycki. Image composition and grayscale conversion and image processing with Adobe Photoshop and/or Corel PaintShop Pro)

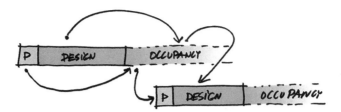

FIGURE 1.8 BIM platforms have the potential not only to facilitate better building design, construction, and management, but also allow for experience building and knowledge transfer between various projects. Predictive versus actual performative data from past projects could and should inform future design practices.
(Image by Andrzej Zarzycki. Image processing with Adobe Illustrator and/or Corel Draw)

However, a more significant repositioning of BIM and the design process is necessary. Design by its nature is a proposition (intent) that is realized by a contractor erecting the building and later tested by the owner and users. In any effective design process one would expect a number of feedback loops connecting users, builders, and designers to validate initial design assumption and techniques used to realize them. This design-build-test approach is prevalent in other design disciplines and is effective in improving product quality. Unfortunately, architecture does not follow this model, and when it claims it does, it does so in a very loose and unsystematic way, relying on scattered information gathering and sharing. This situation creates an opportunity and necessity for future BIM platforms to address the need for validation of assumption, simulation, and projection used to design the building. When done properly, designers will be able to learn from past projects in a clear, quantified way and transfer this knowledge into future designs (Figure 1.8).

Imbedded sensors monitoring buildings' operations could feed data gathered back into the BIM model and verify this against initial simulation models. This would not only provide an opportunity to verify design assumptions and simulations but also to reflect upon the construction techniques and material quality. In such a scenario, the BIM platform would emerge as a broader virtual building model that parallels its physical counterpart and is continuously used to fine-tune building performance throughout the life of the building. In this new role, virtual models become software components that operate physical hardware of an actual physical structure. Digital models that were used to design, analyze, and simulate performance continue their existence as a building operating software.

The predictive value of current simulation tools is limited unless it can be closely tied to actual building performance monitoring and is later used to refine future BIM-driven designs. Iterative design processes that include feedback from constructed buildings incorporated into future designs are important for good design practices. Presently, the architectural profession depends on human designers to accumulate knowledge about specific building efforts. However, in actual practice, designers, architects, and engineers often are not involved in post-occupancy lives of their project. They may lack the time or expertise to comprehensively evaluate their design.

Finally, information modeling and data sharing refocuses the design process from the one-of-a-kind creativity to an iterative and sequential process of prototyping and knowledge building. It facilitates the development of design(er) memory encoded into data model that can be passed from one building into another, from one designer to another, continuously and progressively refining the outcomes.

1.8 CONCLUSION

Emerging computational technologies are the latest in the long line of agents informing the way we work, innovate, and ultimately how we think and who we are. Creativity is perhaps the most cherished and unique of all human attributes. As such, an intersection of creativity and technology becomes a critical opportunity that informs design professions and provides great promise toward our future.

While technology redefines the surrounding world, it also needs to reflect/consider it with its various intricacies, physical behaviors, and materiality. Designers not only need to model materials, energy usage, or lighting but also follow up on built designs and learn from previous work.

Remote building monitoring interconnected with building information models can provide an effective creative feedback loop to improve designs we build and help us to understand a broader impact on the environment. It can quantify the quality of construction labor and material performance as well as our own designs.

This accumulated knowledge can benefit all members of the building delivery team if it persists beyond the life span of a single project in the form of a shared experience that can be passed between various individuals asynchronously and feed into other construction disciplines and the outside world. The experiences gained by clients, architects, engineers, contractors, and facility management personnel throughout the project can be useful to policy makers, residents, or first responders. A recently constructed building may become an important player in the neighborhood for the resource sharing and providing new services for other buildings.

The emerging common denominator to these propositions is a broader unified building information modeling platform that reflects the complexities and aspirations of professionals involved in the building delivery process as well as the social and cultural roles. Current BIM products represent early stages of the ultimate platform that are progressively advancing their scopes and the role they play in practice.

DISCUSSION QUESTIONS

1. What criteria should/could be considered in a building information model to improve its usefulness in the design phase of a building?
2. What are some of the dangers of relying on single-optimization or algorithmically generated solutions to building design?
3. What long-term opportunities may arise from extending BIM beyond the life of a single project and sharing data?
4. What opportunities are there to integrate augmented reality into building information models and in what ways could this prove useful?

BIBLIOGRAPHY

Clayton, M.J., O. Ozener, J. Haliburton, and F. Farias. "Towards Studio 21: Experiments in Design Education Using BIM." In K. Goosens. and L. Agudelo. eds., *SIGraDi 2010 Proceedings of the 14th Congress of the Iberoamerican Society of Digital Graphics*, SIGraDi, Bogota, Columbia, 2010, 43–46.

Decker, Martina. "New Materials Compositions." In Rashida Ng and Sneha Patel, eds., *Performative Materials in Architecture and Design*. Chicago: Intellect, University of Chicago Press, 2013.

Goldman, Glenn. "Digital Media and the Beginning Designer." In *IEEE Computer Graphics and Application*, vol. 32, no. 2 (March/April 2012), pp. 14–21.

Pasquarelli, Greg. Closing Keynote, *ACSA 101: New Constellations/New Ecologies. Annual Conference*. March 23, 2013. San Francisco, CA, https://vimeo.com/63902910.

Zarzycki, Andrzej. "Dynamics-based Tools: An Unusual Path to Design Integration." *ACM SIGGRAPH 2009 Asia Proceedings*, Yokohama, Japan, 2009, (DVD ROM).

CHAPTER 2

Necessity of Cognitive Modeling in BIM's Future

Ömer Akin, PhD, AIA, Carnegie Mellon University

2.1 INTRODUCTION: SOME USEFUL CONCEPTS

Human beings cognize their daily tasks through mental models. Normally these cognitive functions appear to be fluid and painless since these skills are honed over decades of training that often takes place spontaneously as we act to achieve goals (Newell and Simon 1972). In most cases these mental models are tacit (Polya 1973), and we do not have to be self-conscious about them. Building information modeling, on the other hand, is one of the most challenging cognitive tasks that designers face (Akin 1989). We cannot deal with these tasks with our tacit and intuitive cognitive skills alone. While the tools and methods at our disposal allow us to explicitly represent all that that is needed during the long and tedious design delivery process (i.e., all of the processes and products of design, construction, and facility management) there is nothing intuitive about these tools and their interface functions that are supposed to connect our mental models to the internal functions of the computer code by which they are governed. When it comes to the capital project delivery (CPD) process, our cognitive skills for daily problem solving, while still necessary, are not sufficient (Figure 2.1).

The average CPD problem involves at least one million physical products, thousands of person-hours, months of dedicated work, expenditure of millions of dollars, and a plethora of expert consultants who rarely speak each other's language or share each other's tacit mental models. Building information modeling (BIM) technology attempts to mediate all of these challenges. It is no wonder that it has taken more than half a century and dedicated work by individuals as well as product vendors in computer aided design, drafting, and manufacturing (CAD-D/CAM) to make a dent in this challenge.

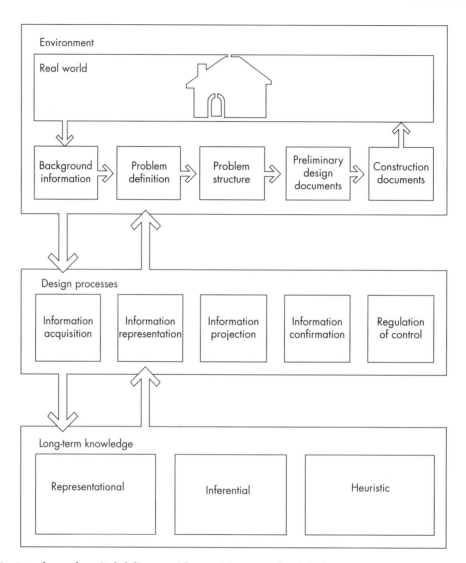

FIGURE 2.1   Interface of capital delivery with cognitive models of design.
(Akin 1989; Figure 4.2, p. 57)

In spite of this mammoth effort, the task is still incomplete. One of the most challenging and rarely addressed aspects of this mission is how to intermarry digital models of building information with cognitive models of designers.

It is important to stress that this is only one of the many challenges of BIM. Clients and users require that products provide reliable performance, are delivered on time, and are within resources available (Akin 2012). In order to address this, the industry has risen to the occasion by targeting *lean delivery* of *green products* (Klotz and Horman 2007). The integrated design process (IDP) approach is but one

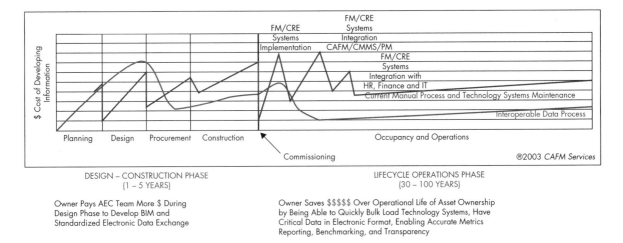

DESIGN – CONSTRUCTION PHASE
(1 – 5 YEARS)

LIFECYCLE OPERATIONS PHASE
(30 – 100 YEARS)

Owner Pays AEC Team More $ During
Design Phase to Develop BIM and
Standardized Electronic Data Exchange

Owner Saves $$$$$ Over Operational Life of Asset Ownership
by Being Able to Quickly Bulk Load Technology Systems, Have
Critical Data in Electronic Format, Enabling Accurate Metrics
Reporting, Benchmarking, and Transparency

FIGURE 2.2   Saw-tooth model of information acquisition and loss in CPD.
(Courtesy of Fuhrman. (2004), "Pay now or pay later," diagram, International Facility Management Association, Houston, TX)

of these approaches that promises to address the historic challenges of the industry: budget, performance, and schedule (Larsson 2009). Interoperability—the ability to use results of each step in the CPD with the next stages seamlessly—is paramount in addressing these goals (Figure 2.2). Finding problems earlier rather than later in the process is a significant time and money saver (Figure 2.3). Naturally, BIM, because of its ability to deploy intelligent tools for design, appears to be the appropriate choice for addressing these issues. This further heightens the importance of solving the problems endemic to the interaction of digital models with cognitive ones.

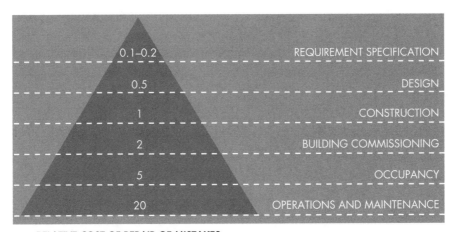

RELATIVE COST OF REPAIR OF MISTAKES

FIGURE 2.3   Cost of repair in phases of design delivery.
(Based on Kelley et al. 1993)

2.2 BUILDING INFORMATION MODELING: THE BRAND NEW WORLD OF DESIGN COMPUTING

The idea of BIM, neither novel nor new, is extremely timely. It has advanced quite rapidly, past the emergence stage of a paradigm shift, and has become a full-blown movement. The context for its support is present and robust. In BIM, as is the case in all movements that enjoy unprecedented coalescence of support from diverse quarters, its context is the key to its persistent success. This context is defined by some of the factors already described earlier: the need for management of large data repositories, intra-task collaboration, and smart representations. Existing systems, such as Autodesk's Revit, provide evidence to make a case for interoperability, while not along horizontal lines crossing entire facility lifecycles, but at least along "vertically integrated business functions" (NIBS 2007).

The lack of lifecycle interoperability is probably the most acute productivity issue that the AEC (architecture, engineering, construction) sector faces. In the current manual process, there are repeated information buildup efforts required at the beginning of each phase and major information loss at the end. By and large, this can be avoided in the "interoperable data process" modality (Figure 2.2). This point underscores both the promise and the challenge this movement currently faces. Even as professionals witness the publishing of a standard for BIM by NIBS-FIC and the authoritative handbook on the subject by Eastman and colleagues (2008), the direction and prospects for success of BIM are still being hotly debated, even by those who are responsible for its inception.

The *BIM Handbook* by Eastman and colleagues provides good coverage of the tools that are available and their interoperability and data standardization rages. It also considers the future of BIM and how it can help transform the future of this effort in the AEC industry. This is a fast-moving target, and it is still being formed by the market forces and nearly three decades of research started by Eastman and Fenves back in the early 1970s at Carnegie Mellon University.

However, some claim that BIM exhibits the classical signs of what is currently wrong with the AEC sector: disjunctive and distributed data, practices, and "standards" (Tardif 2008). While there appears to be some consensus around this position, ideas about potential remedies seem to be uncertain. Should there be a standard BIM practice and ontology centrally maintained and controlled? In the near future, how realistic is it to achieve such a centrally placed BIM system? For the sake of realistic expectations, should a coordinated but distributed BIM be supported? Is this difficulty an artifact of the culture and turf of building construction, rather than digital technology? Are there existing organizations and systems that can become the "natural" stewards of the centralized BIM, like *buildingSMART* alliance of NBIMS? This intense debate around BIM has been fueled by several concurrent technologies, including the modeling software offered by CAD vendors, the process and product model standards offered by international agencies, such as Standard for the Exchange of Product Model Data (STEP), International Agency for Interoperability (IAI), their third-party contributors, and the communication networking enabling remote operations, through the Internet.

In an effort to implement these concepts underlying BIM in the CAD marketplace, many software vendors are taking preliminary but serious steps toward object-oriented (OO) modeling and exchangeable data formats. The challenges that remain include the seamless extension of these capabilities to tasks outside of the core architectural ones, such as mechanical, structural, electrical, egress, emergency, and cladding systems. Further extensions are needed to cover other CPD stages that are not currently covered, like requirements engineering and building commissioning. The challenges are in the volatility of product and process information, lack of standards and standardization, lack of interoperability protocols, and industry's slow acceptance of digital data standards and exchange strategies.

Advancements in building performance simulation over the past two decades have been significant, including new and improved computational tools that address the changing needs of architectural design throughout the CPD life cycle. The ultimate goal of BIM is evolving into the support of sustainable architecture and the creation of healthy, comfortable, and productive habitats for human activities. Ironically, defining such human activities accurately in performance modeling remains probably the single most complex and challenging task.

While the above areas of application signify the core developments in the domain of BIM there are several important developments they do not cover: intelligent graphics, architectural robotics, requirements modeling, performance evaluation, requirement specification, construction site modeling, building commissioning, operations maintenance and management, and economic modeling. Graphics has been a bulwark of early computational design. In fact it has been almost a synonym for BIM from very early on (Sutherland 1963, Chan 1994, Moustapha and Akin 2004). One of the intellectual extensions of the work in the graphic realm into pioneering applications can be found in the physical manifestation of design by digital technology. This includes digital fabrication technologies at one end and architectural robotics applications at the other.

One of the critical areas of CAD emergence in the AEC sector is in the area of modeling for construction site management and planning (Akinci et al. 2008). This is one of the most critical phases of CPD that potentially impacts a building's cost, schedule, and quality most significantly. There is a plethora of application areas in BIM, including construction process planning, modeling, prediction, and control through the use of remote sensing, data encoding, laser technology, simulation, solid modeling, and the like (Akin 2012). Once a building is turned over to the owner, its operation, maintenance, and management challenges begin in earnest (Lee and Akin 2009). Often from the first day there are insurmountable issues of setup, calibration, diagnosis, repair, alteration, as-built records, user requests, inventory record keeping, emergency intervention, and routine maintenance, some of which are excellent candidates for BIM applications.

Finally, there is a great need to develop intelligent assistance for economic decision making in BIM for all facets of the CPD process. New economic models are emerging that take into account not only the traditional economic modeling issues like discount rates, net present value analysis, and value engineering, but also the real estate and design added value analysis (Akin 2012).

2.3 COGNITIVE STRATEGIES FOR BIM: CHALLENGES AND OPPORTUNITIES

In 1956, George Miller, a cognitive scientist at Princeton University, published his seminal work describing the span of human short-term memory (STM). The details of his findings notwithstanding, this

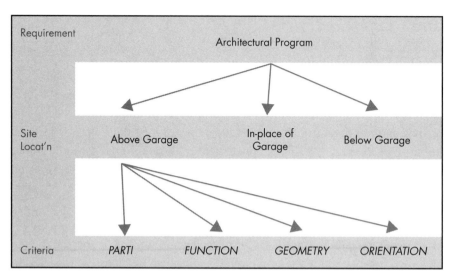

FIGURE 2.4   Decomposition of the design problem.
(Akin 2010)

was the beginning of understanding that humans are able to attend to a very limited number of bits of information at any given point in time (i.e., 3 to 7). Subsequently it has also been learned that people use clever methods like mnemonics and employ the vast resources of their long-term memory (LTM) to extend their information-processing capabilities considerably (Chase and Simon 1973).

This may be the most significant singular reason to pay attention to cognitive factors in improving the performance of BIM systems. Whereas recent advances in human-computer interaction have had a significant impact on software and product development in many areas of commerce and marketing (John et al. 2012), its impact on CPD software has been less significant. In an ethnographic analysis of one of the leading CAD software systems at the time, it was discovered that while around 20,000 different commands were at the disposal of each designer, on the average they used around 20 commands to address most if not all design tasks before them (Bhavnani 2000). Clearly the model of design in the BIM world is one of maximizing choice, whereas the designer tries to reduce variables that cause cognitive overload. Thus it is necessary to recognize that designers in a BIM environment would want to

1. *Apprehend stimuli, selectively.* This is a form of built-in bias that protects the cognitive system from information overload. In fact, the limited span of the STM is a "structural" device to create an intentional bottleneck to slow down the free flow of information. Thus human cognitive systems make us focus instinctively on certain aspects of our environment while filtering out others. In the case of design, this means that we chose that upon which to attend. There are very few BIM systems that help the designer filter information by using self-defined criteria of elimination. Evidence shows that designers create their own views of things that consist of unique assemblies made of decomposed parts of the design problem (Figure 2.4). In this design episode,

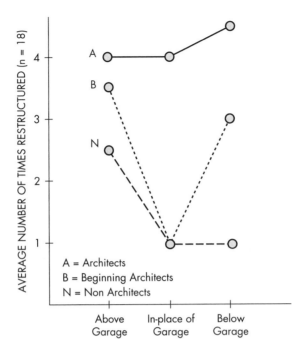

FIGURE 2.5   Iterative approximations of a given design solution decomposition illustrated in Figure 2.4.
(Akin 2010)

the designer first breaks the problem up into three alternative site positions and then into four design criteria: *geometry, function, orientation,* and *concept.*

2. *Use a divide and conquer strategy.* Once the design problem is decomposed into mnemonically sensible parts, the BIM system should also allow designers to engage unique process sequences. This is neither supported by the categories and views one can create by combining the commands presorted into groups, sub-groups, and sub-sub-groups on the menu bar; nor the objects, types or instances, modeled as entities that can be moved around in the database. Furthermore, these cognitive chunks of information do not map onto predefined expertise-related assemblies either—such as energy analysis, LEED compliance testing, emergency egress and movement simulations, structural analysis, clash testing, quantity takeoff data, or scheduling. Designers prefer to create iterative approximations of the same design solution over and over again, each time modifying a limited set of design parameters (Figure 2.5). In this example, expert designers demonstrate that they generate four different solution alternatives within a span of 30 minutes. Rarely do BIM software systems support the designers' "navigation" in a space of potential solution alternatives without resorting to external memory aids. This, at a minimum, requires robust version control functionality.

3. *Integrate distinct but dependent information sets, systematically.* After the design problem is decomposed into parts, the individual partial solutions need to be assembled together to create a singular design alternative. Once again, evidence from cognitive process studies suggests that this is

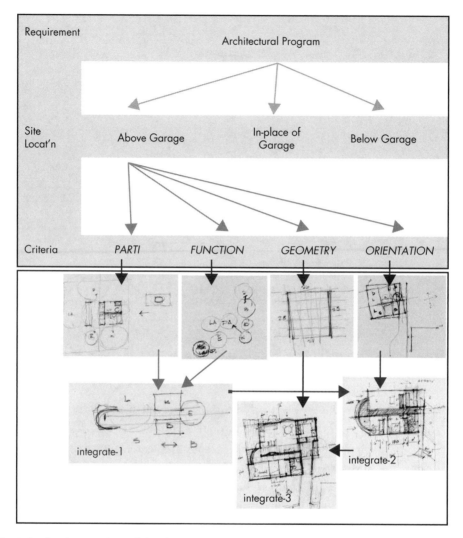

FIGURE 2.6 Pairwise integration of the design problem decomposition in Figure 2.4.
(Akin 2010)

accomplished either in *pairwise integration* (Akin 2010) or *three-way integration* (Akin 2010). In the former case (Figure 2.6), the designer is observed combining the *functional organization* sub-solution with the *design concept* sub-solution, which is subsequently merged with the *orientation* idea, and finally all partial solutions get combined with the *geometry* sub-solution. Whereas, in the latter case, a team of designers, working on a crematorium project, address integrating ideas about issues of *form*, *construction*, and *cost* in a three-way assembly attempt (Figure 2.7). The flow of design actions is indicated by the directed arrows. Here, all three subsolutions are combined at once, rather than the more laborious approach of pairwise integration shown in Figure 2.6. This is attributed to the increased cognitive power of the team design situation.

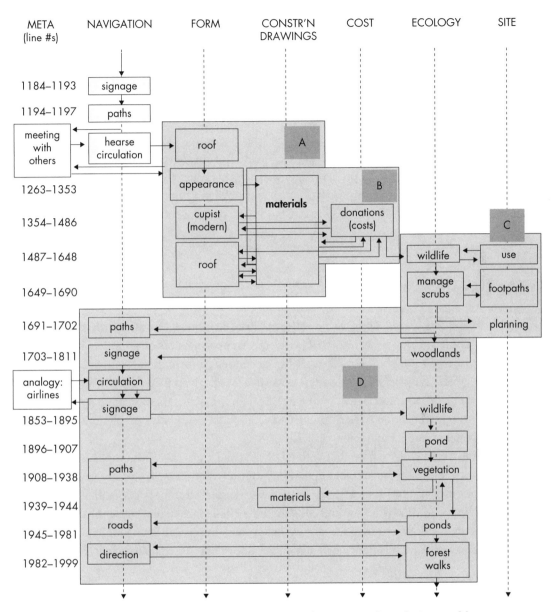

FIGURE 2.7   Three-way integration of the decomposition of a crematorium design problem.
(Akin 2010)

Another set of challenges and opportunities for BIM and cognitive model interface has to do with exhaustive and accurate information processing. Humans are notoriously careless, biased, and downright incompetent when asked to handle large quantities of information exhaustively and accurately. Digital devices, on the other hand, are useful because they can be programmed to be exhaustive and accurate.

1. *Early detection of faults.* These functionalities available even in the least capable digital applications—whether statistical analysis, tax return preparation, or visual data recording—must be made available in the context of design with BIM systems as well. Design errors must be detected early and exhaustively during the early stages of design using clash checking, program compliance, code compliance, performance compliance, and so on. This is a zero-tolerance requirement. The consequences of not providing this functionality are inconsistent with the goals of IDP and Lean Design approaches (Figure 2.3).

2. *Seamless flow between phases.* Information created at any given moment in the design space must be readily applicable to prior or later stages. This must be accomplished with little to no loss of information, redundant processes, or backtracking. Often this function is relegated to the designers, whose cognitive systems are not built to undertake such tasks effectively (Figure 2.2).

2.4 CONCLUSION

Several BIM capabilities would improve the effective use of human cognition in the BIM-supported design process. These include assisting the (1) selective apprehension of stimuli, (2) using a divide and conquer strategy, (3) integration of distinct but dependent information sets, (4) early detection of faults, and (5) seamless flow between phases. A cognitively conceived BIM system will go a long way in fulfilling the market expectations of IDP and Lean Design approaches that are aiming at improving: (1) design quality through realization of performance expectations, (2) timely completion of CPD deliverables, and (3) enhancing budget and value of design.

In closing, it is worthwhile to note that with all of the challenges that the complex world of the CPD process offers and the rapidly developing digital capabilities that range from innovative input output of data, to actuation of physical objects, and to innovative software applications that emulate human intelligence, the future of BIM is bright indeed. While the challenges, particularly the current ones professionals are facing in terms of cognition are extremely tough, so are the ingenuity and technological prowess of the academic and business world aimed at addressing these challenges.

DISCUSSION QUESTIONS

1. What is cognitive modeling?
2. What are short-term memory limitations in human cognition?
3. Name three strategies that designers use to overcome their short-term memory limitations in design.
4. What are the key forces in the capital project delivery (CPD) arena that make BIM an attractive technology?
5. How will BIM assist in overcoming AEC market problems?

REFERENCES

Akin, Ö. 1989. *Psychology of Architectural Design*. London: Pion.

———. 2010. "Variants and Invariants of Design Cognition." In Janet McDonnell and Peter Lloyd, eds., *About: Designing—Analysing Design Meetings*. London: Taylor and Francis.

———. 2012. *Embedded Commissioning of Building Systems*. Boston: Artech House.

Akinci, B., A. Pradhan, and S. Kızıltas. 2008. "Analyses of Data Sources for Multi-Source Data Fusion to Support Project Management Tasks." *Proceedings of 2008 NSF Engineering Research and Innovation Conference*, Knoxville, Tennessee, January 7–10.

Bhavnani, S. K., and B. E. John. 2000. "The Strategic Use of Complex Computer Systems." *Human-Computer Interaction* 15, 107–137.

Chan, C. S. 1994. "A Hypermedia Tutoring for Multimedia Tasks." *Second International Conference of Design and Decision Support Systems in Architecture and Urban Planning*, Vaals, The Netherlands, August 15–19.

Chase, W. G., and H. A. Simon. 1973. "Perception in Chess." *Cognitive Psychology* 4, 55–81.

Eastman, C., P. Teicholz, R. Sacks, and K. Liston. 2008. *Handbook: A Guide to Building Information Modeling for Owners, Managers, Designers, Engineers and Contractors*. Hoboken, NJ: John Wiley and Sons.

Fuhrman, A. 2004. "Pay Now or Pay Later." *Diagram*. Houston: International Facility Management Association.

John, B. E., E. W. Patton, W. D. Gray, and D. F. Morrison. 2012. "Tools for Predicting the Duration and Variability of Skilled Performance without Skilled Performers." *Proceedings of the Human Factors and Ergonomics Society Annual Meeting*, pp. 985–989.

Kelley, S. W., K. D. Hoffman, and M. A. Davis. 1993. "A Typology of Retail Failures and Recoveries." *Journal of Retailing*, 69(4): 429–52.

Klotz, L., and M. Horman. 2007. "A Lean Modeling Protocol for Evaluating Green Project Delivery." *Lean Construction Journal* 3(1): 1–18.

Larsson N. 2009. *The Integrated Design Process; History and Analysis*. International Initiative for a Sustainable Built Environment (iiSBE), larsson@iisbe.org, August 21, 2009.

Lee, S., and Ö. Akin. 2009. "Shadowing Tradespersons: Inefficiency in Maintenance Fieldwork." *Automation in Construction* 18(5) (August): 536–546.

Miller, G. A. 1956. "The Magical Number Seven, Plus or Minus Two." *Psychological Review* 63, 2.

Moustapha, H., and Ö. Akın. 2004. "Strategic Use of Representation in Architectural Massing," *Design Studies* 25(1): 31–50.

Newell, A., and H. A. Simon. 1972. *Human Problem Solving*. Englewood Cliffs, NJ: Prentice-Hall.

NIBS. 2007. National Building Information Modeling Standard (NBIMS) Version 1.0 Part 1 Overview, Principles and Methodologies. Washington, DC: National Institute of Building Sciences (NIBS) and Facilities Information Council (FIC).

Polya, G. 1973. *How to Solve It: A New Aspect of Mathematical Method*. Princeton, NJ: Princeton University Press.

Sutherland, Ivan Edward. 1963. "Sketchpad: A Man-machine Graphical Communication System (courtesy Computer Laboratory, University of Cambridge UCAM-CL-TR-574 September 2003)." PhD dissertation, Massachusetts Institute of Technology. Retrieved 2006-12-26.

Tardif, M. 2008. "BIM Implementation: Applying Lessons Learned." Featured article, *AEC Café*, (http://www10.aeccafe.com/nbc/articles/view article.php?section=CorpNews&articleid=405748).

CHAPTER 3

Modeling Architectural Meaning

Mark J. Clayton, Texas A&M University

3.1 INTRODUCTION

A premise of artificial intelligence research is that software is the formalization and storage of knowledge that, furthermore, transforms knowledge into procedures. In this context, BIM can be considered a compendium of architectural theory that assists and guides the designer to act like an architect. Rather than being a supplemental and practical skill, expertise with BIM tools is inextricably linked to the core knowledge of architecture and the age-old conversation about theory and meaning in architecture. Although the keystrokes and mouse movements necessary to initiate commands and control operations may be unfamiliar, a contemporary architectural designer who is current with architectural theory and professionally competent already knows the concepts expressed in BIM. Architectural knowledge is the starting point to learning BIM for the professional. For the student, BIM helps to make architectural knowledge both explicit and actionable and thus is an aid to retention of knowledge and its incorporation into behavior.

This point of view is elaborated through four examples: the use of an ontology of architecture expressed through the software; the notions of regulating lines, symmetries, proportions, and alignments; the use of diagrams to clarify semantic expressions in a design; and the use of templates that capture the essence of architectural types. Other examples could be explored, such as the expression of basic construction materials and methods, the knowledge of drawing and rendering, or the knowledge of building performance, but these are beyond the scope of this chapter.

3.2 ARCHITECTURAL ONTOLOGY

At a fundamental level, a conversation about architecture depends on sharing a basic ontology that includes a taxonomy and relations among taxonomic items to define semantics. Theorists throughout history have formulated the vocabulary of architecture, by which, to some extent, they have defined architectural styles. The classical style consists of columns, walls, pilasters, roofs, pediments, arches, domes, porches, doors, windows, and other elements organized into the classical orders (Adams 1990). Modernism emphasizes different ontological parts and relations, with primary ideas such as ribbon windows, pilotis, and the free plan (Le Corbusier and Jeanneret 2008). Post-modernist theory attempted to reassert a traditional ontology that includes concepts such as façade, towers, courtyards, and corners (Krier 1988). Classification schemes such as the Uniformat II provide more prosaic but highly practical taxonomies of physical objects (Charette and Marshall 1999).

Every software system must employ an ontology to provide collections of commands that connect the manipulation of abstract computational data structures to more concrete domain knowledge of a practical task. BIM systems tend to use a rather direct and unpretentious ontology of architecture from the standpoint of defining a shelter. Table 1 compares the items in Krier's ontology with the command interfaces of Graphisoft ArchiCAD and Autodesk Revit (Graphisoft n.d.).

BIM tools are distinguished from CAD systems largely by incorporating and enforcing architectonic relations that are also ontological. One way this is expressed is the "host" relation; in the most obvious example, a window must be hosted by a wall. When the hosting object is transformed geometrically or deleted, the hosted object is transformed or deleted too. Many objects in BIM are also given behavior that corresponds to expectations in the real world. For instance, a hinged door is defined to include handedness and direction of swing. These "properties" are special nongraphic fields or parameters that work with the software routines in special ways to model our expectations from the real world.

Although these concepts of an architectural ontology may seem obvious and trivial to the practicing architect, for the student and others learning BIM, it is crucial to change the ontology from being tacit to being explicit. A discussion of architectural ontology in conjunction with basic BIM commands can be a first step to grasping that architecture can have associated meanings and expressions.

3.3 REGULATING LINES

Architectural theorists have long suggested that architectural beauty is closely related to geometric constructs, alignments, and proportions. In the famous essay "Mathematics of the Ideal Villa," Colin Rowe discussed the similar and differing attitudes to proportion between the Renaissance Villa Malcontenta by Palladio and the modernist Villa Garches by Le Corbusier (Rowe 1947). The term "regulating line" is used to refer to the conceptual axes or edges that determine the placement of physical objects in the composition (Le Corbusier 1924). Constraint modeling is a software approach that expresses the ideas behind the use of regulating lines.

Table 3.1 Comparison of ontologies described by Krier and expressed by ArchiCAD and Revit

Krier ontology	ARCHICAD 3D tools	Revit Architecture tools
Interior spaces	Zone	Room
Ceilings and floors	Slab	Ceiling, floor
Columns and piers	Column	Column
Doors	Door	Door
Door handles	—	Component
Windows	Window	Window
Staircases	Stair	Stair
Façades	Wall, curtain wall	Wall, curtain system
Entrance and portals	—	—
Arcades	—	—
Ground floors	—	—
Bay windows, balconies, and loggias	—	—
Railings	—	Railing
Roof and attic storey	Roof	Roof
Towers	—	—
Building corners	—	—
Courtyards	—	—
Outside staircases	—	—
—	—	Ramp
—	—	Mullion
—	—	Curtain grid
—	—	Area
—	—	Opening
—	—	Shaft
—	Beam	Beam
—	Shell	—
—	Skylight	—
—	Lamps	Component
—	Wall end	—
—	Corner window	—
	. . .	. . .

Constraint modeling has been a topic of architectural research for many years. In one exploration of a sketching tool for architects, the software user can apply constraints such as tangent, top-aligned, aligned to grid, parallel, point-on-line, and fixed length (Gross 1992). The notion of regulating lines was used explicitly in a working software prototype to control line segments of the composition itself through relations and constraints (Kolarevic 1994). Transformation of a parent line can propagate to child lines recursively.

Constraint capabilities in BIM tools enable one to explicitly explore and manipulate designs using regulating lines. Levels, grids, reference planes, and various dimensional constraints are available to the designer through the BIM tools.

Perhaps the most fundamental notion of alignment is the idea of a level. Buildings inherently consist of floors, stories, or levels that establish horizontal planes upon which people live their lives, as illustrated in Figure 3.1. Metaphorically, each level is a ground plane that lowers or elevates us through the vertical dimension. In Autodesk Revit, levels are a fundamental notion. By default, most objects are hosted by the level of the plan view that was current when the object was created. If the level is moved, the objects hosted by it move in relation.

Reference planes and reference lines are a more general notion than a level. Grid lines (Figure 3.2) are commonly used in professional architecture to achieve order and control over the building form and anticipate the survey that allows for construction.

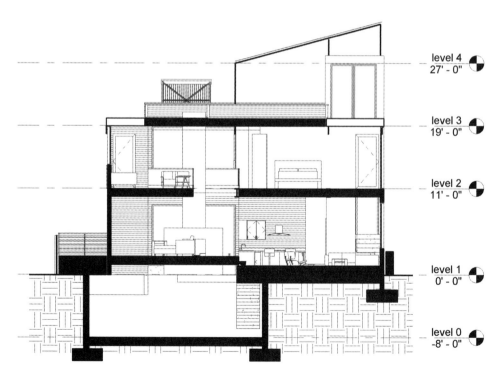

FIGURE 3.1   Levels. The subject is the first LivingHomes model home, designed by Ray Kappe.
(The Revit model was built by Jacob Richie)

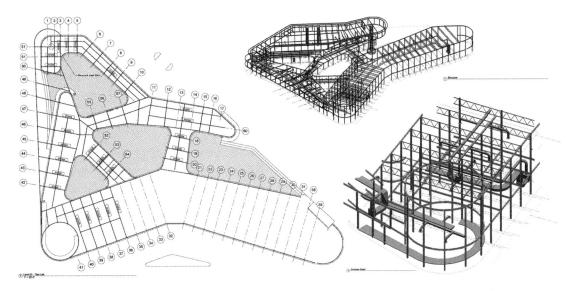

FIGURE 3.2 Grids. The drawing was modeled using Revit and provided by Eliseo Fernandez.
(USC, studio project, diagrams for professional practice course)

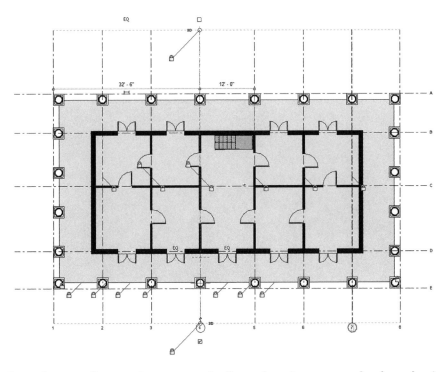

FIGURE 3.3 Extensive use of constraints to control a floor plan. As an example of neoclassical architecture, a Louisiana plantation house is organized by symmetries.

A constraint modeling design approach associates the building form elements to the levels, reference planes, and grid lines through locks and offsets.

In addition to the host relation described earlier, one element can also be "locked" to another element so that they move together. A dimension defining a distance between two elements may also be locked. Mirror or glide symmetry can be established by using an equal constraint on a continuous dimension line. An anchor constraint can force measurements to be made from one element and applied to others. One object can be pinned so that other objects can only be moved in relation to the pinned object.

An example of extensive use of constraints to impose classical design principles is shown in Figure 3.3 illustrating an American neo-Palladian plantation house drawn with Autodesk Revit. The walls are constrained to reference planes and the reference planes are constrained to a centerline so that the symmetry of the design is enforced as the dimensions are changed.

In Autodesk Revit, massing extends the notions of reference planes into the third dimension. The faces of a mass can be used to control the location and shape of walls, roofs, floors, and other elements (Figure 3.4).

Constraint modeling is the basis for parametric modeling in which the design can vary through a range of dimensions or other parameters. By explicitly defining relations among geometric elements, it becomes possible to define how they must move or change as the parameter values vary. Variation may be defined by formula and then the input to the formula varied systematically or randomly to create new designs. Enormous variation can be produced, as shown in the model of the Kaohsiung Stadium in Taiwan (Figure 3.5).

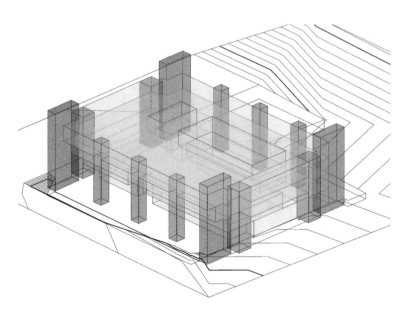

FIGURE 3.4 Use of mass model as constraint modeling. A mass model can be used to control the location of walls, roofs, floors, and other objects.

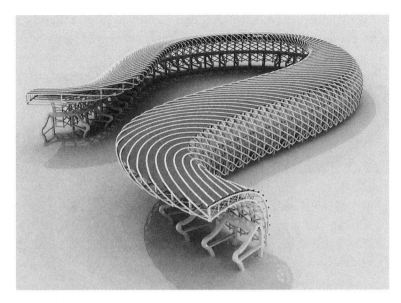

FIGURE 3.5 Complex form modeled with Rhinoceros and Grasshopper. The model was built and rendered by Tim Wofford, for a course offered by Dr. Wei Yan at Texas A&M University. It represents the logic behind the Kaohsiung Stadium, designed by Toyo Ito, and can be reshaped to follow different curves.
(Timothy Wofford)

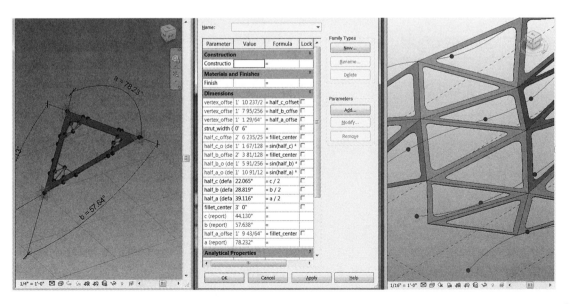

FIGURE 3.6 Constraints and parametric modeling. Values are extracted from parametric dimensions and used to compute other dimensions.

A special case of parametric design is the faceting of a curved surface. Each panel may be unique in dimension, angle, or curvature. Connectors and struts may also vary depending on the continuously changing orientation of the surface. The description and definition of the elements for constructing the surface may not be defined in terms of dimensions, but must be defined in terms of constraints, relations, and formulas. Figure 3.6 presents a triangular panel with a cutout that must adjust itself to the size and orientation of the panel.

3.4 DIAGRAMS AND SEMANTICS

The theory of "graphic thinking" suggests that the architectural concept and composition are developed through a process of abstract sketching and diagramming (Laseau 1989). Diagrams also have been used to isolate concepts in the description of architecture after the completion of the design phase (Clark and Pause 2012). Diagrams depend on either formal or ad hoc graphic languages that encode semantics into line weight, line style, color, shape, and other attributes.

Drafting itself is a highly sophisticated diagramming language. Orthographic projections abstract out one dimension so that scale is preserved in the dimensions that are parallel to the projection plane. Conventions such as wall "poché," dashed centerlines, thin hidden lines, and thick profile lines encode additional information and help to suggest the third dimension in the two-dimensional drawing (Porter and Goodman 1985).

BIM largely eliminates the tedium of drafting, drawing, and diagramming by enabling the creation of rules to generate the graphics. Plans, sections, or elevations may be generated simply by placing a marker to define the cutting plane, while three-dimensional projections such as isometrics or perspectives can be easily composed by setting a camera or vantage point. Graphic conventions such as line

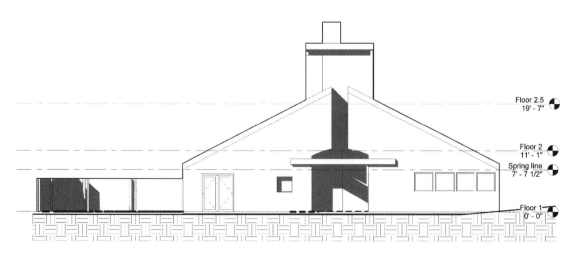

FIGURE 3.7 Elevation showing a profile around the edge of the structure. The subject is the Vanna Venturi House, designed by Robert Venturi.

style and weight, color, transparency, or wireframe representation may be set to focus attention on some aspect of the design (Figure 3.7). Multiple images may be arranged on a sheet to overlap and compose even more complex composite drawings. The set of rules to generate the drawing may be applied to multiple views to enforce a graphic style and even be employed in multiple projects.

By introducing parameters onto objects in a BIM it is possible to interject explicitly the intended experiential semantics of the design. Autodesk Revit provides commands to add parameters to any category of element. Through the use of graphic filters, the parameters interact with the visibility graphics settings to change the view of the model (Figure 3.8). Essentially, once the intended semantic content is encoded into the parameters of the elements of the design, the software can generate a diagram that highlights the semantic content of the design.

To illustrate this idea, works of architecture have been modeled in Autodesk Revit. By manipulating the visibility/graphics settings and filters, view definitions were created to produce diagrams illustrating symmetry, circulation, indoor and outdoor relations, and private versus public spaces. Upon adding parameter values from the standpoint of these semantic topics to the room elements, the software produces a standardized diagram of each work of architecture.

While at a most basic level, diagrams can be used to express the geometry and proportion of the design, diagrams can also be used to express more emotional and associative semantics of the design. This notion became more prominent in post-modern theory of architecture that emphasizes less the rationality and functionalism of modernism and emphasizes more the interpretive and evocative quality of a composition. For example, a diagram could highlight elements of a design that are quotations from historical precedents or stations in a sequence of movement.

This method of diagramming arguably obviates the graphic thinking that diagramming is intended to support. A counterargument is that the designer can think more directly about the semantic intentions

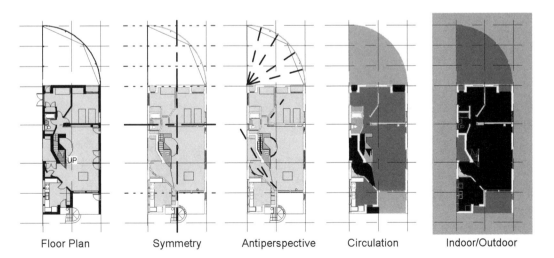

| Floor Plan | Symmetry | Antiperspective | Circulation | Indoor/Outdoor |

FIGURE 3.8 Diagrams produced with visibility filters in Revit. The subject is the Vanna Venturi House, designed by Robert Venturi.

of the design, and the computer produces the resulting diagram in a rigorous, objective way. The technique enables incorporation of aesthetic and expressive intent into the BIM. As the view definitions may be saved as templates and shared, the approach also reduces or eliminates the differences among designers in graphic ability. Many designs can be portrayed with the same graphic style. Perhaps the approach factors out graphic quality so that it is more possible to focus on architectural quality in assessing competing designs. As further research explores how best to model expressive semantics of architecture, new capabilities will enable BIM to be better able to store and integrate this new content.

3.5 TYPES

The notion of building types is used widely in architecture. The International Building Code defines ten basic occupancy groups and several subgroups for classifying buildings (ICC 2009). It also defines five basic construction types that are also broken into additional classifications. Most design firms focus upon a limited range of functional types. Architectural theory also considers formal types that may derive from the shape of a building. Vernacular American houses have been distinguished into types such as "I" houses, dogtrot houses, row houses, and plantation houses, among others (Holl 1983). Notions of type and style are not fully differentiated. Many architects have established signature styles (Figure 3.9)

FIGURE 3.9   Signature styles. A constrained palette of materials and forms enables rapid design within a signature style, such as the casa at Riva San Vitale, by Mario Botta.
(The model was done in Revit by Astrid Santos)

that may even elevate to a new building type, such as Wright's Usonian Houses, Gehry's museums, or Botta's Ticino houses.

BIM systems are inherently organized by notions of type: A type designates a general concept while an instance is a particular element that varies in limited ways from the type. Using terminology from Autodesk Revit, one can also design and model a new "family" consisting of geometric elements that are constrained in a particular way using parameters to represent geometric and nongeometric attributes and relations. A type in Revit is a family that has been further constrained to particular parameter values. Some parameter values may be unconstrained until the object is placed or instantiated in the model. Families may include other families and control the parameters of these "nested" families. Parameters may have values calculated from other parameters or computed through a formula.

Carrying this system of parametric modeling further, a family can define an entire building, representing a building type. A limited palette of materials, assemblies, and components may be applied to a parametrically constrained mass family to produce a composition that follows formal and constructive rules. Figure 3.10 depicts a BIM that has been purged of all unused family types. Only the objects that are used in the model appear in the project browser. The BIM can be used as a template for making new compositions using the same palette of families.

Architecture in the future may be largely the result of instantiating building types that have been represented in BIM (Clayton et al. 2012). At first acquaintance, this idea may imply a depressing sameness to building, but it may also promise a general improvement of quality. Furthermore, the threat of sameness can be overcome by a profusion of variations and competing BIM templates.

FIGURE 3.10 Project browser showing the families used in the model. The model depicts the Horiuchi House, designed by Tadao Ando.

(Modeled in Revit by Nathanielle Sybico)

3.6 CONCLUSION

This discussion presents a collection of small experiments using BIM to explore architectural theory. However, it is also an example of how ideas from architectural theory have been progressively and continually adopted into computational methods of design. Furthermore, computational methods drive the development of theory, such as in the exploration of complex, curvilinear form through parametric modeling, the generation of form through parametric modeling and scripts, the formalization of rules for collaborating on shared models, and the integration of powerful performance analysis tools. In the twenty-first century, learning about architecture requires attention to BIM. It should be evident that BIM can be considered a repository of architectural knowledge made explicit through computational devices of algorithms and data structures. While clearly BIM is not yet a perfect medium for designing architecture, identification of what BIM cannot do suggests that further work is needed on formalizing and making explicit architectural theory. Perhaps future BIM will answer the criticism with additional capabilities.

Understanding and learning how to use BIM can be aided by situating the new knowledge within architectural theory. For the experienced architect, the familiarity and comfort of architectural theory can demystify the concepts expressed in BIM. For the student, discussion of architectural theory can make BIM both more approachable and more intrinsic to education. Modeling with BIM may thus be a way to stay in touch with the inspiration and meaning in architecture that originally inspired one to be an architect.

DISCUSSION QUESTIONS

1. What are the parts of a classical temple such as the Parthenon, and how are they related to each other in an architectural ontology?

2. Given the façade of a building, how would you define the regulating lines of the composition? Choose a façade and define the regulating lines. How does this relate to modeling in BIM software?

3. If you were to create a circulation diagram for a religious, ceremonial building, what items or features would you highlight? Create an annotated circulation diagram of a well-known religious building.

4. How could you use constraints and families to define a gas station building type? Search the Web for "gas station architecture" to find some inspiration. Develop an ontology for gas stations: pumps, canopies, lanes, restrooms, store, cashier station, and so on. Define dimensional constraints and alignments to establish relations of parts to each other, such as to allow cars and trucks to align to pumps. Draw and annotate diagrams to explain your answer.

5. Considering a curtain wall of glass, what are the parts or components of the assembly and what relations do they have to each other?

REFERENCES

Adams, R. 1990. *Classical Architecture: A Comprehensive Handbook to the Tradition of Classical Style*. New York: Harry N. Abrams.

Charette, R. P., and H. E. Marshall. 1999. "UNIFORMAT II Elemental Classification for Building Specifications, Cost Estimating, and Cost Analysis," *National Institute of Standards and Technology*, NISTIR 6389. Retrieved from http://fire.nist.gov/bfrlpubs/build99/PDF/b99080.pdf. Last accessed August 6, 2013.

Clark, R. H., and M. Pause. 2012. *Precedents in Architecture: Analytic Diagrams, Formative Ideas, and Partis*, 4th edition. Hoboken, NJ: John Wiley & Sons.

Clayton, M. J., O. O. Ozener, E. Barekati; J. Haliburton. 2012. "Signature Architecture Franchising: Improving Average Architecture Using BIM," *Proceedings of Digital Aptitudes and Other Openings*, ACSA 100th Annual Meeting, March 1–4, Boston.

Graphisoft. n.d. "General ArchiCAD Brochure," http://download.graphisoft.com/ftp/marketing/ac17/pdf/General_ArchiCAD_Brochure.pdf (accessed August 6, 2013).

Gross, M. 1992. "Graphical Constraints with CoDraw," *Proceedings of IEEE Workshop on Visual Languages*, Seattle WA, pp. 81–87.

Holl, S. 1983. *Pamphlet Architecture 9: Rural and Urban House Types in North America*. San Francisco: Pamphlet Architecture and William Stout Architectural Books.

ICC. 2009. "Quick Reference Guide to Fire Safety: Occupancy Based Requirements of the 2009 IBC." International Code Council, Country Club Hills, IL.

Kolarevic, B. 1994. "Lines, Relations, Drawing and Design." *Reconnecting: ACADIA Conference Proceedings*, Washington University, St. Louis, pp. 51–61.

Laseau, P. 1989. *Graphic Thinking* (2nd ed.). New York: Van Nostrand Reinhold.

Le Corbusier. 1924. *Toward an Architecture*. Translator J. Goodman. Getty Research Institute, Los Angeles, 2007. Originally published as *Vers une architecture*. Paris: G. Cries.

Le Corbusier and P. Jeanneret. 2008. "Five Points for a New Architecture." In H. F. Malgrave and C. Contandriopoulos, *Architectural Theory, Vol. II: An Anthology From 1871—2005*, pp. 218–222. Excerpted from text originally published in Bau and Wohnen Stuttgart: Fr. Wederkind & Co., pp. 27–28, M. Bullock, translator. In *Programs and Manifestos on 20th Century Architecture*, E. Conrad, ed. Cambridge, MA: MIT Press, 1970, 99–100.

Krier, R. 1988. *Architectural Composition*. New York: Rizzoli.

Porter, T., and S. Goodman. 1985. *Manual of Graphic Techniques 4*. New York: Charles Scribner's Sons.

Rowe, C. 1947. "The Mathematics of the Ideal Villa, Palladio and Le Corbusier Compared." *Architectural Review*, March.

CHAPTER 4

Knowledge-Based Building Information Modeling

Hugo Sheward, University of Missouri, Georgia Institute of Technology
Charles Eastman, Georgia Institute of Technology

4.1 THE POTENTIAL OF BUILDING INFORMATION MODELING (BIM) TO CAPTURE DESIGN EXPERTISE

Design expertise is the result of years of design practice and learning from design problem solving. Although some of this experience is based on the application of explicit rules or codes, design expertise is also based on the development of a vast number of nondeclared rules that come from individual experiences in solving particular issues (Eastman et al. 2011). For many architecture engineering and construction (AEC) organizations, a huge challenge is the process of transferring this individual design expertise through the entire organization and to reuse it to improve design processes within a company.

Having the capability of capturing and transmitting design expertise not only eliminates the need for expert designers to be involved in every relevant project, it also allows for the reuse and optimization of this knowledge, allowing for it be applied by novel designers. In traditional practice most of the reuse of design expertise is based on a mentorship system. The process of capturing design expertise, if any, is done by the generation of design guidelines or best-practice compilations. One of the problems with the traditional model is that the application of these design heuristics is limited to the capability of novel designers to learn them and apply them effectively.

Contemporary BIM tools offer an extraordinary potential for embedding a wide range of types of design expertise in computational systems. Through the use of features such as parametric modeling, object relational databases, and application programming interfaces (APIs), contemporary BIM can easily become a viable platform to rationalize and formalize design heuristics. This chapter shows different approaches on how to use BIM software to support the capturing and deployment of design expertise and to provide knowledge-based design assistances embedded in computational design environments.

4.2 "VANILLA BIM" VERSUS KNOWLEDGE-BASED BIM

BIM applications have produced a profound change in the way AEC organizations process designs. In most cases this change is the result of the application of BIM technologies as an advanced tool for the documentation of design data. The capabilities of contemporary BIM have the potential to improve design processes by providing designers with timely design evaluation capabilities in knowledge-based computational design environments.

BIM tools are transforming the way in which design processes are developed in contemporary architecture. They have given designers a great level of control over design change propagation, automated drawing extraction, 3D modeling capabilities, automated material take-offs, and parametric behavior of building components. BIM technologies have also allowed for better coordination and interoperability across the AEC domain. In most cases BIM tools are used for these purposes, the traditional practices in BIM or "vanilla BIM."

Knowledge-based BIM is when BIM applications are used to carry design knowledge information. This information has been made explicit in the form of design rules, parametric constraints, and/or parametric objects. The implementation of knowledge-based BIM provides automated design support without the need of either migration of design data to external assessment software or the presence of domain experts to supervise design activities. There are two main areas in which knowledge-based BIM is being currently used: to assess design requirements compliance and the automation of content generation.

4.3 WHAT IS DESIGN EXPERTISE?

Designers deal with ill-defined problems (Eastman 1969). Designers learn by developing their own strategies and rules of thumb to solve these. In most cases what separates novel from expert designers is the result of years of practice and the development of these design heuristics. Often design knowledge is not explicitly formalized and lives mostly in one individual, who is considered the domain expert. The process by which design expertise is transferred to other designers has traditionally been done applying a one-to-one mentorship model, which requires the direct contact between the novel designer and the domain expert. This type of expertise transfer can take a long time to be completed. When design organizations grow larger and one-to-one mentorship might not be possible, the necessity for formalization of design expertise is commonly documented in what are known as design guidelines.

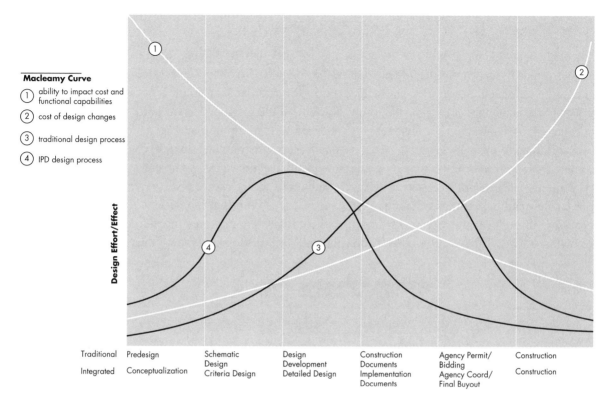

FIGURE 4.1 MacLeamy curve.
(Adapted from Eastman et al. 2011)

4.3.1 Heuristics Applied to Design Processes

Design evaluation is an intrinsic part of any design workflow; designers continuously evaluate features in their work. The evaluation is done regarding specific performance targets or compliance of domain specific requirements. The noncompliance of the performance targets commonly produces new design iteration. The later in the design process these revisions arise the higher cost will be to solve them (Eastman et al. 2011).

For many AEC organizations, the effort then is to develop mechanisms to bring a wide range of design assessment capabilities as early as possible in the design process (Sanguinetti et al. 2012). The principle is based on the MacLeamy curve, which shows the relationship between BIM enabled design processes, compared to traditional design processes (Figure 4.1). The curve shows how the rich semantics of BIM can enhance the decision-making process in early stages of design and reduce the cost of design changes, effectively enhancing the design workflows regarding the cost and the impact of design decisions.

4.3.2 Design Workflows and Knowledge-Based BIM

Although many design workflows incorporate the use of design assessment tools, most of the time these are performed by using tools that are not part of the design environment (external tools), requiring design data to be translated or even remodeled. The model for external assessment is not well suited for every design phase and might be detrimental for the efficiency if the design workflow particularly in early stages of design. Design variations can happen at such speed (sometimes in a matter of minutes) that the time available to perform externally supported assessment is extremely limited. In most cases once the feedback coming from external sources arrives, the design might have moved in a completely different direction.

Traditional BIM practices already support enhanced design workflows by providing semantically rich models and better interoperability. Yet it still requires both that the designer includes all the data necessary to perform the assessment and that the design data migrates to external assessment tools. Knowledge-based BIM, on the other hand, not only brings the assessment capabilities directly in to

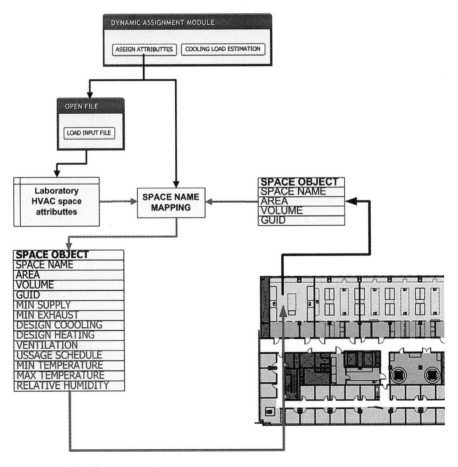

FIGURE 4.2   Automated attribute mapping.
(Sheward, 2012)

the design environment (eliminating the need for data migration) but also implements mechanisms for automatically enhancing the correctness of the semantic content of the model, in the form of predefined parametric constraints (Eastman et al. 2011) or by applying automated attribute mapping (Sheward 2012) onto model objects (Figure 4.2).

4.4 CAPTURING AND DEPLOYING DESIGN EXPERTISE

The need for capturing and deploying design expertise is given by the need of and organization of expand the use of the intellectual capital acquired through years of experience of a domain expert. The possibility of capturing and reproducing this knowledge eliminates the demands on the single individual. This section describes traditional practices developed for this purpose.

4.4.1 Capturing Design Expertise

The process of formalizing and capturing design expertise requires different types of efforts. It might be the results of extensive studies of commonly accepted practices in a specific field as in the case of design guidelines (Eastman et al. 2011) or the formalization of technical requirements, such as codes. Or it might be the result of an organization's effort to standardize their own practices or to make reusable their expertise. Eastman describes how an organization captured and documented parametric variations in Excel spreadsheets (Figure 4.3) that later were used to feed parametric objects in Gehry Technologies Digital Project (Eastman 2012).

The forms of design knowledge being captured vary depending on the area of expertise being documented. For instance, in some areas of architecture, it might be the size of service areas in a building regarding the usable square footage; in engineering, it might be the types of connectivity that a precast beam might need to have when installed under particular conditions; or it might be even the result of a combination of multiple forms of representation, which when combined represent complicated areas of design knowledge (Kimura et al. 2004).

4.4.2 Embedding Knowledge in BIM

Unlike traditional CAD, where design data was mostly geometric in nature, BIM provides the potential to extend semantic contents for building data. In these data structures, building objects can be associated with attribute or parametric information. These capabilities provide the potential for holding different types of design knowledge.

4.4.2.1 User-Level Knowledge-Based BIM Implementation

Some of the functionalities capable of being embedded in BIM tools can be implemented by users without knowledge of computer programming. These users can take advantage of BIM applications

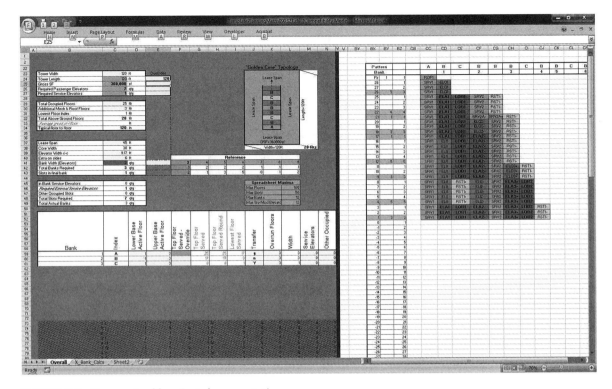

FIGURE 4.3   Parameter libraries' documentation.
(Eastman et al. 2011)

capabilities such as parametric control of geometry, hierarchical building database queries (schedules), and customized parametric objects (Sheward 2011). A combination of these forms of embedding expertise described above can provide feedback regarding the performance of the design even in early stages of development (Sheward and Eastman 2011). Even though different BIM tools might have different mechanisms to customize their operations, the capabilities described above can be commonly found among most BIM authoring tools.

4.4.2.2 Developer-Level Knowledge-Based BIM Implementation

Most of contemporary BIM applications support functional extensibility by providing what is known as application programming interface (API). By using these expert users with knowledge in computer programing languages such as C#, C++, or Visual BASIC can create customized functions. The developer can go as far as to create functions that might not be part of the BIM platform default configuration by attaching proprietary geometric functions (Bernal and Eastman 2011) or by integrating external analysis tools to the BIM environment (Sanguinetti et al. 2012).

The developer-level-based implementation can provide high levels of sophistication to the knowledge-based BIM; its reusability is supported by the possibility of producing domain specific plugins.

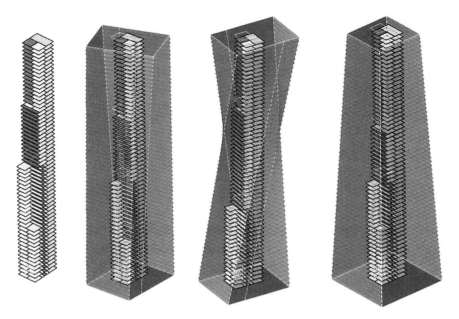

FIGURE 4.4 Building service core, elevator drop off sequences in different types of conceptual massing.

4.4.3 Example 1: Building Service Core

This section describes the use of design heuristics based on one AEC organization and the use of BIM for the automated generation of design content in the form of parametric objects.

4.4.3.1 Background and Need

In order to develop a building core service, an expert provided a compilation of design practices that described the formalization of parametric relations and constraints. These then had to be implemented into usable parametric objects. The system informs designers of both sizing and drop off sequences for service core units in high rise office buildings during massing studies (Figure 4.4). By embedding the expertise developed in the design of service cores by a well-known architectural company, the developer was able to automate the generation of the service core, allowing fast support of different typologies of buildings (Bernal and Eastman 2011).

4.4.3.2 Implementation Methodology

The implementation of this knowledge-based BIM was done in two stages. First, the concept was proven by using a manual data transfer between McNeel Rhinoceros and Gehry Technologies Digital Project. At this stage the concept design data was extracted from Rhino and passed to Digital Project to generate the parametric variations of the service core object. For the second stage of development, the entire process was automated via the construction of a plugin operating in Autodesk Revit; the plugin was developed in Microsoft Visual Studio (Figure 4.5).

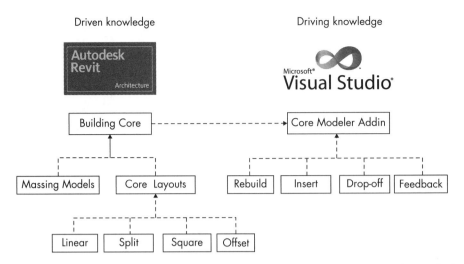

FIGURE 4.5   Implementation diagram showing the interface between the plugin and Autodesk Revit.

This knowledge-based BIM analyzed the geometric properties of the massing study and inferred the number of required elevators for it. The system is based on the expected floor occupancy and the drop-off sequence for the elevators. Then it automatically instantiates the adequate parametric building core object into the building massing being developed by the designer.

4.4.3.3 Results

This study showed the possibility of constructing interactive and reusable parametric objects. It automated the generation of the service core object for massing studies and informed designers regarding the feasibility of their preliminary concept design massing studies. It provided an optimum solution based in the rules predefined by the design heuristics. The automatically instantiated service core object can be modified if necessary during the design process.

The results of this knowledge-based BIM implementation was constrained from the beginning to a very specific building typology, which was office buildings ranging from 60 to 80 stories high. The reason for this specific type was given by the relation between building height and the number and position of the mechanical rooms, which for this type of building requires two mechanical rooms located directly above the first level and at the top level of the building.

4.4.4 Example 2: Ventilation in Laboratories

This section describes the automation of the estimation of one particular building system structure that is critical for the correct design and operation of laboratory facilities. This knowledge-based BIM is based on the use of API's to derive information that supports design assessment.

4.4.4.1 Background

This knowledge-based BIM implementation studied the possibility of developing scientific approaches to replace the industry's current practice of applying rules of thumb when analyzing the implication of ventilation systems in preliminary concept design (PCD) of laboratory buildings. The importance of establishing a rigorous approach is given by the impact of ventilation requirements for both the safe operation of the facility and the energy consumption of it. In the case of laboratories the ventilation systems can account for up to 50 percent of the overall energy consumption (Weale 2001).

4.4.4.2 Implementation Methodology

The implementation of this knowledge-based BIM uses the Autodesk Revit API to channel a wide variety of operations that would enable the system to provide significant design feedback during PCD. Among the functions implemented were the following: automated assignment of domain specific attributes to building objects, normative calculations for energy estimation, and the design and optimization of ventilation system layout. The result is a BIM environment that allows for the evaluation of several performance aspects that are critical for the design of laboratory buildings (Figure 4.6).

During the implementation phase, multiple approaches were developed to extend the capabilities of Autodesk Revit to achieve the goal of automating the assessment. For example, the estimation of the ventilation system energy consumption made it necessary to build an algorithm capable of processing the psychometrics required for the calculation of the cooling requirements of the system. The calculation

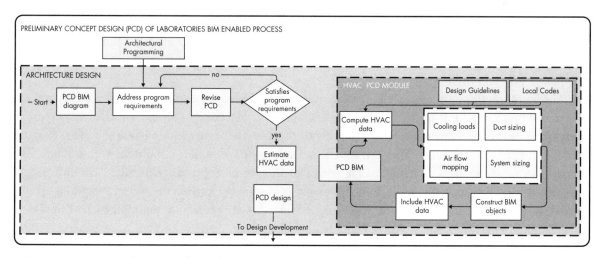

FIGURE 4.6 Process diagram of ventilation in laboratories.
(Sheward 2012)

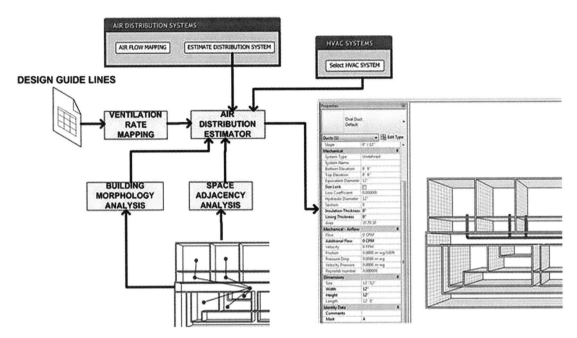

FIGURE 4.7   Spatial adjacency derivation for the purpose of ventilation routing.
(Sheward 2012)

of psychometrics enabled the plugin to calculate the cooling loads required for PCD laboratories in less than 5 seconds. This is vastly faster than manual calculations, which might take from a couple of hours to a day depending on the type of design data extraction protocols prior to the calculation.

Another significant implementation effort was made in the development of the automated layout of the ventilation system. For this purpose, it was necessary to implement geometrical functions not available in hosting applications, such as metric graph algorithms to analyze space adjacency structures and ventilation system morphology.

The automated derivation of spatial adjacencies is critical for the correct estimation of the ventilation distribution system. It allows for the identification of those spaces that are intended to be part of each of the distribution branches; at the same time it enables the software to analyze the space to space ventilation pressure structures. These structures are critical for the safety conditions within the facility as negative pressures help contain leakage of gasses in case of chemical accidents. This knowledge-based BIM will warn designers if ventilation pressure issues are detected in the model and automatically instantiate in to the model and optimize routing for the ventilation ducts required in each of the levels of the laboratory BIM model (Figure 4.7).

4.4.4.3 Results

This project is an ongoing effort in which the energy estimation engine has proven accurate when compared with traditional methods for estimating energy consumption. The system also helps designers to analyze the ventilation system performance among multiple design alternatives by embedding the results of each design assessment within the knowledge-based BIM user interface.

The two main building typologies applied to the design of laboratory buildings were service shafts and the interstitial space. This system was developed to work within the domain of service shafts typologies, which is the most commonly used type. For it to be able to operate effectively in interstitial typologies, it will require form modifications.

4.5 EXAMPLES OF DEPLOYMENT

Although new for architectural design, the concept of knowledge-based computer aided design (CAD) environments has been applied in other areas of engineering such as manufacturing and construction engineering.

4.5.1 Deployment in Manufacturing

The process of deploying design expertise through computational means has been applied to multiple areas of productive processes including part manufacturing. Developing more efficient processes for design and manufacturing of parts lead to the deployment of parametric models based in clear design expertise (Myung and Soonhung 2001). Myung describes a parametric model that is based on predefined rules (design knowledge) that can effectively constrain the design of new mechanical parts. The described knowledge-based system operates as a plugin within a CAD tool. It allows designers to evaluate new parts within the context of part assemblies and the parameters contained in the assembly. The parametric object design is automatically solved for the constraints defined within the assembly.

4.5.2 Uses in Architecture, Engineering, and Construction

Compared with many areas of manufacturing and engineering, AEC has been slow in adopting parametric models for the purpose of modeling and fabrication (Eastman 2003). This is the same for systems capable of deploying expertise to support design activities.

Recently there has been the development of knowledge-based systems capable of deploying design heuristics being used for the performance-driven models for structural optimization (Shea et al. 2005) and systems that support the detailing and specification of components to support the manufacturing of these (Eastman 2003). Such is the case of the effort developed by the Precast Concrete Software Consortium; they developed and supported the implementation of a semantically rich BIM environment capable of assisting in the design and specification of precast components.

This is done through the definition of an extensive library of parametric objects that document both the specifications and the behavior of precast concrete building components. The definition of geometric parameters in the components can be seen in Figure 4.8.

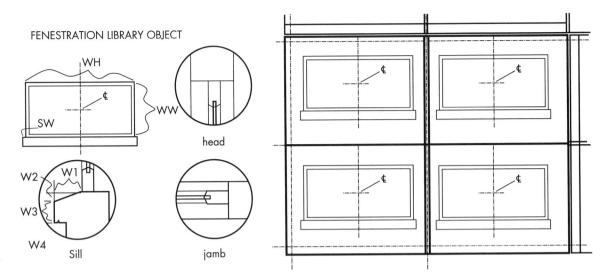

FIGURE 4.8   Fenestration library for the project including the panel.
(Sacks 2004)

4.6 SUMMARY

Knowledge-based BIM has a number of implications regarding design performance and is helping AEC organizations to document and reuse expertise they consider important for the development of their projects. This technology can also positively influence the workflows of design processes by pushing assessment capabilities upstream in the design process and reduce the number of design iterations and revisions.

Knowledge-based BIM will also allow architects to gain a higher level of control over technical aspects of buildings, particularly in construction and performance-level technologies. The development of a wide range of knowledge-based plugins, all operating within the BIM platform and dealing with different types of specific knowledge or assessment, could help designers to develop their tasks in a more efficient and effective way.

DISCUSSION QUESTIONS

1. What are the types of formalization commonly used to document design heuristics in BIM?
2. What is the importance of documenting and reusing design expertise?
3. At what stage of the design process evolution can knowledge-based BIM produce the biggest impact in design outcome?
4. What types of assessment might not be implemented in knowledge-based BIM, regarding the nature of design processes?

REFERENCES

Bernal, Marcelo, and Charles Eastman. 2011. "Top-down Approach to Embed Design Expertise in Parametric Objects for the Automatic Generation of a Building Service Core." *CAAD Futures 2011: Proceedings of the 14th International Conference on Computer Aided Architectural Design*, pp. 149–164.

Eastman, Charles M. 1969. "Cognitive Processes and Ill-Defined Problems: A Case Study from Design." *Proceedings of the International Joint Conference on Artificial Intelligence: IJCAI*, vol. 69, pp. 669–690.

Eastman, Charles, Paul Teicholz, Rafael Sacks, and Kathleen Liston. 2011. *BIM Handbook: A Guide to Building Information Modeling for Owners, Managers, Designers, Engineers and Contractors*. Hoboken, NJ: John Wiley & Sons.

Kimura, F. H. Ariyoshi, H. Ishikawa, Y. Naruko, H. and H. Yamato. 2004. "Capturing Expert Knowledge for Supporting Design and Manufacturing of Injection Molds." *Cirp Annals-Manufacturing Technology* 53 (1): 147–150.

Myung, Sehyun, and Soonhung Han. 2001. "Knowledge-Based Parametric Design of Mechanical Products Based on Configuration Design Method." *Expert Systems with Applications* 21(2): pp. 99–107.

Sacks, Rafael, Charles Eastman, and Ghang Lee. 2004. "Parametric 3d Modeling in Building Construction with Examples from Precast Concrete." *Automation in Construction* 13(3): pp. 291–312.

Sanguinetti, Paola, Sherif Abdelmohsen, Jaemin Lee, Jinkook Lee, Hugo Sheward, and Charles Eastman. 2012. "General System Architecture for BIM: an Integrated Approach for Design and Analysis." *Advanced Engineering Informatics* 26(2): pp. 317–333.

Shea, Kristina, Robert Aish, and Marina Gourtovaia. 2005. "Towards Integrated Performance-Driven Generative Design Tools." *Automation in Construction* 14(2): pp. 253–264.

Sheward, Hugo. 2012. "The Development of the Laboratory Concept Design Assistant." *2ISL*, Labs 21 Annual Conference, San Jose, CA.

PART 2

BIM ANALYTICS

Parametric BIM SIM: Integrating Parametric Modeling, BIM, and Simulation for Architectural Design

Wei Yan, PhD, Texas A&M University

5.1 EXECUTIVE SUMMARY

With the advancement of Building Information Modeling (BIM) technology, the applications of BIM to building energy simulation are promising. Concurrently, more creative, free form, and large-scale buildings are designed using parametric design methods. Parametric methods are also an important part of the BIM technology, helping to manage the relationships among building objects and to explore design options. Integrated together, parametric BIM becomes a powerful design method for architects, and parametric energy simulation enables engineers to search for optimal building energy solutions and design options. An integrated process of parametric modeling, BIM, and building energy simulation for energy efficient building design will be discussed in this chapter. Issues addressed in this chapter are model complexity, computability, and user and system interfaces, followed by case studies.

5.2 INTRODUCTION

Buildings consume about one-third of the world's energy (NSF 2009, DOE 2006). The use of electric power and heat in the building sector also accounts for about 40 percent of the world's greenhouse gas emissions (NSTC 2008). Sustainability with efficient energy use and minimal environmental impact has become a major building design goal. Building parametric modeling, BIM, and performance simulation have great potentials to benefit sustainable building design. Parametric modeling enables design intent to be implemented through identifying parameters and establishing their relationships. Parametric design can generate a building form using physical parameters (e.g., weather data, which has a significant impact on building energy performance). Enabled by parametric modeling, design options can be studied by parametric simulation to achieve better or optimal building performance. BIM is at the center of the workflow from paramedic modeling to simulation, because it helps advance parametric modeling–supported conceptual design to construction and provides input for building energy simulation. Parametric modeling, BIM, and energy simulation act together to optimize building performance.

5.2.1 Parametric Modeling

Parametric modeling is a general methodology for defining models with constraints and variable parameters (Eastman et al. 2011). In architecture, parametric modeling enables generative form-making through the use of parameters and rules based on aesthetic and performance metrics of buildings and allows objects to automatically update based on changed contexts (Aish and Woodbury 2005, Qian 2007). It is a change of architectural design method through designing a system that designs a building (Stocking 2009). It is also a change from designing one solution to designing a system to generate multiple solutions, and the multiple solutions can then be used for optimization. For example, Building Integrated Photovoltaics (BIPV) can utilize parametric models and genetic algorithm (GA) to optimize the design of curtain panels that serve as both PV components and glazing components affecting thermal and daylighting performances (Charron and Athienitis 2006, Kalogirou 2004, Wright et al. 2002). Existing parametric geometry modeling tools used in building design include SolidWorks, Rhino/Grasshopper, GenerativeComponents, and others. Most of the tools employ change propagation modeling methods and some employ visual programming methods, such as Grasshopper (Eastman et al. 2011, Woodbury 2010). Parametric design is going mainstream in architecture as demonstrated by leading global architectural practices—for example, in the construction of two major stadiums used in the 2008 Olympics: Beijing National Stadium and National Aquatics Centre (Stocking 2009, Krish 2011) and high-rise buildings (Park et al. 2004, Gane and Haymaker 2007).

5.2.2 BIM and Parametric BIM

BIM is a process to facilitate the exchange and interoperability of building information (Eastman et al. 2011) and a product of physical and functional characteristics of a building.[1] Semantically rich and object-based, BIM facilitates the creation and management of comprehensive building data, including objects and their properties used in design, simulation, cost estimation, construction, and operation, increasing the AEC process efficiency. In addition, BIM's parametric modeling capability enables quick,

---

[1] "About the National BIM Standard—United States." (www.nationalbimstandard.org, accessed on February 21, 2014).

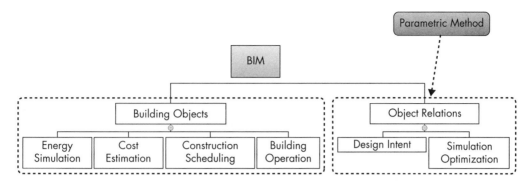

FIGURE 5.1 The relationship between BIM and the parametric modeling method.

interactive, and real-time design changes (Lee et al. 2006). The relationship between BIM and parametric modeling lies in that BIM contains building objects and their relationships, which can be used to express design intent, and the parametric modeling method helps establish and manage these relationships (Figure 5.1).

In a BIM project, objects are defined by built-in and user-specified parameters, and external data such as physical, aesthetic, functional data accessed through databases, or entered in graphical user interfaces (GUI). Parametric modeling enables parameters to be processed by mathematical formulas and computational algorithms before being passed among objects. The formulas and algorithms can be designed based on research and creative design thinking. Integrated together, parametric BIM becomes a powerful design method for architects. Figure 5.2 shows the structure of parametric BIM.

Professional examples that integrate parametric modeling and BIM include the Shanghai Center project designed by Gensler and Tongji Architectural Design Institute (Chen and Zhang 2012) and Hangzhou Olympics Stadium designed by NBBJ and CCDI (Miller 2010, Ji and Zheng 2010). In both projects, Rhinoceros (a 3D modeling tool) and Grasshopper (a visual programming tool) are used for parametric design of the mass and the skin of the building. The resulting forms are then translated into BIM in Autodesk Revit for detailed design and construction. Parametric studies benefited the projects significantly. For example, in the Shang Center project, "by modeling various options and conducting wind-tunnel tests, the design team discovered that a 120-degree twist and 55 percent taper combination reduced wind loads by 24 percent and material costs by $58 million." (Wujec 2011).

5.2.3 Building Energy Simulation

Building energy simulation assists in the prediction of energy performance of buildings in the architectural design process. Existing tools for energy simulation include TRNSYS, ESP-r, Ecotect, EnergyPlus, DOE2, and IES<VE>, among others, which offer thermal, daylighting, and/or BIPV simulation functions and shading analysis. A comprehensive review contrasting capabilities of existing whole-building energy tools is made by Crawley and colleagues (2008).

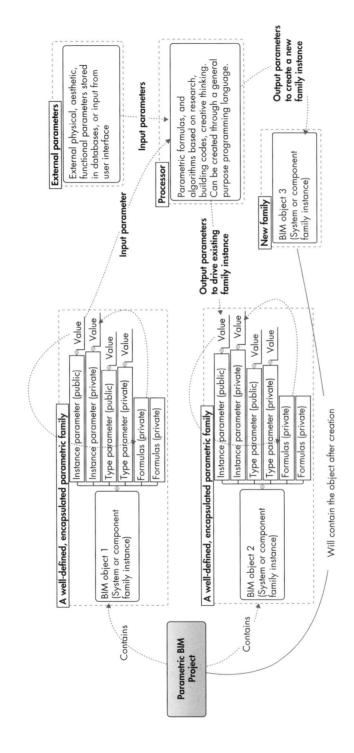

FIGURE 5.2 Structure diagram of parametric BIM showing relationships among BIM objects and external processes.

5.2.3.1 BIM to Object-Oriented Physical Simulation

Use of object-oriented physical modeling (OOPM) is a new trend in energy simulation. OOPM is better structured than the procedural programming method used in the legacy tools (Fritzson 2004). Modelica is a unified OOPM language used for differential algebraic equation (DAE)-based simulation, where the topology of a component connection diagram in Modelica directly corresponds to the structure and decomposition of the modeled physical system (Fritzson 2004).

The Building Library of the Lawrence Berkeley National Laboratory (LBNL) is a Modelica-based building thermal modeling and simulation system (Wetter 2009). The library is validated (Nouidui et al. 2012) and under continued development. The execution time of Modelica building system models can be comparable with TRNSYS (Wetter and Haugstetter 2006). Because both BIM and OOPM are object-based, integration of BIM and OOPM-based energy simulation is better enabled (Yan et al. 2013).

5.2.3.2 Parametric Simulation

Parametric modeling-based simulation (parametric simulation) enables optimizing energy solutions based on different design options. Zhang and Korolija (2010) created a scripting tool to generate 34,560 EnergyPlus simulation sample runs with varying parameters of insulation, glazing, climate data, and so on for a building design. All the simulation results can then be compared for energy performance. This large amount of work is impossible to do manually, while parallel computing (using 128 CPUs) made the process efficient. In another example, by manipulating a few parameters, Gane (2004) was able to obtain 83,500 different design options, enabling the search for optimal solutions in a systematic manner.

However, parametric energy simulation presents a risk of errors for simulation results because the energy models are not parametric internally. There are no parametric relations among objects in energy models (in contrast to BIM); for example, if a wall is transformed in an energy model, windows, shading devices, rooms, zones, roofs, and floors associated with the wall should be updated automatically, but they are currently not updated in the energy model. In other words, design intents embedded in BIM are not embedded in the energy models. As a result, manual update of model data is needed before running the simulations, but that is tedious and error-prone. The recent use of BIM and its parametric change capabilities improves the process because the parametric changes are initiated in BIM and propagated parameter changes are passed from BIM to energy simulation, which allows the change of building geometry in the process (Welle et al. 2012).

5.2.4 A Streamlined Modeling Process

In light of the great potentials of modeling technologies facilitating energy efficient building design, there is a significant need for a new integrated parametric modeling, BIM, and energy modeling that can provide easy-to-use and accurate simulation at the early design stage, when design strategies have the major influence on the building performance. Figure 5.3 shows a streamlined modeling process that is integrated into the general architectural design process, including conceptual design, schematic design, design development, and construction documents. In conceptual design, parametric conceptual modeling of a building mass can be created using tools like Rhinoceros/Grasshopper, conceptual energy simulation can be conducted using tools like Green Building Studio, and optimization algorithms such as genetic algorithms can be applied using tools like Galapagos (a Grasshopper plug-in). In schematic design and design development, a parametric BIM is created using tools like Revit, which can generate multiple, detailed design options. More accurate, iterative simulations for the design options can then be conducted, and the final, optimized design option can be obtained and passed to construction documents. It can be seen that parameter changes, at conceptual design, schematic design, or design development, are not done directly in the simulation models. Instead, the parameter changes are initiated in the architectural models and then passed to the simulation models. This way the parametric relationships of the building objects can be maintained to enable efficient, accurate simulation and optimization results.

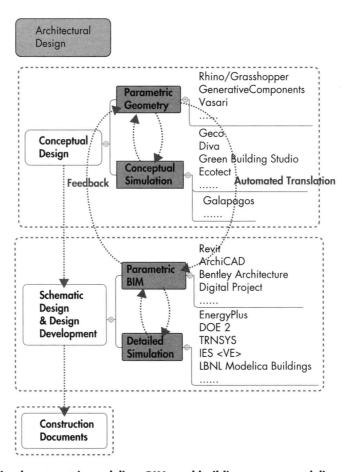

FIGURE 5.3   Streamlined parametric modeling, BIM, and building energy modeling.

5.3 COMPLEXITY AND INTERFACES

Though having great potential, the streamlined, integrated parametric modeling, BIM, and simulation process will involve sophisticated models that may contain freeform geometry and a large number of parameters and their relationships. Improved user interface and visualization for the models are important for designers to understand the design models and better embed design and engineering knowledge into the models to reflect design intent. The streamlined process should also incorporate a new human-computer cooperation system to enable the exploration of the maximum design space for optimization based on available resources. New system interfaces that improve interoperability among parametric modeling, BIM, and simulation are also needed to facilitate the optimization process.

5.3.1 Complexity and Computability

Sustainable building design is a highly complex problem for modeling and optimization. Without a comprehensive understanding of the complexity and computability of the problem, computer modeling tools cannot be used effectively to achieve optimized design options.

5.3.1.1 Complexity

The complexity of the design problem results from the large quantity of interrelated parameters such as building geometry, space layout, materials, sites, weather data, functions, user behavior, and so on. In building energy simulations, an extensive database of building geometry and material properties, climatological information, and thousands of engineering calculations based on differential algebraic equations (DAEs) are used to predict the energy performance of the buildings (ANSI/ASHRAE 2007, Torcellini et al. 2006, Bazjanac 2001). In building simulations, the number of possible design combinations is of the size of billions due to the numerous design parameters such as window areas, the thermal and optical properties of glazing systems (e.g., R-value and transmittance); PV array area; solar thermal variables; thermal storage; control strategies and comfort range; heating, ventilating, and air conditioning (HVAC) system variables; and interzonal air flow, even with a limit of four to six allowable discrete values for each parameter (Athienitis et al. 2006). In addition, building design needs to fulfill traditional requirements of architecture: structural, functional, aesthetic, social, cultural, historical, and behavioral. The quantity of the interrelated parameters in all these disciplines can be extremely large. The complexity of building projects result in the complexity of modeling tools. For example, participants of a survey on the use of daylighting simulations in building design named complexity of tools and insufficient program documentation as weaknesses of existing programs (Reinhart and Fitz 2006).

Parametric modeling increases complexity of both the designers' tasks and the human-computer interface because designers must model an additional process consisting of the parameters and rules that generate the design variations (Woodbury 2010). Meanwhile, the structure of the design work using parametric systems continues to be poorly understood (Aish and Woodbury 2005) and changes to these models are difficult to make (Erhan et al. 2009). In the meantime, the complexity of BIM requires simplification in order to form thermal envelopes and zones for thermal simulation (Bazjanac and Kiviniemi 2007). Research such as Geometry Simplification Tools (Bazjanac 2008) and ASHRAE 1468 project (Clayton et al. 2009) began to provide guidelines and methods for model simplification and translation from BIM to thermal modeling.

Complex building forms enabled by parametric BIM present a significant challenge to energy simulation. As a result of complexity, design mistakes are very common (Jesus et al. 2005) and in many cases significant mismatches exist between the predicted performances and the actual performances of these buildings (Majumdar 2008).

5.3.1.2 Computability

Ideally, for a given design project, all of the parameters in all domains relevant to architecture can be considered in order to achieve an optimal design solution. Currently, however, no comprehensive research is completed on the estimation of the parameter quantity and the computability of design optimization. Given the large number of parameters, the computing time for parametric optimization can be very long. For example, 34,560 simulations of building energy performance take 27 hours on a parallel computing facility with 128 CPUs (Zhang and Korolija 2010). The number of design options explored is far less than that is needed in practice, and the computing time is already far beyond reasonable during the design process.

Because of the high complexity, a global optimization for building energy simulation may not be achievable within a reasonable timeframe during the design process, given the current or near-future computing power available to designers. Thus designers' intervention may be needed to make critical and creative decisions in order to direct the optimization toward desired solutions and achieve the solutions within reasonable time. During this process, the system should provide visualization for designers to better understand the models and the expected outcomes and provide the user interface for them to make changes to the models, in terms of parameter bounds and parametric relationships.

In existing optimization frameworks, such as those using Phoenix Integration's ModelCenter (Welle et al. 2012), the optimization system requires an extensive manual process to link parameters' output from BIM to the input of a downstream simulation tool (e.g., EnergyPlus) before running the optimization process. A new system should eliminate manual processes as much as possible. New OOPM-based energy simulation may eventually replace legacy simulation tools for better integration with BIM, which will assist in speeding up the optimization process.

5.3.2 User Interfaces and System Interfaces

Well-designed user interfaces of the modeling, simulation, and optimization tools can enhance the utilization of the tools in the complex design process. Knowledge embedding and visualization with parametric BIM and simulation are two major issues of user interfaces.

5.3.2.1 User Interfaces: Knowledge Embedding

Standard practices and codes in construction can be adapted and embedded to define object behaviors through knowledge embedding (Eastman et al. 2011). However, a lack of physical properties in BIM limits BIM's direct use in simulation. For example, in existing BIM authoring tools, materials' thermal properties are included in the building element material libraries, but there are missing parameters, such as solar and infrared absorptivities, which are needed by new thermal simulation engines (Yan et al. 2013).

In existing BIM tools, certain design and engineering knowledge can be directly embedded into geometry components through tabular forms. For example, in Autodesk Revit Architecture, dimensions and materials are stored in the objects' property forms. Simple mathematical functions can be defined in the forms too. For more complex relationships between objects, including complex physical processes, mathematical equations, and computational algorithms with conditional statements and loop-based relationships, textual programming or scripting can be utilized through the modeling tools' application programming interface (API), such as Revit API. However, textual programming is beyond the access of most designers. For example, using LBNL's Modelica Buildings library to program a building model for thermal simulation is a challenging task.

In contrast, visual programming lets users create computer programs by manipulating program elements graphically rather than textually (Myers 1990). Based on a survey of 50 visual programming languages (Myers 1990), it is clear that a more visual style of programming could be easier to understand for nonprogrammers or novice programmers (architects normally fit into these categories). For parametric design, Grasshopper is a widely used visual programming tool that is embedded into the 3D modeling software Rhinoceros. It uses nodes and edges in a 2D graph to link parameters and pass values among model components to establish the parametric relations. In BIM, Dynamo as a visual programming tool is a new development by Autodesk. Figure 5.4 shows the different user interfaces for parametric modeling and BIM.

5.3.2.2 User Interfaces: Visualization

While most existing visualization research in architecture is focused on visualizing the visible: the geometry and materials of building design, there is a need to significantly expand the visualization to visualize the invisible: building parameters and their relationships. Visual programming can display the connection of parameters. However, when models become complex, the 2D graphs used in visual programming can be difficult to cognize and manipulate. For example, in the project of Hangzhou Olympics Stadium, the building's free form is defined by the complex model description in Grasshopper (Miller 2010). Without extensive assistance from the creators of these complex model graphs, one can hardly understand and work with the models. Even more, Grasshopper models are geometry-only, and when considering physical and functional parameters, the model complexity will be increased significantly, in which case an improved visualization for the parametric relationships is much needed.

Another type of invisible model aspects are the simulation results, such as thermal performance of the entire building and individual objects, which can be used to inform the design decision. Research

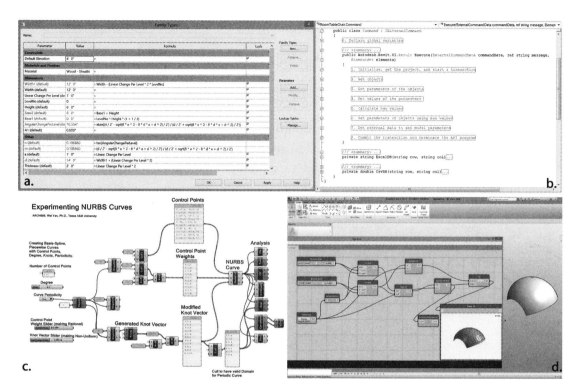

FIGURE 5.4   Current user interfaces for embedding design and engineering knowledge: (a) tabular form (Revit); (b) programming (Revit); (c) visual programming (Grasshopper); (d) visual programming (Dynamo).

efforts to visualize energy simulation results (Sreshthaputra et al. 2004, Haberl and Akleman 2010) have been made for supporting a better understanding of building energy performance analysis. However, the feedback provided by simulation, typically displayed as a series of tables and numbers, is difficult for understanding the causal relationship between building component design and simulation results (i.e., which components are performing well and which are not), information that is needed to improve the design. Information visualization after conducting building energy simulation will increase the effective use of simulation results in developing sustainable design (Jeong et al. 2013).

5.3.2.3 System Interfaces: Interoperability

Interoperability has always been a major issue in the AEC industry, as different applications and model formats across different domains co-exist in a building's lifecycle. Parametric modeling is geometry-based, while BIM is both geometry and object-based, but each has different underlying mathematical constructs. For example, architects may create NURBS curved geometry as a building form with a parametric modeling tool such as Rhinoceros/Grasshopper, but the geometry needs to be translated into mesh elements in a BIM tool such as Revit. In addition, with default graphic user interface (GUI) in existing BIM tools, only limited parametric capabilities at the building object level (e.g., the ratio between a window's height and width) are enabled, but not at the project level (e.g., the relation between weather data and building geometry or between a room's area/number of occupants and the width of its exit respecting fire egress regulations). As a result, current design practice has to employ parametric modeling and BIM separately, which presents significant problems of interoperability. For example, in both the Shanghai Center and Hang Zhou Olympics Stadium projects, the interoperability between parametric modeling and BIM was a major problem during the design process (Ji and Zheng 2010, Chen and Zhang 2012). The interoperability problems result in undesired modification of data structure (e.g., from NURBS to specific meshes) and the loss of parametric editing capability.

When considering design modeling and energy simulation tools, data exchange requires acquisition of building geometry from CAD or BIM tools (Bazjanac 2001) and geometry simplification (Bazjanac and Kiviniemi 2007). Both thermal and daylighting simulation require complicated building geometry and materials entered into simulation based on architectural models. A lack of interoperability between architectural models and building energy models prevents the efficient use of simulation in the building design process. Although both BIM and new energy modeling using the OOPM method are object-based, they are still significantly different in terms of object semantics, ontologies, data formats, and input/output user interfaces used by architecture and engineering software tools, reflecting the different perspectives between architects and engineers when looking at the same buildings (Yan et al. 2013). As computing power increases rapidly, simulation run times will likely be a less important concern, but data interoperability will remain a bottleneck in the design-simulation flow (Maile et al. 2007). Case studies presented below provide some experimental solutions for interoperability.

5.4 CASE STUDIES

Two case studies explore the direct application of BIM to parametric simulation: *Physical BIM (PBIM) for Building Design and Simulation* (Yan et al. 2013) and *BIM-based Parametric Simulation and Optimization* (Rahmani Asl et al. 2013).

5.4.1 Physical BIM for Thermal and Daylighting Simulations

The project aims to integrate physical simulation capabilities into BIM through the development of system interfaces (Physical BIM or PBIM) between BIM and multi-domain simulations for thermal and daylighting simulation. The approach to access BIM data is based on Revit's API. This is an alternative approach to the use of the inter-exchangeable BIM data format Industry Foundation Classes (IFC). Although IFC has several benefits, the advantages of the PBIM method make it a better solution for some cases: (1) the method allows more seamless and direct design-simulation integration without the translation from BIM to IFC and to simulation models, which increases process complexity significantly; and (2) the method preserves the parametric modeling capability that exists in the BIM tools, but not in IFC data. As design changes parametrically, objects modified in BIM can be updated automatically in the simulation models; thus design options can be tested quickly with this approach. From a design and simulation software user's point of view, both BIM and OOPM are object-based modeling approaches. From a design and simulation software developer's point of view, similar object-oriented programming methods used in BIM and OOPM facilitate the development of system interfaces between the two representations.

5.4.1.1 BIM to Thermal Modeling

The project created *Revit2Modelica*—a BIM to thermal modeling mapping prototype using Revit API and LBNL Modelica Buildings library (Wetter 2009). Based on BIM information (geometry, materials, location, etc.), the prototype can output a building energy model file in Modelica, start the simulation, and produce results, including heat flow of each building element, room temperatures, and annual heating and cooling loads.

5.4.1.2 BIM to Daylighting Modeling

The project also created *Revit2Radiance*, which is a BIM to daylighting prototype using the Revit API. Based on BIM (geometry, materials, location, date/time, a camera view, and sensor points), the prototype extracts the building surfaces in triangle meshes and other data needed to generate input files of Radiance and DAYSIM. Once the input files are created, Revit2Radiance calls Radiance and DAYSIM to run daylighting simulations. The results include Radiance-generated illumination images, human sensitivity images, isolux contour plots, and DAYSIM-generated annual illumination data.

Figure 5.5 shows the workflow of the project. Figure 5.6 shows a sample BIM model and thermal and daylighting simulation results. The thermal simulation results are validated using ASHRAE Standard 140 and by comparison with LBNL Modelica Buildings library models. The daylighting simulation validation is made by comparing the BIM model with the generated Radiance model displayed in a Radiance model viewer. The sample demonstrates that BIM models can be converted into thermal models and daylighting models through automated steps with high efficiency and accuracy.

The project demonstrates a new method (BIM to OOPM) for enhancing the interoperability between architectural design models and energy models. BIM becomes a common user interface for architectural design, thermal simulation, and daylighting simulation. There are several advantages of using BIM as the common user interface for simulations: it helps maintain data integrity among different models; BIM's interactive 3D modeling environment is easier to use for creating simulation models than creating building description files through coding (e.g., in Modelica) or through other inter-exchangeable file formats (e.g., converting BIM to CAD models and then converting CAD models to Radiance models). After BIM is created, both thermal and daylighting simulations can be completed quickly. Furthermore, the approach enables each building element's thermal performance to be visualized and examined separately. Architects can then be better informed to improve their design and design optimization may be achieved faster.

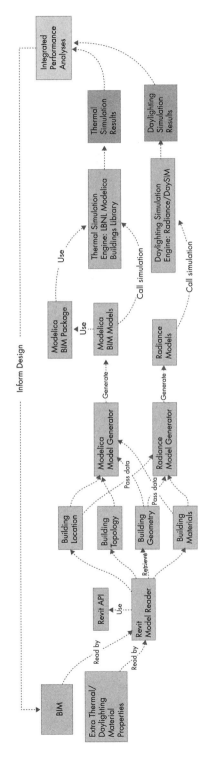

FIGURE 5.5 Workflow of BIM to multi-domain (thermal and daylighting) simulations. In the diagram, the components of Integrated Performance Analyses to Inform Design is expected to be implemented in the future.

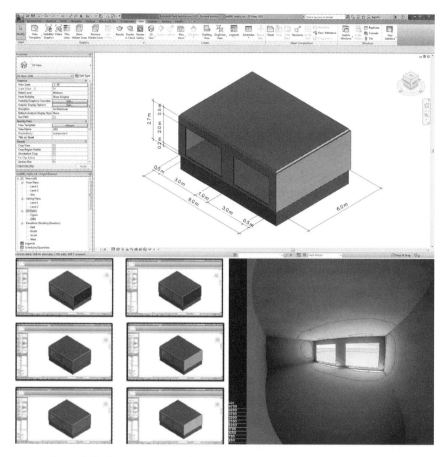

FIGURE 5.6 Top: Revit model of ASHRAE Standard 140 BESTEST Case 600. Lower left: Thermal simulation results (color-coded thermal transfer) using Revit2Modelica. Lower right: Radiance illumination result and rendering for the same BIM model using Revit2Radiance.
(Images courtesy of JongBum Kim [top]; WoonSeong Jeong [lower left], and Sandeep Kota [lower right])

5.4.2 Parametric BIM-Based Energy Optimization

This project prototypes a parametric BIM-based tool to optimize the energy performance of building design using cloud resources (Rahmani Asl et al. 2013). It uses Autodesk Revit for BIM creation, Green Building Studio (GBS) supported by cloud computing for thermal and daylighting simulations, and their respective APIs for extending existing functions in the two programs. The prototype enables parametric simulation runs for finding the optimal solution that fits the project's multiple objectives. All the operations from BIM to parametric simulations are inside a single user interface through the use of a custom Revit plug-in called Revit2GBSOpt (Revit to Green Building Studio optimization). Revit2GBSOpt creates gbXML files for a BIM model with parametric changes (value ranges specified by users) and uploads these files to GBS in the cloud through the Web for efficient energy analyses. It then retrieves the energy simulation results and finds the optimal solution for the project.

A simple sample building model is used for testing. For multi-objective optimization including day-lighting performance and the whole-building energy cost, the goal of this study is to find the optimized window size for minimizing the building energy consumption and at the same time achieving the LEED daylight credit. LEED requires the project to achieve a minimum glazing factor of 2 percent in 75 percent of all regularly occupied areas of the building.

In order to create design alternatives, a parametric window family is created with "width" and "height" parameters. Revit2GBSOpt sets a range of values for each of these two parameters based on user input and creates various alternative designs. By changing these two parameters of the window, 54 design options have been created. Revit2GBSOpt generates the gbXML files for all of the design options. A new project is

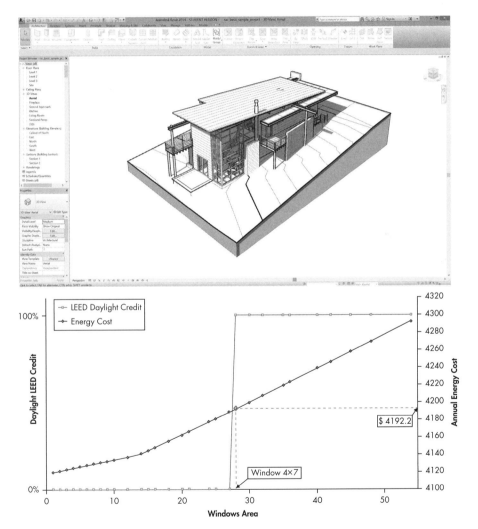

FIGURE 5.7   Top: A sample model of Autodesk Revit for the case study. Bottom: parametric optimization of windows sizes to receive the LEED daylighting credit and minimize the energy use.

(Image courtesy of Mohammad Rahmani Asl)

created in GBS with the project information gathered from the BIM model, including building location and building type. For each design option, a base run is created on GBS and its gbXML file is uploaded. GBS then runs the simulations in the cloud. Revit2GBSOpt retrieves the results from the GBS website. Using the building energy costs and LEED daylight results, the optimum size of the window is calculated. In this case, with the increase in the window's area, the building energy cost increases. Therefore, the design option with minimum window size that receives the LEED credit is the desired solution (Figure 5.7).

While existing experiments of building energy optimization require extensive manual translation from CAD or BIM models to energy models using multiple different software tools, this case study shows that Revit2GBSOpt can provide a single BIM user interface for parametric building modeling and performance simulation and optimization with automated model translation and cloud computing. It demonstrates the potential of making complex parametric simulation and optimization easier and tightly integrated with architectural modeling. In the future, advanced optimization algorithms, such as multi-objective genetic algorithms, can be integrated into the process.

5.5 CONCLUSION

A streamlined process of parametric modeling, BIM, and building energy modeling has great potential to facilitate sustainable building design and optimization. Important research questions exist in the areas of model complexity and computability, user interfaces for knowledge embedding, visualization of the building parameters and their relationships, and system interfaces or interoperability between architectural modeling and multi-domain simulations. Extensive future research and development of parametric modeling, BIM, and energy simulation tools and related computing technologies (e.g., new visual programming tools for parametric BIM, object-oriented physical modeling for energy simulation, and cloud computing for optimization) are expected to address these questions.

ACKNOWLEDGMENTS

The Physical BIM project (Case Study 1) described in the paper is based on work supported by the National Science Foundation under Grant No. 0967446. The Parametric BIM-Based Energy Optimization project (Case Study 2) is supported by Autodesk, Inc. The author also would like to thank the members of the BIM-SIM Lab in the Department and College of Architecture at Texas A&M University for collaboration on the case studies.

DISCUSSION QUESTIONS

1. What is the relationship between BIM and parametric modeling?
2. How can parametric BIM facilitate building simulation and optimization?

3. Describe a current method of interoperability between BIM and energy modeling. How can this be improved? How might this be enhanced for coordination and interaction between different simulations, such as thermal and daylighting?

4. Describe a theoretically possible BIM with the full power of parametric modeling for conceptual massing of arbitrary complexity (e.g., when the form being NURBS surfaces) that enables a significantly larger design space searchable for more optimal solutions.

5. How can one combine tabular forms, visual programming, and textual programming into a seamless multifunctional interface and allow designers, engineers, and software developers to embed design and engineering knowledge into models and design tools?

6. How can cloud computing be utilized for optimization calculation? In other words, explain how to distribute the computing resources for energy performance calculation based on parametric changes, how to enable incremental changes to be sent from the local computers where the building models reside, to the cloud where the simulations run, and how to enable incremental changes to be made in the simulation calculation, without a complete recalculation for the entire building model.

REFERENCES

Aish, R., and R. Woodbury. 2005. "Multi-Level Interaction in Parametric Design." *Smart Graphics*, vol. 3638, 151–162.

ANSI/ASHRAE. 2007. *Standard Method of Test for the Evaluation of Building Energy Analysis Computer Programs*. Atlanta, GA: American Society of Heating, Refrigerating and Air-Conditioning Engineers, Inc.

Athienitis, A. K., T. Kesik, I. B. Morrison, M. Noguchi, A. Tzempelikos, R. Charron, P. Karava, et al. 2006. "Development of Requirements for a Solar Building Conceptual Design Tool." Proceedings of Joint 31st Solar Energy Society of Canada and 1st Solar Buildings Research Network Conference.

Bazjanac, V. 2001. "Acquisition of Building Geometry in the Simulation of Energy Performance." *Building Simulation*, 305–311.

———. 2008. "IFC BIM-Based Methodology for Semi-Automated Building Energy Performance Simulation," CIB-W78: 25th International Conference on Information Technology in Construction, Santiago, Chile, July 15–17, 2008.

Bazjanac, V., and A. Kiviniemi. 2007. "Reduction, Simplification, Translation and Interpretation in the Exchange of Model Data." *CIB W78*: 25th International Conference on Information Technology in Construction, Santiago, Chile, July 15–17, 2008, 163–168.

Charron, R., and A. Athienitis. 2006. "Design and Optimization of Net Zero Energy Solar Homes." *Transactions*. American Society of Heating Refrigerating and Air Conditioning Engineers, 112(2): 285.

Chen, J., and D. Zhang. 2012. "BIM Technology in Shanghai Center Design" (in Chinese). In *Building Structure*, vol. 3, www.buildingstructure.com.cn/Item/4381.aspx.

Clayton, M., J. Haberl, and W. Yan. 2009. "Development of a Reference Building Information Model (BIM) for Thermal Model Compliance Testing." ASHRAE Research Project 1468 Proposal.

Crawley, D. B., J. W. Hand, M. Kummert, and B. T. Griffith. 2008. "Contrasting the Capabilities of Building Energy Performance Simulation Programs." *Building and Environment* 43(4): 661–673.

DOE. 2006. *Annual Energy Review 2006*. Washington, DC: U.S. Department of Energy.

Eastman, C., P. Teicholz, R. Sacks, and K. Liston. 2011. *BIM Handbook: A Guide to Building Information Modeling for Owners, Managers, Designers, Engineers and Contractors*. Hoboken, NJ: John Wiley and Sons.

Erhan, H., R. Woodbury, and N. Salmasi. 2009. "Visual Sensitivity Analysis of Parametric Design Models: Improving Agility in Design." *Joining Languages, Cultures and Visions: CAADFutures*, pp. 815–829.

Fritzson, P. A. 2004. *Principles of Object-Oriented Modeling and Simulation with Modelica 2.1*. New York: Wiley-IEEE Press.

Gane, V. 2004. "Parametric Design: A Paradigm Shift?" Thesis, Massachusetts Institute of Technology.

Gane, V., and J. Haymaker. 2007. "Conceptual Design of High-Rises with Parametric Methods." *Predicting the Future*. 25th eCAADe Conference Proceedings, pp. 978–80.

Haberl, Jeff, and Ergun Akleman. 2010. "Demonstration of the Use of Multimedia Electronic Information Enhancements." For a chapter handbook CD-ROM: 3D Modeling and Animation (Report), ASHRAE *Transactions*.

Jeong, W., J. Kim, M. Clayton, J. Haberl, and W. Yan. 2013. "Visualization of Building Energy Performance in Building Information Models." Proceedings of the Association for Computer Aided Design in Architecture (ACADIA), October 24–27. Cambridge, Ontario, Canada.

Jesus, L., M. G. Almeida, and E. Pereira. 2005. "The Difficulties of Implementation of Bipv in Portugal: Rejection or Abstention?" In S. Kyvelou and K. Katerina (eds.), *Sustainable Construction: Action for Sustainability in the Mediterranean Region: Proceedings of the International SB05MED Conference, Athens, Greece*. Athens: SD-MED Association

Ji, C., and C. Zheng. 2010. "Utilization of Parametric Design in the Main Stadium of Hangzhou Olympic and International EXPO Centre" (in Chinese). *Architectural Art and Technology* 1; available at www.cqvip.com/QK/98474A/201101/1001962998.html, accessed on February 21, 2014.

Kalogirou, S. A. 2004. "Optimization of Solar Systems Using Artificial Neural-Networks and Genetic Algorithms." *Applied Energy* 77(4): 383–405.

Krish, S. 2011. "A Practical Generative Design Method." *Computer-Aided Design*, 43(1): 88–100.

Lee, G., R. Sacks, and C. Eastman. 2006. "Specifying Parametric Building Object Behavior (BOB) for a Building Information Modeling System." *Automation in Construction* 15(6): 758–776.

Maile, T., M. Fischer, and V. Bazjanac. 2007. "Building Energy Performance Simulation Tools: A Life-Cycle and Interoperable Perspective." *Center for Integrated Facility Engineering (CIFE) Working Paper 107 (2007)*.

Majumdar, A. 2008. "Buildings That Think Green." Science at the Theater Lecture Series, Lawrence Berkeley National Laboratory, Berkeley, CA. Presented on September 22, 2008. Video, available at http://eetd.lbl.gov/video/14123/science-at-the-theatre-buildings-that-think-green.

Miller, N. 2010. "[make]SHIFT: Information Exchange and Collaborative Design Workflows." *Proceedings of the 30th Annual Conference of the Association for Computer Aided Design in Architecture (ACADIA)*, New York, pp. 139–144.

Myers, B. A. 1990. "Taxonomies of Visual Programming and Program Visualization." *Journal of Visual Languages and Computing* 1(1): 97–123.

Nouidui, T. S., K. Phalak, W. Zuo, and M. Wetter. 2012. "Validation and Application of the Room Model of the Modelica Buildings Library." Proceedings of the 9th International Modelica Conference, Munich, Germany.

NSF. 2009. "The Challenge of Sustainable Energy." Arlington, VA: National Science Foundation.

NSTC. 2008. "Federal Research and Development Agenda for Net-Zero Energy." *High-Performance Green Buildings*. National Science and Technology Council, October. www.bfrl.nist.gov/buildingtechnology/documents/FederalRDAgendaforNetZeroEnergyHighPerformanceGreenBuildings.pdf.

Park, S. M., Mahjoub Elnimeiri, David C. Sharpe, and Robert J. Krawczyk. 2004. "Tall Building Form Generation by Parametric Design Process." *Proceedings of the CTBUH 2004 Conference*, October 10–13, Seoul, Korea.

Qian, C. Z. 2007. "Design Patterns: Augmenting User Intention in Parametric Design Systems." *Proceedings of the 6th ACM SIGCHI Conference on Creativity and Cognition*, pp. 295–295.

Rahmani Asl, M., S. Zarrinmehr, and W. Yan. 2013. "Towards BIM-based Parametric Building Energy Performance Optimization." Proceedings of the Association for Computer Aided Design in Architecture (ACADIA), October 24–27. Cambridge, Ontario, Canada.

Reinhart, C., and A. Fitz. 2006. "Findings from a Survey on the Current Use of Daylight Simulations in Building Design." *Energy and Buildings* 38(7): 824–835.

Sreshthaputra, A., J. Haberl, and M. J Andrews. 2004. "Improving Building Design and Operation of a Thai Buddhist Temple." *Energy and Buildings* 36(6) (June): 481–494. doi:10.1016/j.enbuild.2003.12.010.

Stocking, A. W. 2009. "Generative Design Is Changing the Face of Architecture." Available at: www.cadalyst.com/cad/building-design/generative-design-is-changing-face-architecture-12948 (accessed September 6, 2013).

Torcellini, P., S. Pless, M. Deru, B. Griffith, N. Long, and R. Judkoff. 2006. "Lessons Learned from Case Studies of Six High-Performance Buildings." Washington, DC: National Renewable Energy Laboratory.

Welle, B., M. Fischer, J. Haymaker, and V. Bazjanac. 2012. "CAD-Centric Attribution Methodology for Multidisciplinary Optimization (CAMMO): Enabling Designers to Efficiently Formulate and Evaluate Large Design Spaces." *CIFE Technical Report #195*, Center for Integrated Facility Engineering, Stanford, CA

Wetter, M. 2009. "Modelica-Based Modelling and Simulation to Support Research and Development in Building Energy and Control Systems." *Journal of Building Performance Simulation* 2(2): 143.

Wetter, M., and C. Haugstetter. 2006. "Modelica Versus TRNSYS—A Comparison between an Equation-Based and a Procedural Modeling Language for Building Energy Simulation." *Proceedings of Simbuild*, 2nd National Conference of IBPSAUSA.

Woodbury, R., 2010. *Elements of Parametric Design*. New York: Routledge.

Wright, J. A., H. A. Loosemore, and R. Farmani. 2002. "Optimization of Building Thermal Design and Control by Multi-Criterion Genetic Algorithm." *Energy and Buildings* 34(9): 959–972.

Wujec, T. 2011. "Imagine Design Create." *Autodesk*.

Yan, W., M. Clayton, J. Haberl, W. Jeong, J. Kim, S. Kota, J. Bermudez Alcocer, and M. Dixit. 2013. "Interfacing BIM with Building Thermal and Daylighting Modeling." 13th International Conference of the International Building Performance Simulation Association (IBPSA), August 25–28, Chambery, France.

Zhang, Y., and I. Korolija. 2010. "Performing Complex Parametric Simulations with iEPlus." Set2010-- 9th International Conference on Sustainable Energy Technologies; Shanghai, China, 24–27 August 2010.

CHAPTER 6

Models and Measurement: Changing Design Value with Simulation, Analysis, and Outcomes

Phillip G. Bernstein, Autodesk Strategic Industry Relations,
*   Yale School of Architecture*
Matt Jezyk, Autodesk Software Engineering

6.1 INTRODUCTION

In the first decades of the twenty-first century, the wide availability of powerful, scaled computers with sufficient storage and graphic capabilities to architects, engineers, and builders has enabled a transition in the fundamental means of building representation from two-dimensional drawings as diagrams of design intent to three-dimensional, behaviorally dynamic digital prototypes or building information models (BIM). This shift is significant for reasons beyond the entry of construction into the more modern paradigms of digital modeling and computer-controlled fabrication that has been well understood in manufacturing for decades. Building design that is predicated on such models becomes transformed by other equally powerful changes in design methodology, in particular the easy availability of simulation and analysis, optimization by parametric manipulation, and direct-to-fabrication representation that translates design intent immediately into a constructed artifact. In combination, these technologies will redefine the structures and outcomes of the design act itself. With that change comes the potential to transform the value proposition of the design disciplines to the building industry marketplace.

6.2 BIM 1.0

A decade after the introduction of BIM to the mainstream architecture, engineering, construction (AEC) marketplace, BIM adoption in mature markets has reached 70 percent of architects, engineers, and builders (Jones, 2012). This first iteration of model-based work has focused primarily on the generation of more accurate and well-coordinated production drawings and relied on the self-integrated database representation of a building described in BIM in which drawing information is derived as a report from that database. Much like the transition from manual drafting to CAD that fully matured in mainstream practice in the 1990s, this shift served the same ends (detailed technical drawings) by different means (BIM-based representation and CAD respectively). CAD-based production empowered more precise drawing, integration of representation at various scales, and a certain facility with new geometries like complex curves and three-dimensional geometric exploits. Digital representation in AEC prior to BIM was CAD-based drawing, with more esoteric digital explorations left mostly to the experimental and academic work of a few avant garde designers using tools original created for gaming or visualization purposes outside of the building disciplines.

While purpose-built for architectural design and engineering, the first commercial applications of BIM, or what is referred to here as "BIM 1.0," focused in large part on the most challenging problems of production and documentation precision—to wit, the creation of better working drawings. As BIM platforms for architectural, structural, MEP (mechanical, electrical, plumbing), and construction representation matured through the first decade of the twenty-first century, the tool was largely understood to be aimed at these ends, rather than the creation, ideation, or generation of original design concepts or the necessary insights to refine or iterate them. Rudimentary analysis, in the form of rapid quantity calculations like materials or areas, was a byproduct of BIM work, but was seen as a secondary benefit of the real thrust of BIM usage under 1.0, making better drawings through multidisciplinary collaboration. The digital transparency of a BIM-based project encouraged such work.

Such an adoption pattern was anticipated forty years earlier by Nicolas Negroponte at what was to be the predecessor of the MIT Media Lab, the "Architecture Machine" project (Negroponte 1970). In that work, Negroponte asserted that the first implementation of a new technology emulates its predigital process and that only through the evolution of use and understanding can that tool truly transform the processes it supports. BIM 1.0 demonstrated that the pattern holds, even today.

The evolution of BIM 1.0 saw both "horizontal" development of capabilities in the creation of capabilities across building disciplines and "vertical" elaboration of the representational models through increased precision and description of physical systems and their relationships. These developments laid the groundwork for further analysis and simulation capabilities as the technology matured.

6.3 ANALYSIS AND SIMULATION THROUGH BIM 1.0

Even as BIM 1.0 became mainstream, methodologies for analysis and simulation—the processes by which an AEC can reason inferentially about a design—remain largely isolated to pockets of domain experts deployed with specific evaluative tasks in the development of a design. Energy analysis, structural evaluations, lighting design, and acoustic performance are each provided to an architect through specialty consultants working in a largely transactional model of propose/evaluate/dispose/repropose. Results of these analyses are reported back to the requesting architect, who attempts to reconfigure the emerging design in response to the constraints and implications of this outsourced evaluation. Analytical inference is limited at best, and the nature of the transactional information exchange inhibits the free flow of ideas and the integrated interaction of technical disciplines in the service of progressing the design. The iterative design process of the architect, especially during the early stages, did not mesh well with the slower exchange of information with consultants, and opportunities for changes informed by analysis, design decision feedback, and studies of trade-offs were often lacking.

As BIM 1.0 methodologies were overlaid on traditional scopes of design service (schematics through construction) some simulative and analytical capabilities came to the fore, the first of which was changes in the way project costs were calculated by architects based on material take-offs that could be easily generated from a BIM. Extracting these quantities rapidly and precisely reduced both the cycle time and uncertainty of cost estimating, allowing builders to estimate an evolving design with greater accuracy much more quickly, and reducing the variability of the results accordingly. Confidence in cost estimating in BIM rose rapidly as a result.

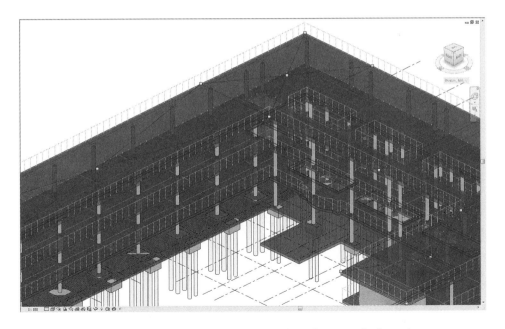

FIGURE 6.1   Structural physical and analytical models combined in Autodesk Revit.
(http://bimcurriculum.autodesk.com/exercise/exercise-5-revit-robot-link)

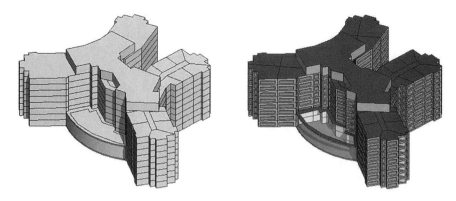

FIGURE 6.2   Physical and energy analytical models as two representations of same model in Autodesk Revit.

Structural engineering as a discipline has used purpose-built analytical models for structural calculations long before the advent of BIM. But under BIM 1.0, the connection of the physical architectural and structural representations to analytical models made finding specific structural solutions and coordinating the resulting design implications considerably more efficient (Figure 6.1).

Early, rudimentary energy analysis was possible by connecting, through various means, outputs from BIM data to energy analysis systems such as EnergyPlus or DOE 2.0. Cost estimating, structural calculations, and energy analysis (Figures 6.2, 6.3, 6.4) were early indicators of the potential for analysis and simulation that more developed implementations of BIM-based process might make possible.

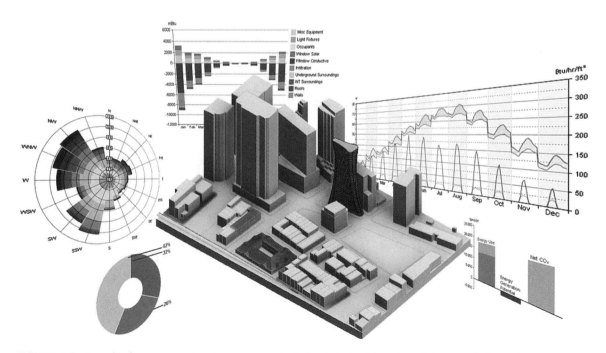

FIGURE 6.3   Results from conceptual energy analysis in Autodesk Revit and Autodesk Vasari.

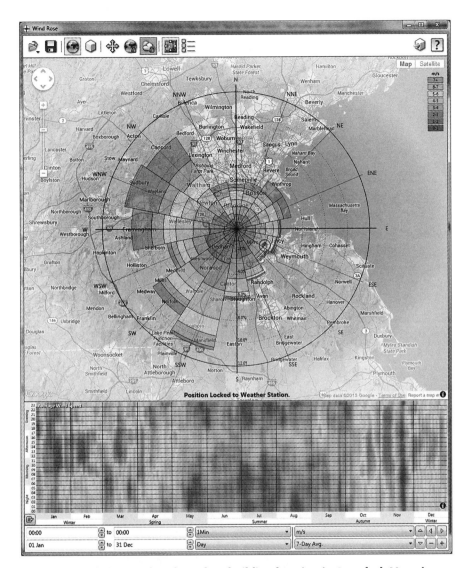

FIGURE 6.4 Wind rose and climate data based on building location in Autodesk Vasari.

6.4 BIM 2.0

As the industry absorbs BIM 1.0 and, as anticipated by Negroponte, new process possibilities become apparent, a second generation of BIM comes to the fore, "BIM 2.0," the intersection of three related evolutionary characteristics of maturing modeling approaches. First, multidisciplinary, integrated, higher-resolution versions of BIM make much more complete digital prototypes of building designs possible and create a robust representational platform for design analysis and investigation. Models under BIM 2.0 comprise both complex geometry that is the skeleton of the digital prototype, the detailed

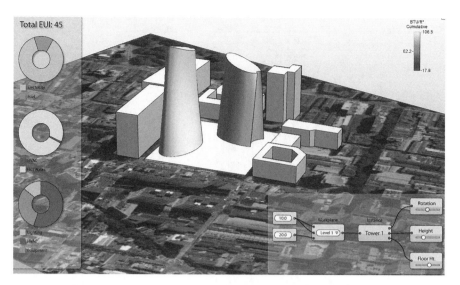

FIGURE 6.5 Energy analysis results overlaid on an Autodesk Vasari parametric model.

characteristic data described above, and fixed settings (like the dimension of a window) as well as parameters that vary by circumstances (where that dimension might be derived computationally from adjacent geometry or meta-data in the design). Computational access to these setting allows the designer to manipulate the design by both direct intervention (changing the dimension itself) or by algorithmic manipulation (accessing the variable that represents the dimension through a script and adjusting its value).

The resulting data-rich environment, likely combined with the computational and storage potential of the cloud, will make possible a second characteristic, software-based analysis procedures and evaluation algorithms tied to model-based meta-data (Figures 6.5 and 6.6). More complex computer-based

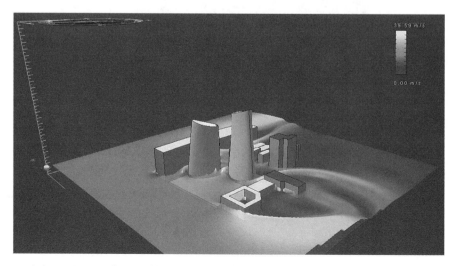

FIGURE 6.6 Real-time CFD wind tunnel based on an Autodesk Vasari parametric model.

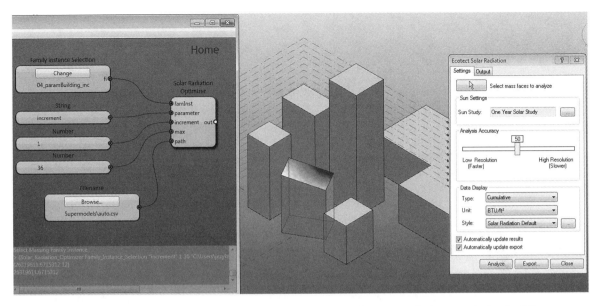

FIGURE 6.7 Using Dynamo Visual Programming and solar insolation analysis to optimize building orientation.

assessment can result from the more detailed digital description of BIM 2.0, since such second-generation models contain considerable additional information from which calculations can be made. Several of the authors of this book explore the specific technical implications and options of such analysis and simulation.

Finally, BIM 2.0 meta-data stored as parameters can be combined with computational scripts that can manipulate that data to both generate new design solutions and, by virtue of the results of digital analysis, evaluate and optimize selected design decisions related to both the form and performance of a building, and this is a critical distinction. While scripting and algorithmic design generation has largely been focused on the creation of formal solutions like specific geometric shapes and topologies (Schumacher 2012), such "parametricism" deployed in the service of design creation writ large opens up an entirely new realm of design methodology (Reinhart 2011). It will also make possible completely new types of design strategies and solutions that will directly address both formal objectives of the designer and measurable, performance-based results of the resulting decisions (Figures 6.7 and 6.8).

6.5 GEOMETRY, BEHAVIORAL PROPERTIES, PARAMETERS, AND ANALYSIS

BIM 2.0 as defined by enhanced resolution, level of detail, and computational power necessary to exploit parametric design combined with robust analysis and simulation results in a powerful new set of strategies for designers. Consider by contrast the case of structural analysis, which under BIM 1.0 was

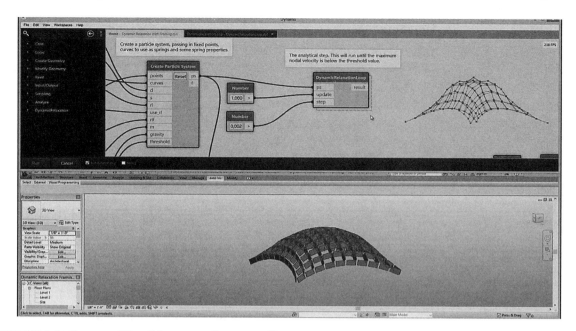

FIGURE 6.8   Dynamo Visual Programming controlling a Revit Structure model.

reasonably robust but based only on analytical models that represented the underlying mathematics of basic structural forces in a building (lines of force, moments, shear connections, etc.). The designer's control of the building structure becomes considerably more refined under BIM 2.0, where the model representation can be interrogated and manipulated based on the following far beyond the simple three-dimensional geometry of the underlying building design:

- **Single material definitions** comprising useful aesthetic and performance characteristics based on, for example, the choice of concrete or steel or specific connection assemblies.
- **Assemblies of materials** that describe the interaction and relationship of adjacent systems and solutions, such as combinations of glazing and framing materials at the intersections of the building enclosure that create specific structural dynamics.
- **Objects connected to make a system** where the physical properties of the material (steel, concrete, timber) contribute to the structural performance of a building as a system of performative elements operating in a connected topology that creates an integrated model of the building structure itself. The interaction of the system itself becomes part of the explicit intent of the designer at the outset of the design, and that interaction at all three levels of detail is transparent to the designer and her collaborators.

There are many other examples of the complex interaction of systems where this construct can enhance designer insight. The design strategy for daylighting, for example, affects the users' experience of the building, its energy use, and its carbon footprint. The combination of glazing, lighting, heating/cooling, and sunlight control systems simulated explicitly in a model and combined with numerical analysis of lighting levels, energy consumption, air flow, and shadowing is a "system of systems." Before BIM in any form these interdependencies were simply too complex to understand in detail without extensive manual calculations or use of rules of thumb, but can now be manipulated—and design ideas rapidly iterated—in concert.

Mathematical analysis of the results of such manipulations is a critical part of the changing process that will result. The parametric manipulation of form and geometry is well-trod ground, but the use of parametric scripting in combination with analytical results from digital simulation tools broadens the designer's power considerably. The size, location, and proportion of a building's windows, for example, could be generated not only from the designer's compositional intent for the façade but based on the implications for daylighting levels in the building interior, the resulting demands on the heating/cooling system, and the embedded carbon in the glazing itself. A complex multi-variable equation results that can be solved computationally through adjustment and iteration that far exceeds the power and grasp of designers unempowered by modeling and allows the designer to see, understand, and select from a wide range of potential options. Information displayed with the design model itself, as suggested in Figures 6.9, 6.10, and 6.11, guides the designer in choosing an optimal solution.

When the characteristic parameters of systems are accessible by scripts or algorithms, an even more powerful strategy emerges for their definition through further automation. Digital scripting allows the manipulation of parameters of the design based on the results of analytical evaluation of the model during the development of the design itself and thereby changes the nature of the design process. In the example above, the aggregate size of the windows might be constrained by the total target carbon footprint of the glazing, bounding the solution in a certain way. By creating a script that controls and manipulates the characteristics of the design, the designer both rationalizes the solution space of potential answers and embeds the characteristics of her design intent within the solution itself, with important ramifications for how design strategy and methodology will unfold under BIM 2.0.

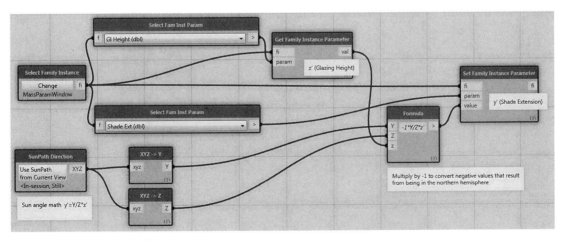

FIGURE 6.9 Dynamo Visual Programming graph connecting altitude and azimuth to a window component.

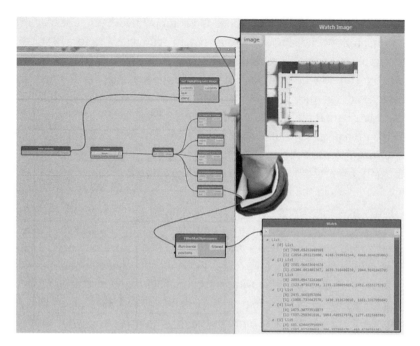

FIGURE 6.10   Dynamo Visual Programming graph driving cloud daylighting calculation.

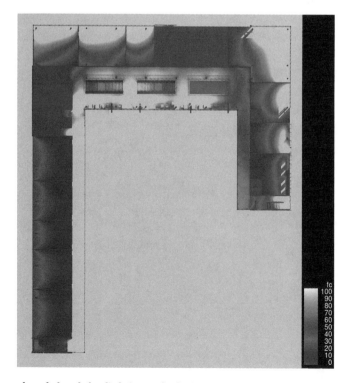

FIGURE 6.11   Visual results of cloud daylighting calculation.

6.6 IDEATION AND DESIGN PRODUCTION UNDER BIM 2.0

The traditional ideation strategy comprises the sequence {Create} {Test} {Evaluate} {Refine} {Repeat}. The complex representation of the design under BIM, the resulting insights of automated analysis and simulation, and the ability to define and manipulate design intent through the powerful combination of parameters and scripting challenges this in several important ways.

First, the definition of design intent, previously instantiated in two-dimensional diagrams display through drawings, becomes considerably more robust, dynamic, precise, and important under the BIM 2.0 construct and not simply because the resulting representation is of higher detail. If drawings were thin proxies—mere diagrams of intent—of a resulting building, a building information model writ large is a digital simulation of the building itself, and under BIM 1.0 that data results in mostly better, less thin drawing representations. But BIM 2.0 defines intent by overlaying far greater detail in combination with the analytical simulative results of that detail. The possibility of goal-oriented procedural scripts clearly set out the limits of the design itself. Tacit, implicit design objectives are made explicit by the objective function of declaring a design goal that is represented by a script, as shown in Figure 6.12; intent is thus imbued in both the creation and the result of the design process.

Second, even without the dynamic of scripting and parametric control, the results that model-based analysis make immediate to the designer shorten the cycle time between ideation and understanding (the design "feedback loop"), making iteration much more rapid and insightful. Prior to BIM 2.0 analytical

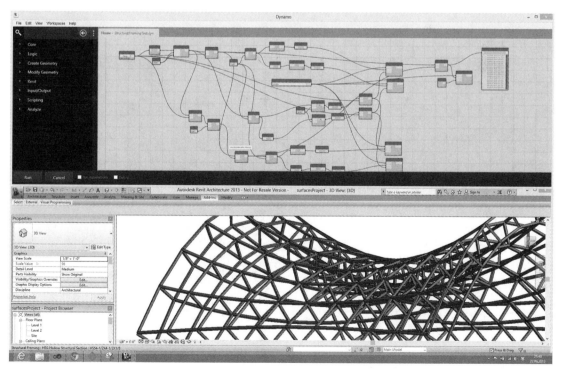

FIGURE 6.12 Dynamo Visual Programming optimization of a space frame truss.

implications of digital simulations of the design were "outsourced" to consultants or largely unavailable without special intervention. For example, an energy consultant would run simulations of the current building design and report the results back to the architect in a cumbersome, time-consuming, and expensive sequence. Under more modern BIM 2.0 protocols such evaluations are immediately served up to the designer by software that reports implications in real time as the design develops. The power of the cloud, where much simulation software is moving under current software development strategies, will free designers from the computation constraints of a desktop computer, making it possible to perform simultaneous development of the design in parallel with the resulting analysis of implications, essentially in real time as ideas are developed.

Third, the resolution and materiality of BIM 2.0 bridges the gap between design ideation and actual construction. The detailed, procedural definition of the design and its accompanying analysis makes the transfer of digital design information to the factory floor and project job site much more direct than traditional translation through design drawings. The resulting information is both more accurate and more valuable to the entire building enterprise. The example in Figure 6.13, where structural members are generated parametrically within the BIM, indicates how such information then becomes immediately available for subsequent definition and fabrication of steel elements.

The importance of these three developments in design process cannot be understated, as they make measurable, explicit results available to the designer as an implicit part of the design process and will move the evaluation and understanding of the implications of a design far away from pure "designer's judgment" and into the realm of performance-based processes. Engineers and builders will likely

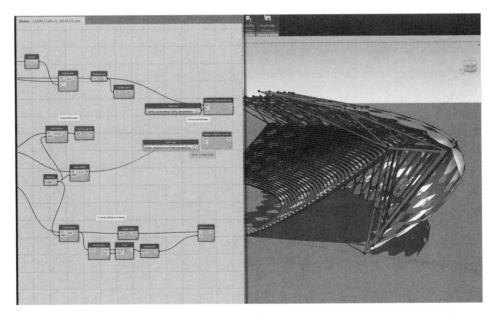

FIGURE 6.13   Stadium parametric model created in Dynamo Visual Programming for Revit.

welcome such a change with enthusiasm, architects with trepidation as the former see the potential of accuracy and productivity while the latter assume typical concerns of simultaneous loss of control and increased risk. But the fear that computer-based building design software will replace architects is largely unfounded if architects embrace, rather than summarily reject, these newfound capabilities.

6.7 DESIGN EMPOWERMENT

Peter Rowe, has argued that architectural design is a process of solving "wicked problems" (as originally defined by Horst Rittel) that are largely unsuited to procedural methodologies:

> Architectural design problems can also be referred to as being "wicked problems" in that they have no definitive formulation, no explicit "stopping rule," always more than one plausible explanation, a problem formulation that corresponds to a solution and vice versa, and that their solutions cannot be strictly correct or false. Tackling a problem of this type requires some initial insight, the exercise of some provisional set of rules, inference, or plausible strategy, in other words, the use of heuristic reasoning. (Rowe 1982)

Heuristic reasoning defined here is an implicit strategy employed the human designer to see and affect the ineffable synthesis to a design problem beyond mere solution. Is heuristic reasoning, and to a large extent the pursuit of the ineffable qualities of architectural design, enhanced or compromised by the advent of BIM 2.0 and its capabilities? Inasmuch as design process is a combination of both heuristic and procedural thinking, there is the possibility that heuristics will be overwhelmed with procedures, algorithms, analytical results, and data, and the resulting buildings will be energy efficient, cost-effective, and banal. One might argue, however, that such challenges have faced architects since the advent of complex engineering demands on building, and that the availability of the added performative insights of BIM, analysis, and parametricism empowers, rather than enfeebles, an architect to understand, manipulate, and control the development and implications of her design explicitly and in doing so can create even better work. And as the power and capabilities of BIM 2.0 expand with the advent of the cloud and its unlimited supply of computational power and storage, the more mundane aspects of design process—cost modeling, code analysis, energy performance—will become increasingly automated and immediately available, giving designers more time to do what they do best—understand and interpret the world and express their ideas through architectural design. It is a choice that architects must make as technology is increasingly integrated into their design processes.

6.8 CONCLUSION: AVENUES TO ALTERNATIVE VALUE GENERATION

Designers are empowered, rather than constrained, by the capabilities of the transformative technologies of modeling, simulation, and analysis, and parametric scripting as the industry moves from BIM 1.0 to 2.0. The implications of these methods could be more profound than an incremental change in design methodologies and outcomes. Design services in modern construction economies are largely bought and sold as commodities become disconnected, in the main, from the value they deliver to the marketplace. The business models of construction are based on lowest first cost procurement across the supply chain, from the "purchase" of design services through selection of general contractors to competitive bidding of subcontractors, suppliers, and fabricators. Buildings themselves are treated largely as complex, risky commodities that are critical to their users but designed and built by service providers who struggle to correlate the resulting value those buildings deliver to the value they receive for designing and building them. Design and construction is complex, risky, and not very profitable. The marketplace usually rewards such assumption of risk with reward, but this equation is largely broken in the building industry.

Architects in particular tend to correlate their value with the ineffable aspects of their work and bemoan the fact that "design" as a service is largely unappreciated by the public or their clients. It might be that "design" is not unappreciated but rather assumed to be a given by those clients who are commissioning buildings to serve other more prosaic ends (like delivering health care or creating research infrastructure) and presuming that "good design" will come as a result. The overlay of BIM 2.0 described here, however, creates a value opportunity for architects, engineers, and builders that might otherwise confront the heavy commoditization of their services by introducing the concept of measurement and outcomes to their work.

Project delivery methods that have evolved under BIM 1.0 challenge traditional commoditized work by introducing the idea of measurable outcomes that are correlated to profit by design and construction providers. Rather than purchase design services and construction by fixed price determined by lowest bid, these models define specific outcomes desired by the client, such as budget, energy, or quality performance, and pay designers and builders based on achieving these ends (Ashcraft, 2012). As the simulative and analytic capabilities of BIM 2.0 provide design and build teams with the opportunity to anticipate and optimize a wider array of such possible outcomes, business models will evolve accordingly and clients will be more willing to tie contract structures and compensation strategies to those outcomes. That approach decouples design and construction work from its commoditized basis today and reconnects it directly to the outcomes that clients value most, the performance of their projects. The resulting buildings will be more effective and beautiful, and their providers paid more appropriately for creating that value, an outcome that is richly deserved.

DISCUSSION QUESTIONS

1. Explain the major differences between BIM 1.0 and BIM 2.0 with respect to opportunities for analysis and simulation.
2. How can BIM 2.0 help architects provide acknowledged value for their design services?
3. How can parametric design be used beyond form-making?
4. What types of questions can be answered by incorporating analysis into the design process?
5. What techniques can be used to connect parametric design with analysis?
6. What is visual programming? What is scripting?

REFERENCES

Ashcraft, Howard. 2012. *The IPD Framework* at www.hansonbridgett.com/Publications/pdf/~/media/Files/Publications/IPD_Framework.pdf, accessed August 2013.

Jones, Steve. 2012. "Business Value of BIM," *Smart Market Report 2012*. New York: McGraw Hill Construction Analytics.

Negroponte, Nicolas. 1970. *The Architecture Machine*. Cambridge, MA: MIT Press.

Schumacher, P. 2012. "Parametricism as Style—Parametricist Manifesto." Lecture presented and discussed at the Dark Side Club, 11th Architecture Biennale, Venice 2008, www.patrikschumacher.com/Texts/Parametricism%20as%20Style.html.

Reinhart, C. F. 2011. "Simulation-based Daylight Performance Predictions." In *Building Performance Simulation for Design and Operation*, J. Hensen and R. Lamberts, eds. New York: Spon Press.

Rowe, P. G. 1982. "A Priori Knowledge and Heuristic Reasoning in Architectural Design." *Journal of Architectural Education* 36 (1): 18–23.

CHAPTER 7

Energy Modeling in Conceptual Design

Timothy Hemsath, University of Nebraska—Lincoln

7.1 INTRODUCTION

The 2012 American Institute of Architect's *Guide to Integrating Energy Modeling in the Design Process* (AIA 2012) expresses a critical professional need to more clearly understand and utilize energy modeling. In addition to the business benefits energy modeling provides the architecture profession, there is the transformative potential of conceptual energy modeling to produce energy-efficient buildings. Today this is accomplished using specific software often utilized by energy consultants. Building information modeling (BIM) could expand energy modeling use beyond these experts. BIM plays a critical role for assisting designers in making the best decisions about energy savings in building design. It enables evaluation of energy considerations to occur early in conceptual design. BIM brings significant change to the architectural design process by introducing energy modeling early and thereby shortening the distance between evaluation and design.

The benefits of BIM for modeling energy in conceptual design are built on understanding what building performance simulation is, the role of BIM in the design process, conceptual design decisions, sensitivity analysis and design optimization, and how BIM affords assisting designers to evaluate design decisions. Key decisions about when and what to simulate during design is important to understand to reduce energy consumption of buildings.

7.2 BUILDING PERFORMANCE SIMULATION (BPS)

Building performance simulation (BPS) is not new to the process of building design. Like a virtual simulation, physical handmade models and drawings are key abstractions representing functions of particular building elements. Building energy modeling (BEM) is an aspect of BPS representing energy performance within a building. For architects, BEM considerations include the proper use, application of the simulation tool for design evaluation, and determining when to use the tool effectively.

Proper use requires ". . . sufficient domain knowledge by the user of the software" (Hensen 2004) in order to effectively simulate energy performance. However, in BEM, "this expert knowledge is limited by the accumulation of knowledge and current workflow directed to the energy modeler" (Schlueter and Thesseling 2008), putting distance between the architect and his ability to evaluate energy performance implications of his design ideas. Due to the specific knowledge required for BEM, energy modeling remains primarily the domain of specialized engineers. For the proper use of BEM the architectural design community needs expertise in the evaluative aspects to improve and maximize a building's energy performance. This provides the impetus for energy modeling; "beginning the design in this simulation environment is a means by which the architecture profession can address its responsibility, for the betterment of all involved" (Butler 2008) and meet the challenge to reduce carbon emissions. As architectural practice gravitates toward a more effective use of energy modeling (Hensen 2004), it will require the understanding to simulate the proper information (Donn 2009) and how to apply in building design.

Proper application of BEM in building design requires identification of specific energy saving measures and associated energy metrics. Since simulation isolates a small range or one building feature for evaluation, it allows design analysis to objectively identify the right building element or energy-saving measure from analysis of the results. Isolating an energy-saving feature prioritizes a specific design objective for further study. For instance, orientation of a basic form on the site early on during conceptual design would establish a building site location that could minimize or maximize solar exposure depending on which is most beneficial. In the design process, when to use BEM will determine what energy-saving measure is most critical.

The energy design process starts in predesign and continues through the building's occupation (Hayter et al. 2000). Analysis opportunities throughout the design process rely on what information is available at the time. In predesign the project team can set goals and identify key energy savings strategies that influence subsequent design decisions. Energy goals used in BEM establish a best-case building model determining performance targets and identify the energy saving design strategies, build energy-use profiles, and annual energy use results. Additionally, use of this information can communicate and engage the project team throughout the design development. Therefore, because of the amount of data, advanced visualizations, and BEM outcomes that BIM brings to design, energy decisions move to points earlier in the design process. This requires designers to leverage BEM for design analysis.

Validating design decisions early, shown as the modified MacLeamy Curve in Figure 7.1, will require BEM analysis points along the design development curve. If early BEM can have an impact on building design, then evaluating the right information with the right tool is important to the accuracy or fidelity of the BEM. However, in many ways the fidelity or resolution of the BEM follows the trend line representing the cost of design changes.

Potentially using BEM at several key points in the design process can have a significant impact on initial design decisions. Designers must use energy simulation more effectively than they do today in order to maximize a building's energy performance. To expand the use of building energy modeling

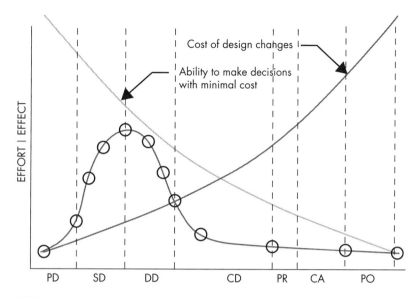

FIGURE 7.1 Key BPS analysis points in the design process.
(Modified HOK MacLeamy Curve identifying the idealized design curve based on Lévy 2011)

in architecture, understanding when and what to simulate is critical in order for widespread adoption in the architectural discipline. Sustainability issues aside, building codes are requiring better-performing buildings and architects can achieve these goals but remain dependent today on the additional expertise of consultants. But this trend is changing. The American Institute of Architects (AIA) realizes this and in 2012 issued *Integrating Energy Modeling in the Design Process* for architects. The guide explains why energy is a design problem, explores the role of performance modeling, and reviews current tools. It provides a good snapshot of why, how, and where to ingrate energy modeling in the design process. However, BIM's use is covered only superficially in this document, thus missing an opportunity to enhance the use of BEM in the early phases of design.

7.3 BIM'S ROLE IN THE PROCESS

BIM currently has a crucial role in reflecting the intent of the engineer or architect. Inputting information into a model takes time and is an integral part of the design process. BIM shortens the distance between building energy modeling and evaluative design decision by encoding information in parameters, making iterations easier, creating advanced building visualizations, and streamlining software interoperability.

Energy-based performative aspects of BIM rely on the modeler's ability to define the shape, volume, and material properties of an interior environmentally conditioned space establishing parametric relationships within the model. Space properties include performative aspects such as occupancy, temperature settings, lighting conditions and controls, and energy use assumptions about plug loads, all of which affect the mechanical and electrical design. Volumes of spaces and their organization, defined by room elements, determine the amount of conditioned space and establish the zoning and load of mechanical systems. Next, materials properties within a model have thermal characteristics, which influence the range of BEM results. These aspects of a space, volume, and material dictate the energy-based criteria leveraged by the designer to make decisions. Energy-based design can use BEM to aid designers to set formal priorities for energy performance. Using material properties, space, and volume attributes the parametric relationships established in the model moves energy evaluation of a building into multiple points of the process.

What is critical with BIM, due to the upfront loading of a project with more data, is iterative use of BEM for design optimization of energy savings measures throughout stages of the design process. Of the range of significant decisions made in early building design, how does one know which will have the most impact? Determining this would allow for confident identification of key design traits to save energy and further optimization of the design to maximize the potential for improved performance. Cycling through the design process professionals can test the various measures against the design intent with BEM and move forward. Aiding these decisions is the advanced visualizations BIM provides to represent the building.

BIM's visualizations of design intention allow evaluations to be clear and easier to understand. For instance, many BIM platforms simulate sun position and can calculate this information real-time during design. At any point in the design process, the correct positioning of the sun can help the designer understand shade, shadows, and daylight penetration. Since BIM knows the project location, the sun system enables visual representation of heliothermic planning and passive design rules.

File exchange formats between BPS software, such as .gbXML for Ecotect and Green Building Studio (GBS), allow transfer of consistent formal (space, volume, and material) properties for simulation. Interoperability is a traditional barrier to streamlining energy evaluation in architectural design. To translate architectural models into energy modeling software, the abstracted simple surfaces of the building geometry import into a BPS platform. The process disconnects a design from the resulting evaluation due to time of translation, possible inconsistencies, and human interpretation of the information. BIM brings three advances to eliminate all three disconnects: first, integrating the evaluative process into the same platform; second, linking together models with interoperable file exchange formats or plug-ins allowing greater play and evaluation of the design simultaneously; and third, advancing the range of BPS software specifically tailored to the designer. These three interoperability advances in BIM bridge energy evaluation into design decisions. The interoperability of software enables designers to use simulated energy results as decision-making feedback for conceptual design.

7.4 CONCEPTUAL DESIGN DECISIONS

Conceptual design is an intuitive and creative design phase of a project. It involves design of the basic building plan, massing, general appearance, siting, orientation, structural organization, and programmatic layout. Using BIM from the beginning enables use of BEM software. A software comparison by Bambardekar (2009) comparing Ecotect, IES, and Green Building Studio as part of evaluating the energy simulation protocols in early design, found that there is a need to define the simulation scope (what to simulate) to guide energy modeling. Thoughtfully defining this scope can aid conceptual modeling to address key design goals in order for architects to make more intelligent design decisions based on energy-saving features (Wilde and Augenbroe 2002).

Determining what to simulate during conceptualization of a project involves understanding the relevant information available. Project size, geometry, materials, assemblies, building site, and program define explicit building information modeled via BIM during conceptual design and are directly relevant to evaluation of energy performance. However, it is necessary to determine what specifically to simulate from this building data and how to analyze the results to improve energy efficiency and streamline design decisions. The simulation therefore depends on the energy goals and conceptual design objectives. For example, orientation of the building, the amount of solar radiation, energy consumption, and daylighting versus electrical lighting might be initial questions used for evaluating design objectives. Alternatively, studying many orientations of a basic form on the site early during conceptual design would help in establishing a building site location, whether the goal is to minimize or maximize solar exposure depending on which is most beneficial.

This example highlights a starting point for energy modeling in conceptual design and demonstrates the importance of determining specific simulation goals to analyze. Determining these goals is a function of the specific building design, which is located in a specific climate and influences which metric is most sensitive. One common metric to analyze is solar insolation (kWh/m2), the amount of the sun's radiation energy striking the building surface. Predicting this value helps designers understand the thermal performance of the building's mass as affected by site orientation or shading. A designer wanting to understand shading devices and overhangs can test incident solar radiation during conceptual design to provide a proof-of-concept and embed early ideas into the design model. Incident solar radiation represents one simulation of design criteria related to shading early in design. This simulation feedback provides designers with evaluative analysis to make informed energy-based decisions affecting the building design and BIM.

Verification of the conceptual design energy intent, for example, to use shading devices to reduce the amount of sun on the south and west facades, allows the designer to translate the conceptual building massing and shading strategy into the BIM. Figure 7.2 shows the analysis of the BIM final shading strategy that evolved from evaluating the radiation of conceptual massing iterations, as shown in Figure 7.3. The early analysis of shading enabled the designer to verify design intentions. From here the conceptual shading strategy evolved into the working BIM where modification of the building mass turns into more detailed building components and the shading device built with a defined family. The model used at the beginning study was from a BIM, translated to .gbXML and imported into Ecotect for BEM simulation. This process of translation into BEMs imports abstracted 3D data from BIM for evaluation. Today, interoperability through file exchange formats allow the BIM and BEM to synchronize, saving valuable time.

In a second example, once the interior layout was complete, the interior lighting fixtures were added. Combining the day lighting from the exterior with the electric lighting on the interior, an iterative

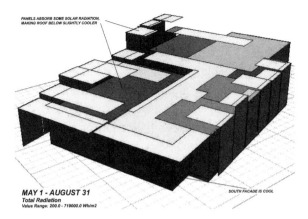

FIGURE 7.2   Simulation of incident solar radiation of shading devices on conceptual mass.

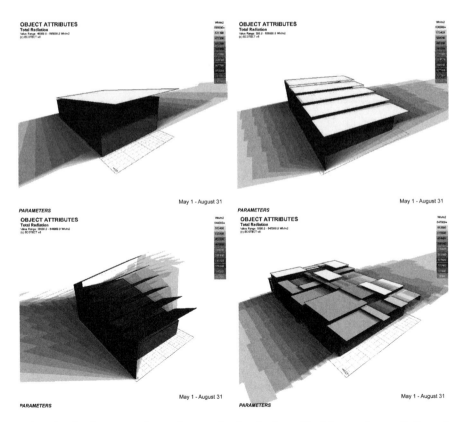

FIGURE 7.3   Conceptual massing study simulation of incident solar radiation of shading devices.

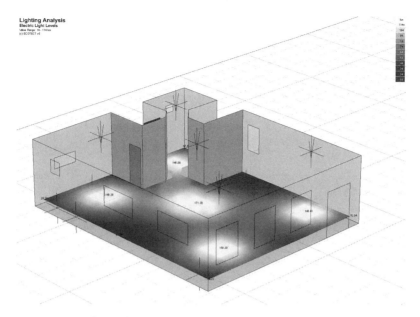

FIGURE 7.4   Electric light levels analysis of a housing interior.

process can find the best location of the lights based on the desired electric light design levels (Figure 7.4). Conversely, based on the lighting needs of the interior spaces, lighting analysis can help determine interior partition locations or programmatic layout options based on daylight levels.

These design examples show how conceptual design decisions relate to what design information is available and how key design goals simulated early inform the building solution. Exploring iterations based on this early information, BIM allows the designer to operate more quickly and have more feedback, achieving greater success at matching design intent with energy savings. From here, BEM aids in further screening and optimization of the building design. For example, the designer might explore the trade-offs between having more windows (for daylighting) and saving energy from electrical lighting versus losing operational energy from the window. Completing a sensitivity analysis and design optimization can further refine the building design and increase energy savings.

7.5 SENSITIVITY ANALYSIS AND OPTIMIZATION

7.5.1 Sensitivity Analysis

Designers can break down early building features through a screening analysis to identify the design sensitivity of specific material properties and geometry to optimize formal design decisions.

Design sensitivity of material considerations is a function of the linear relationship between building performance and a material's thermal properties. The BIM embodies thermal properties of a specific building form enabling a design sensitivity based on the range of possible properties. Thus Green Building Studio (GBS) can quickly evaluate the sensitivity of window glass, lighting, daylight, infiltration, wall, and roof insulation. The model analysis is a result of the range of material, operational, mechanical, and thermal properties for a given building form. In the case of GBS the building's overall shape and form is set in the BIM and is not subject to change based on the results of analysis, making the impact of geometric choices (the building form and shape) that designers typically control not a part of the parametric evaluation of that building.

In order to analyze the geometric implications of building proportion (a mass's aspect ratio, for example), investigation of stacking, compactness, orientation, and eave overhang is required. It is crucial to maintain the volume of the base model to have consistency in the conditioned space used to calculate a type of annual energy performance called load-based sensitivity. To remove unwanted load variation due to footprint changes along with the constant volume, the window sizes stay proportional in relation to the wall area.

Iterative testing of geometry using Grasshopper, a parametric modeler, and evaluation of energy with DIVA for Rhino results in a range of energy performance loads and thus the sensitivity of building geometry. The resulting graphs (Figure 7.5) compare the sensitivity of both geometry and material characteristics screening for what energy saving measures are most impactful. Quantification of the building design in this way enables designers to use and analyze differences to make the best decisions.

Sensitivity information is project specific and would not correlate or transfer to other projects that are larger in size, have different contextual and micro-climatic considerations, and are composed of different materials. A building project's sensitivity and location produces a range of specific results, highlighting different design possibilities and conceptual design approaches one could pursue. Proper use of a sensitivity analysis requires understanding the differences in variables such as building orientation and proportion. Therefore, screening for energy-saving measures and setting energy goals to prioritize the key design features is important to efficiently progress in building design.

7.5.2 Conceptual Design Optimization

Digital optimization uses BEM analysis to further refine specific building design elements seeking the best available energy-saving option. Optimization of building materials, systems, and geometry occurs by isolating specific design features and using a simulation to analyze building performance, maximizing energy savings. Where conceptual design decisions using BEM explore possibilities, optimization targets the conceptual decision made to advance the energy savings of this choice. However, often optimization of a particular building element is not a linear process involving singular simulations discussed previously. Instead, architects must weigh the complexity and interaction of multiple variables to optimize building energy performance.

Managing this complexity is ideal for BIM, which defines, stores, and manages building parameters. The complex decision-making process to conserve energy is aided in the definition of parameters in the model. Technically, design objectives for an optimization analysis are a collection of parameters (genes) that provide for the algorithm objectives to test in order to reach a target optimization level (fitness

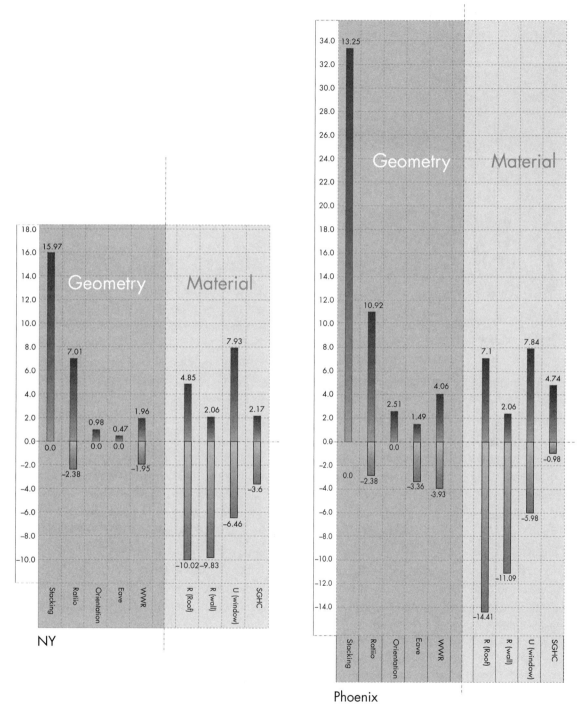

FIGURE 7.5   Annual load-based design sensitivity analysis for the same geometry and materials in two different locations.

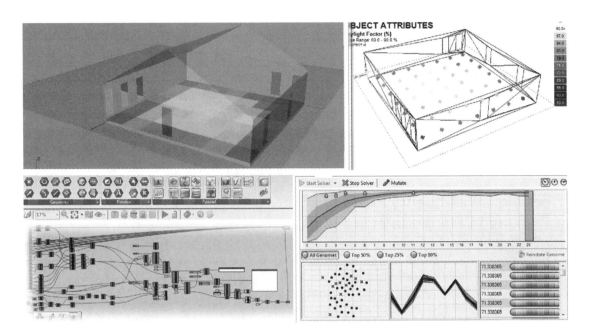

FIGURE 7.6 Daylight factor simulation iteratively testing window locations using an evolutionary solver using Rhino, Ecotect, Grasshopper, and Galapagos.

level). The building form and footprint use parameters of volume, height, length, and width to establish an associated definition of the building model. Since the designer easily and quickly changes these associations, the numeric data produces a range of design alternatives with close approximation to the optimized energy performance.

Leveraging the parametric definition built in the model, evolutionary computing (a process through which a genetic algorithm automatically searches the range of potential outcomes for the best option) transforms data to optimize building form and shape. For example, a designer trying to achieve good interior daylight but also balance energy consumption has multiple dimensions to consider since increasing windows for daylight often also increases energy consumption. Design optimization helps to understand the balance between these conflicting outcomes. Evolutionary computing processes search a range of defined changes, window locations, in the design model iteratively testing them against results from the BEM simulation, daylight levels, until it reaches the best available choice. Because BPS software determines the daylight factor on the interior to a predetermined metric, the algorithm tests results against the desired design intent. Optimizing these factors, the algorithm—with the goal of maximizing interior daylight levels (Figure 7.6)—searches a sample of window locations on the exterior until achieving the design objective. Using the parametric model to evaluate energy performance early during conceptual phases of design is efficient because of the ability to iteratively test a wide range of possible solutions quickly. The results vetted against the design intent helps optimize energy savings in the design.

Exploring many parameters—whether through the use of an evolutionary solver above, or through a sequential technique—allows designers to investigate a broad range of design possibilities. For example

Settings and Parameters

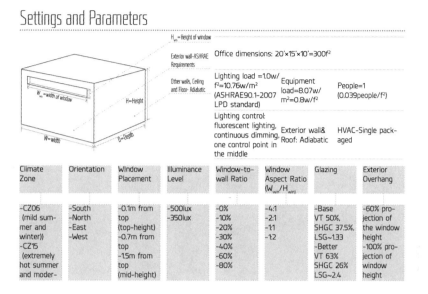

Office dimensions: 20'×15'×10'=300f²

Lighting load =1.0w/ f²=10.76w/m² (ASHRAE90.1-2007 LPD standard)

Equipment load=8.07w/ m²=0.8w/f²

People=1 (0.039people/f²)

Lighting control: fluorescent lighting, continuous dimming, one control point in the middle

Exterior wall& Roof: Adiabatic

HVAC-Single pack-aged

Climate Zone	Orientation	Window Placement	Illuminance Level	Window-to-wall Ratio	Window Aspect Ratio (W_{win}/H_{win})	Glazing	Exterior Overhang
-CZ06 (mild summer and winter)) -CZ15 (extremely hot summer and moder-	-South -North -East -West	-0.1m from top (top-height) -0.7m from top -1.5m from top (mid-height)	-500lux -350lux	-0% -10% -20% -30% -40% -60% -80%	-4:1 -2:1 -1:1 -1:2	-Base VT 50%, SHGC 37.5%, LSG~1.33 -Better VT 63% SHGC 26% LSG~2.4	-60% projection of the window height -100% projection of window height

FIGURE 7.7 Designers can test for a range of values very early in the design process.
(Image courtesy of Geman Wu, USC MBS thesis)

(Figures 7.7 and 7.8), window orientation, height, aspect ratio, window-to-wall ratio, lighting design level, and glazing can be varied to find the best balance for daylight harvesting and energy demands of fenestration in the early design stage for office buildings in multiple climate zones (Wu et al. 2012). Searching the range of options for the ideal design intent and energy performance match is conceptual design optimization.

Recent advancements of parametric modeling and evolutionary computing support digital optimization during conceptual design and assist in integrating energy savings in the conceptual design process. By establishing the necessary communication between software, one can achieve a parametric model that instantly reflects the energy performance of the design (Jakubiec and Reinhart 2011). Moreover, the data used in an evolutionary algorithm to reach a desired level of design optimization early in the process potentially solves the informational overload inherent in optimizing multiple design variables. Designing and planning for energy performance is the goal of digital optimization using sensitivity analysis and parametric optimization algorithms.

7.6 BIM AFFORDANCES

Advances in BIM and related technologies will improve the opportunity for designers to be more effective in conceptual energy modeling and optimization and have better understanding that their design intent is energy efficient. BIM optimizes conservation of energy, thereby reducing carbon emission

Software-DIVA for Grasshopper (Viper Component)

	Company	Features
Diva for Grasshopper (Viper Component)	GSD	-EnergyPlus engine; -More open to users in modeling and input variables; -Limitation: some parameters are not shown in Grasshopper interface, but users can make changes through EnergyPlus basic settings;

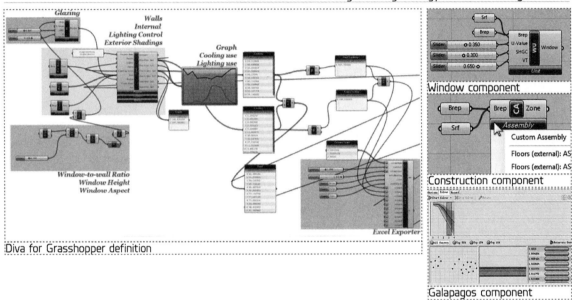

FIGURE 7.8 Genetic algorithms search for optimized solutions; in this case minimum summer energy use based on a trade-off of daylighting and heat gain based on window parameters.

(Image courtesy of Geman Wu, USC MBS thesis)

through the singularity of the BIM and BEM, increased simulation fidelity, and analysis of a larger range of performative criteria.

The design model and energy model could be one and the same if the associative objects and definitions between the two are in synchronization. The resulting fluidity between the analytical and design models streamlines navigation, modification, and evaluation of the design being considered and helps the designer make informed decisions. However, in some cases the BPS of energy performance still occurs in the cloud or through external software, both using another format. This opens up room for miscommunication and inaccuracies. The user needs to be able to efficiently make changes to and run simulations in one mode and not be forced to navigate back and forth between the two. Often, for this to work efficiently, the building model needs to begin with evaluative intentions, making the model accurate for translation to the evaluative assessment with BEM.

Since a simulation is only a representation of a specific function of a building, it will not accurately reflect the real world performance of what is actually built and operated. How nearly the simulation reflects reality is known as its fidelity. However, the fidelity of simulation is increasing as modeling technologies improve and more accurately reflect reality. One affordance of BIM is the ability to input actual utility information into a post-occupancy energy model. Since the BIM contains the theoretical design model, linking it to the operational model allows comparisons between the virtual and real.

7.7 CONCLUSION

Since designers have a range of information at any given time during the design process, knowing what information is key and having flexibility to leverage information in a variety of digital formats strengthens the architect's ability to evaluate design performance. Deciding when and what to simulate during design is important for designers to make clear design choices. Filtering information during design helps to shape a clear objective to simulate, clarifying design objectives and selection of alternatives.

Examples looked at simulating energy-based design objectives of shading, daylight, and form using different metrics to evaluate energy performance and the relationship to conceptual design decisions. Elaborating an energy model early in design allows evaluation of design intentions using sensitivity and conceptual design results for the building. BIM enables this to occur earlier, optimizing building design and allowing the energy savings of design intentions to be clear. Interoperability of software allows data exchanges between design and BPS software, affecting the simulation fidelity and the fluidity of the design process. Within the design process, parametric associations capture energy performance criteria early, allow iterative testing, and carry intentions through design development into post-occupancy, allowing better building operations and management of energy performance. Advances in software like BIM improve designers' ability to make decision for energy efficiency.

ACKNOWLEDGMENTS

Thanks to the AIA UpJohn Research Fellowship for support in funding some of the work discussed in this chapter. Gratitude also needs to be given to Bryce Willis and Kaveh Alagheband, whose work as research assistants at the University of Nebraska-Lincoln, College of Architecture, informed the discussion and graphics.

DISCUSSION QUESTIONS

1. Explain three reasons why it is important for architects to use building simulation software.
2. What simulations can be completed in order to understand daylight based space programming?
3. Download the American Institute of Architects (AIA) *Integrating Energy Modeling in the Design Process* (www.aia.org/practicing/AIAB097932). Explain how BEM can be used with BIM to assist in energy modeling at the earliest stages of design.

REFERENCES

American Institute of Architects (AIA). 2012. *An Architect's Guide to Integrating Energy Modeling in the Design Process*. Accessed Feb 23, 2014. http://info.aia.org/aia/energymodeling.cfm.

Bambardekar, S. and U. Poerschke. 2009. "The Architect as Performer of Energy Simulation in the Performance Based Design." *Building Simulation: Eleventh International IBPSA Conference*, pp. 1306–1313.

Butler, T. W., 2008. "Design in a Simulation Environment." Master's thesis, Georgia Tech University.

Donn, M., S. Selkowitz, and B. Bordass. 2009. "Simulation in the Service of Design: Asking the Right Questions." *Building Simulation 2009*: Eleventh International IBPSA Conference, pp. 1314–1321.

Hayter, S., P. Torcellini, R. Hayter, and R. Judkoff. 2000. 'The Energy Design Process for Designing and Constructing High Performance Buildings." *Climate*.

Hensen, J.L.M. 2004. "Towards More Effective Use of Building Performance Simulation in Design." Seventh International Conference on Design and Decision Support Systems in Architecture and Urban Planning Proceedings, Technische Universiteit Eindhoven.

Jakubiec, J. A., and C. F. Reinhart. 2011. "DIVA 2.0: Integrating Daylight and Thermal Simulations using Rhinoceros 3d, Daysim and Energyplus." *Building Simulation 2011*: 12th Conference of International Building Performance Simulation Association, Sydney, pp. 14–16.

Lévy, F. 2011. *BIM in Small-scale Sustainable Design*. Hoboken, NJ: John Wiley and Sons.

Wilde, P. D., and G. Augenbroe. 2002. "Managing the Selection of Energy Saving Features in Building Design." *Engineering, Construction and Architectural Management* 9(3): 192–208.

Wu, G., K. Kensek, and M. Schiler. 2012. "Studies in Preliminary Design of Fenestration: Balancing Daylight Harvesting and Energy Consumption." *PLEA 2012* (28th International PLEA Conference—Design Tools and Methods), Lima, Peru (November).

CHAPTER 8

Performance Art: Analytics and the New Theater of Design Practice

Daniel Davis, CASE
Nathan Miller, CASE

8.1 INTRODUCTION

The understanding of building performance continues to advance. Recent technological innovations have delivered improvements to building materials, energy generation, building analysis, facilities management, and building information modeling (BIM). Architects have never been in a better position to achieve better building performance, and yet the buildings they create remain expensive, environmentally damaging, risky, and enormously time consuming to design and build. They devour vast amounts of energy and money. Just the energy used to control air temperatures inside buildings accounts for 19 percent of all the energy used in the United States (U.S. Energy Information Administration 2011). While the understanding of building performance continues to advance, attempts to design more energy-efficient buildings have sometimes resulted in buildings that "actually performed worse" (Mehaffy and Salingaros 2013). As such, performance remains an enigmatic target of the architecture, engineering, construction, and owner (AECO) industry.

BIM brings with it vast amounts of data. Designers have access to more information about the performance of their project than ever before. They can query the model to extract quantities, measurements, and costs. Project partners can collaborate by extracting subsets of the data to base their own discipline-specific models upon, which gives them insights about the project that contribute yet more data to the model. Data on top of data on top of data. Most will have no bearing on the project, but there are pieces and patterns that will come to define the project. In this seemingly overwhelming situation, the designer's role is to provide structure and sense to the noise and disorder.

This chapter explores the instruments, analytics, and interactions that help bring meaning to the data overflowing from BIM. Drawing upon CASE's experience in helping clients with BIM implementation, five case studies have been selected to showcase how performance is evolving within the practice of design. The first group of case studies involves the instruments designers use to appraise performance; the second group concerns how these instruments are being applied as analytics across all project phases; and the final group illustrates how these instruments and analytics are influencing the larger design process. In doing so the aim is to discuss performance not as a target of the AECO industry but rather as a process of the AECO industry.

8.2 INSTRUMENTS

Instruments transform data into measurements of expected building performance. With the advent of computer-aided design in the 1960s, computers were quickly harnessed to automate calculations that would otherwise be done by hand: walking distances, static structural analysis, and basic energy calculations (Keller 2006). While the instruments revealed aspects of performance that were previously infeasible to calculate, they also obscured the assumptions and calculations that were underlying these revelations (Turkle 2009). Many worried that designers would misapply the tools if they could not see the inner workings, but there were also those that found it liberating to apply an instrument without needing to know the precise details of how it worked (Turkle 2009). The initial mistrust of digital tools was somewhat placated by the fact that they could be verified by the original nondigital equation. Yet as instruments grew more sophisticated, so too did the methods for verifying them. Many contemporary digital instruments have advanced to the point where their transformations of data into measurements of expected building performance can no longer be verified through an analog equation.

A recent example is the CASE/Autodesk comparative energy instrument (Figure 8.1). The prototype originated from the observation that while the user is able to perform quick conceptual energy analysis on models within Revit and Vasari, the presented results do not allow for effective comparative metrics, nor do they reveal the underlying mechanisms by which the results are derived. The comparative charting add-in extracts data from multiple results files and provides clear comparative charts to reveal the variations in performance among many options. Decades of research have gone into the equations powering the instrument. These equations are arguably the most significant part although their mechanisms remain hidden behind the user interface. Like another project partner, instruments often come to embody knowledge far outside the designer's expertise. The charting instrument is not just about making data more accessible to the designer, but also about providing visualizations that endow the designer with greater clarity for the decision-making process.

Like the CASE/Autodesk comparative energy instrument, the CASE/Snøhetta daylight instrument is about finding potentials in a range of design possibilities (Figure 8.2). The CASE/Snøhetta daylight instrument lets users set twenty-three parameters that control the rotation, spread, and depth of a series of louvered panels on a building's facade. The instrument returns a daylight analysis, an energy analysis,

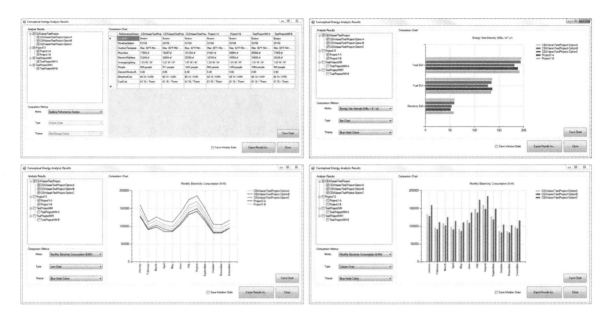

FIGURE 8.1   CASE, Autodesk—comparative energy analysis prototype compares data from multiple runs of a Green Building Studio energy model.

and a sensitivity analysis. This focus on relative potentials rather than absolute ideals is a subtle but important shift in emphasis compared to earlier computational instruments.

Sean Keller explains that researchers developing instruments in the 1960s were doing so because they "hoped that the application of the correct algorithms to sets of building requirements could produce architectural forms that were objectively 'best'" (Keller 2006). The structural instrument would tell the designer the best beam size; the walking distance instrument would tell the designer the best room adjacencies; the energy analysis instrument would tell the designer the best window size. These early tools largely failed because, according to Keller, "at best, quantitative approaches have a limited use for certain very complex problems, and must always rely on many assumptions that cannot be quantified and on inherited typologies" (Keller 2006). In other words, there will always be aspects of a building's performance that lie outside the quantification of instruments. Turkle says that designers can become vulnerable when using digital instruments because "sometimes it can be hard to remember all that lies beyond a simulation, or even acknowledge that everything is not captured in it. An older generation fears that young scientists, engineers and designers are 'drunk with code'" (Turkle 2009).

The CASE/Autodesk comparative energy instrument and the CASE/Snøhetta daylight instrument do not pretend to offer a designer an objectively "best" solution. Instead, they present a range of possibilities. Rather than the designer being subservient to the instrument (being told the best option), the emphasis shifts toward the designer being empowered by the instrument (being able to see a range of possibilities). In the CASE/Snøhetta daylight instrument this manifests as a sensitivity analysis.

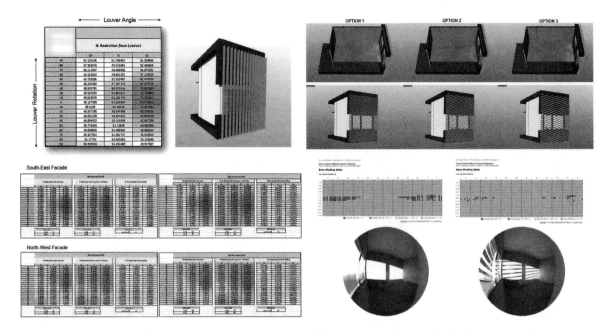

FIGURE 8.2   CASE, Snøhetta—design and analysis workflow for shade and daylight optimization.

In a spreadsheet the designer can see the best louver angle, as well as the range of values that produce results near or indiscernible from the best. The designer is then able to explore a range of near Pareto Optimal solutions, satisficing the instrument's analysis against the designer's own knowledge of things like patterning, constructability, and cultural meanings—things largely outside the quantification of an instrument. When this works well, the instrument enters into a dialogue with the designer that helps find performance potentials rather than dictate what these are. Instruments are about bringing structure and sense to data; they are about making knowledge more accessible, but ultimately they are about designers and computers coming together to achieve a performance unimaginable by either.

8.3 ANALYTICS

With the advent of web-based BIM file servers that track project changes, every design iteration on a project becomes accessible. As a result, instruments can be applied to the entire lineage of a project instead of just a single design instance. This is a relatively new strategy for achieving building performance. Rather than trying to analyze the performance of the completed building, the analytics are applied to the performance trends across the design process.

Although a project's entire lineage may be saved on a server, this history can be difficult to access. In a sketchbook every drawing, every erasure, every hesitation of the pen is captured page by page, accessible with a simple page turn. In a BIM each variation writes over the last. The model is in a constant

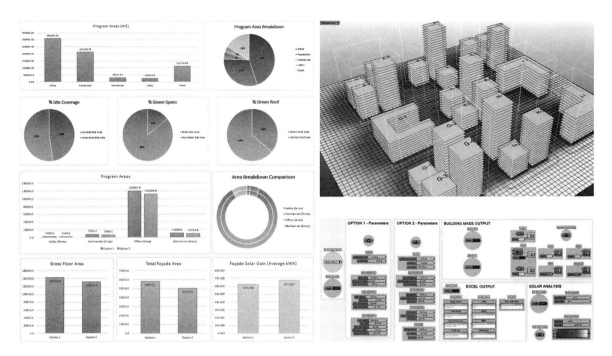

FIGURE 8.3   CASE—Design Iteration Dashboard for tracking metrics about major design features at the conceptual stage.

state of newness with the project's history only accessible by either undoing or opening an old version of the model. Often designers will rely on their memory to recall past instances of the model. A wide range of research has shown that humans are generally unable to accurately recall changes not immediately visible (Simons and Levin 1997), the implication being that if they are unable to recall the changes between design options, they are even less likely to appraise them accurately. Analytics offers designers a way to evaluate past design instances and to bring to this appraisal a consideration of the building's performance. An example is the CASE Design Iteration Dashboard, which enables designers to track how key metrics like a project's size, façade area, and solar gain have changed over the course of a project (Figure 8.3). Using the dashboard designers can recall and compare the major design features of various conceptual models, a comparison that is often difficult in the perpetual newness of a BIM model.

Typically the design history of a project ends with the handover. The project's archive begins with conceptual decisions and concludes with a document set or some staged photos just prior to the official occupation. Analytics offers the ability to trace the history of a project beyond the handover. Plastarc, for example, is a company that performs post-occupancy observation and analysis (Figure 8.4). Recordings of activities are stored within spreadsheets and are sequenced with plan layouts. CASE worked with Plastarc to create data visualizations of the recorded observational data and reveal dynamic visual patterns that are not apparent through tabular views. The combination of data and visualization might inform future space utilization and business decisions about facility expansion. As more sensors

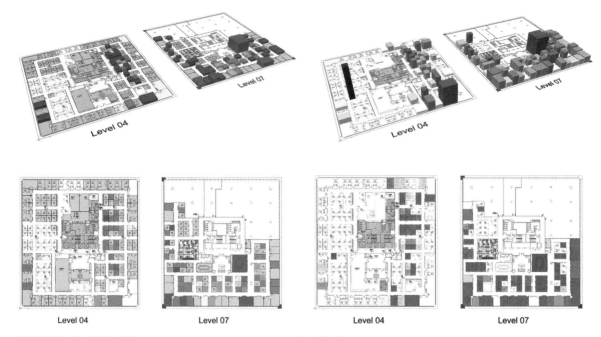

FIGURE 8.4 CASE, Plastarc—post-occupancy data visualization.

are embedded within ever more "intelligent" buildings, and as BIM begins to integrate better with building operations, it is conceivable that architects will have detailed, real-time access to how their buildings are performing. They might be able to discover how much energy is being used, which blinds are constantly closed, what equipment was replaced, perhaps even the various room occupancy rates. In doing so these systems promise to close an important information gap between anticipated performance and actual performance.

While some aspects of analytics extend into building performance post-occupancy, others extend into the performance of the design team. In a survey of 429 AECO professionals, approximately two-thirds were gathering accounting analytics around key statistics like monthly expenditure, open leads, and employee hours on projects (CASE 2013). Beyond these basic enterprise resource planning statistics, a small number of firms are beginning to gather more general data about their organization's performance with BIM. To facilitate this growing need, CASE has developed a Building Analytics Framework for monitoring file open rates, file sizes, errors, standards conformance, and other modeling data (Figure 8.5). Using this dashboard, anyone within the company can monitor a project's progression at a glance and look for trends in model evolution. These types of analytics are still in their infancy when applied to architectural practice. It remains to be seen how these new insights conclusively affect team performance, software utilization, and architectural quality. Nevertheless, meta-level analytics of an organization's BIM data undoubtedly brings to the surface new measures of performance and can provide views into data that has, until now, been left within a black box.

FIGURE 8.5   CASE—Building Analytics Framework used for presenting and tracking project information and model performance.

8.4 INTERACTIONS

Instruments and analytics are informing not only the performance of design but the performance of doing design. At a superficial level the colorful diagrams produced by instruments and analytics serve as props in discussions of performance that, at times, take on a theatrical quality. At their worst, the instruments are used as devices to post-rationalize a project or to give a false appearance of authority, which leads some to dismiss analytic methods like computational fluid dynamics—CFD—as "color for designers." At their best, the instruments help catalyze interactions that help inform directions, validate hypotheses, and interpret results. In these instances, the instruments and analytics are ultimately about communicating what lies within the data overflowing from BIM. Given the vagueness that surrounds the performance of a project, these conversations—however crude an expert observer finds them—are pivotal in revealing aspects of the project's performance within the landscape of uncertainty. They are the props around which individuals from different disciplines can communicate their ongoing appraisal of a project from the point of view of their respective discipline.

From the uncertainty that surrounds a project, "the designer sets off to explore, to discover something new, rather than to return with yet another example of the already familiar" (Cross 2006). These design journeys are not ones of repeatable scientific exploration so much as they are an artful, iterative

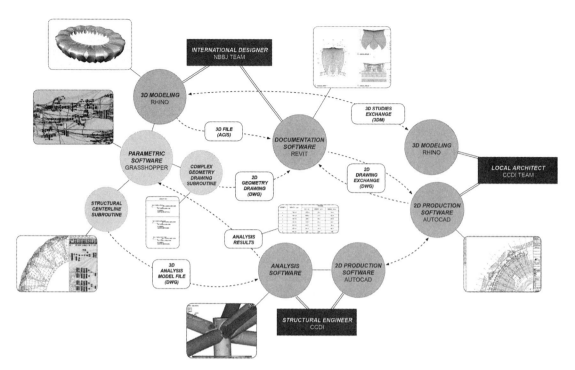

FIGURE 8.6   ACADIA 2010, Nathan Miller, NBBJ—project team interoperability, Hangzhou Stadium.

meandering into the angst of unknowing (Schön 1983, Lawson 2005). Instruments and analytics serve to facilitate these iterations by compressing the time between making a design decision and receiving feedback from it. The scope widens to include not only the intuitive feedback of the designer, but the feedback of an ensemble of colleagues who have embedded their knowledge within the instruments or who have helped set the courses of action through the interactions enabled by effective data management. Take, for example, this diagram of NBBJ's process on the Hangzhou Stadium (Figure 8.6). The design does not follow a straight path, but rather is pushed iteratively through a network of software, instruments, and people. Three members of the project team from different disciplines anchor the sides of this network, communicating by exchanging models, data, and analytics. The performance of the design depends on these interactions. The instruments are about supporting the design practice of performance as much as they are about achieving design performance.

8.5 CONCLUSION: ALGORITHMS ARE THOUGHTS

In 2004 a group of live-coding performers known as TOPLAP wrote a short manifesto that reframed computation in the context of theatrical, extemporaneous performance. They listed six "demands" that outlined their philosophy toward computation. The final demand reads: "Algorithms are thoughts, chainsaws are tools" (TOPLAP 2005). It is a demand that asks designers to reconsider the role of computation in creative thinking. Rather than computation being a means of achieving a particular performance, TOPLOP suggests that computation serves as a performance in and of itself.

In the past decade, BIM has become the new favorite "chainsaw" in the AECO industry. As a tool, it has undoubtedly enabled new enhancements for building production and provided new efficiencies for well-established conventions and representations. However, the introduction of information-based capabilities into the mainstream architecture lexicon has set the stage for new modes of ideation and collaboration—new modes of performance. Instruments are becoming increasingly sophisticated, more conversational, and shifting from finding optimums to finding potentials. Analytics are being applied across the design process; they are beginning to incorporate post-occupancy as well as the performance of the design team itself. These instruments and analytics are facilitating interactions that are becoming less linear and more iterative. But for all that the instruments and analytics reveal, for all that they communicate, for all the interdisciplinary knowledge that they embody, they still only reveal a narrow range of what makes a building successful. It remains unlikely that "the application of the correct algorithms to sets of building requirements could produce architectural forms that are objectively 'best'" (Keller 2006). Performance has become less about identifying the best solution—the most performative solution—and more about supporting the performance of doing design.

DISCUSSION QUESTIONS

1. Simulation software returns different types of information. Explain the differences between generating a prediction, finding an optimal solution, and presenting a range of possibilities. How, in these cases, does the nature of the simulation affect the designer?

2. What constitutes optimal building performance? In what ways can a design team go about achieving this?

3. Given the range of people involved in an architecture project, and given that each likely has a differing understanding of performance, how can these individuals best transfer their specialized knowledge to one another? How should divergent or conflicting appraisals of the project be handled?

4. Buildings quite often fail to perform as predicted. How can designers close the gap between simulation and reality? Do you expect this will improve in the future? Why or why not?

REFERENCES

CASE. 2013. *Managing the AEC Industry: A Survey of Technology Applied to the Management of Projects, Knowledge, and Resources*. New York: CASE.

Cross, Nigel. 2006. *Designerly Ways of Knowing*. London: Springer-Verlag.

Keller, Sean. 2006. "Fenland Tech: Architectural Science in Postwar Cambridge." *Grey Room 23*, April.

Lawson, Bryan. 2005. *How Designers Think: The Design Process Demystified* (4th ed.). Oxford: Elsevier.

Mehaffy, Michael, and Nikos Salingaros. 2013. "Toward Resilient Architectures 2: Why Green Often Isn't." *Metropolis*, April 4, www.metropolismag.com/Point-of-View/April-2013/Toward-Resilient-Architectures-2-Why-Green-Often-Isnt/, last accessed August 13, 2013.

Schön, Donald. 1983. *The Reflective Practitioner: How Professionals Think in Action*. London: Maurice Temple Smith.

Simons, Daniel, and Daniel Levin. 1997. "Change Blindness." *Trends in Cognitive Sciences* 1 (7): 261–267.

TOPLAP. 2005. "Manifesto Draft," July 31, http://toplap.org/wiki/ManifestoDraft, accessed August 13, 2013.

Turkle, Sherry. 2009. *Simulation and Its Discontents*. Cambridge, MA.: MIT Press.

U.S. Energy Information Administration. 2011. "Use of Energy in the United States: Explained," EIA Energy Explained, www.eia.gov/energyexplained/index.cfm?page=us_energy_use, accessed August 13, 2013.

CHAPTER 9

Automated Energy Performance Visualization for BIM

Paola Sanguinetti, University of Kansas
Pasi Paasiala, Solibri, Inc.
Charles Eastman, Georgia Institute of Technology

9.1 INTRODUCTION

Researchers working to facilitate business processes and information exchange in the architecture, engineering, construction (AEC) field have made progress toward interoperability between design and energy analysis models in the later stages of the design process (Madhavi 1999, Bazjanac 2004). Mapping engines have been proposed to link a building information model (BIM) to an energy analysis model, where each building space is mapped to a thermal zone, including an interface for drawing the building spaces (Lam et al. 2006), or algorithms to decompose the BIM geometry into a finite element mesh (Van Treeck et al. 2006). This type of solution often requires the designer or consultant to develop a new custom model for the analysis, separate from the model developed by the architect to facilitate exploration and resolution of the wide variety of design issues. One of the hurdles to automation and interoperability has been the introduction of sophisticated simulation tools dealing with complex thermal exchanges at the stage when building design models are early stages of development, where the amount of design information is not fully defined.

Another aspect of interoperability involves the use of the simulation results to quantify performance and provide feedback for design decision making (Foliente 2000). The analysis of design concepts using simulation tools in conjunction with the prevailing use of data analytics to monitor performance has led to a variety of tools to aggregate data and support decision making. Most of these tools provide a dashboard interface for stakeholders to make decisions based on a set of performance indicators.

These visualization environments do not integrate with the representation and context used by architectural designers for decision making. A case study is presented where the design model from the architect is automatically post-processed for the needs of the energy analysis. This implementation accepts a model generated by any of the General Services Administration (GSA) validated BIM authoring tools whose model is exported into the neutral file format IFC (buildingSMART).

9.2 CASE STUDY: AUTOMATED ANALYSIS OF U.S. COURTHOUSE MODELS FOR GSA

The GSA's BIM program is advancing the use of information technology (IT) in construction. The case study focuses on automated assessments for federal courthouses in the preliminary concept design (PCD) phase. In this stage, the architectural team generates multiple project concepts (at least three) and assesses them against one another, to select one, as final concept, for further development. The assessment includes the review of the building spaces against the GSA federal courthouse design guidelines, an evaluation of building circulation based on three levels of security, a preliminary construction cost analysis, and an energy performance evaluation based on preliminary heating and cooling loads. Automating feedback for energy performance is a critical part of this work.

9.2.1 Preliminary Concept Design (PCD)

PCD building models are modeled using BIM tools to define information related to spaces and building objects for preliminary review. The information contained in a PCD building model includes massing to show how the building program is composed into an overall building configuration. Floor-by-floor spaces represent departments and some individual spaces, to be validated against program requirements. Other than space names, only a few properties are associated with building objects. PCD building model geometries tend to be moderately complex, including multiple ceiling heights, atrium spaces, and often courtyards. PCD building models can have multi-story walls that continue across multiple interior and exterior spaces. Roofs, balconies, and mezzanines are usually defined as simple slabs. The external shell materials are only loosely defined. General considerations regarding fenestration and basic envelope conditions, such as thermal insulation and mass, are largely determined at this stage. Glazing is not detailed beyond general layouts or percent glazing. The decisions made after preliminary review, such as the building footprint and massing, the general conditions of spatial orientation and siting, and the sizing and location of atrium and courtyards, have critical impacts on lifetime energy costs.

9.2.2 Post-Processing for Energy Analysis

9.2.2.1 Thermal Zone Generation

Because individual spaces and their detailed thermal requirements are only partially known, the development of thermal zones is directed to provide feedback on the energy loads on different sides of the building envelope and the predicted energy use intensity (EUI). Three general geometric operations are used to translate the PCD building model geometry into thermal zone geometry:

1. Aggregations of building spaces into thermal zones with same internal loads (Figure 9.1)
2. Subdivision of perimeter and core zones (Figure 9.2)
3. Subdivision and solving of building zone geometry to resolve first- and second-level space boundaries as required for a zonal model (Figure 9.3)

9.2.2.2 Space Boundary Geometry

The energy zone abstraction of a building is called a 3D tessellation structure by geometers, roughly equivalent to a crystal lattice (Pauling 1929). The crystals (packed 3D forms) have no thickness between them. In addition, thermal zone surface boundaries must be homogeneous with regard to the spaces on both side and their internal transition properties. Bjork (1992) identified these homogeneous regions as needed for energy analysis and called them space boundaries. Two steps are needed to realize the tessellation structure for space boundaries: determining the centerline location of horizontal and vertical space partitions and resolving the homogeneous bounded surface condition of space boundaries.

1. Determining the centerline location of horizontal space partitions (mostly for walls) and determining the vertical space partitions (usually of a slab) is important because it includes the volume of the walls in the thermal zone calculation. The centerline line location algorithm is implemented by performing the following actions:
   o Take each polygon surrounding the spaces.
   o For each segment in the polygon, find the neighboring segment from neighboring spaces.
   o Split segments if a segment has several neighboring segments, so that neighboring segments are not overlapping.
   o Move the segments to their common centerline.
   o Solve the corner situations so that polygons meet at the vertices.

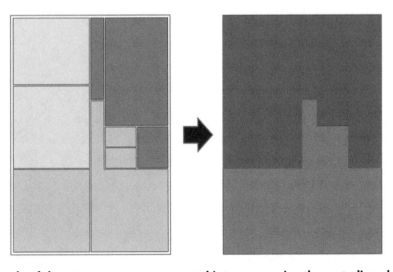

FIGURE 9.1 Example of department space aggregated into zones using the centerline algorithm.

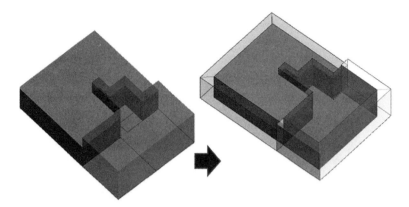

FIGURE 9.2   Example of the subdivision of zones to create perimeter zones.

2. Resolving the bounded surface condition of space boundaries, so that their conditions on both sides of the boundary and transition through boundaries are homogeneous with regard to energy flow behavior. The resolution of homogeneous space boundaries is very similar to the intersection operations in solid modeling. A fundamental step in solid modeling is face-face intersection so that every face of one solid is completely inside or outside of the other solid (Mantyla 1988). The operation consists of partitioning one face into as many sub-faces needed as to obtain the homogeneous regions. The first set of partitions applies the test of zonal boundaries on both sides of the face-face intersection. These conditions respond to both boundaries between two zones and also changes between inside and outside. If one zonal face is not at the edge of its opposite zone face, the zonal faces must be partitioned so that this zone-to-zone condition is satisfied. These are called "first-level space boundaries." The second step applies to changes of building construction within a zonal face. Such changes of construction generate new thermal transfer surfaces with their own properties. If such a partitioning exists within a face, these also partition the zone boundaries.

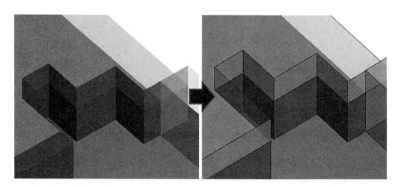

FIGURE 9.3   Example of surface subdivision to resolve first-level space boundaries.

Table 9.1 Mapping of building information to energy input data

BIM Data Set	Data Mapping for Energy	Default Values Assigned Based on BIM Mapping				
Wall (thickness)	ASHRAE construction types	Number of material layers	Material thickness	Conductivity	Density	Heat capacity
Department (name)	Internal gains by occupancy type	Occupants/floor area	Sensible heat/ occupant	Lighting load	Receptacle load	Operation schedules

First-level space boundaries are the bounding faces of the space looked from its inside. A first-level space boundary can have more than one space on the opposite side of its boundaries. The second-level space boundaries are constructed by splitting the first-level space boundaries so that they have only one space on the other side. Operations were developed to traverse the IFC building model structure and apply the described operations to each anomalous condition encountered.

The corrected building model generates the proper geometry needed for the IDF input to EnergyPlus.

9.2.3 Building Model Property Definition

Many properties for a building are not defined in the building model itself. PCD building models are usually not defined down to each individual space. Thus some of the building information is assigned by reference. Table 9.1 shows the mapping of information from the PCD building model and the energy simulation input data. The internal load requirements for all alternative concepts are obtained from the GSA building spatial program. Operating schedules for the building and internal load assignments for spaces are assigned to each thermal zone by matching the building space name to an occupancy type. A database stores a set of values for internal gains specified in GSA's guidelines and complying with the ASHRAE 90.1 standard. The envelope physical properties such as the thermal resistance of the external walls and other surfaces are assigned to each thermal zone surface by matching the model wall thickness to a construction type. A database stores a set of values for construction types, also complying with the ASHRAE 90.1 standard (Table 9.1).

The geometric transformations for building spaces (i.e., zones) are generated automatically. The assignments to the data in Table 9.1 are largely automated, based on space names. Thus alternative designs can be easily generated and their energy behavior automatically simulated.

9.3 PERFORMANCE VISUALIZATION

The aggregation and visualization of the energy simulation results is the final step in providing useful design feedback (Figure 9.4). The output from the energy simulation is a spreadsheet file containing raw numerical data organized by thermal zone. Performance visualization outcomes explore the aggregation of the results as performance indicators and the visualization of performance within the design environment for performance verification.

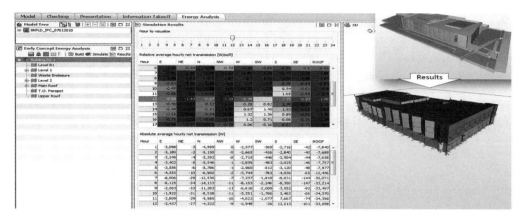

FIGURE 9.4 **Visualization of heat transfer through the building envelope.**

9.3.1 Aggregation of Simulation Output Variables

The simulation output is saved with the BIM model using the interface of the Solibri Model Checker as a tool for comparative analysis. The raw simulation data file is collected and classified to remap the output results for each thermal zone to the spaces in the design model. The results are quantified into performance indicators—in this case, the energy use intensity (EUI) for each zone—and compared against performance targets predetermined by GSA.

9.3.2 Visualization of Thermal Flows

The raw simulation output file is also queried to match the building surface with the heat transmission values for each hour of the day for a specific month of the year. Part of this step includes the aggregation of the raw data to calculate the average heat transmission for each surface of the building envelope. The visualization of the envelope thermal performance is based on the surface average hourly heat transmission. The quantitative data is color-coded to facilitate performance feedback to the designer (Figures 9.5 and 9.6).

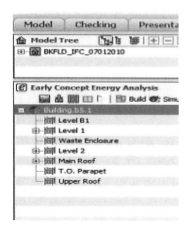
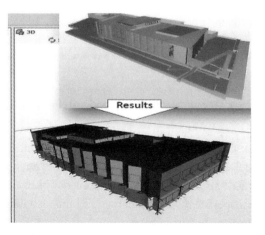

FIGURE 9.5 **Detail showing model visualization in Solibri Model Checker.**

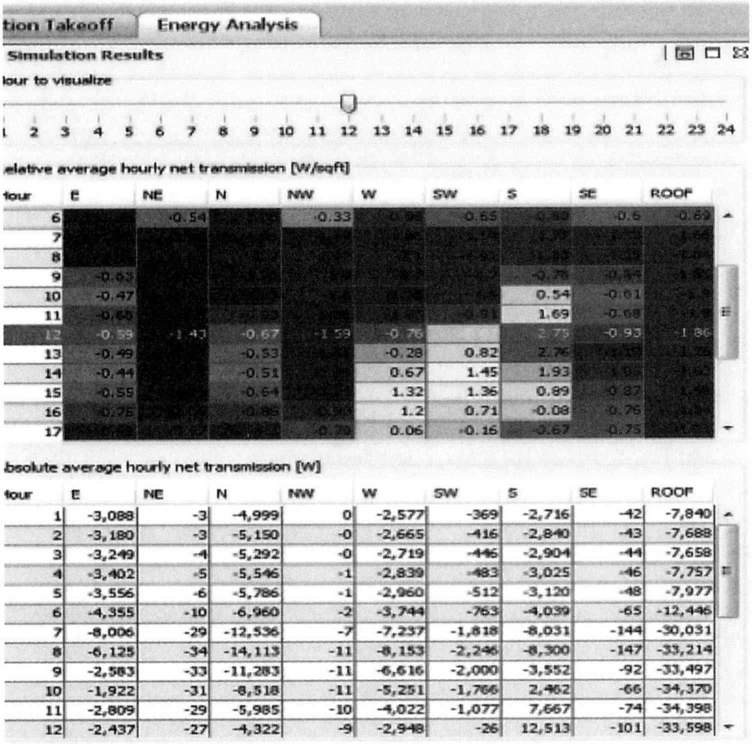

FIGURE 9.6 Detail showing color gradient for heat transmission values.

The figure shows a software interface with tabs "tion Takeoff" and "Energy Analysis", titled "Simulation Results", with an "hour to visualize" slider numbered 1–24.

Relative average hourly net transmission [W/sqft]

hour	E	NE	N	NW	W	SW	S	SE	ROOF
6		-0.54		-0.33		-0.65		-0.6	0.62
7									
8									
9	-0.63							-0.54	
10	-0.47						0.54	-0.61	
11	-0.65						1.69	-0.68	
12	-0.59	-1.43	-0.67	-1.59	-0.76		2.75	-0.93	1.86
13	-0.49		-0.53		-0.28	0.82	2.76		
14	-0.44		-0.51		0.67	1.45	1.93		
15	-0.55		-0.64		1.32	1.36	0.89	0.87	
16	-0.76		-0.86		1.2	0.71	-0.08	0.76	
17					0.06	-0.16	-0.67	0.73	

Absolute average hourly net transmission [W]

hour	E	NE	N	NW	W	SW	S	SE	ROOF
1	-3,088	-3	-4,999	0	-2,577	-369	-2,716	-42	-7,840
2	-3,180	-3	-5,150	-0	-2,665	-416	-2,840	-43	-7,688
3	-3,249	-4	-5,292	-0	-2,719	-446	-2,904	-44	-7,658
4	-3,402	-5	-5,546	-1	-2,839	-483	-3,025	-46	-7,757
5	-3,556	-6	-5,786	-1	-2,960	-512	-3,120	-48	-7,977
6	-4,355	-10	-6,960	-2	-3,744	-763	-4,039	-65	-12,446
7	-8,006	-29	-12,536	-7	-7,237	-1,818	-8,031	-144	-30,031
8	-6,125	-34	-14,113	-11	-8,153	-2,246	-8,300	-147	-33,214
9	-2,583	-33	-11,283	-11	-6,616	-2,000	-3,552	-92	-33,497
10	-1,922	-31	-8,518	-11	-5,251	-1,766	2,462	-66	-34,370
11	-2,809	-29	-5,985	-10	-4,022	-1,077	7,667	-74	-34,398
12	-2,437	-27	-4,322	-9	-2,948	-26	12,513	-101	-33,598

9.4 DISCUSSION

The aggregation of simulation output variables is usually represented in a graph or bar chart displayed as a performance dashboard. One drawback in the use of dashboards for design feedback is that the numerical data is separate from the design model.

The method described challenges this approach to performance feedback for architectural designers. Figure 9.7 shows a diagram of the automated process implemented in this case study, where a building information model is post-processed in two steps: first, to automatically generate a thermal zone model for energy simulation; second, to aggregate the raw simulation data and visualize the information for feedback. Performance indicators are used to provide a normalized approach to performance assessments. This type of reporting can be applicable to various design phases, providing critical information to track the decisions made during the design process.

The multi-dimensional visualization enhances the building information model layering performance information, qualitatively and temporally. This combination of quantitative information in qualitative terms facilitates the explorations of what-if scenarios in concept design. The challenge to integrate design exploration and analysis feedback within a single interface is solved using a color gradient scale to display thermal flows, at different points in time, through the external surfaces of the preliminary conceptual design model.

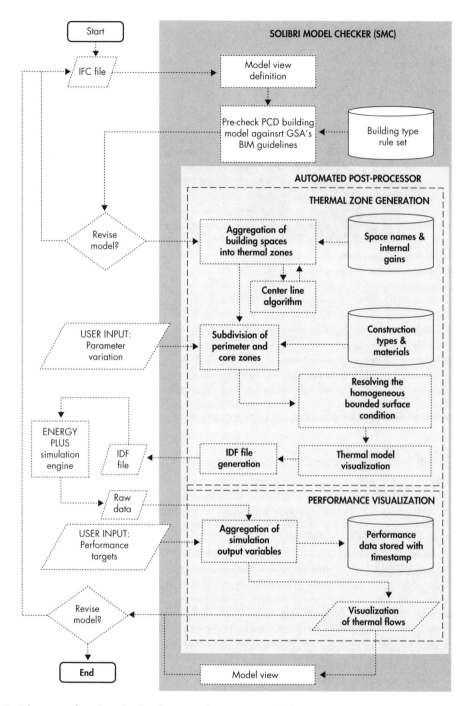

FIGURE 9.7 Diagram showing the implemented post-processing.

9.5 CONCLUSION

Energy evaluation of building designs is important to many stakeholders with different interests. Owners are interested in aggregate costs and performance, while designers are interested in disaggregated performance regarding façades and fenestration. The approach presented here relies on building model post-processing to transform a design model to one that supports energy analysis, minimizing the setup for analysis (Sanguinetti et al. 2012). The implemented energy module automates the data exchange between building models and the necessary input data for energy simulation. The approach maps the heat transfer data back into the BIM visualization tool, which integrates multidisciplinary perspectives to represent both the building model and the environmental performance of the model as color-coded surfaces.

ACKNOWLEDGMENTS

This work was carried out for the U.S. General Service Administration, one of the main facilitators of the building industry's move to Building Information Modeling. This project has been funded by the GSA to automate energy simulation and reporting in a contract with Georgia Institute of Technology.

DISCUSSION QUESTIONS

1. List the information typically represented in a preliminary concept design model. Also identify the properties defined in a preliminary concept design model for GSA.
2. Explain why a preliminary concept design model must be broken into thermal zones for energy simulation.
3. Explain the concept of a first-level space boundary.
4. Describe how the visual representation of thermal flows is used to provide performance feedback to the architectural designer.

REFERENCES

Bazjanac, V. 2004. "Building Energy Performance Simulation as Part of Interoperable Software Environments." *Building and Environment* 39: 879–883.

Björk, B. 1992. "A Conceptual Model of Spaces, Space Boundaries and Enclosing Structures." *Automation in Construction* 1(3): 193–214.

buildingSmart "Terms and Definitions," http://buildingsmart.com/resources/terms-and-definitions/?searchterm=ifc, accessed on 09–13–2013.

Foliente, G. 2000. "Developments in Performance-Based Building Codes and Standards." *Forest Products Journal* 50(7/8): 12–21.

Lam, K. P., N. H. Wong, L. J. Shen, A. Mahdavi, E. Leong, W. Solihin, K. S. Au, Z. and Kang. 2006. "Mapping of Industry Building Product Model for Detailed Thermal Simulation and Analysis." *Advanced Engineering Software* 37(3): 133–145.

Mahdavi, A. 1999. "A Comprehensive Computational Environment for Performance Based Reasoning in Building Design and Evaluation." *Automation in Construction* 8: 427–435.

Mantyla, M. 1988. *Introduction to Solid Modeling.* Rockville, MD: Computer Science Press.

Pauling, L. 1929. "The Principles Determining the Structure of Complex Ionic Crystals." *Journal Am. Chem. Soc.* 51(4): 1010–1026.

Sanguinetti, Paola, Sherif Abdelmohsen, Jaemin Lee, Jinkook Lee, Hugo Sheward, and Chuck Eastman. 2012. "General System Architecture for BIM: an Integrated Approach for Design and Analysis." *Advanced Engineering Informatics* 26: 317–333.

CHAPTER 10

Urban Energy Information Modeling: High-Fidelity Aggregated Building Simulation for District Energy Systems

Nina Baird, Carnegie Mellon University
Shalini Ramesh, Carnegie Mellon University
Henry Johnstone, GLHN Architects & Engineers, Inc.
Khee Poh Lam, Carnegie Mellon University

10.1 INTRODUCTION

The promise of the smart grid in the building sector is time-of-use energy management to better match supply and demand, encourage conservation, improve resilience, and allow use of more diverse, distributed, and variable energy sources. To some extent, however, this is retroactive planning for existing infrastructure. What if time-of-use grids were visualized and planned at a community scale and could integrate energy demand and supply to support local energy planning and ongoing management? This extension of building information modeling (BIM) to a district scale could provide new ways of looking at sustainable design.

10.2 UNDERSTANDING DISTRICT ENERGY SYSTEMS

Most buildings get their electricity from remote centralized plants that lose as much as two-thirds of their input energy as "waste" heat in the plant cooling towers and in transmission and distribution line losses. These buildings are then heated and cooled at the site by stand-alone HVAC (heating ventilation air-conditioning) equipment, which may also generate "reject" heat. Each building is a terminal point on the network, and systems are oversized at every point based on assumptions of ongoing inefficiency and loss. As pressure for new energy supplies grows, the inefficiency of centralized supply and conventional electricity generation seems increasingly extravagant. Better time-of-use management within centralized grids is one possible improvement; well-integrated district energy systems are another.

A district energy system is a system that serves more than one building. A district system will have a thermal plant that generates steam or hot water and/or chilled water to condition the buildings it serves. A pipe network circulates the steam/hot/chilled water to the buildings and back to the plant. Such a system may use boilers and chillers powered by natural gas and centralized electricity to meet district demand. Alternatively, thermal energy may be generated with more varied energy sources timed in—solar, geothermal, wind, biomass, ground-coupled heat pumps—and with on-site cogeneration (generation of electricity and the associated hot water) or trigeneration (generation of electricity, hot water, and chilled water). The time-dependent nature of demand and supply can also be addressed with heat recovery and thermal energy storage.

District systems have long been recognized as a key consideration in community energy management (Jaccard et al. 1997). They offer opportunities to integrate local renewable energy resources—solar, geothermal, biomass, wind—and energy-focused strategies such as energy recovery, energy cascades, and industrial ecology. Depending on their configuration and management, they can provide substantial energy savings, reduced air emissions (CO_2 and NO_x), and life cycle cost savings. Within the individual buildings they serve, district systems reduce floor area required for building mechanical systems, typically improve HVAC system operation and maintenance, and may reduce energy costs. Where cogeneration or trigeneration is involved, a district system can substantially increase the efficiency of electricity generation (Figure 10.1).

Of course, the infrastructure investment can pose challenges. The energy plant must be sited, permitted, and built. Installing underground pipe is a substantial expense and can be difficult in existing developments. The plant may be regulated as a utility and must interconnect with existing utility infrastructure and procure fuel. In many cases, the plant must also acquire and manage customer accounts. Although fuel prices and load on the system may vary, the equipment must be continuously maintained, and service must be as reliable as that offered by the central grid.

10.3 COMMUNITY ENERGY PLANNING

Despite these challenges, community energy planning and management is rapidly gaining traction as a means to increase livability and environmental performance at a micro- to macro-scale, and geographic information systems (GIS) can make community options visible. As an example, in 2008 the City of Calgary contracted with the Canadian Urban Institute to conduct an energy mapping study. The stated purpose of the study was "to provide clear direction to the City and inform the private sector about the potential to reduce greenhouse gas emissions and encourage the use of alternative energy systems

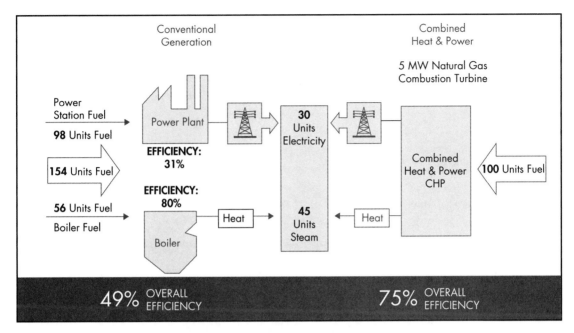

FIGURE 10.1 Comparison between conventional and combined heat and power generation.
(US EPA)

through considerations such as the design of buildings and encouragement of more compact, mixed-use and high density communities." The resulting Calgary Energy Maps show comparative energy intensity per hectare in 2036 for a "business as usual" approach and an "ultra-high efficiency" approach to development and building design. There is also an "Alternative Energy Source by Land Use" map that indicates potential areas for solar hot water systems, solar air, energy recovery/sharing in industrial sectors, and district energy systems in dense developments.[1]

The City of London commissioned a study, published in 2011, to identify sources of decentralized energy to meet 25 percent of the city's demand. The London Heat Map is an interactive tool intended to help identify district energy opportunities based on collocation of large heat users, large heat producers, and existing heat networks.[2] In 2012, Columbia University prepared an NYC Heat Map that represents estimated annual energy use intensity at the block and lot level in an interactive, color-coded map (Howard et al. 2012) and in a study similar to London's, the Energy Island Study for Minneapolis/St. Paul maps facilities that produce excess or waste heat, areas of concentrated thermal energy demand, and areas that are being developed or redeveloped.[3]

---

[1] See pp. 48–52 at www.calgary.ca/PDA/LUPP/Pages/Municipal-Development-Plan/Plan-It-Calgary/Plan-It-Calgary-research.aspx.

[2] The London Heat Map is available online at www.londonheatmap.org.uk/Content/home.aspx

[3] *Energy Island Integration Study*. 2013.
http://reconnectingamerica.org/resource-center/browse-research/2013/energy-island-integration-study/ (accessed August 23, 2013).

These energy mapping studies and tools are very useful in helping to visualize opportunities for energy conservation and integration and can motivate consumers to act.[4] They are static maps, however, and as such are primarily suggestive. They do not illustrate the time-dependent nature of demand and supply, enable district system sizing, or allow exploration of specific system alterations within the map. They definitely do not support ongoing system operation and management. A more advanced tool is needed for this.

10.4 DYNAMIC ENERGY MAPPING

A dynamic local energy map could show

1. An 8,760 hourly time-of-use energy profile for individual buildings and for aggregate demand in an existing community or planned development
2. A corresponding 8,760 profile of local energy supply

It would reveal the patterns of heating, cooling, and electricity demand over time. It would show the source and timing of peaks and troughs in thermal and electricity demand and the ability of existing or new local supply sources to meet this demand. Coupled with the analytical capability of simulation tools, it could offer the power of BIM on a district scale: holistic, integrated design at a community scale with the potential for ongoing integrated system planning and management throughout its operating life cycle.

10.4.1 An Initial Example: Pittsburgh's Lower Hill District

Although not fully realized, many elements of dynamic energy mapping already exist. In 2011–12, with financial support from the International District Energy Association, the Department of Energy, and Pittsburgh Gateways, a baseline simulation of a 28-acre urban mixed-use redevelopment of the Lower Hill District in Pittsburgh, Pennsylvania, USA was created (Johnstone and Baird 2012). It was used to analyze the feasibility of a district system for the site. As a complete site redevelopment, this *tabula rasa* example is easier than the effort to retrofit a district system into an existing site. However, it illustrates fundamental approaches and would certainly be applicable to rapidly developing areas in other countries (Raufer 2009).

A site master plan provided detail about the preliminary design development program of the Lower Hill District. The mixed-use redevelopment comprises approximately 3.5 million square feet in 35 buildings, including midrise multifamily and townhouse units, offices, retail space, a community center, a hotel and structured parking, and 5.8 acres of open space. A GIS map was created using the 2D layers

---

[4]www.reuters.com/video/2010/08/16/infrared-maps-highlight-energy-use?videoId=138861038&videoChannel=74 "Infrared maps highlight energy use: Thermografishche Kaart" (accessed August 28, 2013).

FIGURE 10.2   2D map of Lower Hill District site.

of the land parcels, roads, topography, building blocks, and hydrology for Pittsburgh. The layers were then imported into ArcMap to create a 2D base for the building blocks. In order to model a realistic topography for the base, a triangulated data structure was created using the 2D contours and the extrusion function in ArcMap. Figure 10.2 shows the site plan of the Lower Hill District.

10.4.2 Urban Energy Simulation of the Lower Hill District

A baseline energy simulation of the actual buildings on the site was created in EnergyPlus with DesignBuilder as the interface. Although this was not necessary for the preliminary screening analysis described below, energy simulation is essential in design and site-specific simulation with the surrounding buildings in context will better inform district system assessment. 3D models of the buildings of the Lower Hill District site were then linked to the map along with the 8,760 energy use data from EnergyPlus. To accomplish this, the Google Sketchup file of each building, which was provided by the planning firm for the site, was exported as a collada file format from Sketchup and imported into ArcScene version 10.0 as a geodatabase for every building. The building geodatabase contains the building attributes: building name, total conditioned area, annual energy consumption, energy use intensity, and annual and monthly peak demand. After the 3D map was created in GIS, the data from the energy

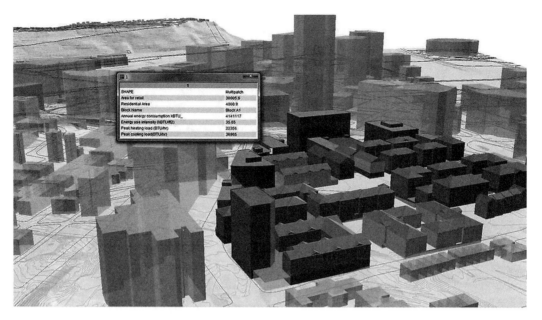

FIGURE 10.3 3D view of the Lower Hill District with building attributes displayed in an HTML pop-up window.

simulation was imported from an Excel file as building attributes in ArcScene. The building attributes for each building can be viewed in a HTML pop-up window using ESRI ArcScene (Figure 10.3).

10.4.3 Future Improvements Using Cloud Services

An improvement on this strategy would be making the map available online using GIS Cloud.[5] Cloud services can speed computer-intense tasks and offer greater accessibility and flexibility for shared data analysis and data mapping. Currently, GIS Cloud has limited 3D visualization and data communication; all mapping on GIS Cloud is in 2D format. The maps are directly imported from ArcMap with the individual layers as cloud data and the 3D components such as buildings and other land features can be coded into the GIS Cloud website using JavaScript API. Newer software such as ESRI's CityEngine or Autodesk's BIM 360 could streamline the mapping function, including the importing of the 8,760 hourly building energy use data. Autodesk BIM 360 Glue is a cloud-based multidiscipline model coordination application. The 3D neighborhood/city model can be integrated from Autodesk Revit, Sketchup, Google Earth, and other modeling software (Figure 10.4). BIM 360 Glue is used to display individual building data (e.g., building type, building area, number of residential units) and summary simulation results (e.g., annual end use energy consumption, peak design loads, energy use intensity) for each building.

---

[5]www.giscloud.com, "Step by Step Guide for GIS Cloud Applications."

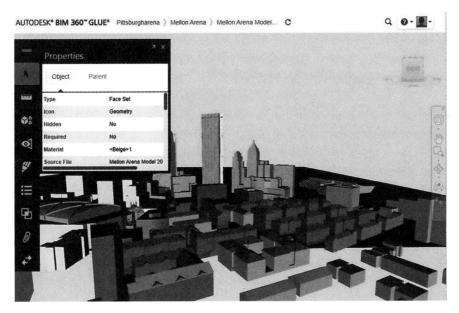

FIGURE 10.4   3D view of the Lower Hill District development using Autodesk BIM 360 Glue.

10.4.4 First-Order District System Analysis

Ideally, an urban-scale BIM tool would allow dynamic mapped display and analysis of energy demand and supply for all buildings and for individual buildings within the same software. For this project, however, the preliminary assessment of district system potential and subsequent detailed parametric analysis were performed in a separate Excel-based district system screening tool being developed by GLHN Architects and Engineers, Inc., with funding from the International District Energy Association and the Department of Energy. The screening tool contains the 8,760 hourly energy use data for each of the 16 building types in each of the 16 IECC/ASHRAE climate zones provided by the DOE 90.1–2010 commercial prototype building models (www.energycodes.gov/development/commercial/90.1_models). Currently, additional features of the screening tool include the following:

- Inputs for fuel prices, utility rates, and charges
- Inputs for the type and size of buildings within the development
- Modifiable assumptions about stand-alone HVAC equipment cost and efficiencies and about district energy plant efficiencies and operating costs, size, and location
- Choices of equipment for cogeneration and trigeneration and their properties
- Inputs for phased development of the district

- Modifiable assumptions for the discount rate, the rate of inflation, escalation of rates for electricity and natural gas, and interconnect charges for district plants
- Inputs for existing site equipment and energy consumption
- A variety of charting and graphing functions

For the preliminary assessment of the Lower Hill District site, one of the DOE 90.1–2010 EnergyPlus prototype models for Climate Zone 5a was chosen to represent each type of building on the site. The prototype models were not modified, but a sizing factor was used to adjust the energy consumption of the model to the square footage of that building type on the site. This approach allowed rapid progress toward a first-order district energy system analysis by providing a time-dependent load profile of all the individual buildings or types of buildings (e.g., midrise residential space, townhouses, midrise office space) within the district, as they are affected by climate and orientation, envelope characteristics, ventilation, the occupancy schedule, internal gains, equipment type, and efficiency.

For a higher-resolution approach, the 8,760 energy use profile from site-specific building simulation models could be imported into the software. Although that was not done for this project because of the timing of available funding, it would be a necessary step if the end goal is similar to what is proposed above: a dynamic energy map coupled with the analytical capability of simulation tools that could support holistic, integrated design at a community scale and ongoing integrated system planning and management throughout the district's operating life cycle.

10.4.5 Data Visualization for Time-of-Use Aggregate Load Profiles

Figures 10.5, 10.6, 10.7, and 10.8 show some of the graphing capabilities of the screening tool and suggest how time-dependent load data can be used for district system planning. The load profiles make

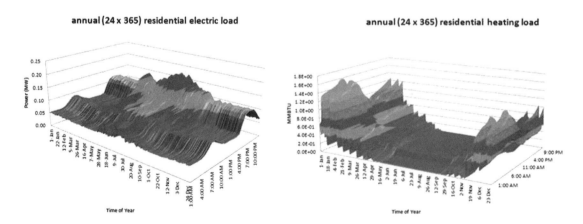

FIGURE 10.5   Detailed annual electric load and heating load profiles for site residential buildings, based on DOE 90.1–2010-compliant models for Climate Zone 5a.

visible the peaks and valleys of energy demand and the times at which these occur. This information allows the user to assess the reasonableness of the building models, an important step if generic models are used at the outset. It also indicates the types of fuel needed and the required capacity of district system equipment. Together with the GIS map functions, it can also begin to suggest possible configurations of a district system.

The 24 × 7 composite site load profile, shown in Figure 10.7, integrates time-dependent energy demand across the site. Composite demand by fuel type allows the user to assess district energy requirements and to explore an investment in cogeneration or trigeneration by showing the base electric demand and the opportunity to use heat from electricity generation for building conditioning and DHW.

10.4.6 Interpreting Lower Hill District Results

With embedded assumptions about fuel pricing, stand-alone HVAC equipment performance, and district system plant operations and production efficiency, the screening tool allows testing of various

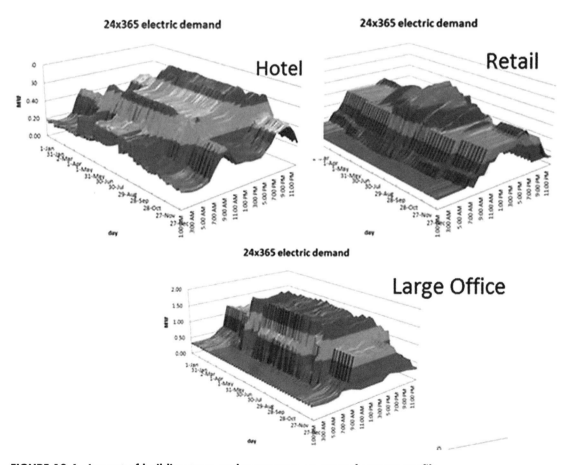

FIGURE 10.6   Impact of building type and occupancy on annual energy profile.

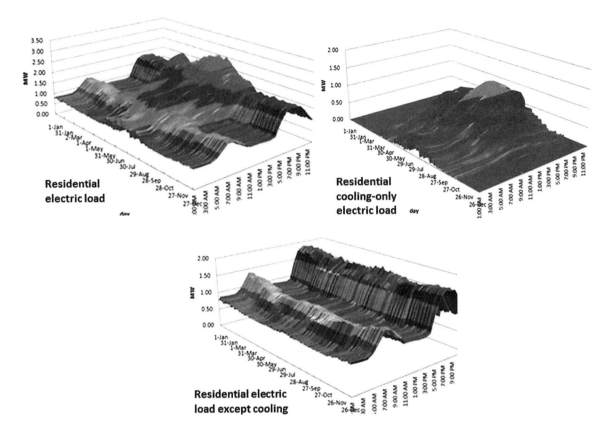

FIGURE 10.7 Site residential electric load, residential cooling-only electric load, and electric load minus cooling.

energy production, conversion, and storage techniques against hourly demand. Annual gas, electricity, and CO_2 emissions, and estimates of annual operating cost can be calculated and estimates of life-cycle costs, NPV, and ROI for various system configurations are possible.

For the Lower Hill District project, the screening tool was used to provide an initial assessment of the economics of a district thermal or district cogeneration system compared to individual HVAC systems for each building. Ultimately, the 10-year development phasing and limited initial energy demand from efficient buildings suggested that the return on investment (ROI) for a district system approach at the outset might be marginal for private investment, but possibly attractive enough to warrant consideration as a publicly funded utility. In such cases, it is possible to design buildings to be "district ready" with hydronic HVAC systems. Another option still under consideration is the possibility to join loads from energy-intense adjacent properties to a Lower Hill District system, providing sufficient base load to support the initial private infrastructure investment.

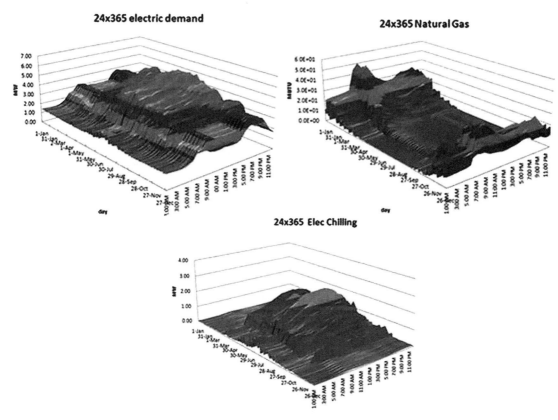

FIGURE 10.8   Composite annual electric demand, natural gas demand, and cooling-only demand for 35 buildings on 28-acre site.

10.5 THE FUTURE: BIM IN URBAN ENERGY INFORMATION MODELING

From this applied example, it is not difficult to imagine future developments that would make BIM possible at a district scale to facilitate community energy planning and ongoing energy management. Those developments would likely involve a cloud-based GIS platform that would facilitate data access and speed data analysis. Each building in the district would have among its attributes high fidelity estimates of hourly energy use to identify demand. It could also include high fidelity estimates of hourly solar insolation and HVAC heat rejection to identify opportunities for surplus heat transfer and the potential for solar energy generation within the district.

The GIS platform would be coupled with a calculation engine to allow users to construct composite district energy demand profiles for site power, heating, and cooling and would make these profiles visible as a dynamic energy map. The energy map would reveal the patterns of heating, cooling, and electricity demand over time. It would show the source and timing of peaks and troughs in thermal and electricity demand and show baseline demand. Ideally, it would also integrate time-of-production energy supply sources, including renewable and recovered energy (e.g., wastewater heat recovery).

Such a dynamic energy map and calculation engine would then be coupled with the analytical capability of a simulation tool that could produce, at a minimum, first order assessments of energy production, distribution, and storage alternatives for the district and fundamental cost/benefit analysis. It would allow consideration of different development phasing schedules, variations in the building mix, and variations in the juxtaposition of building types that might improve overall system efficiency and/or lower cost. And in experienced hands, such a tool could even be used to plan a modular district energy system, one that would grow with the development.

Ultimately, of course, the dynamic mapping, calculation engine, and simulation tool would become BIM on a district scale: a suite of data integration, processing and visualization tools to support holistic, integrated thermal and power system design at a community scale with the potential for ongoing integrated system planning and management throughout its operating lifecycle. Similar to BIM on a single-building scale, this vision is not yet fully realized. Yet as we look to smarter grids to improve future energy management, it seems reasonable to plan smarter grids from the start: grids that assume energy recovery and reuse as the norm, that accommodate a range of fuel sources where options are available, and that integrate and reflect the loads they serve.

DISCUSSION QUESTIONS

1. What is the relationship between BIM and aggregated energy simulation or energy mapping?
2. What is the difference between static and dynamic energy mapping?
3. How might time-of-use energy visualization be useful in planning and design for (a) single buildings? (b) a group of buildings on a district system?
4. Can you think of ways to incorporate alternative energy supply sources (e.g., solar, "reject" heat) into a dynamic energy map?

REFERENCES

Howard, B., P. Parshall, J. Thompson, S. Hammer, J. Dickinson, and V. Modi. 2012. "Spatial Distribution of Urban Building Energy Consumption by End Use." *Energy and Buildings*, Volume 45, pp. 141–151. Available at www.sciencedirect.com/science/article/pii/S037877881100524X (accessed March 3, 2013).

Jaccard, M., L. Failing, and T. Berry. 1997. "From Equipment to Infrastructure: Community Energy Management and Greenhouse Gas Emission Reduction." *Energy Policy* 25(13): 1065–1074.

Johnstone, H., and N. Baird. 2012. "Combined Heat and Power District Energy Screening Tool." International District Energy Association 28th Annual Campus Energy Conference, February 6, www.districtenergy .org/proceedings-25th-annual-campus-energy-conference/ (accessed August 23, 2013).

Raufer, Roger. 2009. *Proposal Concept—Energy System Integration in Asian Cities: Promoting Change for Development and Sustainability*. United Nations ESCAP. Beijing, China. www.unescap.org/esd/Energy-Security-and-Water-Resources/energy/lowcarbon/2009/forum/LCDP-PolicyDialogue/ESCAP-DraftProposal forEnergySystemIntegration.pdf (accessed July 21, 2013).

www.reuters.com/video/2010/08/16/infrared-maps-highlight-energy-use?videoId=138861038&video Channel=74 "Infrared maps highlight energy use: Thermografishche Kaart," accessed August 28, 2013.

Yamaguchi, Y., Shimoda, Y. and Mizuno, M. 2007. "Proposal of a Modeling Approach Considering Urban Form for Evaluation of City Level Energy Management." *Energy and Buildings* 39(5): 580–592.

CHAPTER 11

BIM and the Predesign Process: Modeling the Unknown

Michael Donn, Centre for Building Performance Research, Victoria University of Wellington

11.1 INTRODUCTION

You can never plan the future by the past.

> Attributed to Irish politician and conservative philosopher
> Edmund Burke, 1729–1797

Current implementations of building information modeling (BIM) are buried in a historicist mode of thinking. This mode sees writers about BIM and practitioners identifying how current and past building design processes can be made more efficient through this technology. The role of the players in the design team is viewed in a frame that expects design to follow traditional paths. In the early days of the "common building model" the nature of the BIM representation was speculation, and the research goal was typically to improve the means of integration of digital design performance analysis into the typical architectural design process (Amor, Groves, and Donn 1991). Two decades later, BIM technology has reached a level of development that makes it accessible to general practitioners, and yet the nature of its role in architectural design is still ill-defined and mired in tradition. The role and nature of the model in BIM and how this affects the design process is still very much a work in progress.

11.1.1 Current BIM Concepts Limit Performance Analysis

The problem facing practitioner and researcher alike is the nature of this common building model. Building the shared mental model of what a BIM is upon traditional views of the design process limits full exploration of the potential of the concept. As owners and users become more demanding of accurate prediction of a building's performance, the need for the true integration of performance analysis into the design process has become more critical (UK Carbon Trust 2012). The perception of a BIM as a comprehensive and detailed representation of all the parts of a real building makes performance analysis difficult. This is because the data required by this detailed representation makes the BIM unwieldy and inflexible.

This problem is critical for developers and users of BIM early in the design process when the most critical design decisions are made (Petersen and Svendsen 2010). BIM seems essential because the integrated design process is reported by designers of high-performing buildings as critical to successful performance (Gordon, Kantrowitz, and Estoque 1987, Antoni 1986). But, during early design, rapid testing of many design options with a BIM is difficult because there is insufficient data to build a complete model.

11.1.2 Performance Analysis in Early Design

The key advantage of the application of digital design decision support tools (DDSTs) in early design is that they provide feedback about performance that is useful for the designer-client discussion early enough in the process that key decisions can be made based on the planned mode of operation and exact site conditions. For example, a quick performance sketch can report the temperature indoors on a cold winter's day if the owner turns off or turns down the heating system overnight—will it be cool but not cold? Similarly, a sketch of several typical rooms at several heights in a potential office tower can inform the developer of the likely potential of daylighting making a useful contribution in a complex urban environment. Rules of thumb get the building generally right but provide no assistance to the design team on the value of their design decisions. A sketch of the various shapes that might be employed in auditorium design can be explored in conjunction with other ideas about access, ceremony, and display that might be investigated by designers of a concert hall.

The potential that sophisticated metrics offer is that design decisions can extend well beyond the barely legal minima of the simplistic measures written into codes and standards. Ultimately performance analysis early in design encourages the following and will not fail to perform when weather, use patterns, or controls are slightly different from those assumed during design:

- Design for quality, not just a minimum (code) quantity
- Designs that are truly responsive to the way clients plan to use the building
- Tests of design ideas that ensure they are robust in many different conditions

11.2 LIMITS OF TRADITIONAL EARLY DESIGN ANALYSIS

Walton (1989) and Feustel (1989) explain that most existing tools are either too "simplistic" or too "complicated" to provide effective design support. The simplistic ones are often too limiting, in that they apply only to highly generic situations regarding building geometry and operation. Complex models may only be able to be created by experts and take longer to simulate.

Traditional approaches to the inclusion of performance information into the early phases of architectural design have involved heuristics like rules of thumb. The problem with rules of thumb and similar prepackaged information was succinctly summarized in 1986:

> [I]nformation which actually reaches the profession and is assimilated . . . is highly selective and carefully pre-digested [into rules of thumb and guide books etc.]: I am suspicious of selected, processed information. It is a last resort. . . . One never knows what criteria lie behind the choice made and how competent those doing the processing are (Antoni 1986).

11.2.1 The Promise of BIM in Early Design

The original dream of BIM was, and remains, the integration of many different digital design decision support tools (Donn 2009). The focus of much research and development effort has been on the ways in which the building representations can carry some intelligence and can share common information. The promise of BIM is that it eases design teams' access to sophisticated digital DDSTs (CIB 2009). It is intended to provide them with complete flexibility to model all design options, but offers the promise of reduced complexity of data input due to the shared common building model. The extension of this proposed benefit of the BIM to the early design process, replacing the rigid and simplistic limits of the rule of thumb, offers the promise that the performance analyst can pose and develop answers to sophisticated design questions, rich in detail and depth.

11.2.2 Performative (Generative) Design as a Solution

Performative processes, where the performance of the building is as much a generative design technique as more formal considerations of proportion or context, have been posited as enriching architectural design (Kolarevic, Branko, and Malkawi 2007). This generative process is argued to be responsive to the environment and leading to consequent enhancement of the potential to meet the needs and desires of the occupants (Oxman 2008). Performative design is used to suggest (generate) form, not to analyze ideas generated by other means. For example, the argument can be developed that the equations representing the flow of light in a space can be easily reversed (Tourre and Miguet 2010). Thus one might identify a daylighting target and with these reversed equations calculate the nature of the construction (the building and its windows) that will produce the target lighting quantity. The seductive attraction of this idea is that the designer paints the surfaces in a building with the desired light qualities,

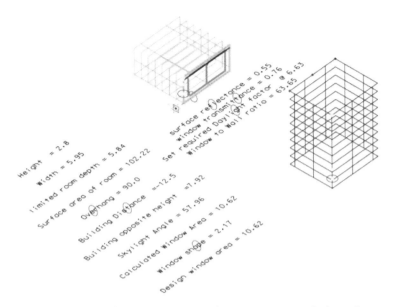

FIGURE 11.1 Performative "GC" script generates a window size that produces a target daylight level (room with window top left) given a shading building (outlined to the right).
(Image from script by Quinten Heap, 2009)

and performative software then develops window opening solution sets that are capable of providing this light.

Figure 11.1 illustrates the seductive power of this performance-based approach to the generation of a building design. It shows a 2009 student exercise from the Victoria University of Wellington School of Architecture. It encapsulates the window design sequence proposed by Joe Lynes (Lynes 1979). The formulae proposed by Lynes enable the calculation of the daylight factor (DF), a measure of daylight quantity, inside a room given certain input data on the reflectances and dimensions of the room, the window area, and the amount of shading outside from overhangs and from building(s) across the street that might obscure the amount of light coming from the sky. Reversing these formulae the student created a script in the Bentley MicroStation parametric design product "generative components" (Heap 2009).

The windows in the room outlined in the shape show the required window area to produce the desired daylight factor. The circles overlaid on the text indicate named parameters that can be adjusted by sliding the circle along the text. Thus it is possible to vary the size of the room, the size of overhang shading the sun, the distance to the building across the road, and the reflectance of the surfaces in the room and watch the required window area change to meet the desired daylight level.

Unfortunately, these equations are only simple if a series of simplistic assumptions are made about the design situation. These reversible formulae are based on rules of thumb. Therefore, the generation of a building design through some form of performative process remains problematic at best and potentially misleading.

Also, the integration of performative design into a BIM is a concept without a theoretical foundation at present. Performative design typically generates a family of designs that meet the design criterion. Imagine a real situation where there are sliders for multiple rules of thumb. Even if these were limited just to four rules representing structural, thermal, acoustic, and lighting goals, the likelihood of these four single factor rules of thumb dealing adequately with the interaction between factors is minute.

11.2.3 Daylight Design Example of Limits of Traditional Analysis

The simplicity of traditional rules of thumb in daylight design arises from their focus on diffuse daylight, but this is also their fundamental weakness. They can work quite well for those days when there is very little direct sun or in generally overcast conditions. In many climates, they are therefore only relevant for a small portion of the whole year. This leads to windows optimized for the diffuse light of a completely cloudy day and assumes not only that the direct shadow-casting light of a sunny day will be excluded but also that it is not a useful source of daylight. Whilst possibly true of some offices, this assumption of the total exclusion of the sun, and reliance on a standard overcast sky that will be the same on every cloudy day not only ignores what real climates are like but also ignores the potential analytical power of the digital model (Muneer, Fairooz, and Zhang 2003).

The seductive power of the multiplicity of design ideas produced by the performative/generative processes based on such rules of thumb hides their weakness: they are limited to a single sky condition and may therefore represent only a small fraction of the 4000 or so potential daylight hours each year.

11.2.4 Modern Performance Metrics in Daylight Design

The rich and detailed analysis promised by BIM is nowhere clearer than in daylight design. The field of daylight analysis has been revolutionized in the past decade as researchers have developed "climate-based performance metrics." The following paragraphs detail the current debate about climate-based performance metrics in daylighting.

Much of the work of the last 100 years of daylight science has focused not on modeling buildings but on the appropriate modeling of the sky (Kittler and Darula 2008). Predicting the performance of a window as a source of illumination requires a good knowledge of the hugely varying qualities of light experienced minute by minute every day and in every climate. There is a well-documented need for more sophisticated metrics of daylight performance than have been used in the past (Mardaljevic, Heschong, and Lee 2009).

Over most of the hundred-year history of daylight design science, the approach adopted to making daylight design relevant to more than just cloudy days has been to supplement the diffuse day calculations with calculations based on calculations for standard times of the day and year. The design then becomes a hybrid of windows that suit cloudy conditions and those that suit the sunny (clear sky) conditions for a few particular times of the day and year. The hybridization process relies on assuming that cloudy conditions can be represented by some quasi-mythical standard overcast sky and that morning,

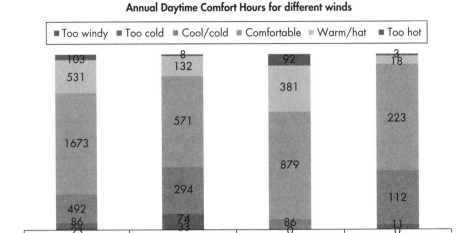

FIGURE 11.2   Graph reporting annual hours comfort index for a sketched urban site combining temperature, wind, and sun from student project at VUWSoA.

(Walton, Dravitzki, and Donn, 2007)

Daylight Autonomy

Average   96%

	1	2	3	4	5	6	7	8	9	10
J	96%	91%	91%	91%	91%	86%	82%	81%	81%	82%
I	100%	100%	100%	100%	100%	100%	100%	100%	100%	100%
H	100%	100%	100%	100%	100%	100%	100%	100%	100%	100%
G	82%	84%	91%	91%	91%	90%	91%	91%	95%	100%
F	95%	91%	91%	91%	90%	84%	82%	82%	82%	82%
E	100%	100%	100%	100%	100%	100%	100%	100%	100%	100%
D	100%	100%	100%	100%	100%	100%	100%	100%	100%	100%
C	81%	85%	91%	91%	91%	91%	91%	91%	96%	100%
B	93%	91%	91%	91%	91%	83%	82%	82%	82%	82%
A	100%	100%	100%	100%	100%	100%	100%	100%	100%	100%

Useful Daylight Illuminances

Average   6%

	1	2	3	4	5	6	7	8	9	10
J	6%	3%	9%	15%	18%	14%	11%	18%	18%	19%
I	0%	0%	0%	0%	0%	0%	0%	1%	9%	9%
H	9%	9%	6%	0%	0%	0%	0%	0%	0%	0%
G	12%	13%	18%	18%	19%	13%	6%	0%	6%	9%
F	5%	3%	9%	18%	18%	13%	11%	18%	18%	18%
E	0%	0%	0%	0%	0%	0%	0%	2%	9%	9%
D	9%	9%	5%	0%	0%	0%	0%	0%	0%	0%
C	11%	15%	19%	18%	18%	12%	5%	0%	7%	9%
B	4%	5%	9%	18%	18%	11%	13%	18%	18%	19%
A	0%	0%	0%	0%	0%	0%	0%	3%	9%	9%

FIGURE 11.3   Graphs from a 10x10 grid daylight analysis showing on the left daylight autonomy: percentage of daylight greater than target 300 lux and on right useful daylight index: percentage of daylight above 300 lux and below 2000 lux glare limit; from student exercise VUWSA.

noon, and evening sun conditions for spring, summer, and winter are sufficient to represent clear skies. It also more crucially assumes that windows that work for these two (cloudy and sunny) conditions will also work for partially cloudy conditions.

Modern climate-based design tools therefore allow a more precise definition of how much light is available (Table 11.2, 11.3). They permit the development of more subtlety in the use of daylight: for example, balancing glare from the sun with need for light or quantifying the amount of light available over the whole year. Statistically examining the availability of daylight for the more than 4000 hours of daylight in a normal year produces a climate-based daylight analysis (Reinhart, Mardaljevic, and Rogers 2006). The state of the art in daylight design is to report on all these 4000 hours; statistical analysis of the proportion of the year that daylight is sufficient to replace electric light is merely the beginning. Other statistics routinely reported are the following: documentation of what proportion of each day glare might be a problem; plotting of variations of illuminance and luminance ratios for differing viewing positions within any building from art galleries and offices; and maps on any surface of lighting quality, not just the traditional desktop illuminance of building codes (see Figures 11.2, 11.3).

The promise of BIM is to make these metrics easily available from analysis of the base building (BIM) model. The challenge for BIM developers and practitioners is to facilitate the construction of BIMs quickly that have sufficient building information that performance can be assessed in early design.

11.3 BIM-BASED DETAILED PERFORMANCE ANALYSIS

The future cannot be predicted, but futures can be invented.

Dennis Gabor, inventor of holography and Nobel Prize for physics recipient, in *Inventing the Future* (1964, p. 207)

The historicist approach to developing the role of BIM limits its potential. Nowhere is this clearer than in daylighting performance analysis. The following paragraphs propose (invent) a change in approach, one that also implies a change in the approach to BIM. What is required of a BIM by this approach is that the focus of the modeling process is not on interoperability, but on accurate performance modeling. The question of accuracy is paramount: interoperability seems to focus more on precision, the number of decimal places in the model, whereas accuracy asks that the model's predicted performance represents reality.

11.3.1 A BIM Is More than a Representation of a Building

A model is required that represents the performance of a building for a much wider range of days of the year and times of the day than has been acceptable in the past. This requires recognition that the BIM is not only a model of the building, but also includes a model of the sky driving the daylight performance. In general, all models used in building performance analysis are a closely intertwined combination of the model of the building and the model of the environment in which it sits. For example, a very detailed model of the thermal performance of a building is dependent crucially on the "typical" weather file used to calculate the heat losses and gains over all 8,760 hours in the year (Crawley and Huang 1997).

The key to quick, accurate, and sophisticated early design performance analysis is that the model used contains sufficient information about the major elements of the building that the future performance is accurately represented.

11.3.2 The Role of the Analyst in Performance Simulation

BIM offers the promise of the added analytical power of a reliable digital model. Systematic analysis of model quality has identified the features of a BIM dataset that have an influence on the reliability of the daylight performance simulation (Osborne and Donn, 2011). This analysis argues for a high degree of care and detail in model construction. The features were developed in a study designed to develop a validation dataset for daylight simulation computer programs. In descending order of influence on the performance simulation results the features are

1. Model material detail
2. Model external geometric detail
3. Internal reflectance measurements
4. Model opening geometric detail
5. Glazing transmittance
6. Dimensions of the room
7. Size and dimensions of glazed opening
8. Measurements of mullions or other simple obstructions

From the above list, the most critical elements of any daylight simulation dataset are the reflectances, both internal and external. Without precise reflectance data for most surfaces in the simulation model, it is unlikely that a reliable prediction can be achieved. Of unexpected importance is the model detail, particularly the setbacks and shaded areas found in the validation dataset used in the analysis.

The validation dataset was created to extend existing daylight validation for 3ds Max Design (Reinhart and Breton 2009). The validation comprised two parts: simple validation against analytic solutions published by the CIE of Radiance and 3ds Max Design (CIE 2006) and comparison of measured data in a test cell and in a complex building in very different climates.

The illustration in Figure 11.4 shows the monitored complex building whose daylight performance data formed the basis of the validation dataset. The building is shown in what is normally considered design configuration—the surfaces are represented as varying shades of white, black, and gray. It is common to recommend that, for design studies where the surface colors are unknown, inside rooms the ceiling should be modeled as white with a reflectivity of 0.8, walls as mid-gray with reflectivities between 0.5 and 0.7, and floors dark gray with reflectivities of 0.2–0.3. Given that these reflectivity values inside

FIGURE 11.4   3ds Max daylighting model used for analysis of the LPBS Net Zero Building at the University of Reunion, St. Pierre, Reunion.
(Rendered by Jacob Osborne)

the room can have a significant influence on indoor light levels, the design decisions about how big windows need to be could be crucially in error.

In the case of buildings like the validation dataset building, the reflectivities of the outside walls that face into the atrium and the detail with which the atrium is modeled are also highly influential. Reflectivities of the internal surfaces were shown to have one of the largest effects on internal illuminances. For a 3 percent change in reflectances for all surfaces in the model, predicted internal illuminances rose by between 1 and 14 percent, depending on the measurement point. The effect was smallest at the measurement points nearest the window where the number of reflections are least.

In addition, it was demonstrated during this validation exercise that the sky model used by the software has significant limitations near sunrise and sunset when the sun is at a very low angle of elevation above the horizon.

What this means for the BIM modeler is that accuracy of the daylight predictions based on a model of a building like this depends crucially on the skill and prior knowledge of the modeler. A BIM promises precise matches to the nth decimal place between the architect's, the structural engineer's, and the daylight analyst's models, but the analyst needs to understand the relationship between the BIM representation of reality (paradigm) and the predicted performance. This will include in the case of daylight design knowledge of the limitations in the applicability of the performance predictions. The problem is not the accuracy of the prediction, but the knowledge of what that prediction represents.

It is easy to see these limits include the relevance of "typical" sky models to performance on an individual day; or the effects of color choice on likely outcomes. However, each design team member has a different paradigm of building behavior. This paradigm is the relationship between the BIM and reality and therefore between the BIM and actual performance. For example, in daylight autonomy (DA) calculations for LEED and other sustainability assessments, it is common to assume that if the target illuminance is met 80 percent of the time over 50 percent of the floor area, then the electric lights will not be used over this floor area. This is assumed to be a nearly 50 percent saving in lighting energy use. The reality of many offices is that they have blinds for times when the light from outside is too bright, and these are not adjusted because it is easier to switch on and off the lights. It is also common to find that the lights are on when the daylight is well above the target level.

The architect and the structural engineer have similar paradigms with similar crucial underlying relationships to likely performance. It is this balance in the early concept stages of design that a BIM must facilitate. A single central BIM representing information about a building with this level of sophisticated analysis has been the dream since the 1980s. What seems to be missing from the typical representation of the BIM is a specific role for the modeler. The focus of BIM development seems firmly on the model in the BIM label. The role of the modeler, the modeler's intelligence, and the ability to weigh design options is less clear. To sketch enough of a building to analyze the energy, daylight, or acoustic performance requires BIM cameos. Not full models of the whole building, but sufficient detail to sketch the likely performance of the whole.

To meet the needs of the informed analyst, the BIM paradigm requires that the BIM aid the analyst to assess the significance of their modeling assumptions on the predicted performance. In daylight, for example, it must aid the analyst in determining the reliability of the performance prediction in the face not only of likely variation in building features like reflectance and room dimensions but also in the likely effect of the assumed sky model. Sky models represent partially cloudy skies as a perfectly even distribution of slightly diffusing cloud across the whole hemisphere of the sky when in reality a cloudy sky might have some dark clouds and a large area of blue sky. A BIM cameo has sufficient geometrical detail for the small part of the building model to be representative of the whole building, but also contains a representation of nonuniform skies to assist the parametric analysis of how much the asymmetry of a real sky might lead to a different design conclusion.

Typical analytical approaches to determining the scale of these potential influences (sensitivity analysis) use quickly sketched alternatives. At many stages in design, but particularly during early design, the robustness of the design recommendations should be tested quickly. To the experienced analyst, such tests are often single-factor analyses conducted on single rooms or even single facades. The information weight of the complete building information model is a paradigm that does not help this type of analysis. Worse, the current BIM paradigm encourages new users of the technology to focus on this complex whole building paradigm, not on the rapid answering of design questions.

11.3.3 Tools for Rapid Evaluation of Design Scenarios

During all phases of design, but especially during the critical early design decisions about type, scale, and design quality, the client needs high-quality data about design scenarios. They need more than rules of thumb. They need analyses that look statistically at the risk the building will only work in certain situations: for example, if the weather file represent a wide range of "average weather" scenarios, how will the building work in a week or two of peak summer or winter conditions? While a detailed BIM can be used for this type of analysis, strategic planning involving design option evaluation during early design often requires this type of sophisticated analysis when the design team has only a "sketchy" idea of the final design and thus cannot construct a complete BIM.

The simulation world is full of interfaces that encourage the analyst to sketch just enough of a building definition that a sophisticated analytical model can be constructed. SU2CATT and SU2ODEON permit building data to be exported from SketchUp to highly sophisticated ray-traced models of sound dispersion in a room such as CATT-Acoustic and Odeon; SU2DS and SU2RAD permit building data to be exported to highly sophisticated daylight models like DAYSIM and Radiance; OpenStudio and the IES SU Plugin allow building data to be exported to EnergyPlus or IES VE, which model the thermal performance of buildings for all 8,760 hours in a year. All these exporters permit the informed modeler to sketch rich and nuanced analyses of building performance. Used by informed design teams, they readily fit into the early design process (Donn, Selkowitz, and Bordass 2012). None is a BIM representation, so none encourages interoperability.

11.4 CONCLUSION: INVENTING A NEW BIM FOR EARLY DESIGN ANALYSIS

Unfortunately the strictures of a BIM currently limit the speed of these modeling exercises and thus restrict the ability of BIM to contribute to sketching performance. The speed issue arises in two ways. First, the overhead of the combination of information even just for acoustics, light, and energy is difficult to remove in the translation to the analytical tool, so the acoustic analysis, say, is slowed by the details that are only necessary for the light analysis. Second, the inevitable "reality" of the model's wall thicknesses, window details, and material finishes requires far more thought than a quick study of the sun shading options on a living room warrants. Yet the promise of the improved teamwork and thus improved building performance of the "common building model" remains. There is a need to invent a BIM paradigm that retains information from one analysis to the next, but can function with incomplete information providing sufficient support for the informed analyst to "sketch" the performance of many design scenarios. A quarter century after Walton and Feustel noted that design tools are either too simplistic to provide useful design input or too complicated to be used early in design, DDSTs are largely unchanged.

Some researchers are working on design tools that provide design advice rather than simulate design alternatives (Petersen and Svendsen 2010, Ochoa and Capeluto 2008). These have a didactic role in the classroom, but do not facilitate use of sophisticated analysis tools like Radiance or 3ds Max Design in daylight or SuNREL or Energy Plus in thermal performance or CATT or Odeon in acoustics.

The challenge facing BIM program developers today, looking to invent the future of building design, is to improve the sketch modeling capability of their products—to make a BIM cameo possible. The equivalent challenge facing researchers in this field is to demonstrate modes of operation of BIM that encourage rapid performance analysis (sketching performance) to assess the difference between the predicted performance of a BIM cameo against the performance of a full building information model and the measured performance of the real building. The challenge facing design teams is to see beyond the superficial "reality" of the BIM software representation to the real model, to distort the current BIM paradigm and work with multiple malleable representations of reality, each of which can show how the building might perform, and to develop their own BIM cameos.

DISCUSSION QUESTIONS

1. What is the critical limitation hindering the use of a standard BIM model in early design?
2. What are some of the broader determinants of the accuracy of building performance simulation beyond the precise representation of the dimensions and materials of the BIM?
3. Why is early design analysis important in building performance simulation?
4. Imagine you are developing a BIM cameo definition for a design office. Choose a design approach (such as daylighting or noise control) and an appropriate performance goal (such as glare-free 300 lux on the desktop or keeping highway noise out of an apartment) and list the minimum number of rooms, wall materials, and other building components required to produce an accurate performance prediction.

REFERENCES

Amor, Robert, Lindsay Groves, and Mike Donn. 1991. "Integrating Design Tools: An Object-Oriented Approach." Building Systems Automation-Integration Conference, Dallas, Texas (June 2–8). In *Building Systems Automation-Integration*, August 1993, University of Wisconsin-Madison, pp 717-730.

Antoni, Nils. 1986. "Editorial." *Building Research and Practice (CIB Journal)* May/June.

CIB. 2009. *CIB White Paper on IDDS "Integrated Design and Delivery Solutions."* Robert Owen (ed.). CIB publication 328. Rotterdam: International Council for Research and Innovation in Building and Construction. Available at http://cibworld.xs4all.nl/dl/publications/IDDS_White_Paper.pdf.

CIE. 2006. *Test Cases to Assess the Accuracy of Lighting Computer Programs*. Publication no. CIE:171, Vienna: International Commission on Illumination (CIE).

Crawley, Drury B., and Y. Joe Huang. 1997. "Does It Matter Which Weather Data You Use in Energy Simulations?" *Building Energy Simulation User News* 18(1) (Spring). Available at http://simulationresearch .lbl.gov/dirpubs/1801_weath.pdf (accessed September 2013).

Darula, Stanislav, and Richard Kittler. 2002. "CIE General Sky Standard Defining Luminance Distributions." Proceedings of International Building Performance Simulation Association (IBPSA) Canada, Montreal 2002. Available at Bratislava: Institute of Construction and Architecture, Slovak Academy of Sciences. www.ustarch.sav.sk/ustarch/download/Darula_Kittler_Proc_Conf_eSim_2002.pdf.

Donn, Michael. 2009. *Simulation of Building Performance: Environmental Design Decision Support Tools in Architecture*. Berlin: VDM Verlag.

Donn, Michael, Steve Selkowitz, and Bill Bordass. 2012. "The Building Performance Sketch." *Building Research and Information* 40(2): 186–208.

Feustel, H. E. 1989. "The Comis Infiltration Model." *IBPSA Proceedings on Building Simulation*, Vancouver, 1989, available at www.ibpsa.org/?page_id=134.

Gabor, Dennis. 1964. *Inventing the Future*. New York: Alfred A. Knopf.

Gordon, Harry, Min Kantrowitz, and Justin Estoque. 1987. *Commercial Building Design: Integrating Climate, Comfort and Cost*. New York: Van Nostrand Reinhold Co.

Heap, Quinten. 2009. "Generative Components Script Exercise." Building Science Honours 400 level course in computer applications. Wellington, New Zealand: Victoria University Wellington, New Zealand. Available at www.victoria.ac.nz/architecture/centres/cbpr/publications.

Kittler, R., and S. Darula. 2008. "Historical Developments in Practical Predicting of Sunlight and Skylight Availability." *Przeglad Elektrotechniczny* 84(8): 15–18.

Kolarevic, Branko, and Ali Malkawi. 2007. *Performative Architecture*. London: Taylor and Francis.

Lynes, J. A. 1979. "A Sequence for Daylighting Design." *Lighting Research and Technology*, 11(2): 102–106.

Mardaljevic, John, Lisa Heschong, and Eleanor Lee. 2009. "Daylight Metrics and Energy Savings." *Lighting Research and Technology* 41(3): 261–283.

Muneer, T., F. Fairooz, and X. Zhang. 2003. "Sky Luminance and Radiance Distributions: A Comparison Based on Data from Bahrain, Israel, Japan and Europe." *Lighting Research and Technology* 35 (1): 11–17.

Ochoa, Carlos Ernesto, and Isaac Guedi Capeluto. 2008. "Advice Tool for Early Design Stages of Intelligent Facades Based on Energy and Visual Comfort Approach." *Energy and Buildings* 41(5): 480–488.

Osborne, Jake, and Michael Donn. 2011. "Defining Parameters for a Duality Daylight Simulation Validation Dataset." 12th Conference of International Building Performance Simulation Association. Sydney: 12–14 Nov. 2011. Available at http://www.ibpsa.org/?page_id=44.

Oxman, Rivka. 2008. "Digital Architecture as a Challenge for Design Pedagogy: Theory, Knowledge, Models and Medium." *Design Studies* 29(2): 99–120.

Petersen, Steffen, and Svend Svendsen. 2010. "Method and Simulation Program Informed Decisions in the Early Stages of Building Design." *Energy and Buildings Journal* 42(7): 967–1164.

Reinhart, C. F., J. Mardaljevic, and Z. Rogers. 2006. "Dynamic Daylight Performance Metrics for Sustainable Building Design." *Leukos* 3(1): 1–25.

Reinhart, Christoph F., and Pierre-Felix Breton. 2009. "Experimental Validation of Autodesk 3ds Max Design 2009 and Daysim 3.0." *Leukos* 6(1): 7–35.

Tourre, Vincent, and Francis Miguet. 2010. "Lighting Intention Materialization with a Light-Based Parametric Design Model." *International Journal of Architectural Computing (IJAC)* 8(4): 507–524.

Walton, Darren, Vince Dravitzki, and Michael Donn. 2007. "The Relative Influence of Wind, Sunlight and Temperature on User Comfort in Urban Outdoor Spaces." *Building and Environment* 42(9): 3166–3175.

Walton, G. N. 1989. "Airflow Network Models for Element-Based Building Airflow Modelling," *ASHRAE Transactions* 95(2): 613–20.

CHAPTER 12

Analytical BIM: BIM Fragments, Domain Gaps, and Other Impediments

Karen M. Kensek, University of Southern California

12.1 INTRODUCTION

Building information modeling (BIM) and simulation tools are converging into "analytical BIM," the ability to use the model for analysis and predictions about the future performance of the building. However, this process is incomplete and fragmented. Feedback loops are not closed, and file standards are still immature. To understand where improvements can be made, three methods of categorizing BIM are discussed. One is an extension of the LOD (level of development) model used by building industry professionals. A second bases its categories on the level of information in the BIM, and the third is based on the FDEIC (factual, deontic, explanatory, instrumental, conceptual) framework of knowledge. Each suggests directions and trajectories about the future development of analytical BIM and the critical importance of feedback loops for informative iterative design. Three case studies are then explored, where bridging the gap between BIM and simulation provides opportunities for designers, builders, and facility managers.

12.2 ANALYTICAL MODELING

Architects have traditionally used both geometric modeling, a description of what a building would look like, and analytical modeling, a representation created for simulation purposes. Formerly, these types of models were distinct from each other, but modern tools have blurred the separation between the geometric and analytical models.

Before inexpensive computing and powerful software became generally available, architects provided graphic directions on how buildings were to be constructed by way of hand-drawn sketches and physical models. Drawings and "analog" models are still extremely useful and can convey certain types of information more clearly than renderings from digital models. Some common examples are

- Site models: How the building will look in context
- Massing models: To study shadow casting and wind flow in wind tunnels
- Structural models: For understanding seismic behavior on shake tables
- Presentation models: For clients and marketing, to show the completed building design
- Partial models: For many diverse purposes (for example, a partial model of a library reading room to study day lighting issues)

These models can be made from cardboard, wood, plastic, metal, plaster, and even fabricated from data in digital models. What is critical is that the important details are modeled accurately. For example, in a lighting mock-up, accurate scale reproductions of materials, color, textures, and geometry of the model will help provide accurate results. The size of the replica is often less crucial. However, a lighting model created with only these attributes exactly represented would not likely be accurate for acoustic calculations. Determining what to encode is important; adding too many unnecessary details will slow down the time it takes to build the model without providing additional useful information.

There are many software programs that are used by architects to predict the future performance of the proposed building (Krygiel and Nies 2008, Lévy 2011). These overlap and supplement the use of physical models. Some of these programs address sustainable design, code compliance for state energy codes, and green building compliance verification, and generally help to produce buildings that respond to the environment with less impact. It would be inaccurate to say that these simulation software programs are new. Early energy simulation software can be traced back to 1967 (Milne 2008). Many programs used today were developed from the early 1970s to the 1990s. Other types of simulation tools have an equally long history of development.

Increasingly, the computer has been used to analyze virtual models, but similar limitations and guidelines remain as compared with physical models. It is still critical to model the specific characteristics that are important for the analysis, giving enough information and detail for the results to be accurate within the tolerances that the user feels are appropriate. BIM can be used to provide geometric and parameter data to these programs.

12.3 BUILDING INFORMATION MODELING

Recently embraced by the architecture and construction industries, building information modeling has been proselytized by its evangelists as a completely new, innovative, breakthrough technology. However, the current incarnations of building information modeling reflect the latest stage of a continuous evolution of computer tools that started in the 1960s. The unevenly paced, but nonetheless steady evolution, has seen both the growing sophistication of graphical depiction from two dimensional (computer aided drafting–CAD) to three-dimensional modeling and the addition of specialized architectural components (Eastman et al. 2008). By the 1990s, most larger architecture firms were converting to CAD programs, which metaphorically translated pin-registered drafting media from hand-drawn documents to digital files. Concurrently, from the mid-1970s on, building description software was being developed that used a different metaphor. The structured database described building components and their relationship to each other. Early attempts embedded components with data produced proto-BIM software. By the turn of the twenty-first century, building information modeling was making deep in-roads in both architecture and construction firms.

At its best, a BIM provides an integrated, structured database, informed by the building industry, and consisting of 3D parametric objects. BIM is often used as a method for achieving 2D/3D coordination, and it can be used as a graphic interface between the building design intent and performance-based software. A BIM ecosystem currently commonly includes software programs for rendering and animation, clash detection, trade coordination, construction sequencing, and cost estimating. Innovative firms are doing much more, and scopes of services are reaching into facilities management and operations, but that is not the usual extent. It has only fairly recently that designers, contractors, and facilities managers, among others, are expecting that their building information model data flow seamlessly into simulation software.

12.4 LEVELS OF BIM

While some people distinguish between BIM and 3D modeling, it is more helpful to think of these technologies as points on a continuum. A 3D model is a "proto-BIM," a digital model of a building without the associated data. It does not even need to be component based and still be useful. There are many software programs that fit into this category, their major purposes being for 3D modeling, rendering, and animation. They can still be used for several types of limited analysis that depend only on geometry: for example, shadow casting, simple clash detection, and as a basis for 2D drawings. In contrast, one theoretical pinnacle of BIM is that of a solitary, super database. It includes all the geometry (3D digital models), information, and decisions that went into the creation of the building. It could be conceived as a virtual description of the building where the geometry is created for architecture components and linked to manufacturer databases with up-to-date specifications (Harfmann 2013). A single BIM is an exemplar that also embraces the real building itself, which holds a different set of data in a physical form. This might be an unrealistic goal, perhaps an unreasonable one, especially considering the current state of software development.

Most architecture firms and construction companies have achieved an intermediate level in their implementation of a BIM. The lowest-level true BIM is an integrated component database that achieves relatively seamless coordination between the 3D model and 2D production drawings where the 3D model serves as a database and any output, such as a 2D drawing, can be regarded as the result of a query of this database. The level of BIM is somewhat ambiguously associated with the level of development of the components that it comprises; it is somewhat confusing that LOD has also been referred to as "level of detail." In either case, the level being referred to is about the richness of the component and its data, not usually its graphic complexity. A building information model might also contain objects at varying degrees of "completeness" depending on the intended use of the model. The American Institute of Architecture (AIA) describes these levels of development in article 2 of the "Project Building Information Modeling Protocol Form."

The Level of Development (LOD) describes the minimum dimensional, spatial, quantitative, qualitative, and other data included in a Model Element to support the Authorized Uses associated with such LOD (AIA 2013).

The definitions have changed somewhat since the original AIA 2008 specifications, but a simplified description is as follows:

LOD 100: The component may be represented by a symbol or other generic description. Because of the type of data, only very conceptual analyses can be made.

LOD 200–400: The component is created as an object. It probably will contain attributes that are nongraphic data. Graphic development from LOD 200 to 400 has to do with the specificity and accuracy of the geometry of the object in terms of quantity, size, shape, location, and orientation. By LOD 400, it is the intent that the level of detail is equivalent to that traditionally supplied by shop drawings. Attribute data might include items like cost (from estimates to actually cost), scheduling information, manufacturer, and so on.

LOD 500: The component has been field verified in terms of its geometry. It may also include attributes (for example, specifications and product data) that are useful for the operation and maintenance of the facility.

From LOD 100 to LOD 500, the AIA defines a clear progression for the geometric representation, expected accuracy, and existence of associated data. It is clear that the standard identifies the level of development, not the level of geometric complexity of the object.

However, as with any system of categorization, other methods are illustrative in different ways. The following taxonomy focuses on the entire BIM rather than the component. It privileges data over geometry and proposes that the type of data that is associated with the model is extremely relevant for analytical BIM.

1. Pre-BIM
2. BIM Light
3. BIM + information
4. BIM + knowledge
5. BIM + decisions

12.4.1 Pre-BIM: Planning Stages

Pre-BIM is any organized set of nongraphic data that is used in the planning stages of a design project. The nature of the pre-BIM depends on the user, for example:

- Developer. A real-estate pro forma with leasing information and projected costs that tests if it is economically feasible to create and operate the building.
- Client. A spreadsheet with room information including square footage, program elements, and proposed tenant.
- Architect. Cost estimation spreadsheet; preliminary LEED Scorecard or other green rating system preliminary goal form; weather and climate data.

12.4.2 BIM Light: A Component-Based 3D Model

BIM Light consists of 3D building components that collectively describe a virtual digital model of a building. As a direct successor to computer-aided design, the component-based 3D BIM is incredibly useful. Instead of lines, circles, surfaces, solids, and the like creating an image of a building, architectural components are assembled into a 3D model, which provides significantly more utility. It can be used for

- Rendering and shadow casting
- Creating plans, sections, elevations
- Making schedules. Building components can be quantized and spreadsheets automatically generated by the software; for example:
  - ○ amounts (e.g., number of doors or windows)
  - ○ perimeter and length (e.g., how much wood trim to install)
  - ○ area (e.g., amount of gypsum wallboard that needs painting)
  - ○ volume (e.g., conditioned space that is heated or cooled)
- Interference/clash detection, with reports listing the virtual clashes of objects with other objects. More sophisticated clash detection is possible if there is also nongraphic information in the model.

12.4.3 BIM + Information

The "I" in BIM refers to information, more precisely data that are associated with the 3D objects. Data are supplied to the architecture components that can then be used for analysis. The data do not have to be contained within the object; they just have to be associated with it. Analytical BIM refers to this addition of specialized data that are within the BIM or another simulation software program that can be used in conjunction with the 3D model. Building performance can be predicted based on the data plus building model. The breadth of potential analysis targets is wide; a short list includes

- Interference checking that includes tolerances around specific types of objects (e.g., fireproof insulation around steel columns; this is not usually modeled directly)
- Acoustics, sound mitigation
- Water resources, runoff, harvesting
- Quantity-based cost estimating
- Code compliance such as handicap accessibility, exiting, stairs, and parking requirements
- Smoke modeling, fire evacuation
- Structural analysis
- Energy consumption, renewable energy production, CO_2 footprint, life cycle assessment, thermal comfort
- Ventilation (natural and artificial), sizing of ductwork and HVAC equipment
- Daylighting, electrical lighting, glare

For the most part, current simulation algorithms are reasonably accurate. What varies is the quality of data that the user supplies, the default assumptions, and the sensitivity of missing information. For example, will the building owner actually open the windows for nighttime flushing of heat, as was assumed in the software program, and how much difference will that make to the predicted energy savings when the owner turns on the air conditioning instead? As the software program might not even ask about occupancy behavior, the user might not realize that it could be an important factor when predicting the performance of the building.

12.4.4 BIM + Knowledge

Knowledge is information and skills acquired through experience or education. This is more than just facts or parameters that are associated with a BIM component. At present, knowledge is usually in the brains of the designers and consultants and not in the BIM. But there are applications where this could happen. In some cases it already has been:

- Cost estimates have gone beyond simple quantized schedules. Sophisticated software can use the building information model for schematic and conceptual cost estimating. Data mining and analysis of previous comparable projects' hard costs, overruns, and savings insert past knowledge to assist in predictions.
- Fabrication of real architecture components is often based on the 3D model. This allows for tasks such as automatic shop drawings from 3D models, including complex parameterized structures, constructability analysis, panel rationalization for curved surfaces, and machine tool path optimization.

- Location-based project management using BIM allows for the visualization of the budget, the schedule, and multiple design options towards enabling target cost driven design.
- Modeling of rental properties combined with real estate and tenant-oriented software can assist with lease administration, portfolio management, and strategic planning.

Building information models can morph into building management models. This is useful during the occupancy stage for operations and maintenance including building performance monitoring and data logging, fault detection, real-time sensing and response, simple decision making algorithms (for example, air change rates based on weekends versus weekday occupancy), and renovations.

12.4.5 BIM + Decisions

"The ability to have all relevant information about a window or other building component or system, along with the decision-making process that led to the choice, is of great value for all team members throughout the life of the building" (Epstein 2012, pp. 57–58). Epstein precedes this comment with a thorough example that explains how to embed data into the parametric objects (BIM + information), but does not provide suggestions as to how past decisions and hindsight might be included in the building information model. In addition, how can the author tag the data as to the quality and intended use? "Weeding" the model might become necessary; while appropriate data should remain in the model, bad data should be removed.

Knowledge and hindsight together provide the opportunity for foresight. Yet not all hindsight is useful, and all the decisions that went into the design and construction of a building are not equal in importance. What tracks the critical decisions that went into the design of the building? For instance:

- Which decisions are not worth recording beyond their immediate use? For example, the client requested that the wall in the hospital room be painted white.
- What information is useful for only a short period of time? The amount of paint used is approximately 300–400 sq. ft. per gallon, depending on surface conditions and application techniques.
- And what decisions need to be incorporated into the BIM for future reference? Dunn Edward "ENSO Low Odor, Zero VOC Interior Eggshell Paint ENSO30" was chosen for the hospital room's walls.

A building information model is currently structured to hold data (color of paint) and calculate the areas (the approximate number of gallons used), but it does not usually contain information about *why* the decision was made (eggshell white provided a good reflectance value for daylighting and the zero VOC was important for LEED credits and the health of occupants). In renovations, the wall might be painted with a dark blue generic paint because the initial decision-making reasoning was no longer available. The daylight availability would go down, and perhaps the amount of VOC would go up. Past decision processes have been lost to the detriment of the building owner and occupant.

12.5 FDEIC KNOWLEDGE

Both the AIA LOD and the pre-BIM to BIM + decisions taxonomy recognize the importance of data and information. Understanding more about types of knowledge would provide a different framework for understanding BIM. The FDEIC taxonomy (explored by Horst Rittel) categorizes knowledge into five categories: factual, deontic, explanatory, instrumental, and conceptual. It could help answer the question of how a building information model could move beyond being a repository of geometric and factual data.

One critical goal is that the BIM aids effortlessly and directly in the design, construction, and occupancy process. Appropriate to the scope of the project, it will need to respond to knowledge of several forms:

1. *Factual.* This is what is known about the virtual building that can be put in dialogue boxes or calculated from other data, geometric or specified. The roof is rated R-30 and has a slope of 4 in 12. The wall is structural and is made of concrete. The window faces south, is 3′ deep, and has a 3′ overhang. Often relationships can be specified. If the window is made wider, the length of the overhang increases. However, more complex relationships are often not explicit. For example, a pair of windows, their location, height, and lack of walls between them may be crucial to a ventilation scheme. Yet this relationship's importance is not usually saved, and the details could be lost in a later renovation.

2. *Deontic.* Deontic knowledge acknowledges that solutions might be the best one can do for now, but given additional resources, something else ought to be done. For example, when the money becomes available, install a cool roof or upgrade the fixtures to those that are EnergyStar rated.

3. *Explanatory.* Similar to BIM + decisions. An explanatory knowledge base contains information about why something was done. This is especially useful for combinatorial innovations that might be counterintuitive. For example, a Trombe wall is painted black; the maintenance person observes the heat buildup and paints it white to reduce heat gain. There should have been some way that the maintenance person could have learned why the wall was black to begin with. This leads to instrumental knowledge.

4. *Instrumental.* In some cases, directions and explanations are given as "user guides." These can be tied to the BIM. How to fix something, maintain it so that it works well, warnings about what not to do, and so on are types of instrumental knowledge. The BIM might not be the correct place to hold this information. When saved, this information is commonly in three-ring binders stacked in the maintenance and operations office or sometimes ties to facilities management software systems. Perhaps the building and its components are another place where the information could be stored (e.g. a light fixture has an RFID tag or QR code that links to manufacturer, warranty, and maintenance information).

5. *Conceptual.* This set of knowledge refers to what is meant or intended. If an architect refers to a highly sustainable building material, are they including embodied energy and end-of-life energy? Lack of clarity about terms and concepts can lead to misinterpretations.

12.6 FEEDBACK LOOP

The presence of a feedback loop is important at every level of design, but the examples discussed below are for approximately LOD 300, BIM + information, and factual knowledge. As the building information model is theoretically a database containing all the information about the building in addition to its geometric characteristics, it is entirely suitable to be used with simulation software to help predict the performance of the future building. There is a common myth that there will be a single virtual building model. Instead, partial models for different uses might be a more appropriate strategy especially as a way to keep file sizes manageable and complexity contained (Johnson 2013). With interoperability standards becoming more robust, it should be possible to take the information from the BIM to the simulation software, add other significant data, and perform a simulation. Currently, professionals and academicians write specific translation software such as *Revit2Modelic* and *Revit2Radiance* and *Revit2GBSOpt* (Yan 2013) for this.

A design process problem asserts itself when trying to use BIM and analysis software together; this is related to the simulation feedback loop. The design process is iterative. An architect might locate fenestration; evaluate their position based on interior daylighting, aesthetics, cost, and other factors; then move, resize, specify a new type of glazing; and make another set of evaluations. Old ideas are reintroduced, new information is discovered, and the design changes again. The intent of using simulation software is that the results of the study are used to predict the behavior of the building, inform the designers of possible alternatives, and have them make changes to the digital model. Then it is back to the simulation software for more studies, and the looping continues until the designers are satisfied or time and money run out. This is the feedback loop, a series of iterations between the software programs until a resolution is reached. To maximize the effectiveness of simulation tools in the design process, there must be a seamless way to go from BIM to simulation back to BIM while keeping the changes that have been made in each program.

Sometimes there is a nearly seamless feedback loop. This is often the case when the simulation tool is embedded within the building information modeling software (Lin et al. 2010). Wind studies on digital building masses provide almost instant response. The user can move the wind direction arrow or change the building design, and the colors and animation of the wind flow will react immediately. The feedback is clear, instantaneous, and the information made to the model and wind conditions is saved in the file. Or the designer can change the date and time; the sun moves, shadows are cast, and the designer can use this information to inform decisions. One can edit the BIM, and the results are saved within the same file. The viewpoint can also be changed for studying the impact in interior spaces.

Unfortunately, the effectiveness of the feedback loop is usually not this clear. Buildings are often modeled in one software program and analyzed and evaluated in another. For example, the project BIM could be exported to an artificial lighting analysis tool. Information specific to artificial lighting is added. Often, this specific information is directly entered into the lighting program because the BIM was unable to hold the data or exporting the detailed lighting data was not possible or the data was just not present because up until that point the designer did not need it.

Usually more domain-specific data are entered in the analysis tool. Simulations are run with different data, alternatives studied, decisions made. However, often the data, alternatives, and decision-making process cannot be exported back to the BIM. The feedback loop is not complete; one cannot "round trip." Eventually, interoperability standards such as IFC will help in the transfer of data, but currently, any changes made to the design in lighting or energy tools, for example, have to be manually reentered into the BIM. Many other simulation programs have this same undesirable feature. This limits their usefulness during the design process. And to complicate matters, there is usually not a single BIM or a "complete" partial BIM containing all the necessary data that are needed for the simulation.

Versioning and historiography could also be embedded in the building information model. These would allow users to trace their choices back in time, follow different timelines of development of the model, and be able to select paths that they might have first discarded. A different type of "feedback loop," these could also allow knowledge and decisions made by others working with the model be made more transparent.

12.7 FRAGMENT BIMs AND THREE GAPS

There rarely exists a single unified project BIM that is used during the life cycle of a building project. Instead, there are many BIMs used for diverse purposes that evolve over time:

- Design BIM. This is a building project BIM held by the architect that links the design intent model with those of the consultants.
- Consultant BIMs. This includes those models created by the consultants: structure, MEP, fire protection, and so on.
- Constructability BIM. This is a building project BIM developed by the contractor that links the design BIM and those from subcontractors and fabricators if they exist. Often this includes a range of file types from 2D CAD drawings to fully 3D BIMs.
- Facilities Management BIM. This is an intermediate step toward a BIM becoming fully included into a computerized maintenance management system (CMMS).

Partial BIMs come into existence for a specific purpose. For example, designers might use part of the design BIM for sun shadow analysis. This implies that the users know what they need to run the analysis software and employ the subset of data useful for completing that task. This is in contrast to "fragmented BIMs" where not all the information that is needed is contained in the BIM, and it is unclear who is responsible for including the data.

Fragmented BIMs have led to gaps in the handoff of models. Three short examples explore gaps that exist between the architect and consultant, architect and contractor, and the architect and contractor to facilities manager and owner. Determining ways of bridging gaps provides opportunities for future development of building information modeling.

12.7.1 Architect to Energy Consultant

BIM to BEM or BEP (building energy modeling or building energy performance) is a relatively small gap. With the addition of appropriate information (essentially moving up from "BIM Light") architects can use their BIM for conceptual whole building analysis and determination of EUI (energy use intensity), heating and cooling loads, and approximate carbon footprints. The same file can provide geometric information and some limited data that the energy consultant can use to create more sophisticated simulations. Unfortunately, this is one area where the feedback loop is often broken, and changes to the consultant's energy models (usually not BIM) are not sent back to the designer.

Overall, however, even at the current state of development, for the conversion of BIM to BEM the advantages outweigh the disadvantages, and quirky workarounds have been developed. In one mostly successful example, the NASA Ames Sustainability Base, the original contractor's BIM had to be completely rebuilt, and the IFC file format used to exchange data resulted in minor errors. The overall conclusion was "that adequate training in the design of BIM for the purposes of BEM could resolve the majority of the issues encountered and a remodeling would not (have been) necessary" (O'Donnell et al. 2013).

Better software compatibility and file interoperability standards are critical. These can be improved and will be over time. However, BIM to BEM/BEP is primarily a knowledge gap. Complex energy software relies on experienced users to provide appropriate and accurate data that will produce accurate simulations. Other suggestions for improvement:

- Insure that the software that is available to designers is not just easy to use but also leverages BIMs that are already being created for other purposes.
- Provide error bars or ranges on the simulation results.
- Supply information in a way that is helpful for design. Generous use of graphs will often help achieve better understanding than charts of numbers.
- Provide sensitivity analyses and give design guidance. List the main parameters that are applicable to the software and how they affect the results. For example, the designer might be studying the trade-offs of many features. It would be helpful to know that the type of window glass is more critical (or not) for energy savings than the use of occupancy sensors for electrical lighting. Having many common parameters as part of a sensitivity analysis with explanations on how to interpret them would be incredibly useful.

12.7.2 Architect to Contractor

The gap between the design BIM and the constructability BIM is a modeling gap and is often a wide chasm. The former describes the design intent, the latter how the building will be built. The standards and norms for the architect and contractor are different, historically and contractually. The transformation of traditional 2D paper drawings to a BIM (and what that means) is still largely undefined in the architecture profession, especially when one also considers that the design intent model needs to become the contractor's and fabricator's models (Hardin 2009, pp. 107, 110). Communication during the process, deliverables that address the problem rather than avoid it, and a strong BIM execution plan can help. In addition to standards and workflows, the plan often includes specific details about model authorship, LOD, and often a BIM use analysis chart. If both the contractor and architect have agreed on LOD-based milestone definitions, have clearly defined the allowable uses and components' accuracy, and have communicated intended uses of the model, it is possible to bridge the gap between types of BIMs and avoid the necessity of the contractor rebuilding the BIM from scratch (Bedrick 2013).

This second example instead addresses a small subset of the architect to contractor gap that focuses on information, not modeling standards: the addition of tolerances and a time component to interference checking. Interference detection is easily achievable even with just a "BIM Light" model, with reports listing the clashes of objects with other objects. More sophisticated clash detection is predicated on additional nongraphic information in the model, for example, tolerances and time.

Tolerances are a modeling issue. For example, clash detection has more utility when the information supplied is not merely that "object A" intersects with "object B," but is very specific to the building design that is described in the BIM. For example, there is a conflict between a specific column and HVAC duct that results in a change order. Or that because of tolerances, a door swings into a restricted space in front of an electrical panel, and one or the other has to be moved because of code restrictions. Although tolerances are a modeling issue, more critically, they are an information issue. The modeler does not need to create the fire insulation around columns or boxes in front of electrical panels—specifying tolerance data for a "soft" clash is more effective, especially if the data can be component specific.

A time component can also be added to avoid future clashes. The BIM's components should know how they change over time. Some examples of clash detection that depend on a time component:

- Multiple cranes are positioned on a large building site. The logistics need to be established so that they do not intersect each other while working. Or if it is unavoidable that their arcs intersect, operating procedures need to be put in place to ensure that they do not physically crash into each other.

- Trees grow. In doing so, they might make a building more energy efficient, but they also may become tall enough to shade the solar collectors on a roof, which would decrease their efficiency.

- Maintenance staff enter a mechanical room to replace a panel. To do so, they need a ladder, but the ladder cannot be brought into the room because it physically cannot be moved into place. There is space inside the room for it, but the process of getting it into the proper location cannot be resolved.

- Construction sequencing of complex MEP layouts in small plenum spaces can be resolved. A static BIM shows that all components fit, but not how they got into the space. This type of analysis, or lack thereof, was actually the basis of a court case involving the architect, contractor, and others (Stewart and Nicole 2011).

12.7.3 Architect and Contractor to Facilities Manager and Owner

The gap between BIM and building management systems can be solved with better software and hardware. To bridge the gap, the architect and/or contractor must supply the gathered data in an appropriate format to be integrated into the facilities management software. The staff who use the computerized maintenance management system need to be involved in the process; they can feel overwhelmed by new technologies and may not even trust the data supplied. "Once transferred, the subsequent use and maintenance of the COBie and BIM data is not a trivial problem" (Anderson et al. 2012).

Several successful examples show how this can be done. For example, the U.S. Army Corp of Engineers since 2005 declared in its vision statement that the "USACE will be a leader in using Building Information Modeling to improve delivery and management of facilities for the nation" (Brucker et al. 2006). University campus managers, the General Services Administration (GSA), and other owners with large portfolios are requiring (or are at least researching the idea) "record" building information models as deliverables at the end of a design project. These are similar to the record drawings (sometimes referred to as "as-builts") that are often created after the building is constructed.

Even more inventive, a BIM can be a 3D control system or a test bed for a real building. This example is not far beyond current progressive practice. Here is one scenario. Sensors are used to detect solar radiation, indoor and outdoor temperature, interior lighting levels, and location of occupants. Algorithms combined with real-time weather data decide when and where to move shading devices on the building. The BIM holds the knowledge of who in the past preferred the shades partially open or closed in similar conditions. It considers the current sky conditions, energy usage, and time of day pricing recently implemented by the power company. The BIM reflects on-screen what will happen, and the building responds.

The building can be "taught" how to do this if it has sensors, access to data, control systems, and actuators. The building has passive components (i.e., overhangs and light shelves), active systems (i.e., occupant sensors and switches for turning of/off lights), and very active systems that are often overlooked—the occupants of the building. They can also be "trained" to operate the building efficiently, even as simply as opening and closing blinds to increase comfort level. The building's control management system can make adjustments if energy prices go up or down or occupants place complaints. By knowing the occupants' calendars, it can even determine office temperatures and conference room set points before a meeting begins.

The building information model could provide the core for a building and occupancy health model. The building records its own health fitness (e.g., real versus simulated energy usage), diagnoses any problems (e.g., faulty fan on the third floor), and prescribes a treatment (e.g., email to the maintenance crew that includes the specifications of the fan, what is broken, and directions on how to fix it). It could also give itself yearly checkups (fire sprinkler and alarm checks), have triggers in the software for age-related issues (boiler has a 20-year warranty), and know where hazardous materials are stored.

The building could be an actual physical and virtual database that is in constant communication with its "smart" neighbors. In this scenario, it can "correspond" with neighboring buildings. The building (with appropriate oversight by the building information management team) finds out if the midrise office next door is willing to "pay" for a shadow and deploys a shading device at midday, transfers waste heat and gray water via a commercial venture, and bargains for a fair price for that week's trash for gasification. The building itself contains data about its eventual retrofit and demolition, recycling information for how to take apart the façade and what metallic coatings are in the glass, hazardous materials that it contains, and what building code versions it is in compliance with. It could even provide information to the public (energy usage, CO_2 footprint, water resources, fun activities that are happening within, etc.) as part of the civic information (or disinformation) network.

The building plus its databases of information and knowledge create the building information model. Or more succinctly, the building is the definitive BIM.

12.8 CONCLUSION

Analytical BIM starts with the premise that the building information model can and should be used for building simulation. Time, effort, desire, fee structure, nonusability of software, deficient feedback loops, and a lack of a common language for communicating between the BIM and the simulation software are all culprits holding designers back from realizing the ideal. And, of course, analytical BIM is useless without a knowledgeable person who can interpret the results of the simulations and a competent designer to create the architecture forms.

Between disciplines, gaps exist that hinder the handoff of the BIM between stakeholders. Some of these are small and are in the process of being solved now. Others are deep chasms that have been carved by the different expectations and historical division of tasks between team members. Discovering ways of overcoming these gaps may also provide new opportunities for expanding the use of software, offering new services to clients, and transforming BIM plus appropriate data into the building and its associated databases.

ACKNOWLEDGMENTS

Thanks to Greg Smith and Anthony Colonna of Skanska USA Building, Inc. for their support in exploring the BIM "gap" between the design and constructability models.

DISCUSSION QUESTIONS

1. How is BIM similar or dissimilar to CAD? What is analytical BIM? Discuss three specific examples.
2. Think of a specific building or construction problem. How can BIM be used to help mitigate this problem?

3. What other BIM gaps exist in the handoff of information from the initial client ideas for a building to occupancy of a building? Suggest a solution for one of them.

4. How can BIM be used by a historic conservationist? Landscape architect? Interior designer?

5. Look up and define the following terms: gbXML, ICF, COBie. How do they relate to analytical BIM and interoperability as discussed in this chapter?

6. How can the actual building be the building information model for the occupants?

REFERENCES

American Institute of Architecture (AIA). 2013. "Guide, Instructions, and Commentary to the 2013 AIA Digital Practice Documents." www.aia.org/groups/aia/documents/pdf/aiab095711.pdf, p. 11 and pp. 34–37.

Anderson, Anne, Andrew Marsters, Carrie Sturts Dossick, and Gina Neff. 2012. "Construction to Operations Exchange: Challenges of Implementing COBie and BIM in a Large Owner Organization." *Construction Research Congress 2012@ Construction Challenges in a Flat World*, pp. 688–697; ASCE, 2012, p. 689.

Bedrick, Jim. 2013. "A Level of Development Specification for BIM Processes." *AECbytes Viewpoint #68* (May 16), www.aecbytes.com/viewpoint/2013/issue_68.html. Aaccessed July 12, 2013.

Brucker, Beth A., Michael P. Case, E. William East, Brian K. Huston, Susan D. Nachtigall, Johnette C. Shockley, Steve C. Spangler, and James T. Wilson. 2006. "Building Information Modeling (BIM): A Road Map for Implementation to Support Milcon Transformation and Civil Works Projects within the Us Army Corps of Engineers." No. ERDC-TR-06-10. Champaign, Ill.: Construction Engineering Research Lab (Army).

Eastman, C., P. Teicholz, R. Sacks, K. Liston. 2008. *BIM Handbook: A Guide to Building Information Modeling for Owners, Managers, Designers, Engineers, and Contractors*. Hoboken, NJ: John Wiley & Sons.

Epstein, Erika. 2012. *Implementing Successful Building Information Modeling*. Norwood, MA: Artech House.

Hardin, Brad. 2009. *BIM and Construction Management*. Hoboken, NJ: Sybex (an imprint of John Wiley & Sons).

Harfmann, Anton C. 2013, "Component-Based BIM: A Comprehensive, Detailed, Single Model Strategy." BIM Futures 2013: The Seventh Annual BIM Symposium on Building Information Modeling, USC School of Architecture (July 15–16).

Krygiel, Eddy, and Bradley Nies. 2008. *Green BIM: Successful Sustainable Design with Building Information Modeling*. Hoboken, NJ: Sybex.

Johnson, Brian. 2013. "One BIM to Rule Them All: Future Reality or Myth?" *BIM Futures 2013: The Seventh Annual BIM Symposium on Building Information Modeling*, USC School of Architecture (July 15–16, 2013).

Lévy, François AIA, AIAA. 2011. *BIM in Small-Scale Sustainable Design*. Hoboken, NJ: John Wiley & Sons.

Lin, Eve, Karen Kensek, and Laura Haymond. 2010. "Analytical Building Information Modeling: What is the Gap between BIM and Energy Simulation Tools' Performance Feedback Loop?" *Ecobuild 2010: Proceedings of the BIM-Related Academic Workshop*. Washington DC (December 7–9).

Milne, Murray. 2008. "Building Performance Simulation Models. A Subjective Chronology of Computer Simulation Models and Design Tools from 1967 to 2007," white paper.

O'Donnell, James T., Tobias Maile, Cody Rose, Natassa Mrazović, Elmer Morrissey, Cynthia Regnier, Kristen Parrish, and Vladimir Bazjanac. 2013. *Transforming BIM to BEM: Generation of Building Geometry for the NASA Ames Sustainability Base BIM*. Report No. LBNL-6033E (January) Berkeley, CA: Lawrence Berkeley National Laboratory.

Stewart, Brian K., and Nicole Tinkham. 2011. "BIM: Risk and Rewards for Design Professionals." *Extreme BIM 2011: The Fifth Annual USC Symposium on Extreme BIM: Parametrics and Customization*, USC School of Architecture (July 11).

Yan, Wei. 2013. "Parametric BIM SIM: Integrating Parametric Modeling, BIM, and Simulation for Architectural Design." *BIM Futures 2013: The Seventh Annual BIM Symposium on Building Information Modeling*, USC School of Architecture (July 15–16).

PART 3

COMPREHENSIVE BIM

CHAPTER 13

One BIM to Rule Them All: Future Reality or Myth?

Brian R. Johnson, University of Washington

13.1 INTRODUCTION

One of the most appealing and fundamental concepts of building information modeling (BIM) is the notion of the "virtual building," the unambiguous digital model that exists from ideation through construction and operation, all the way to decommissioning. On the face of it, a single model simply reflects the singular reality of the actual building; it seems a natural next step as increases in computing power and networking draw ever more tasks under digital management. However, there are centrifugal forces as well that are pushing the pieces apart. Whether these forces create temporary hurdles or fundamental limits remains unclear, but they should be investigated. BIM and related business practice changes are already changing the trajectories of individuals in the profession of architecture, and may well change the trajectory of the profession itself. This chapter briefly reviews the history of BIM and raises concerns about limitations to BIM unity arising from three broad areas of consideration: complexity, cognition, and culture.

13.2 A BRIEF HISTORY OF THE SINGLE MODEL

The notion of a single computable representation of a building actually had its start in the 1960s, at the dawn of architectural computing. At that time computers had very limited (and expensive) graphic input or output and relatively little total data store. Early visionaries had to really address the question

"What's *computable* about architecture?" As contemporary thought tended toward metaphors of "electronic brains" and "artificial intelligence" it is not surprising that they turned to floor-plan layout, optimization of circulation, structural calculations, and the like. These are "whole building" computations, though often at reduced levels of detail.

The single model approach grew throughout the 1970s and 1980s. In his 1977 book, *Computer-Aided Architectural Design*, Bill Mitchell described several single model systems developed in the early years, devoting twice as much space to "BIM-like" topics as to 2D or 3D graphics. In his "Foreword" to the *BIM Handbook* (Eastman et al. 2008) Jerry Laiserin credits a 1986 paper by Robert Aish with the first use of "Building Modeling" to describe a single model from which various representations could be extracted as "views" or "reports," but others pursued the idea as well (Bergin 2011). Unfortunately, this direction of development was largely displaced by 2D CAD during the PC revolution, before resurfacing in the twenty-first century as building information modeling.

13.3 THE 2D INTERREGNUM

The demise of the "proto-BIM" systems also had its roots in the 1960s. Ivan Sutherland's 1963 "Sketchpad" project demonstrated how constraint resolution, repeated elements, and an engineering application could leverage graphic information, but it also demonstrated what is now called a "direct-manipulation" interface for rapidly and interactively editing a graphic representation. This represented a giant step forward in terms of enhancing interaction between a human and the computer, paving the way for developers of 2D drawing editors during the personal computer (PC) revolution.

13.3.1 Drawings versus Models

The projection of a 3D object onto a 2D medium invariably reduces information. While multiple projections from a single model will be consistent, ambiguities arise when attempting to interpret these representations "backwards" into a singular object, as must happen during construction. Even worse, if the representations are created independently, they may be individually ambiguous (see the many works of M. C. Escher) or collectively contradictory due to errors in their creation. On top of all this, architectural drawing conventions are more symbolic than geometric in places (doors: open in plan, closed in elevation; electrical wall outlets in plan: next to the wall, 1-2' in diameter; line weights and pochés, etc.). All of this makes it difficult for programs to automatically produce conventional drawings from a 3D model.

Unfortunately for the development of BIM software, the 1980s saw the rise of the personal computer, causing a two-decade detour. Early PCs were underpowered, yet inexpensive and still able to run direct-manipulation programs, editing individual documents such as 2D drawings. In contrast, proto-BIM systems required central data storage in order to provide multi-user data coordination, and mini-computers were expensive. They did not perform well economically in head-to-head competition with PC-based drawing production systems.

During the 1990s, as PCs rapidly expanded in computing power, their wider and wider acceptance in the marketplace meant that economies of scale brought introduction of new hardware, including bigger RAM chips, powerful graphic processors, faster and larger hard disks, and eventually (once TCP/IP won the networking wars) inexpensive network connections. Then came laptops, Wi-Fi, and the cloud—in short, the return of the centralized single model.

13.4 WHAT'S WRONG WITH THIS PICTURE?

It all sounds pretty good, more and more powerful and interconnected computers running robust BIM software are finally bringing us into the era of the single model, right? In a broader culture swept up in "big data" and the implied potential of facts, a computer-based approach to managing the complex design process seems only natural. The modern vision, from the first pages of the *BIM Handbook*, reads:

> With BIM technology, one or more accurate virtual models of a building are constructed digitally. They support design through its phases, allowing better analysis and control than manual processes. When completed these computer-generated models contain precise geometry and data needed to support the construction, fabrication, and procurement activities through which the building is realized (Eastman et al. 2008, p. 1).

But other authors counter:

> The whole single building model (SBM) is really only available in a dream (Day 2011).

13.4.1 Task Complexity

"One or more accurate virtual models" is the first worrisome issue. The BIM isn't really a single model, even if it comes from a single database. Depending on the specific tasks or questions at hand, a consultant or engineer is probably going to (a) simplify some aspects of the design, and (b) add detail to other aspects of the design. Shop drawings, energy analyses, and construction schedules all focus on and enhance certain details while ignoring others.

13.4.1.1 Conservation of Complexity

Larry Tesler (c. 1984) is credited with formulating the "Law of Conservation of Complexity," which states: "Every application has an inherent amount of irreducible complexity. The only question is: Who will have to deal with it—the user, the application developer, or the platform developer?" In the design of a building "implicit" building complexity (decisions that will need to be made) is gradually converted to "explicit" complexity (decisions captured as data) by designers, through the relatively small area of the computer screen and sophisticated software. BIM software seems to enable design without engaging complexity, but one of the common complaints about BIM as a design tool is that it requires too many decisions early in the process, interrupting creative flow with details the user isn't yet prepared to address (you want a wall, it wants to know what kind of wall). It seems likely that managing complexity will remain a challenge.

Further, a BIM user interface is a bit like an airplane cockpit, a very complex environment dedicated to control. The complexity of that visual environment imposes a cognitive load on users. Those who don't make daily use of the software, such as managers, may well be frustrated by this complexity. Inexperienced users may inadvertently change data they shouldn't. Without appropriate mating of task-based operations to disciplinary specialties (i.e., different user interfaces for designers, managers, engineers, etc.), or provision of change management in some sort of federated relationship that creates bounded work-areas for "newbies," BIM won't be able to expand to the full "cradle to grave" range.

13.4.1.2 Data Complexity Explosion

For a single model to function across the many disparate analyses of the AEC (architecture, engineering, construction) industry the model must provision unknown and possibly unforeseen analysis tasks with data. Most specialized tasks involve subsets of the complete model, enhanced with domain-specific information related to the analysis. The tendency has been to include all the detail of every aspect. Storing and transporting all of this is a daunting task, even at a time when data storage costs are rapidly shrinking. Computing with it can be impossible. *AECmagazine* cites the Autodesk Boston building as a case in point:

> Autodesk's HQ building in Boston was modelled in Revit when the firm renovated the interiors. This was an impressive model and allowed Autodesk to practice what it preached. The one thing I could not understand was why clash detection on the project was not done in Revit but in Navisworks Manage, which is a considerable additional price.
>
> I met one of the architects who told me that to perform a clash detection, the geometry of all the disciplines needed to be loaded and this made the Revit model so large that only one of Autodesk's machines was capable of loading the complete model, let alone running clash detection.
>
> Navisworks has the advantage of loading a lightweight version of the model, mainly the faceted geometry without all the memory-hungry BIM data (Day 2011).

Note the implied presence of multiple models and the utility of "incomplete" models. As more disciplines, with more discipline-specific details, are brought onboard, the possible data interaction complexity increases exponentially.

13.4.1.3 Models Are Tailored to Specific World Views

There may be just one finished building, but different actors construct different representations of it depending on the details they care about. The construction model isn't the same as the design model isn't the same as the analysis model. The challenge is to efficiently derive correct analysis models from a single BIM.

The General Services Administration hosted a BIM conference in Seattle in 2009 at which the consensus opinion was that the typical building requires at least three BIMs. Why three? For the designer, the store-front façade is thought of as a system and likely to be created as a single element in the BIM. However, for construction purposes, the contractor may divide the façade into floor-to-floor slices to interface with scheduling software. Finally, the building operators don't need all the geometric detail, but need to schedule routine maintenance and occasionally replace broken glazing units. These differences are not just different levels of detail; they are different data organizations.

Similarly, the architect designs the geometry of poured concrete, and the engineer will need to show reinforcing steel and expansion joints, but formwork design is left to the contractor, and once the wall is poured, the owner probably doesn't care where the formwork was, and most facilities tasks won't require knowledge of the reinforcing steel.

13.4.2 Software Complexity

The use of software in design, while reducing some problems, introduces new sources of complexity as well. Unlike paper records that are immediately legible to humans (if fragile in some ways), BIM files reside in proprietary formats mediated by licensed software. Even ignoring hardware failures, this creates forces that act against single-model approaches.

13.4.2.1 Version Variation

Part of the idealized BIM vision is a "handoff" of building design and construction data (the BIM) to the building owner to support operations. The problem is that software evolves, due to competitive pressure, industry change, and increasing sophistication in users and hardware. New versions are almost always "backward compatible" with the old, but that's no guarantee. In the case of the Airbus 380 (discussed further below), "a lack of interoperability between versions of the CATIA software used by Airbus, result[ed] in miles of wiring that didn't fit" (Bowron 2012). Knowing this kind of history, skittish users may delay upgrades during development and freeze configurations to avoid problems (as well as costs), with the result that the database that becomes progressively more out of date rather than serving as a "live" document.

13.4.2.2 Interoperability and Data Exchange

The notion of provisioning secondary analyses with data from the BIM model has another difficulty. Ideally, data changed or added in the secondary software is merged back into the BIM model (often called "round tripping" or "feedback loop").

This ideal may be achieved in a single-vendor environment but there is very little chance that any one vendor will be able to deliver all the computational processes that an evolving industry requires (Hamil 2012), so it will be necessary to move data in and out of the model. If the native file format is proprietary, users will be at the mercy of a vendor-supplied API or export function for access to the data.

"Open" (fully documented public) formats (IFC, XML, STEP, etc.) have been created, but do not always provide for full model transfer. Vendors also hesitate to use one of the open formats as their native format, usually for speed reasons (Stafford 2010).

The representational range of open standards tends to lag the industry. The current data-exchange standards focus on building geometry. Complex data relationships (complex data objects, as well as placement constraints, circulation graphs, etc.) may not be well represented in open formats.[1] The threat of lost information may inhibit users from conducting certain conversions, while conversely; difficulty expressing new data elements using open formats may inhibit developers from implementing new functionality.

13.4.2.3 Longevity of Data and Software

New versions of software generally open files from previous versions. However, if you have ever tried to open really old files—Multiplan files in Excel, Word 3.0 documents in Word 2011, or DXF 1.0 files in AutoCAD—you may have discovered that while these applications once read those formats, vendors rarely preserve the ability to read older formats indefinitely. The lifespan of a building is substantially more than most software product lines, and evolution of the software may mean that even brand identity (e.g., "Autodesk AutoCAD") is meaningless in the face of incremental change. There is a risk that old data can be rendered meaningless by evolution of software.

13.4.3 When a Model Isn't Enough: Data versus Process

A complete data model isn't always enough. Two recent examples from the aircraft industry, which is often held up as an exemplar of what BIM could mean to the AEC industry, might prove cautionary. Though similar, they illustrate different pitfalls: technology problems and human weaknesses.

13.4.3.1 Airbus A380 Problems

German and French companies collaborate in production of Airbus planes. They all use the well-regarded CATIA software, from Dassault Systems. Unfortunately, during production of the A380, the Germans used one version, and the French used another. Designers (and software) spent many hours configuring aircraft wiring harnesses in Germany, only to find that they didn't fit the airframes being assembled in France. Why? "[D]esign software used at different Airbus factories wasn't compatible" (Matlack 2006). For various reasons Dassault had changed the software in such a way that existing models could not be moved to the new software transparently. Further, the new system's clearances and tolerances (arguably a matter of "encoded judgment") in the automated wire-routing software were different, so even with the same geometry, the analysis results of the wiring design might be different.

---

[1] *Wikipedia*, s. v. "AutoCAD DXF."

13.4.3.2 Boeing 787 Problems

Airbus's main rival, Boeing, has also encountered problems with their data-driven production. In the 1990s, the Boeing Company rather famously shifted to an all-digital design process with its 777 aircraft, winning the 1995 "Smithsonian Computerworld Award for digital product definition and preassembly in manufacturing" (Boeing 2013). With the 787 they tried to leverage their digital models even further by distributing design and production activities across their supply chain in a complex scheme that is now frequently cited as being hampered by cultural and interpretive differences that no amount of computer-supported "supply chain integration" could alleviate.

> Outsourcing parts led to three years of delays. Parts didn't fit together properly. Shims used to bridge small parts weren't attached correctly. Many aircraft had to have their tails extensively reworked. The company ended up buying some suppliers to take their business back in house. All new projects, especially ones as ambitious as the Dreamliner, face teething issues, but the 787's woes continued to mount. Unions blame the company's reliance on outsourcing (Rushe 2013).
>
> Boeing [. . .] outsourced that work and weakened its control over crucial systems (Gates 2013).

Much of the blame for difficulties in this scheme will be familiar to architects—the different subcontractors didn't want to reveal too much to their (future) rivals, so they didn't work together as closely as they were expected to.

13.4.4 Limitations on Data as an Expression of Intent

In the end, the building construction process is inexact. Yes, coordinates are recorded to many decimal places, and dimensions are consistently and exactly represented in the model, to the point where some observers have suggested architects could deliver BIMs without dimension strings. However, the building may not be congruent with the geometry model. In traditional dimensioning, this is accommodated by "float" gaps in dimension strings, or intent is asserted through notes (e.g., "EQ") rather than numbers on related dimensions.

> [M]ost BIMs produced can only be used for conceptual development, as a basis for rough bidding and to satisfy the demand for PR flythroughs. Sadly they cannot be used directly for modern, digitally-driven construction (Bowron 2012).

Design rules and constraints in BIM systems are intended to encode and enforce intent, but experience with editing the models shows that there is a lot of room for improvement in terms of controlling this kind of data. One award-winning Seattle firm used BIM in the design of a series of libraries. They found that their dimensional constraints interfered with attempts to recycle parts of models in the "sister" buildings and had to be removed.

13.4.4.1 Drawings: Enabling Process

In fact, AEC, being less well integrated vertically than an assembly-line manufacturing process such as aircraft production, may actually need the data to play a different role:

Architects cannot prepare complete or entirely correct construction documents. What an architect can do is prepare documents that are sufficient for supporting the construction process. Incompleteness, conflicts, coordination miscues, errors, and omissions can and will occur in all documents prepared by human hands. The surviving discrepancies are corrected during construction through communications with the contractor, requests for information, and the change process (Simpson and Atkins 2005).

Often, what is critical is communicating intent rather than numerical fact:

While Architects can use BIM to generate a great building, reducing costs and material, if the thought approach when the building is being designed is not transmitted to the GC, then claims and problems will arise (Rodriguez n.d.).

13.4.5 People and Cognition

BIM is widely recognized as a major paradigm shift in the AEC industry. Taken together these comments describe a very disruptive technology! Subjected to such stress, human systems tend to distort.

BIM will alter your staffing needs, your processes, and your technology requirements (Autodesk Inc. 2011).

Designers need to understand how a building goes together as well as how design data is used by other disciplines (Autodesk Inc. 2011).

Data is not information, information is not knowledge, knowledge is not understanding, understanding is not wisdom (Clifford Stoll).[2]

13.4.5.1 Complexity, Ambiguity, and Cognition

One of the goals of a BIM system must be to eliminate the ambiguities inherent in independent 2D representations. The dominant method to achieve this is to build in or preconstruct semantic elements (walls, doors, windows) and make them available for placement in the design space. In so doing, the architect's design vocabulary is preconstrained. Research from cultural psychology suggests that vocabulary influences cognition (Kitayama and Cohen 2010), and software developer Brosseau frankly acknowledges how software developers respond to complexity:

We cope through employing massive simplifications and the construction of mental models.
Our mental models form the box within which we live and often overly constrain our ability to creatively resolve the issues we face (Brosseau 2008, p. 76).

Brosseau's "box" bears a lot of resemblance to the architectural idea of a "design concept" so some of the implied constraint is probably desirable. However, most designs and designers begin with a diagram

---

[2]BrainyQuotes.com, www.brainyquote.com/quotes/quotes/c/cliffordst212166.htm (accessed July 1, 2013).

of the problem as an idea, not as geometry, and gradually evolve towards geometry, a manipulation somewhat foreign to BIM. Further, when drawing, the designer may take advantage of the serendipitous ambiguity of the image to reinterpret existing marks in new ways. Can BIM be made to accommodate or even support ambiguity?

13.4.5.2 Operator Skill versus Construction Knowledge

BIM systems are intended to put editing power in the hands of their operators. Perhaps unsurprisingly, firm managers show some reluctance to turn new interns loose on their precious BIM data. In the old days interns could be tasked with contributing to the project in ways that were easy to oversee and adjust. As experience and skill developed, they could be entrusted with more and more opportunity to make mistakes. Now, interns are likely to be the ones charged with running the software and while they may know how to get a section cut plotted, they may not know where the most useful section is, or why.

This might be a transitional intergenerational problem, but the industry has been learning to deal with computing for 20+ years and still generally utilizes an "interns first" approach to new technology. While side-stepping reluctant adopters and training, it's worth noting that the Airbus 380 debacle was blamed, in part, on engineers who were still "in training" at the time. Career paths that don't include learning new technology may well sustain a gap between operator skill and disciplinary knowledge and judgment indefinitely.

13.4.5.3 Users: Cultural Congruence, Conceptual Context

> *"Esse quam videri."*
>
> —To be, rather than to seem

"Working smart" with software often involves concepts that might be new. Software presents users with many affordances (Gibson 1977) and some users take maximum advantage of the tools available to complete their task (e.g., styles in Microsoft Word or block libraries when drawing CAD plans), while others use less powerful basic manipulations (ruler changes, copy and paste). The results look the same. Without the appropriate training the software can be used to create "seems" rather than "is."

Setting aside issues of operator training, are different professional cultures (engineer, architect, contractor) sufficiently congruent to share BIM models without the overhead of negotiation that builds shared vocabulary? Integration and collaboration are as much an outgrowth of culture as of software affordance.

13.5 ONE BIM TO RULE THEM ALL?

Building designs involve coordination and repeated use of a very large number of facts and actions both in design and construction. It is hard to imagine that computing will not be applied to managing this complexity.

The preceding paragraphs raised questions about the complexity of resulting models in the face of design tasks, software evolution, as well as human learning, cognition, culture, and organizations, questions at the core of skepticism about any single solution. Individuals and organizations partition and navigate this conceptual space in different ways—producing different designs and workflows. A narrowly defined BIM vision seems destined to overly constrain and frustrate designers and degrade the quality of the product.

What will go a long way to alleviating the skepticism attached to the "One BIM" paradigm is a data-oriented federation model of the sort promised by the OpenBIM initiative and similar efforts, which should offer

- An open-source vendor-neutral elastic data-structure
- Enabling interoperation of applications from multiple vendors
- Sharing data in a design ecosystem without explicit import or export
- Supporting different kinds of users, tasks, workflows, and stages in the design process

It will require significant negotiation and cooperation among vendors, academics, and interested users, in a fashion similar to that of the World-Wide-Web Consortium. Fortunately, there are hints in the marketplace that this is the direction the industry is taking—one BIM to support them all—a Building Information *Medium*.

DISCUSSION QUESTIONS

1. How has complexity been "conserved" (or not) in your own work practices?
2. Who uses BIM? If younger members of a firm do most of the BIM work, do they see themselves continuing to use BIM as they become more senior?
3. Does your BIM (or other) software influence your design process or product in ways that are identifiable?
4. Are you able to reshape your software environment to suit your firm, or must you learn to use the software as it is?
5. In context of the paper, explain the last line: "Fortunately, there are hints in the marketplace that this is the direction the profession is taking—one BIM to support them all, perhaps a Building Information *Medium*."

REFERENCES

Autodesk Inc. 2011. "Realizing the Benefits of BIM." http://images.autodesk.com/adsk/files/2011_realizing_bim_final.pdf. Accessed June 27, 2013.

Bergin, Michael S. 2011. "History of BIM." www.architectureresearchlab.com/arl/2011/08/21/bim-history/. Accessed July 11, 2013.

Boeing Company. 2013. "Boeing 777 Program Awards, Records and Firsts." www.boeing.com/boeing/commercial/ 777family/pf/pf_awards.page. Accessed June 25, 2013.

Bowron, Julian. 2012. "Real BIM: Can Architects Be Master Builders Again?" www.vectorpraxis.com/ information-content-of-drawings-return-to-the-master-builder/. Accessed July 1, 2013.

Brosseau, Jim. 2008. *Software Teamwork: Taking Ownership for Success*. Boston, MA: Pearson Education.

Day, Martyn. 2011. "The Trouble with BIM." *AECMagazine*. Oct, 2011, http://aecmag.com/index.php?option= content&task=view&id=450. Accessed June 26, 2013.

Eastman, Chuck, Paul Teicholz, Rafael Sacks, and Kathleen Liston. 2008. *BIM Handbook: A Guide to Building Information Modeling for Owners, Managers, Designers, Engineers, and Contractors*. Hoboken, NJ: John Wiley & Sons.

Gates, Dominic. 2013. "Electronics Outsourcing Weakened Boeing's Control over 787's Crucial Systems." *Seattle Times*, May 25. http://seattletimes.com/html/businesstechnology/2021045270_boeingoutsourcingxml.html. Accessed June 25, 2013.

Gibson, James. 1977. "The Theory of Affordances." In *Perceiving, Acting, and Knowing: Toward an Ecological Psychology*. Hoboken, NJ: John Wiley & Sons.

Hamil, Stephen. 2012. "Building Information Modelling and interoperability." www.thenbs.com/topics/bim/ articles/bimAndInteroperability.asp. Accessed June 25, 2013.

Kitayama, Shinobu, and Dov Cohen (eds.). 2010. *Handbook of Cultural Psychology*. New York: Guilford Press, p. 678.

Matlack, Carol. 2006. "Airbus: First, Blame the Software." *Business Week* (October 4). Available at www.businessweek .com/stories/2006-10-04/airbus-first-blame-the-software. Accessed June 26, 2013.

Mitchell, William J. 1977. *Computer Aided Architectural Design*. New York: John Wiley & Sons.

Rodriguez, Juan. n.d. *Building Information Modeling Risks: Minimizing BIM Risks*. Available at http://construction .about.com/od/Trends/a/Building-Information-Modeling-Risks.htm. Accessed June 25, 2013.

Rushe, Dominic. 2013. "Why Boeing's 787 Dreamliner Was a Nightmare Waiting to Happen." *Guardian*, January 18. Available at www.theguardian.com/business/2013/jan/18/boeing-787-dreamliner-grounded.

Simpson, Grant A., and James B. Atkins. 2005. "Best Practices in Risk Management: Your Grandfather's Working Drawings." *AIArchitect*, (August). Available at http://info.aia.org/aiarchitect/thisweek05/tw0805/ tw0805bp_risk.htm. Accessed July 1, 2013.

Stafford, Steve. 2010. *Revit OpEd*. "I Speak IFC." Available at http://revitoped.blogspot.com/2010/04/i-speak-ifc .html. Accessed July 10, 2013.

Sutherland, Ivan. 1963. "Sketchpad: A Man-Machine Graphical Communication System." *AFIPS Conference Proceedings*, pp. 329–346.

Tesler, Larry. c. 1984. "The Law of Conservation of Complexity," www.nomodes.com/Larry_Tesler_Consulting/ Complexity_Law.html. Accessed June 25, 2013.

CHAPTER 14

Component-Based BIM: A Comprehensive, Detailed, Single-Model Strategy

Anton C. Harfmann, University of Cincinnati

14.1 EXECUTIVE SUMMARY

The component-based paradigm argues that the digital environment offers the opportunity to electronically design and construct an entire building at the molecular level of individual elements of construction. The emergence of new building information modeling (BIM) tools coupled with exponential advancements in computing capacity over the past decade makes implementation of this paradigm possible. The paradigm presumes that computing potential and programming capabilities will continue to increase and that the profession will continue to progress toward adopting new strategies for architectural practice to replace centuries-old traditions and habits. The component-based modeling concept shifts the responsibility of defining the geometry and attributes of components to manufacturers and utilizes the parametric BIM modeling tools to design, group, manage, and represent the building assembly. This virtual construct would support the development of a single, shared model and would eliminate the conventional practice of producing two-dimensional drawings to describe a future three-dimensional construct. In this paradigm, the contractor would query the model directly for details, assembly information, and specifications of materials and components. The obvious benefits of this approach include better coordination and design integration of the systems in a building as well as the elimination of errors that currently plague the industry due to multiple representations and duplicate information. While the possible limitations are numerous and significant, this paradigm represents a method that could have a significant positive impact on how buildings are designed and constructed and would reunite the currently fragmented building industry.

14.2 THE WICKED PROBLEM OF MAKING ARCHITECTURE

Horst Rittel's definition of a "wicked problem" has often been used to describe the process of designing a building (Rittel and Webber 1993). The wickedness of designing and constructing a complicated building in contemporary society grows exponentially as more knowledge of building physics and behavior is explicated. The result has been a dramatic departure from Christopher Alexander's "craft" model of design to the contemporary design and building environment where it is impossible for one individual to possess all the knowledge and skill required to design and construct a building (Alexander 1979). The modern-day consequence is a very complex and fragmented industry, with an ever-increasing chasm between those who design and those who build.

14.2.1 Design Complexity and Uniqueness

Good design blends distinctive aspects of site and specific user needs with the individual creativity and artistic aspirations of the designer into a unique solution. The distance between the initial poetic concept and the built reality represents one of the most challenging aspects of architectural design—the more unique the solution, the greater the rift between idea and physical reality. Take, for example, the wireframe diagram of the Aronoff Center for Design and Art at the University of Cincinnati by Peter Eisenman, shown in Figure 14.1. This building is arguably one of the first significant architectural

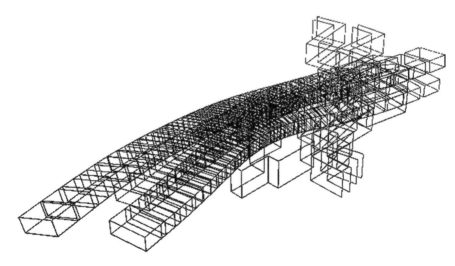

FIGURE 14.1   Wireframe diagram of Aronoff Center for Design and Art.
(Courtesy of Professors Ming Tang and Michael McInturf)

FIGURE 14.2   Photographs of the Aronoff Center for Design and Art.

endeavors to take advantage of computational design to generate form and required sophisticated computer-aided surveying tools and construction techniques for its realization.

All spaces are defined by the myriad of intersecting lines in the wireframe, creating a visually stimulating, highly unique, and energizing sequence of space and form as seen in the photographs in Figure 14.2. This level of complexity and uniqueness coupled with the difficulty in integrating the various mechanical, electrical, communication, and fire protection systems makes for an interesting choreographic challenge, and it will serve as the backdrop for the argument of the component-based, single model strategy.

14.2.2 Fragmentation and Multiple Representations

The numerous individuals with specific expertise in discrete areas of knowledge have led to unprecedented fragmentation of the building design/construction industry. Complicating the issue of fragmentation is the fact that most of the individuals contributing specific expertise to the process are either slow to adopt new technology or have developed their own methods and customized software for analyzing and conveying the specifics about their contributions to the emerging building design (ITIF 2012). For example, while the steel fabricators utilize sophisticated 3D modeling to drive CNC equipment in the fabrication of steel frame components, many architectural firms still rely heavily on 2D drawings. Even when an architectural firm produces a 3D model, the steel fabricators routinely discard it and build a more detailed and accurate model to drive their fabrication processes, wasting time and perpetuating fragmentation.

14.2.3 Redesign and Discovery

Design is iterative, and designers consistently revise concepts in search of a better solution to a problem. Unfortunately, in the current practice climate, it is all but impossible to entertain changes in a design late in the process. While parametric modeling offers great promise for designers who want to revise

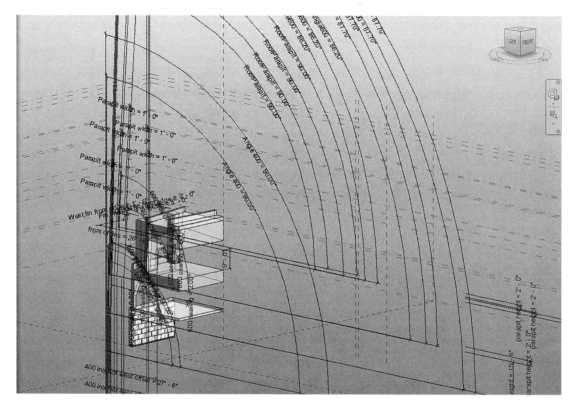

FIGURE 14.3   Parameters describing the complex geometry of a 20-foot-wide section of the north façade of the Aronoff Center.

design late in the game, the process can be rather complex, requiring designers to codify and model their design drivers early in the process (Aish 2005, Woodbury 2010). As a result, the ability to make a significant change in a design and immediately have all of the mechanical systems, electrical systems, structural systems, and construction materials regenerate to the new configuration remains an elusive goal. For example, the attempt to articulate the parameters that drive a small section of the Aronoff Center has proven a challenging task. Figure 14.3 illustrates the nearly two-dozen parameters that drive the relationships of forms of a small section of the Aronoff Center.

14.3 IMPLEMENTING COMPONENT-BASED DESIGN

14.3.1 The Component-Based Paradigm: Overview

A component in this paradigm is defined as an individual, installed element of construction such as a stud, a sheet of drywall, or a fastener. Components can be preassembled and grouped together as an assembly, such as a door hinge, and treated as a single entity within the building model since it is purchased, delivered, and installed as a unit. With this least common denominator of individual components, the strategy proposes the construction of a highly detailed model that sits parallel to the actual building as its virtual counterpart. As a departure from most current BIM trends, the argument here is for a completely separate model that is driven by all the various BIM software that is used throughout the different disciplines. In this paradigm, there is a fundamental assumption that knowledge about any building product should reside outside the actual modeled component (Harfmann et al. 1993). For instance, a 3-5/8-inch metal stud in an assembly should not contain any knowledge or intelligence about itself outside of the description of the geometry and a link to its source. Any structural responsibility or specific information about its behavior, even how it is deployed, should be stored external to the model. The rationale for this approach stems from the reality that any building component can be "seen" or described differently by various disciplines. For example, the metal stud could be used as an exterior backup wall to a rainscreen, as a stud in an interior partition, as a framing member for an exterior soffit, or as an interior ceiling-framing member. While the studs in all these conditions have the same geometry and material characteristics, they have quite different purposes and structural responsibility. Consequently, storing all of the attributes and possible uses as part of the component overly complicates the model. Instead of storing all the information and characteristics as part of the object file of a building component within BIM software, the argument is for separating this intelligence and the parameters from the object, freeing it to be used in multiple situations without having to create a new component type for an alternative orientation or use.

14.3.2 Product/Manufacturer Links

In this strategy, the manufacturer of an individual building product would supply an accurate geometric model of their component or assembly for inclusion in the shared component model. The architect, engineer, and other building design consultants would download components from the manufacturer's sites and choreograph their use in the shared model. Once placed in the model, the component would retain its link to the manufacturer or agency that is responsible for maintaining the most recent information on cost, availability, and other nonconstant mechanical and behavioral properties. Constant data, such as modulus of elasticity, melting temperature, and other nonvariable information could be stored in common tables to streamline analysis. By stripping the variable properties and data from the model and storing constant data locally, analysis would always be done dynamically by retrieving the most recent up-to-date information for each component directly from the manufacturer or producer.

14.3.3 External Reasoning

Divorcing all properties and information other than geometry from the model mimics what occurs in a physical construct. For example, while a structural engineer can look at a simple metal stud and visualize it as a beam, the actual physical stud is not endowed with this intelligence. This makes a strong argument for the separation of these values from the basic, static description of the component. Since the individual metal studs in the assembly previously described do not "know" their own modulus of

FIGURE 14.4   Metal stud wall surrounding projecting structural columns on the north façade.

elasticity, area, weight, or cost, the values are calculated or looked up by the consultant performing an analysis (Schumacher 2013). In the case of the resurfacing of the Aronoff Center, the structural consultant determined that the existing metal studs surrounding the columns on the north façade, as shown in Figure 14.4, were of insufficient gauge to resist the deflection due to wind load and to resist withdrawal of the screws for the new rainscreen. Just as this analysis occurs independently of the actual metal studs, so too should analysis occur independently of the digital component model.

14.3.4 BIM-Driven Component Modeling

At the heart of the paradigm is the concept of a single model driven by the various disciplinary models, such as the structural, electrical, and mechanical systems. For the single model to be effective it must allow for incomplete data and assembly information while design is in a fluid state. At early stages of design, the gesture of a "wall" serves as a sort of "spatial formwork" or placeholder for actual components of construction (Yessios 1987). The spatial model would eventually exist as a parallel overlay that allows components to be grouped together once they are instantiated. For example, the metal stud backup rainscreen wall discussed previously would initially be modeled as a simple mass to serve as a placeholder for the actual tracks, studs, and exterior drywall. Once the components are added, the mass wall simply remains as an overlaid grouping mechanism and as a simple visualization abstraction of the components that make up the wall. This is already possible in most BIM modeling software; however, the abstract view resides as part of the model instead of an external group linking components.

14.3.5 Component-Based Model Example

Figure 14.5 illustrates the concepts previously outlined using the recladding efforts of the north façade of the Aronoff Center as the backdrop to explain the strategies. It shows the emerging component model with an actual photo of construction and links to manufacturer's websites on the left, the table of components that make up the component-based single model in the center, and the various views that drive or extract information from the model.

1. Initially, the architect would construct a design-massing model that drives overall form (number 1 in Figure 14.5). The mass could be parametrically driven and serves as "scaffolding" against which more detail, such as a structural system, walls, and so on can be built. Once the design progresses to the point where the envelope will be constructed out of layers of materials, in

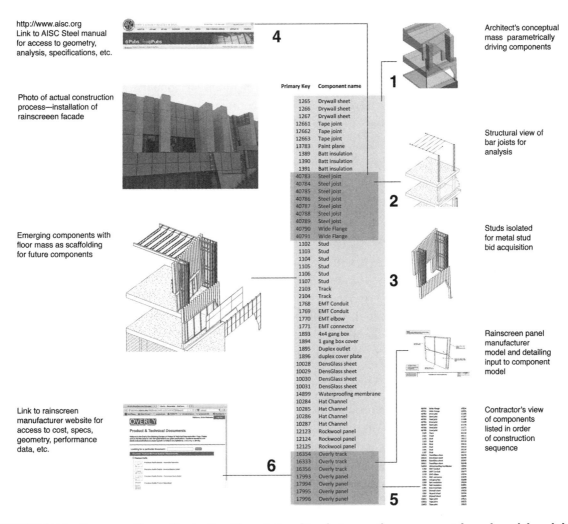

FIGURE 14.5 Summary figure illustrating the relationships between the component-based model and the various interacting authorities.

this case, a metal stud backup wall supporting the rainscreen and interior finishes, a generic wall is constructed in the architect's model and would show up in the component model. This wall would serve as formwork for the metal stud components, then together with the engineer or façade consultant, the components would be designed and instantiated within the placeholder wall.

2. The structural consultant or façade engineer would develop their own "view" of the overall structure and of the emerging wall as a freebody diagram of beams to support the gravity and wind loads being imposed (number 2 in Figure 14.5). Once the size of the studs is determined by the consultant, the three-dimensional model of the studs would be available as a downloadable geometry from the Steel Stud Association website.

3. The metal stud component in the model would retain a link to this site where other information is stored and maintained by the authority for metal studs (number 3 in Figure 14.5).

4. Just as the architect's model of the generic wall retains a link to the studs that frame the wall, the engineer's model of the structural beam system retains a pointer to the beams and studs in the emerging component network, which also contains links to the appropriate resource or manufacturer's website for data (number 4 in Figure 14.5).

5. When analysis of the model, such as determining construction sequence, thermal performance, or material cost, is required, the relevant reasoning mechanism would be applied to assess the assembly. For construction sequence, the contractor will develop an order for the installation of components for the most efficient purchasing and delivery of materials for the job (number 5 in Figure 14.5).

6. As more detail about the assembly emerges, such as the detailed model used by the rainscreen fabricators to drive their CNC processes, their components are added to the emerging component model where conflicts, fit, and construction sequence can be explored and resolved. Cost analysis is accomplished by traversing the component network in the model, then tracing the link to the manufacturer's site where information about cost for each component is retrieved. If price or availability of the hat section specified for the rainscreen changes, this information is passed to the architect or consultant through this query of the model (number 6 in Figure 14.5).

If a link cannot be traced or if a product becomes unavailable, the designer is alerted and has ample opportunity to reconsider changes or alternative manufacturers. By placing more of the responsibility on the manufacturer for producing and maintaining information about their standard components, the reliability of the information and the accuracy of the model should be greatly increased as it is in the best interest of the manufacturer to provide quality data. Furthermore, by separating basic and constant data (such as geometry) from variable data (such as cost), the model can remain very simple in form and will limit the quantity of information stored as part of the model.

14.3.6 Component Model as Authority

Once the components are instantiated, whether through contributions of the architect, engineer, steel fabricator, subcontractor, or consultants, the emerging component model becomes the authority for all analysis and communication. Just as in actual construction, architects, engineers, consultants, and contractors often meet at the job site to solve problems that arise during construction. Disassociating the intelligence from the component model allows each of the contributing members to retain the intellectual property that drives their contribution.

Furthermore, the component model represents the least common denominator for all the trades involved in the building design and construction endeavor and most closely parallels the actual physical construction of the building. The detailed model would lend itself to much more detailed analysis as new knowledge is explicated and as analytical tools improve. Consider, for example, the analysis of the lateral load resistance of the structure. Conventionally, the engineer would only consider the actual structure and diagonal bracing in the calculation of the structure's ability to resist lateral loads. In the component model, however, it would be possible to consider the accumulated resistance of all the exterior drywall as simple shear walls in a more comprehensive analysis. It may not be wise to count on these walls for stability, but a detailed simulation could provide insights to potential building failure, allowing the engineer and architect to design accordingly.

14.4 CONCLUSION

With the exception of direct links to external models that drive component configuration, this strategy is already being practiced by many contractors who are investing in the production of completely separate, detailed component-based models that incorporate all of the work of the architect, engineers, consultants, fabricators, and the like into an accurate electronic construction model. Discarding the models produced by the consultants, they begin the process fresh, creating an entirely new building information model for the purpose of construction, even hiring the architects and engineers who produced the original design to assist with the process. Needless to say, this duplicative effort is wasteful, and if it continues to its logical end, architects will eventually be unnecessary in the process of making buildings beyond the initial artistic or poetic gesture of form-making. Furthermore, the quality of architecture at the detail level will be significantly diminished as architects are pushed further away from details and building knowledge as a means to inform form and reveal the DNA of a building design (Frascari 1984).

Realizing that this secondary modeling process is already occurring and will likely continue to expand, the concept proposed for component-based modeling is to embrace it fully and develop a better strategy for implementation.

While the component-based paradigm offers several clear benefits, the limitations and unanswered questions are equally numerous. None of the difficulties are insurmountable, given the exponential growth of technology in the last decade, but when taken together, they do represent significant obstacles to the full implementation of these concepts.

DISCUSSION QUESTIONS

1. What is component-based modeling? Explain two other approaches to a BIM single-model paradigm.
2. Pick a specific truss from a catalogue. List what data are needed about that truss for it to be incorporated into a building. For each data item, label who is responsible for creating the electronic component and maintaining the data.
3. Look up model element authorship (MEA) and level of development (LOD) by the AIA. How do these two concepts compare favorably or unfavorably versus component-based modeling?
4. Describe how an assembly like a light switch made of many subcomponents, but sold and installed as a single entity in a building, would be modeled in the component-based strategy.

REFERENCES

Aish, R., and R. Woodbury. 2005. "Multi-level Interaction in Parametric Design." *SG 2005 Conference Proceedings: International Symposium on Smart Graphics*, pp. 151–162.

Alexander, C. 1979. *The Timeless Way of Building*. New York: Oxford University Press.

Frascari, M. 1984. "The Tell-The-Tale-Detail." In P. Behrens (ed.), *VIA 7: The Building of Architecture*. Cambridge, MA: MIT Press, pp. 23–37.

Harfmann, A. C., B. Majkowski, S. S. Chen. 1993. "A Component-Based Approach to Building Product Representation and Design Development." In *CAAD Futures '93: Proceedings of the Fifth International Conference on Computer-Aided Architectural Design Futures*, pp. 437–452.

ITIF. 2012. "Bricks and Bits: Transforming the Construction Industry Through Innovation." Washington, DC: Information Technology and Innovation Foundation. Available at www.itif.org/events/bricks-and-bits-transforming-construction-industry-through-innovation.

Rittel, H., and M. Webber. 1973. "Dilemmas in a General Theory of Planning," *Policy Sciences*, vol. 4, pp. 155–169. Amsterdam: Elsevier Scientific Publishing Co. Reprinted in N. Cross (ed.), *Developments in Design Methodology*, Chichester: John Wiley & Sons, 1984, pp. 135–144.

Schumacher, J. 2013. "Thornton Tomasetti Project Case Study." BIM Futures 2013: Seventh Annual BIM Symposium on Building Information Modeling, USC School of Architecture (Los Angeles, July 15–16).

Woodbury, R. 2010. *Elements of Parametric Design*. New York: Routledge.

Yessios, C. 1987. "The Computability of Void Architectural Modeling," in Y. Kalay, ed., *Computability of Design*. Hoboken, NJ: John Wiley & Sons.

CHAPTER 15

BIM Ecosystem: The Coevolution of Products, Processes, and People

Ning Gu, University of Newcastle
Vishal Singh, Aalto University
Kerry London, RMIT University

15.1 INTRODUCTION

Building Information Modeling (BIM) is a systemic innovation in the architectural, engineering, and construction (AEC) sector that impacts all aspects of the industry, beyond just the development and adoption of a specific technology. BIM as a systemic innovation entails interdependencies between technological, process, and organizational/cultural aspects, requiring innovation across all three dimensions. These mutual dependencies across the different aspects has created a BIM ecosystem in which BIM-related products, processes, and people form a complex network of interactions, influencing one another, determined by factors that are internal as well as external to the AEC sector. This chapter describes the BIM ecosystem and explains how the products, processes, and people (PPP) in this ecosystem coevolve.

First, the significance of coevolution of products, processes, and people is explained. Second, the context of BIM and the AEC industry is briefly described to facilitate the understanding of BIM and its development, particularly in relation to the industry perception of the three aspects of the BIM ecosystem: products, processes, and people. Third, the current research and practices in BIM are discussed to explain the implications and approaches to managing the complex dependencies between products, processes and people in BIM enabled projects. In particular two approaches are highlighted: (1) supporting technological advances and facilitating cultural changes in the industry through the development of

BIM "Operational and Support Technical Requirements; and (2) developing BIM adoption and project management guidelines through the "Collaborative BIM Decision Framework." Finally, some of the key internal and external factors and trends that are likely to influence the future development and evolution of the BIM ecosystem are discussed. Accordingly, the chapter concludes the discussion by highlighting the implications of future BIM ecosystem for BIM research, practice, and education, as well as the guidelines to prepare for the future BIM ecosystem.

15.2 COEVOLUTION OF PRODUCTS, PROCESSES, AND PEOPLE

Given the complex dependencies between products, processes, and people in the BIM ecosystem, it is important that the evolution and growth across each dimension remains compatible. That is, the pace of innovation and development across these aspects should be comparable, and they should facilitate one another. Such dependencies of products, processes, and people are well established in the innovation literature (e.g., Abernathy and Utterback 1978, Kotabe and Murray 1990, Moore 1993, Fritsch and Meschede 2001, Damanpour and Aravind 2006). However, compatible growth and equilibrium is challenging because of the continuous strive for innovation and improvement (Schumpeter 1934, Fagerberg and Verspagen 2009). While the constant striving for innovation propels growth, gaps in the development across each of these aspects can lead to different levels of adoption (London et al. 2006) and different levels of performance in the system (Figure 15.1).

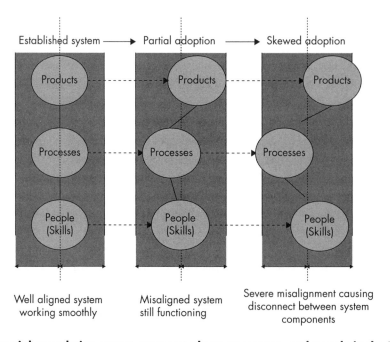

FIGURE 15.1 Potential coevolution stages across products, processes, and people in the BIM ecosystem.

When the ecosystem is in near-equilibrium stable state (when the products, processes, and people have mutually coevolved into an established system), it sets into a routine or tradition. For example, pre-CAD paper-based practice had set into a routine such that stakeholders had a general agreement and understanding of how the construction projects worked. However, in established systems ongoing innovation and innovation adoption across products, processes, or people would require other aspects to realign. For example, when CAD-based drafting was introduced and adopted as a technical innovation, it required people to learn new skills and some procedural changes. However, the misalignment and gap could still be managed even if early inefficiencies were observed as the routine was disrupted. Once again as the industry practices and skills around 2D CAD matured, another tradition was established that set into a routine. Thus, partial adoption requires catch-up and realignment that does not necessarily lead to a system breakdown. On the other hand, if the introduced technical innovation or innovation along any one aspect is radical and entails a paradigm shift, it may lead to system breakdown unless the other aspects are developed within reasonable limits to avoid skewed situation (e.g., Pawson and Tilley 1997, Greenhalgh et al. 2004). Skewed adoption refers to unplanned adoption of a radical innovation in one aspect, without due consideration or assessment of the compatibility of the complementary aspects. For example, BIM applications by design require a paradigm shift in how projects are managed. Therefore, unless the BIM supporting processes or skills are developed or adopted, at least to an acceptable level, BIM projects may not produce desirable outcomes and can be a setback in innovation diffusion.

In an Australian study while some successful cases of BIM adoption and implementation were reported, significant losses were reported in one of the projects where BIM tools were used in traditional ways, leading to erroneous cost estimates and scheduling (CRC 2008). The lack of supporting processes, skills, and awareness in the failed case resulted in substantial cost and schedule overruns. Understanding the significance of compatible coevolution between PPP in the BIM ecosystem will prepare the AEC industry to appropriately and effectively adopt and develop BIM capabilities.

15.3 UNDERSTANDING THE INDUSTRY CONTEXT OF BIM

15.3.1 Fundamental Characteristics of BIM and Their Evolution

BIM is both a tool and a process, with the term increasingly being used as building information modeling and management. At a fundamental level, the capabilities of BIM can be described by the following main characteristics: representation; documentation and information management; inbuilt intelligence, analysis, and simulation tool; and collaboration and integration.

Representation: Clear representation of the design intent is a critical part of the design and construction process. Representation aids design thinking and development. It allows designers to visualize the conceptualized ideas, reflect on them, and improve the design outcome (Schon 1992, Oxman 2006). Representation also provides common ground and a visual language for communication between the multidisciplinary team. Clear representation and high-quality visualization is an important aspect of BIM.

Documentation and information management: While representation and visualization is also part of documenting the project-related information, it is equally important to be able to record, manage, and use all other forms of data generated across the different stages of the project lifecycle.

Inbuilt intelligence, analysis, and simulation tool: The inbuilt intelligence in BIM applications provides the users assistance and proactive tools for managing the complexity and improving the design decisions through analyses and simulations. The ability to provide inbuilt relationships and constraints and to define the functions to use these relationships and constraints to improve the project outcomes is another important characteristic of BIM. Thus, BIM not only allows data management, but it also enables making sense of the data.

Collaboration and integration: Construction projects typically require multiparty collaboration and integration of the project information developed across the different parties. The primary benefits of BIM can only be derived if the building data generated across the different parties are integrated and checked for compatibility and consistency. That is, by design, BIM is envisioned as a collaborative tool as well as a process.

These characteristics of BIM are derived from its underlying object-oriented modeling approach. On one dimension, BIM evolved as an improvement to CAD, along the way progressing from 2D drafting to solid modeling to parametric modeling, and finally object-oriented modeling. On the other dimension, BIM evolved as an improvement to project information management systems, along the way evolving from paper-based filing systems to standalone databases and spreadsheets to linked databases and finally to integration with object-oriented building models that support embedded information. While the history of BIM technology evolution has been documented earlier (Eastman et al. 2008), the following points highlight the key conceptual aspects of this evolution:

Representation has evolved from symbolic representation (i.e., 2D drawings and images) to 3D virtualization. For example, rather than a line representing a wall, a virtual wall model represents a real wall, reducing ambiguity.

Information management has evolved from an independent set of specifications, documents, and spreadsheets to the information that is typically embedded in (and appended to) the objects. Accordingly, there is transition from documentation toward management.

In order to support **inbuilt intelligence and analysis**, these tools have evolved from passive representation and modeling tools to active knowledge-based systems. In BIM, domain knowledge is coded in various forms such as product libraries, object properties, rules, and constraints. Effective utilization of these tools is also determined by the effective use of this inbuilt knowledge base. Accordingly, there is a transition from drafting to modeling to simulation and analysis.

Collaboration and integration: With the increased ability to exchange digital data across different parties, these tools have evolved from standalone design tools to multidisciplinary collaboration tools.

BIM is a collection of various applications such as collaboration platforms and analysis tools. Corresponding process changes that are emerging include concepts such as integrated project delivery and "Big Room" collaborations. At the same time, skills and BIM educational requirements for people are changing. For example, designers are also expected to be managers and tool builders (Oxman

2006). While some of these trends are discussed in the end of this chapter and other chapters in the book, it must be noted that these trends correspond to broader technological evolution such as the emergence of PCs, the Internet, and Information and Communications Technology (ICT) and the resulting social patterns. For example, 2D CAD grew with the emergence of PCs, while commercial BIM followed the widespread use of information systems and ICT across the society in general. That is, external factors contribute as much to the evolution of BIM ecosystem as the needs of the AEC sector. Hence, a review of the current status of BIM and the broader technical trends is important to understand, manage, and influence the evolution of BIM ecosystem.

15.3.2 Industry Perception of BIM-Related Products, Processes, and People

The industry perception and expectation of BIM-related products, processes, and people vary across disciplines (Singh et al. 2011, Gu and London 2010). Through focused group interviews with key BIM players and associates who cover all major sectors of the AEC industry, including architects, engineers, contractors, design consultants, construction/facility management information technology service providers, project managers, facility managers, delegates from government agencies, software application vendors, and academics, it was found that products, processes, and people have had to change.

In terms of products, expectations of BIM technology differ from discipline to discipline. For example, for design disciplines, BIM is an extension to CAD, whereas for non-design disciplines such as contractors and project managers, BIM is more like an intelligent Database Management System (DBMS) that can quickly take off data from CAD packages directly. With evident overlaps, BIM application vendors seem to aim to integrate the two requirements. Users with CAD backgrounds, such as designers, expect BIM to support integrated visualization and navigation comparable to the previous applications they are familiar with. Users with DBMS backgrounds, such as contractors, expect visualization and navigation to be the important features of BIM that were missing in existing DBMS solutions.

In terms of processes, BIM adoption requires a change in the existing work practice. An integrated model development needs greater collaboration and communication across disciplines. A concurrent engineering approach to model development is needed where multiple parties contribute simultaneously to the shared BIM. Standard processes and agreed protocols are required to assign responsibilities and conduct design reviews and validation. Experience from DBMS will be useful for data organization and management; however, organizations need to develop their own data management practices to suit their team structure and project requirements. Different business models are required to suit varied industry needs. A BIM can be maintained in-house or outsourced to service providers. In the latter case, additional legal measures and agreements are required to ensure data security and user confidence.

In terms of BIM-related people, new roles and relationships within the project teams are emerging. An examination of the existing workflow and resourcing capabilities would begin to highlight whether this would be an internally or externally resourced role. Singh and colleagues (2011) suggest that the scale and business models of the different players in the industry mean that organizations need to develop strategies that suit their requirements and practices, contingent upon the capabilities of the firms they work with. In general, dedicated roles such as BIM or BIM system manager will be inevitable for complex projects. Team members need appropriate training and information in order to be able to contribute to and participate in the changing work environment.

As the current industry perception and expectation of BIM differ across disciplines, in order to effectively facilitate BIM adoption and to maximize the impact in BIM, it is important to establish the BIM ecosystem and support balanced coevolution of related products, processes, and people. This requires a collective and integrated approach to manage the complex interdependencies across the three aspects. There are two different means for establishing a BIM ecosystem that can form a part of this collective and integrated approach. There are the concept of "Operational and Support Technical Requirements in BIM" (Singh et al. 2011; Gu et al. 2010) for balancing the technological advancement and adoption of BIM and the concept of the "Collaborative Platform BIM Decision Framework" (London et al. 2010; Gu and London 2010) for facilitating technological, organizational, and cultural changes in the AEC industry.

15.4 ESTABLISHING A BIM ECOSYSTEM: OPERATIONAL AND SUPPORT TECHNICAL REQUIREMENTS IN BIM

So far the technological advancement in BIM has largely focused on the development of the Operational Technical Requirements (OTRs). OTRs refer to the features and technical requirements needed during the usage of the BIM technology in direct support for design and modeling of a building project. OTRs in BIM typically include but are not limited to the following categories:

- BIM management–related requirements
- Design review–related requirements
- Data security–related requirements

Singh and colleagues (2011) and Gu and colleagues (2010) argue the need for both OTRs and Support Technical Requirements (STRs) to balance the advancement of BIM technologies for effective BIM adoption. STRs such as help menus and FAQs have been recognized as an integral part of technological tools, and they are critical to the application and adoption of the technology. For example, the existing building project collaboration platforms and Document Management Systems (DMS) such as Aconex and Team Binder include a wide range of assessment matrices, workflow templates, and the like that are provided as support features to facilitate the set-up and implementation of the collaboration platforms. Similarly, to facilitate the application and adoption of BIM as an information management and collaboration tool, STRs in BIM applications should include project decision support features, besides the routine help menus, FAQs, and tutorials. The decision support features will assist the set-up and implementation of the BIM technology for a particular building project by mapping the products, processes, and people dependencies. BIM decision support features may eventuate as plug-ins to existing BIM tools, get embedded within them, or be developed as standalone BIM project management applications.

15.5 ESTABLISHING A BIM ECOSYSTEM: COLLABORATIVE PLATFORM BIM DECISION FRAMEWORK

There is a lack of formal tools in the field to facilitate the technological, organizational, operational, and cultural changes needed in the AEC industry for BIM adoption. Aids such as the "Collaborative Platform BIM Decision Framework" (London et al. 2010, Gu and London 2010) can facilitate BIM adoption through

- Critical assessment of BIM readiness of key stakeholders by mapping their product (technological), process (cultural, operational, and organizational), and people (organizational, cultural, and skill) dependencies.
- Effective BIM project scoping and work process roadmap definition.
- Informed selection and application of appropriate BIM technologies.

The decision framework can facilitate the collection and dispersion of data across the collaborating firms and supply chain actors that could aid the development of shared understanding across the project team through shared information and enhanced visibility of each other's and the team's roles, responsibilities, and capabilities. In a newly formed project team, the framework is also expected to compensate for the lack of shared experiential knowledge (London and Singh 2012).

The framework aims to achieve the targets of lean design management, through efficient resource utilization, technology adoption, and project information management. It responds to interaction, collaboration, and communication requirements for the implementation of an integrated design and delivery solution across actors that increasingly spend the majority of their time operating within a virtual team (Emmitt and Chirstoffersen 2009). Key elements of the decision framework are briefly described.

15.5.1 Current Scope and Development of the Decision Framework

The framework provides a project life cycle view to support all the stakeholders. The aim is to present a way forward to realize the full potential of BIM implementation. It provides information for clients and facility managers to understand the full resource implications of BIM technologies on projects and the impact of their decision on BIM implementation. The diffusion of innovative technologies is influenced by the positive experiences of adopters and the ability to modify the technologies to suit individual organizational needs to successfully maintain and/or enhance business competitive advantage. This means that the framework needs to be customized for individual organizations or unique projects.

As such, the decision framework is intended to be revised by the following groups to suit their organizational and project requirements:

- Architects, engineering consultants, quantity surveyors, design managers, and the like who may not make project decisions but create, update, review, collaborate, and integrate models. These include all actors who need to know about one another's roles, responsibilities, capabilities, approaches, and perceptions in order to develop a shared understanding of the project.
- Clients, project managers, facility managers—those who make decisions about BIM implementation on a project and who can influence resourcing for project teams.
- Senior technical managers, managers, and executives—those who make decisions about technology investment, human resourcing, project bidding, and organizational strategy.

15.5.2 Sections of the Decision Framework for BIM Implementation

The development of the framework is an ongoing process (Figure 15.2). It is organized into different sections such that each section deals with different decision-making objectives, and each section can be developed incrementally. This allows decomposing the complex task of developing the decision framework into manageable segments.

There are four sections of the decision framework for BIM implementation: defining of scope, purpose, roles, relationships, and project phases; developing work process roadmaps; identifying technical requirements, and implementing the decision framework.

1. Defining of scope, purpose, roles, relationships and project phases: Critical early decisions in the BIM environment are required at the outset to enable a supportive business and cultural environment for streamlined data flow and information management within a knowledge enterprise.
2. Developing work process roadmaps: Guidelines for developing BIM implementation roadmaps.
3. Identifying technical requirements: A comprehensive knowledge of the available commercial BIM applications and their capabilities is important. Tools and levels of interoperability, is dynamic and therefore project-specific requirements regarding tool compatibility for multidisciplinary model sharing need to be defined at the outset.
4. Implementing the decision framework: Guidelines for implementing the framework include evaluating skills, knowledge, and capabilities required mapped against current status.

15.5.3 Applying the Decision Framework in Collaborative Practice

The framework is primarily a tool for reflection on practice. Clearly the challenge is that BIM is not just a technical solution, it is a business process, an education program, a changing of work culture, and a procurement and contractual dilemma. It is a mapping of these dependencies that will facilitate the move to collaborative platforms.

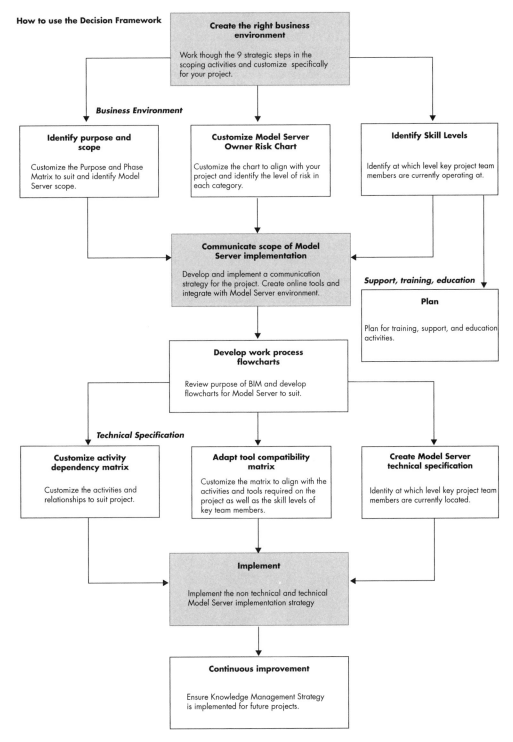

FIGURE 15.2 BIM collaborative platform decision framework customization flowchart (London and Singh 2013.)

In order to achieve the goal of integrated BIM development, BIM supporting technologies should be able to manage all the information related to the project. Increasingly, the BIM approach includes information appended as well as linked to the models and the information embedded in the object properties. Similarly, BIM is moving toward collaboration platforms, including Web-based collaboration technologies. All this while, the number of BIM supporting tools and complexity of BIM projects continues to increase. A variety of tools coexist with specific capabilities and limitations. While ideally interoperability can be achieved at some point, market competitiveness and business alliances may prolong the goal. Hence, the selection of right tools is critical to project effectiveness. A software compatibility matrix is required to ensure that the BIM applications chosen in a project are compatible.

With more distributed design and greater inter-firm specializations, the need for coordinating project resources and capabilities is likely to increase. Ad-hoc processes in technology integration and selection may prove detrimental to project success. The higher role of technology will necessitate better decision making for technology and tool management across the firms and specific to project requirements. This is where a collaborative BIM decision framework will be useful. However, given the increasing number of factors to consider, this framework itself should develop into a BIM management tool (Singh et al. 2010). In general, it is expected that the collaborative platform BIM decision framework can be implemented through one or more of the business channels listed in Table 15.1.

Table 15.1   Examples of business channels for implementing the collaborative platform BIM decision framework

Business Channels	Why?
Client as the driver	To implement BIM and require a report on strategy and analysis of the project collaborators capacity to operate within the environments.
Leadership of parent and dominant organization	To manage the project complexities and avail the benefits of BIM.
Application vendors and market opportunity	To respond to market needs and opportunities. New roles such as BIM managers are emerging. Analogous to project management tools (for project managers), a BIM management tool and plug-in (for BIM managers) implementing the BIM decision framework is a likely possibility.
Government regulation	To promote BIM usage and adoption in strategic and significant projects a BIM decision framework in some format will be critical to development of such a BIM project plan.
Requirements for loans, insurance, and financial agencies	To assess the inherent risks and opportunities in project collaboration and development. 4D and 5D models are desired because they provide greater cost estimation and detail before the construction phase.

15.6 DISCUSSION AND FUTURE BIM ECOSYSTEM

This chapter has presented the BIM ecosystem and explored different approaches for BIM-related products, processes, and people to coevolve in this ecosystem. In particular, approaches for supporting technological advances and facilitating cultural changes in the industry through the development of "BIM Operational and Support Technical Requirements" and for developing BIM adoption and project management guidelines through the collaborative BIM decision framework. To conclude this chapter, the following sections will discuss the key internal and external issues that are influential to the future BIM ecosystem. The discussion is centered on the following critical questions:

- What are the key issues in future BIM evolution in terms of BIM ecosystem?
- What external trends can influence future BIM evolution in terms of BIM ecosystem?
- What are the implications of future BIM ecosystem for practice, research, and education?
- How can one prepare for the future BIM ecosystem?

15.6.1 Key Issues and Implication of Future BIM Ecosystem

The BIM ecosystem is in a continuous flux as a result of the continuous improvements and coevolution across the products, processes, and people dimensions. For example, the current set of BIM tools and applications have created a demand for innovation in BIM education and training, as well the need for new forms of collaboration and contractual agreements. While these new demands are being addressed, at the same time BIM technologies will continue to improve, following broader technical innovations in the related field such as those in computing and digital and networked technologies. Therefore, some of the key external factors that are likely to influence innovation across BIM technologies and processes in the near future are highlighted below, along with a brief discussion on their implications for future BIM ecosystem:

- Developments in the areas such as augmented reality, haptics, 3D printing, and holographic imaging are likely to enhance **representation** capabilities in the BIM ecosystem, with potentially greater role for the use of immersive environments in virtual design and construction.
- Concepts such as BIG data and open source development are likely to influence **information management** capabilities of BIM. At the same time, applications of BIG data approach in the construction sector will potentially feedback into innovations across **simulation and analysis tools**, facilitated by a positive feedback loop from precedence.
- Trends across crowdsourcing, social computing, and cloud technologies are likely to influence the developments in BIM **collaboration and integration** capabilities.

The potential technological innovations resulting from the listed trends will promote corresponding innovation across process and people aspects.

15.6.2 Preparing for Future BIM Ecosystem

The challenge with adoption of BIM has always been varying levels of adoption between key actors on projects. For example, in Australia initially the design consultants were the leaders of BIM adoption, and it has taken some years for the construction companies to embrace and take leadership within their own organizations and also on projects. There are still many major projects that have little or no systematic approach, although BIM Implementation Plans are becoming increasingly common in practice. There are also critical trade-specific construction supply chains that have moved significantly in the development and implementation of standards, industrywide professional development programs, and changed work practices. One of the fundamental assumptions to the decision framework is that an open and transparent discussion will take place in the scoping stage. The key to this discussion is the identification of roles, the purpose of the information model, and the current levels of adoption. Such

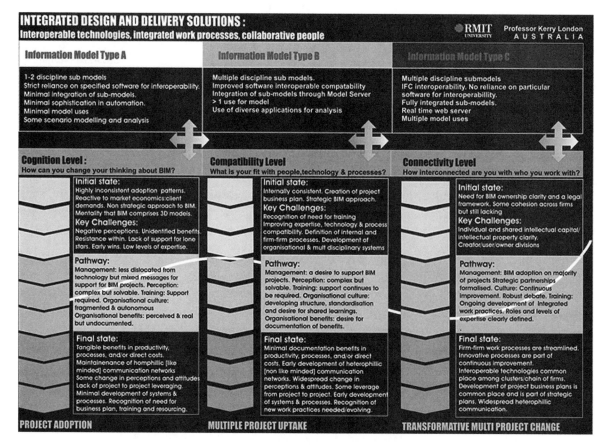

FIGURE 15.3   Integrated design and delivery solutions pathway: interoperable technologies, integrated work processes, and collaborative people.
(London 2014)

a discussion requires a certain level of trust between the key actors leading the project, namely the client, project management consultant firms, lead contractor, and design consultant(s). It is questionable whether such maturity currently exists. We must not forget that this is a business environment and that exposing a lack of knowledge and sharing the true nature of an organization's capabilities may damage that organization's credibility in the marketplace. The decision framework proposed enables a facilitation of the early project discussions needed towards BIM collaborative implementation. However, the framework assumes that all the project team members are a cluster embedded within organizations that have similar adoption patterns. Yet in many cases this is not the case.

Client leadership is thus integral to future adoption, particularly those clients who will manage the facility or asset in its in-use operational phase. Figure 15.3 presents a model of adoption at the organizational level that can enable "conversations" internally within the client organization and externally within their cluster of key business partners. The chart organizes key principles of adoption integrating the technical and social into (a) type and level of information models and (b) states, challenges, and pathways within organizations. The levels of differing states are described in terms of cognition, compatibility, and connectivity, and three fundamental questions. Again it accepts a premise that coevolution will assure project success but in particular a coevolution of the actor network elements.

DISCUSSION QUESTIONS

1. What are the key issues in future BIM evolution in terms of BIM ecosystem? How can designers prepare for the future BIM ecosystem?
2. What external trends can influence future BIM evolution in terms of BIM ecosystem?
3. What are the implications of future BIM ecosystem for practice, research, and education?

REFERENCES

Abernathy, W. J., and J. M. Utterback. 1978. "Patterns of Industrial Innovation." *Technology Review* (June/July) 80(7): 40–47.

CRC. 2008. *Collaboration Platform: Final Report.* Brisbane, Australia: Cooperative Research Centre for Construction Innovation.

Damanpour, F., and D. Aravind. 2006. "Product and Process Innovations: A Review of Organizational and Environmental Determinants." In J. Hage and M. Meeus (eds.), *Innovation, Science, and Institutional Change.* Oxford: Oxford University Press, pp. 38–66.

Fagerberg, J., and Verspagen, B. 2009. "Innovation Studies: The Emerging Structure of a New Field." *Research Policy* 38: 218–233.

Fritsch, M., and M. Meschede. 2001. "Product Innovation, Process Innovation, and Size." *Review of Industrial Organization*, 19(3): 335–350.

Greenhalgh, T., G. Robert, P. Bate, O. Kyriakidou, F. Macfarlane, and R. Peacock. 2004. "How to Spread Good Ideas: A Systematic Review of the Literature on Diffusion, Dissemination and Sustainability of Innovations in Health Service Delivery and Organization." Report for the National Co-ordinating Centre for NHS Service Delivery and Organisation R & D (NCCSDO), London.

Gu, N., and London, K. 2010. "Understanding and Facilitating BIM Adoption in the AEC Industry." *Automation in Construction* 19: 988–999.

Gu, N., V. Singh, C. Taylor, and K. London. 2010. "BIM Adoption: Expectations Across Disciplines." In J. Underwood and U. Isikdag (eds.), *Handbook of Research on Building Information Modelling and Construction Informatics: Concepts and Technologies*. Hershey, PA: IGI Global, pp. 501–520.

Kotabe, M., and J. Y. Murray. 1990. "Linking Product and Process Innovation and Modes of International Sourcing in Global Competition: A Case of Foreign Multinational Firms." *Journal of International Business Studies* 21(3): 383–408.

London, K. 2014. "Integrated Design and Delivery Solutions Pathways Using Information Models: Actor Network Analysis." In K. London, and W. McAdam (eds.), *Building Information Modelling and Management: Legal, Procurement and Regulatory*. John Wiley & Sons Limited.

London, K, N. Bavinton, J. Mentink, and B. Egan. 2006. *e-Adoption Profile Report*. Cooperative Research Centre for Construction Innovation Research Project No. 2003-003-A, Project Name: E-Business Adoption.

London, K., and V. Singh. 2012. "Integrated Construction Supply Chain Design and Delivery Solutions." *Journal of Architectural, Engineering and Design Management*. 8(4), June, pp. 1–21.

———. 2013. "Integrated Construction Supply Chain Design and Delivery Solutions." *Architecture, Engineering and Design Management* (June) 9(3): 135–137.

London, K., V. Singh, N. Gu, and C. Taylor. 2010. "Towards the Development of a Project Decision Support Framework for Adoption of Building Information Modelling." In J. Underwood and U. Isikdag (eds.), *Handbook of Research on Building Information Modelling and Construction Informatics: Concepts and Technologies*. Hershey, PA: IGI Global, pp. 301–320.

Moore, J. F. 1993. "Predator and Prey: A New Ecology of Competition." *Harvard Business Review* 71(3): 75–86.

Oxman, R. 2006. "Theory and Design in the First Digital Age." *Design Studies* 27(3): 229–265.

Pawson, R., and N. Tilley. 1997. *Realistic Evaluation*. London: Sage.

Schon, D. 1992. "Designing as a Reflective Conversation with the Materials of a Design Situation." *Knowledge-Based Systems* 5: 3–14.

Schumpeter, J. A., 1934. *The Theory of Economic Development*. Cambridge, MA: Harvard University Press.

Singh, V., N. Gu, and X. Wang. 2011. "A Theoretical Framework of a BIM-based Multi-disciplinary Collaboration Platform." *Automation in Construction* 20: 134–144.

PART 4

REASONING WITH BIM

CHAPTER 16

BIM, Materials, and Fabrication

Christopher Beorkrem, UNC Charlotte School of Architecture

16.1 THE UBER-DETAIL

Undoubtedly, the greatest advances in architectural discourse over the past fifteen years are due to the widespread availability of advanced software and computer-controlled manufacturing tools. These tools have brought about a windfall of change for the process of design and construction and the expectations for singular architectural works. Architects can now define systemic parameters or networked linkages that value relational logics over traditional, linear methods of design. While infatuated with new automated sculptural capabilities, designers have often lost sight of larger responsibilities to human inhabitation and the phenomenological experience of materiality.

Despite the desire for BIM software to create a broader applicability and develop simpler methods for customization, its tendencies toward verisimilitude continue to pervade the use of most of these types of software. Too often an observer can recognize a filleted edge on a curb in a parking lot or street corner or recognize the software-defined articulations in prefabricated brick panel systems.

BIM's ability to link a manufacturer's specifications to a designer's model is one of its best strengths. This does lead to a propensity for models from within a BIM environment to contain many of the typical details and components (which are built in), removing some (or a lot) of the diversity from traditional expectations for architectural identity. Human instinct tends toward repetition and the familiar, unintentionally creating an environment that, when spread throughout the world, creates a pattern of similar architectural elements and construction systems.

The same technological advances that have brought designers complex tools like BIM have also provided alternative options for creating buildings with new materials and with entirely new ways for manufacturing components. The introduction of these new tools has created the need for architects, and the manufacturers with whom they collaborate, to develop and explore new methods for designing customized componentry and assemblies. There continues to be a broad disjunction between the ability to adapt to wider possibilities and to provide the requisite levels of efficiency. These possibilities can include smarter construction methods, but certainly should include the ability to map material characteristics onto geometry.

16.2 MATERIALS

Manuel Delanda, in his article "Philosophies of Design: The Case of Modeling Software," describes the historic tendency for humans to have valued knowledge over know-how. With the advent of digital technology, that tendency is reversing; machines are fully capable of storing the knowledge necessary to play chess, or to solve a math problem, while engineers struggle to design a "mechanical hand." Delanda is pointing to some of humanity's technological innovations as the actual source for some of the problems society had hoped they would solve, in particular designers' lack of awareness of a material's character (touch, density, and durability) in the production of architectural design.

What made us different from animals and machines is, in fact, the easier to mechanize. And the minor, less prestigious skills that we have always neglected to study are the hardest to transmit to a machine, hence, the least mechanical (Delanda 2001).

Delanda goes on to describe how so often designers first select a "surrendered" material, so that it can be used to create any shape desired. When wood components are sliced into thin veneers and re-adhered into plywood sheets, the new material (plywood) has multiple grains so that there is no longer any knowledge required to use the material for whatever purpose. Further, sheets of plywood are created at a fixed size (typically 4 × 8 feet in the United States), often resulting in enormous amounts of wasted material. Instead of "imposing form upon matter," designers should look for ways to surrender to the material. Alongside new formal possibilities, technology is creating the absence of know-how, compounding the problem. Designers must start to critique the tools of the profession and evaluate what works well within the design sensibilities they value. Ultimately, deciding which parts of the profession can be better completed using automated systems that are inexplicably linked to the fundamentals of design. These choices are further burdened by the changing expectations of our culture.

Architects and designers must respond to the post–great recession standards society is expecting of them. Buildings are no longer built to simply accommodate the relatively simple task of human inhabitation for a particular purpose, but now they must accomplish it with fewer resources, during construction and during the lifespan of the building, all while under the burden of increased potential for litigation. There is no stopping the arc of digital advancement, but there must be a more grounded outlook going forward. The material choices designers make bear the burden of their performative impact (Oxman and Oxman 2010). If designers are to select a particular parameter to define exceptional work, materiality and construction ought to be at the front of the line. All too often construction techniques are post-rationalized layers of the design process. Forms are brought to engineers and consultants to have systems applied to them. This often results in convoluted and piece-meal structural integration, and excessively high construction costs. Alternatively, designers could use inventive material assemblies as the defining logic behind innovative architectural form.

16.3 THE LOGIC OF MATERIALITY

In recent years, designers have developed processes for layering performance-based feedback into the early stages of design development. This is often a response to the tendencies of both a culture and a construction industry that values efficiency (resulting in excessive waste) over environmental steadfastness. However, a systematic design process, applied specifically to material constraints, could frame awareness of the interconnectivity between the mediums of ecology, parametric modeling, and computer-numeric controlled (CNC) fabrication (see Juhani Pallasmaa, "From Metaphorical to Ecological Functionalism" 2003 for an earlier discussion of this methodology). This type of substantive design is defined by tangible knowledge of material characteristics (e.g., dimensional properties, durability, deformation, waterproofing and weathering, connection types, relative costs, color, texture, and finish). These characteristics define the performance criteria, which can and should be layered into the early stages of each design process and linked to their formal expression through parametric design. Patkau Architects provides an excellent example of this material mapping in its Cocoons (Figure 16.1) project, which is based on the original design of its Winnipeg Skate Shelters.

FIGURE 16.1 Patkau Architects Cocoons, Tokyo, Japan, 2011–2012.
(Photograph © James Dow)

FIGURE 16.2   ICD/ITKE Research Pavilion 2010.
(Institute for Computational Design, Prof. Achim Menges. Institute of Building Structures and Structural Design, Prof. Jan Knippers.
© ICD/ITKE University of Stuttgart.)

As materials become more specifically a point of departure for design, architects must recognize that materials aren't ultimately flexible; they come in modules, bricks, blocks, extrusions, and sheets. It is through the aggregation of these materials that experimentation is most rich. From a nail to a custom-fabricated hinge, the detail contains the information for delimiting the articulation and performance of a system.

An excellent example of this type of logic is seen in the Institute of Computational Design (ICD; Professor Achim Menges) and the Institute of Building Structures and Structural Design (ITKE; Professor Jan Kippers) at the University of Stuttgart Research Pavilion from 2010 (Figure 16.2). The pavilion is a dynamic expression of the physical behavior present in a material placed under stress. In this instance, thin birch veneer plywood strips, 6.5 mm (0.25"), are placed in an elastic bend, or "bending active" position, to create a rigid structural arch. The form was developed based on a series of lab tests (Figure 16.3), analyzing the amount of curvature at which the plywood was capable of sustaining strain without eventual failure. Each of the panel strips, once bent, are organized in a circumferential ring of alternating convex (compressive) and flat panels (tension) that resist the elastic compression of each neighboring panel. The model was tested using a finite element analysis (FEA) simulation. The test estimates the energy contained in the bent strips to measure how the entire system would perform. This project extracts a structural parameter by making a simple change (an elastic bend) to an otherwise passive piece of material.

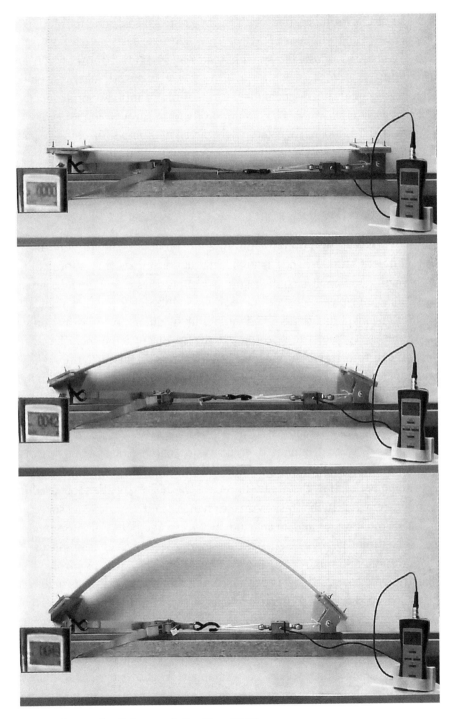

FIGURE 16.3   Testing for ICD/ITKE Research Pavilion 2010.
(Institute for Computational Design, Prof. Achim Menges. Institute of Building Structures and Structural Design, Prof. Jan Knippers. © ICD/ITKE University of Stuttgart.)

The development of this form began through a series of tests, analyzing the amount of force necessary to create particular profiles in bent plywood. Through these tests a series of forms or arcs were determined to be possible solutions. The system creates an integrated form of skin and structure in which each strip alternates from its neighbor to provide the necessary local resistance to keep each bent arch in compression and each flat component in tension, in this case dramatically improving the structural capacity of a material, while also delimiting its form through the know-how of a material's properties. By parametrically mapping a material's characteristics onto a form, the system could become infinitely more adaptable.

16.4 SOFT DATA

In Cynthia Ottchen's article "The Future of Information Modeling and the End of Theory: Less Is Limited, More Is Different" (2009), she highlights the opportunities that information modeling and parametrics can harness when applied to the rigorous complexities of building design and production. She says that "soft" data are typically not considered quantifiable in information models. Ottchen argues that the combination, overlap, integration, and variability of qualitative information can be analyzed and used not only through parametric algorithms but also through the inclusion of underlying and sometimes more difficult-to-perceive information. As a profession, architecture needs to create more awareness for the separation between the tools it has and the ones it desires. Ultimately, the search for solutions must provide designers with tools that are more efficient, but which don't delimit possibility and invention.

Parametric software modeling creates systems defined not by Cartesian coordinate systems, but by linkages and constraints between geometry. By their nature, parametric systems do not have a specific solution but are capable of accommodating a range of possibilities. Design software's capabilities to adapt to soft data initially began as the ability to record the history of the tools used in the software, but then to eventually retreat into that history, make changes, and see all of the subsequent operations adapt. So often parametric linkages to data are made between rigid points of information (solar orientation, zoning and code envelopes, or program); the difficult tasks, however, lie in the use of information, which is changing, information that is soft. Typical computational solutions involve simple calculated possibilities, tying fixed data to geometry; more complex and inventive solutions involve tying geometry to geometry or even entire geometric solutions to flexible information (soft data).

The ability to change a model with explicit history eventually led to the use of scripting languages, which allowed designers to predetermine a set of functions, to be applied to a variety of situations. BIM software and component-based scripting provide more intuitive methods for creating parametric linkages between components and data. McNeel's Grasshopper 3D allows designers to create components using node-based scripting. This type of visual programming creates scripts with a series of components, each of which has an input and output allowing for a more intuitive setup and increasing accessibility for novices. BIM specific software such as Autodesk Revit uses an even more intuitive system, which embeds the logic of external data into each piece of geometry created or drawn. Though this simplifies

FIGURE 16.4 Adaptive components, student project.
(Image courtesy Jeremy Roh)

the entire process, it also ascribes why so much of what is drawn with Revit uses default settings. A user has to deliberately change the settings to customize parts of the system.

In 2010 Revit introduced adaptive components (Figure 16.4) in their software, greatly expanding its operability for creating customized components. Adaptive components were initially built as an expansion of Revit's curtain panel system, used to model curtain walls or storefront glazing systems. Adaptive components use reference levels or drawing planes to link objects internal to the component to external edges. Whatever is drawn given a set of edge planes or levels will scale and shift based on the location of those components. When a user inserts a window into a typical Revit model, the window is drawn with a dimensional reference to one corner of a wall or another object within the model; should that corner or object move, the window moves accordingly. Adaptive components work similarly, giving the designer the ability to create parametric components through geometric definitions.

Adaptive components allow designers to use geometry to delimit the relationships of various instantiations of a piece of geometry, but only as variations within a ruled edge and not as an object defined by its individual relationships to other objects and systems. Typical uses for an adaptive component might be a customized railing or stair detail. These details are drawn as "hosted" profiles onto levels and are often extruded through to other levels using a defined length or simply by hosting on another level, which is then linked to an external object. Solutions created with this tool can be applied to wide-ranging design problems, such a flowing surface conditions, using customized storefront systems or complex railing configurations. However, the primary method for creating shifts in each object is grounded in making scalar and angular shifts to the imbedded components. This results in components that will likely have a singular profile and not be capable of adapting to changing material limitations (the size of sheet of material), structural loads, or aesthetic shifts in the design. Moreover, tools like adaptive components don't have the capabilities to adjust to aggregate conditions, wherein the connections between materials define their relationships. In an ideal world architects would have the flexibility of Grasshopper built into a holistic modeler like Revit. Academics and practitioners have written plugins attempting to connect the capabilities of Revit and Grasshopper (Chameleon and Dynamo, amongst others), but these are only patchwork solutions, and they are rarely accepted as part of the mainstream.

16.5 BACKWARD BIM

Another less widely employed BIM software is Gehry Technologies Digital Project, which is typically used for more complex design problems. Digital Project prepares a conventional system that mimics both structure and geometry with many of the same limitations of Revit. This characteristic is not only evident in the software but is also manifest in Gehry's early design work. The extrusions that make up much of the lattice work trusses behind Gehry's skins are typically composed of only one or two unique profiles and are constructed of typical lengths, resulting in an infrastructure that is rarely made visible despite its organic complexity. However, in the design of the Pritzker Pavilion in Chicago's Millennium Park (Figure 16.5), the rear of each of the proscenium surfaces are open, exposing these extrusions.

Digital Project is a single "silo" of components from CATIA, an aeronautical engineering program originally written in the 1970s. There are a broad range of other silos in CATIA that provide an infinite

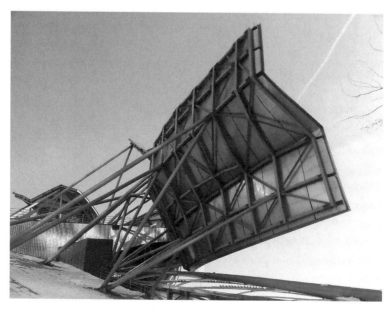

FIGURE 16.5   Pritzker Pavilion, Chicago, Illinois, 2004.

FIGURE 16.6 Digital Project "quilt" screenshot. The underlying light gray surface is the parent to the entire system.

set of possibilities for both analysis and simulation. The software's lack of reliance on Cartesian systems does create interesting possibilities for alternative uses. Though Digital Project typically uses geometric, organizational relationships to calculate components for complex surfaces and custom building systems used by many avant-garde designers, the modeler can just as easily be used "backwards" to design responsive complex systems of off-the-shelf or customized components and link them to yet-to-be-defined surfaces.

The inversion in this situation is brought about by the ability to predefine relationships between each object and its neighbors. This requires the user to conceptualize the model as a sequence of relationships. It must be organized through the capacity for one part of the system to affect another. If the location of a pier under a column is flexible within a certain limitation, then the column attached to it must come after. If the height of that column is flexible then the roofline attached to it must be "drawn" after it in the system. This logic creates a series of grandparent/ parent/child relationships that is continuous throughout the model, whereby no one component is defined independently from the system.

The organizational logic creates a "quilt," a formless parametric model of components, both structure and skin, linked to each other through geometric definitions. Each model is constructed of a pattern, made of fixed objects with variable "hinges" or linkages that gives a designer the ability to "drape" the quilt across any surface (Figure 16.6). If the geometry of the surface does not comply with the built-in geometric limitations of the quilt, it will not update and therefore is beyond the limits of the system. The form can ultimately be defined by its material character and connective definitions.

The underlying geometric limitations within Digital Project can be used to map objects across a surface or across its edges; it can also use limitations to identify when surface deviations become too dramatic for the system. The topological nature of the surface, when combined with the complexities of parametrics, allow for the variation that arises through relations instead of individual components. Another silo built into CATIA, Knowledgeware, can be used to map the maximum deviation of each piece of the system away from the original surface. When the deviation becomes too great compared to predefined standards (for aesthetic pairing or legibility of form), the system will identify the portions of the system that are beyond those limits, so they might be corrected or the surface adjusted. The fabrication of components in this system is simply a byproduct of the model, dependent on the user selecting one version to build. As with other modelers, the data contained in the finished version can be used to directly inform the digital manufacturing of the componentry.

16.6 BIM, MATERIALS, AND FABRICATION

The applications of digital fabrication technologies in contemporary practice have primarily emphasized the ability to connect design and construction in tangible, productive ways. Discourse on digital fabrication has tended toward two poles: on one hand an overly technical framework that uncritically presents the technologies' capabilities as ends in themselves and on the other an overly broad speculative approach that sees these means as metaphors for larger cultural changes. Moving forward the design profession must close the gap between these two unwieldy—and arguably counterproductive—poles. Contemporary designers need to present case studies and theoretical positions that seek to critically assess the roles of the digital in the production of the physical. Going forward, built projects, assessments, and histories, and philosophical examinations of the real possibilities and limitations of these technologies will form the basis for meaningful use of these tools, potentially prompting a discussion that will ask designers to take stock of the current relations between design, production, and the digital. Designers must learn to use manufacturing equipment in responsible ways, minimizing customization while maximizing form.

Responsible use of the machine starts by looking beyond the superficialities of so-called "green" design to a set of strategies that embrace substantive design rather than mundane aesthetics of environmental architecture. To each question there is an ethical answer about the humanistic value of the process. Performance-based architecture needs to be defined by more than the simple building product. It is composed of a complex set of systems, both technological and cultural, made of physical commodities and human effort. Ultimately, the designer is responsible for coordinating this discourse, responsible from the point of conception to the destruction of the building. This responsibility includes not only how the building performs throughout its life cycle, but equally how it performs during construction, through adaptive reuse, and in its eventual demolition. Architects must consider every commodity consumed in the production of building as a part of their design. Through this awareness, with and through technology, architects can create a new definition for sustainable design.

16.7 GOING FORWARD

A systematic design process, applied to ubiquitous options for design and assembly, could bring a new awareness to complex webs of interconnectivity that remain undiscovered through the mediums of ecology, parametrics, and fabrication. In David Gissen's article "APE" (2010), he outlines an architectural ideology based on the acronym APE, or Architectural Political Ecology. Gissen outlines a variety of concepts to accomplish a "production of nature." By applying materials in an informed way designers can be efficient with time and money, but can also deploy materials in a highly inventive and sustainable way. As a profession, architecture will inevitably continue hurtling towards automation; through this, designers must maintain control over the outcomes. It is here that designers can identify one particular aspect of their future, one that holds the most opportunity for them to create more robust tools, through the use of collective intelligence.

Author Mario Carpo has recently outlined three scenarios for collectively developed parametric systems, through the idea of "split agency" (Carpo, 2011). First is an existing parametric environment such as Revit, which has a corporate author (Autodesk). Second is a scenario where the parametric software has a "system author" that customizes the design environment according to a series of rules, parameters, or laws that govern how the system functions, such as Digital Project by Gehry Technologies. Finally is a scenario where the parametric software is defined by multiple users operating through collective intelligence as "virtual authors," customizing the way a system functions. This final scenario could create a fracture, which could redefine the significance and applicability of BIM.

By provoking the question of "authorship," designers can utilize BIM as a design and production tool, which integrates ethical and inventive decision making within parametric design environments. In many ways, Roland Barthes's assumptions about the author have become a reality that must be confronted (Barthes, 1977). The loss of authorship may allow information to become more transparent; however, designers must be careful not to devalue the way that multiple authors access or profit from this "collective intelligence." The culture of open-source software, from the Mozilla Firefox browser to the Linux operating system, to the activist group of hackers known as Anonymous, has proven that no computational task is too complex for a group of people motivated to change the world.

The current collective naivety that the profession has with regard to the use of BIM can result in oversimplified proposals, which all too often result in designers being able to recognize CAD in the constructed environment. As a profession there ought not to be any way in which the identity of a piece of software is visible in a final building product. Any profession—whether artists, lawyers, or doctors—would expect the same. This is a problem driven in part by the lack of familiarity or know-how with the tools, which, as Delanda pointed out, is only a byproduct of the same technological shift that has brought so much opportunity back to the profession.

16.8 CONCLUSION

As a response to societal expectations and as the natural progression of design process evolves, designers are in the midst of a struggle for a clearer control over the parametric relationships that govern their methods. There is undoubtedly a new pragmatism formulated through more meaningful responses to process fostered by the excess and flippant use of digital manufacturing equipment and the incredible flexibility of design software. There is a clear desire to explore how design process is being redefined by complexity through software. The questions remain of how the machine can give designers new solutions to problems they didn't even know existed, and how it can allow them to redefine the processes they use to assemble building components. This new functionalism has been a long time coming, though it is much more broadly accepted today than ever before. The delimitation of process has been accelerated by the wide use of parametric software, providing more flexibility with every new software update.

Design process requires the foresight necessary to compose a solution that properly engages all of the necessary systems for both ethical and inventive proposals. Rather than relying on a select tool defined by particular invested parties, who often have political or economic motivations, architects ought to rely on a system of competing parties, arguing for best practices at that point in time, and for that location. Few would doubt the growing importance of computational methods and thinking within architectural design, but what remains unclear is how a discipline such as architecture *becomes* computational. In other words, how does it arrive at the point of integration, when architects understand that computation is not just a tool for helping design but a way of doing design, a time when all designers—not only specialists—can practice computationally and are able to ruminate on the subject?

DISCUSSION QUESTIONS

1. What other types of parametric constraints can designers employ to make for more responsible uses of technology?

2. What designers have been provoking the profession to make more conscientious decisions about how technology is affecting the products of our profession?

3. What tools do you use that create a sense that you are no longer in control of your design process? What about the tool causes this? Give specific examples of changes in the tools that would make you feel in charge of the design process.

4. What other scientific shifts in the history of design have caused architecture to separate its expectations from culture's expectations for the profession?

REFERENCES

Barthes, Roland. 1977. "The Death of the Author." *Image-Music-Text*. New York: Hill and Wang.

Carpo, Mario. 2011. *The Alphabet and the Algorithm*. Cambridge, MA: MIT Press.

Gissen, David. 2010. "APE." In Lisa Tilder and Beth Blostein (eds.), *Design Ecologies: Essays on the Nature of Design*. New York: Princeton Architectural Press, p. 62–75.

Ottchen, Cynthia. 2009. "The Future of Information Modelling and the End of Theory: Less Is Limited, More Is Different." *Architectural Design* 17(2) (March–April): 22–27.

Oxman, R., and R. Oxman. 2010. "New Structuralism: Design, Engineering and Architectural Technologies." *Architectural Design* 80(4).

Pallasmaa, Juhani. 1993. "From Metaphorical to Ecological Functionalism." *Architectural Review* 193 (June): 74–79.

CHAPTER 17

Communicating Semantics through Model Restructuring and Representation

Ramesh Krishnamurti, Carnegie Mellon University
Varvara Toulkeridou, Carnegie Mellon University
Tajin Biswas, Carnegie Mellon University

17.1 INTRODUCTION

Design is intentional, purposive, goal-seeking, it decisively relies on reasoning. . . . "Reasoning" pertains to all those mental operations we are aware of, can even communicate to others. It consists of more or less orderly trains of thought, which include deliberating, pondering, arguing, occasional logical inferences.

(Rittel 1987)

In the processes of designing and creating buildings, architects and other building professionals explore various configurations for a desired outcome of design, function, and performance. Designers reason about evolving designs through inferences and interpretation of explicit information, processed or gleaned, from drawings, physical and digital models, documents, diagrams, and mathematical models. Design intentions and decisions are communicated to the relevant professionals and stakeholders through a variety of representational medium. Inevitably, during this process, there is information exchange between one form to another such as from sketch to digital model or from one context to another such as from architectural model to energy model.

Commonly used software tools to assist in design essentially provide graphic visualization of geometry where lines, symbols, and annotations are interpreted as definitive objects with definitive meaning. Building information modeling (BIM) has emerged as a significant tool to represent the various building components as objects with semantics (Eastman et al. 2008). A building information model is a digital representation of the physical and functional characteristics of a design. "[It] serves as a shared knowledge resource for information about a [design] forming a reliable basis for decisions during its life cycle from inception onward" (Smith and Edgar 2008). Each proprietary software application specifies its own internal model to capture the relations and intended uses of the various types of data. In order to make these models accessible to applications outside of the proprietary BIM environment, data need to be extracted to nonproprietary applications. Inevitably, during this process there is information loss; on the positive side, the tradeoff is having platform independence. There are public data exchange formats that can be employed to implement tools that support reasoning and decision making. Of these, IFC (Industry Foundation Class) and CIS/2 (for steel) are currently the widely recognized data exchange standards (Eastman et al. 2008). IFC provides a suitable data structure based on concepts and relationships, which can offer a complete and uniform description of the project data, independent of project specifics or proprietary software (Stouffs and Krishnamurti 2001).

For purposes of reasoning about building-domain-related questions, one requires the semantic model encapsulated within the building information model. However, such semantics are hard to access, navigate, and manipulate. Three important issues arise: knowing the kind of data that must be extracted, how effectively the data can be augmented and/or restructured, and how effectively the data can be represented for a specific need. In order to leverage the power of BIM for reasoning and decision making, the inherent semantics of a multidimensional building product model need to be made explicit (Figure 17.1).

Two projects are described, which explore how BIM assists in reasoning and decisionmaking. Each project employs its own kind of "drawing board." One examines the provisions of building information models for analyzing spatial and network topologies through data extraction, data restructuring and representation; and the other explores capabilities for assessing designs for green certification through data extraction, data augmentation, and representation.

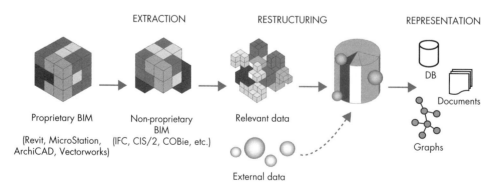

FIGURE 17.1   General process for using information from BIM for reasoning.

17.2 SPATIAL REASONING AND QUERYING

17.2.1 BIM as an Infrastructure for Spatial Reasoning

Understanding spatial relations of building components plays an important role in decision making during the design process of a building. Moreover, querying spatial relations in an existing design solution can facilitate evaluation of the design in terms of meeting specific criteria and requirements. These queries refer to spatial topology requirements. Common questions include:

- Is the bedroom adjacent to the bathroom?
- Are the electromechanical spaces separated from the user spaces?
- What is the shortest egress from this room to the exit?

Building information models offer a promising infrastructure for spatial reasoning. Beyond explicitly representing building components, their properties, and geometric characteristics, BIM additionally represents basic topological relationships among building components. However, current central model management servers, which mediate between user and BIM, are not based on certain spatial semantics of particular attributes and relationships, and therefore information stored in these models cannot be interpreted, adequately, to infer spatial relations.

BIM servers provide ways for the user to select, filter data, perform queries, and constraint checks and even implement custom queries by programming (Mazairac and Beetz 2012). Although it is possible to resolve certain spatial topology queries using these ways, nevertheless, implementing a more complete evaluation tool to compare existing designs against standard building criteria necessitates good working knowledge of the syntax and structure of the underlying building information model.

17.2.2 Extraction, Restructuring, Representation

The title of this section suggests the order in the sequence of evaluating a spatial topology query. For ease of explanation, however, this order is reversed, and representation is considered first. The choice of representation guides decisions relating to the structuring and data extraction steps. The representational needs for a given query imply a certain but appropriate data structure to maintain the extracted data and determine whether the data provided by the building information model suffices or needs to be augmented. Ideally, any tool for spatial reasoning and querying must support representational flexibility, which, in this context, implies models that are scalable and multimodal. A scalable representation model allows for moving effortlessly between scales of three-dimensional space, changing view and granularity. A multimodal representation model enables changing across different perspectives, namely the various spatial topology relationships that might be considered. In the context of BIM, scalability and multimodality are key properties if one considers the differing information and reasoning needs of the various project professionals and stakeholders.

Graph representations have proven to be convenient models of spatial configurations in architecture and other space planning domains (March and Steadman 1974, Hillier and Hanson 1984). A typical example is the graph theoretic application to the space layout problem, namely, generating a layout that meets certain adjacency requirements between activities (Liggett 2000). Nodes in these graphs typically represent spaces, and edges typically connect two nodes to represent spatial topology relationships among spaces. Certain graph models provide greater representational flexibility than others. For example, hierarchical hypergraphs form an infrastructure that may allow through the appropriate user interactions change in scale as well as the capability to extract subgraphs according to user defined levels of detail (Grabska et al. 2012).

The need to extract relevant data from industry foundation classes (IFC) instead of from a proprietary software application has been previously highlighted in the introduction. However, the IFC data structure does not provide an efficient infrastructure on which to base a graph representation. Therefore, the extracted data must be effectively structured *a posteriori* so as to provide the basis for a scalable and multimodal representation model.

Data structures to support graph representations are important. Choosing the appropriate data structure enables certain queries to be effectively answered. In certain cases a simpler representation may suffice. For example, to answer a shortest egress query, Dijkstra's shortest path algorithm (Dijkstra 1959) may be used. This can be implemented with an adjacency list, a data structure where each space-node in the graph references a list of the space-nodes it is connected to (Cormen et al. 1990). There are other design problem situations that require finer-grained layouts of architectural spaces to be queried. For example, to answer queries related to electrical circuitry infrastructure, a schema that represents adjacency among spaces and connectivity between the boundary elements of each space would be required. Such a schema could be implemented with a double-edge list (Berg et al. 2000), a data structure that enables the space boundaries of the spaces to be efficiently traversed in order, either clockwise or counterclockwise. There is usually a trade-off between the complexity of the data structure and the types of the queries that can be answered.

17.2.3 Spatial Topology Data Extraction from IFC

Spatial topology querying is considered in the context of a specific BIM format, namely, IFC, industry foundation classes. IFC is an object-oriented data structure to represent building models. Building components are members of classes; for example, these could be discrete objects such as walls, windows, or abstract objects such as project and process. An IFC model is a collection of such discrete and abstract building components and the relationships between them. Each IFC object has attributes that specify its semantics.

Objects in an IFC model are linked to each other through a complex network of relationships forming a tree hierarchy. An investigation of how IFC conceptualizes space, how it breaks space down into its basic entities, and how it defines relationships among those entities reveals the types of data that are useful for inferring spatial topology relations. Information is stored in the IFC structure either explicitly, available by accessing a simple property of an object, or implicitly requiring complex navigation of the underlying model (Mazairac and Beetz 2012). For instance, deriving networks of adjacency and connectivity relationships belongs to the second category and requires extraction of information involving a significant number of steps in navigating over the IFC tree structure.

The key elements in inferring adjacency and connectivity relations within the context of a BIM are the concepts of bounded space and shared element. Space is defined as "an area or volume bounded actually or theoretically" (buildingSMART 2013). IFC grounds the definition of space on the property of it being bounded by enclosing elements. It objectifies this relationship of the space to its physical or virtual boundaries (referred to as IfcRelSpaceBoundary) by the BoundedBy attribute in the IfcSpace entity. Each physical space boundary references the building element that physically separates the space under consideration from its adjacent spaces. On the other hand, if the space boundary is deemed virtual, it either references a virtual element or none at all.

It is important to note that although an IfcRelSpaceBoundary expresses a unique relationship between an element and the space it bounds, each element is allowed to define many such relationships, and each space is allowed to be defined by many such relationships (buildingSMART 2013). This observation leads to the concept of a shared element, which is the basis for deriving adjacency and connectivity relations. If a building element, either vertical or horizontal, is referenced by more than one space (in other words, it is shared by more than one space), these spaces may be respectively vertically or horizontally adjacent. If, additionally, the building element contains an opening intended for access, these spaces will also be connected.

The concept of shared elements has been adapted by researchers; for instance, implementing shortest path queries on the connectivity network of a floor plan from IFC models (Taneja et al. 2011), and for deriving topological relationships directly from the 3D geometry of spaces based on the Poincare duality (Lee and Kwan 2005). The latter example is instructive; according to the Poincare duality principle, the common 2D face shared by two adjacent solid objects can be transformed into an edge linking two vertices in the dual space of the graph. Thus, the edges of the dual graph represent adjacency and connectivity relationships that may correspond to doors, windows, or walls between rooms in primal space.

17.2.4 Prototype for Spatial Topology Queries

A prototype application that generates and displays graphs representing adjacency, connectivity, composition and containment was developed (Figure 17.2). The prototype has been implemented in Java and has been successfully tested with IFC models of three different building types.

The source application, ideally, is a commercial BIM software (for example, Revit, ArchiCAD, or VectorWorks) that provides options for exporting a model to IFC. The prototype parses the IFC model, determines the building decomposition into floor levels and spaces, and extracts the relevant spatial topology information. The relevant data referring to adjacency and connectivity has been described in the previous section. Once the data are extracted and restructured the spatial topology graphs are generated. The prototype's user interface lets the user select between the available graph representations. The user can navigate over the building composition tree provided by the user interface, select a floor level

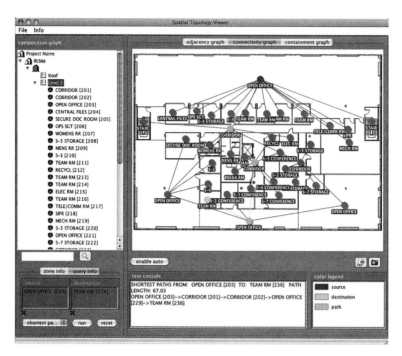

FIGURE 17.2   Spatial topology prototype.

or a specific space, and have the respective graph displayed. By further interacting with the graph nodes a subgraph can be extracted. Additionally, the prototype allows querying the generated graphs by applying a series of graph theory algorithms, namely, all paths and shortest paths among sets of user selected spaces, connected components, and spanning trees (Cormen et al. 1990).

17.3 REASONING FOR GREEN CERTIFICATION

No single computer application can support all of the tasks associated with building design.

(Eastman et al. 2008)

In light of this claim each type of specialty has to be supported and augmented by its own application. In addition to supporting geometry and material specification, additional applications are required for structural and energy analyses, fabrication, and facilities management among others. These added applications obtain data from a basic building information model, then restructured or processed within an augmented data structure in order to address functions necessary for reasoning and decision making. Here, BIM is examined in the context of green certifiability through the lenses of data requirement and extraction, suitable data structures for augmentation, and tools and processes.

A building typically achieves a green certification when it fulfills requirements set by a rating standard. Green or sustainable building rating systems are defined as "tools that examine the performance or expected performance of a 'whole building' and translate that examination into an overall assessment that allows for comparison against other buildings" (Fowler and Rauch 2006). In the process of assessing a project for green certification, design teams are exposed to different types of information (codified as drawings, product models, standards, etc.) and have to use a combination of tools to come to a conclusion using knowledge related to green assessments. Some common requirements are:

- Is the building X percent more water efficient than the benchmark?
- Is the building X percent more energy efficient than the benchmark?

These performance requirements are specified in the building rating standards. BIM-based environments can assist in decision making to comply with sustainable rating standards, in particular, during the early stages of design (Biswas et al. 2013).

17.3.1 Aggregation, Augmentation, Representation

As in the case of querying spatial topology, knowledge necessary to support sustainability could be used efficiently, provided the relevant data can be identified, extracted, aggregated, and restructured, which in this context is for the purpose of checking of certification requirements. Data are aggregated from a combination of sources such as performance data, sunlight, and rainfall (in general, external data), and internal data from BIM, essentially, geometry, pertinent attributes and other BIM-dependent data (Figure 17.3). This data must be stored in a suitable data structure so as to lend the information to checking outcomes according to green assessment criteria.

In practice, no single specification standard provides support for sustainability assessment, nor do these completely suffice as a data structure. In examining building representation models, Huang (2011) concludes:

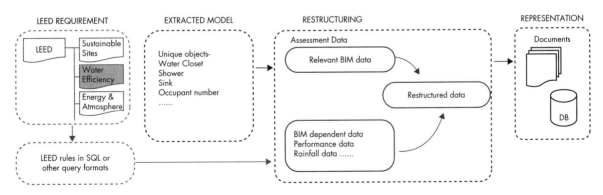

FIGURE 17.3 Data extraction, structuring, and representation for green certification.

There are significant differences between the IFC and gbXML schemas, including comprehensiveness, efficiency, robustness, redundancies, and portability. . . . Both formats are not yet able to represent all information across all building performance domains (p. 6).

In order to use design information and integrate sustainability related information requirement, a number of information exchange formats were explored. COBie (Construction Operations Building Information Exchange) was seen as a suitable candidate for a lightweight building information model, which is derivable from an IFC model. A COBie model saves building owners and occupants from having to rekey information multiple times throughout the life cycle of a project (East 2013). The objective behind the development of COBie is not to specify an alternative model for information for building management, but rather to provide a standard format for common information. COBie was adopted as the data structure because its format offers a structure that could be easily used, extended, and augmented to drive sustainability assessments.

17.3.2 Prototype for Green Certification

Following this approach a prototype application was developed using COBie as the extendible data format (Figure 17.4). The source application ideally is a commercial BIM software that provides options for exporting a model to IFC. The IFC model is then converted to a COBie model via data exchange software provided by BimServices (Nisbet and East, 2013). For the prototype, LEED (Leadership in Energy and Environmental Design) is chosen as the exemplar sustainable building rating system. LEED requirements are represented as a set of executable rules and stored in an augmented COBie database, COBie+. Evaluation rules are taken as input, and these are interpreted for assessment against building data held in the COBie+ model. Storing rules in the augmented COBie+

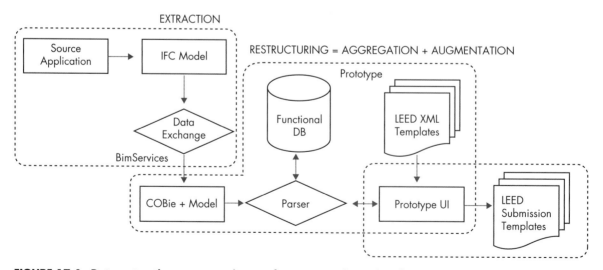

FIGURE 17.4 Data extraction, restructuring, and representation using the prototype.

model allows the application to more readily accommodate future rating requirement updates. It enables multidisciplinary cooperation from sustainable assessment rule mapping to corresponding building data (and vice versa). The prototype generates LEED submittal documents in HTML format, containing the aggregated results. The prototype exemplifies a process where design information can be aggregated, structured, and represented to support the certification of designs according to a green rating standard.

17.4 CONCLUSION

Assumptions, factors, and processes, which are required of a building information model to provide reasoning support, have been explored in the context of two projects: spatial topology querying and green certification. BIM is a rich repository of data that can support exchange between applications and databases. However, understanding the semantics and data structures imposed by industry standards for data exchange is key in developing tools for specific needs. This understanding enables one both to navigate a given building model and to identify data availability. A general process of data extraction from proprietary to nonproprietary BIM, extraction of relevant chunks of data and/or data augmentation, and restructuring and representation in addressing domain specific queries are necessary. These steps are integral for implementing tools that are flexible and adaptable for the differing and changing needs of the different stakeholders and professionals in the industry.

Perhaps, the single most important lesson learned from the two projects on spatial topology querying and green certification is that building information model–based processes need to be more knowledge intensive; this responsibility has been previously placed upon the construction industry (Wetherill et al. 2007). This challenge of making specific project knowledge available to interested parties for purposes of reasoning in a systematic and reusable way may be resolved by developing ontologies, each essentially an "explicit specification of a conceptualization" (Gruber 1995). To this extent, such ontologies become the next relevant step in refining building information models and their relationship to domain specific applications.

DISCUSSION QUESTIONS

1. How can building information models become shared knowledge resources to support decision making about a project?
2. What are the most vital components of a BIM for communication? Which of these are useful in understanding and explaining problems and solutions?
3. How can conceptualization be used in analyzing BIM domain knowledge, in making explicit domain assumptions, and enabling reuse of domain knowledge?

REFERENCES

Berg, Mark de, Otfried Cheong, Marc van Kreveld, and Mark Overmars. 2000. *Computational Geometry: Algorithms and Applications*. Berlin: Springer.

Biswas, Tajin, Tsung-Hsien Wang, and Ramesh Krishnamurti. 2013. "From Design to Pre-certification Using Building Information Modeling." *Journal of Green Building* 8(1): 151–176.

buildingSMART. 2013. "Industry Foundation Classes: IFC4 Official Release," last modified March 25, 2013, www.buildingsmart-tech.org/ifc/IFC4/final/html/index.htm.

Cormen, Thomas H., Charles Eric Leiserson, and Ronald L. Rivest. 1990. *Introduction to Algorithms*. Cambridge, MA: MIT Press.

Dijkstra, E. W. 1959. "A Note on Two Problems in Connexion with Graphs." *Numerische Mathematik* 1(1): 269–271.

East, E. William. 2013. "Construction Operations Building Information Exchange (COBie)." Accessed August 6, 2013, www.wbdg.org/resources/cobie.php.

Eastman, Chuck, Paul Teicholz, Rafael Sacks, and Kathleen Liston. 2008. *BIM Handbook: A Guide to Building Information Modeling for Owners, Managers, Designers, Engineers, and Contractors*. Hoboken, NJ: John Wiley & Sons.

Fowler, K. M., and E. Rauch. 2006. "Sustainable Building Ratings Summary," Technical Report, U.S. Department of Energy: Pacific Northwest National Laboratory. Accessed August 24, 2013, www.usgbc.org/Docs/Archive/General/Docs1915.pdf.

Grabska, Ewa, Andrzej Lachwa, and Grazyna Slusarczyk. 2012. "New Visual Languages Supporting Design of Multi-storey Buildings." *Advanced Engineering Informatics* 26(4): 681–690.

Gruber, Thomas. 1995. "Toward Principles for the Design of Ontologies Used for Knowledge Sharing." *International Journal of Human-Computer Studies* 43(5–6): 907–928.

Hillier, Bill, and Julienne Hanson. 1984. *The Social Logic of Space*. Cambridge, Mass.: Cambridge University Press.

Huang, Yi Chun. 2011. "An Integrated Scalable Lighting Simulation Tool." PhD dissertation, Carnegie Mellon University.

Lee, J., and M. P. Kwan. 2005. "A Combinatorial Data Model for Representing Topological Relations Among 3d Geographical Features in Micro-Spatial Environments." *International Journal of Geographical Information Science* 19(10): 1039–1056.

Liggett, Robin. 2000. "Automated Facilities Layout: Past, Present and Future." *Automation in Construction* 9(4): 197–215.

March, Lionel, and Philip Steadman. 1974. *The Geometry of Environment: An Introduction to Spatial Organization in Design*. Cambridge, MA: MIT Press.

Mazairac, Wiet, and Jakob Beetz. 2012. "Towards a Framework for a Domain Specific Open Query Language for Building Information Models." Paper presented at the International Workshop Intelligent Computing in Engineering, Herrsching, Germany, July 4–6.

Nisbet, Nicholas, and E. William East. "BimServices: Supporting COBIE2 with IFC." www.nibs.org/?page=bsa_ifccobie#bimservices. Accessed August 22, 2013.

Rittel, Horst W. J. 1987. "The Reasoning of Designers." Paper presented at the International Congress on Planning and Design Theory (August) Boston, MA.

Smith, Dana K., and Alan Edgar. 2008. "Building Information Modeling (BIM)." Last modified July 24, 2008, www.wbdg.org/bim/bim.php.

Stouffs, Rudi, and Ramesh Krishnamurti. 2001. "On the Road to Standardization." *Computer Aided Architectural Design Futures 2001*. Dordrecht, The Netherlands: Kluwer Academic, pp. 75–88.

Taneja S., B. Akinci, J. H. Garrett, L. Soibelman, and B. East B. 2011. "Transforming Ifc-Based Building Layout Information into a Geometric Topology Network for Indoor Navigation Assistance." *Congress on Computing in Civil Engineering Proceedings*, pp. 315–322.

Wetherill, M., Y. Rezgui, S. Boddy, and G. S. Cooper. 2007. "Intra- and Interorganizational Knowledge Services to Promote Informed Sustainability Practices," *Journal of Computing in Civil Engineering* 21(2): 78–89.

CHAPTER 18

BIM as a Catalyst to Foster Creativity through Collaboration

Murali Paranandi, Miami University

18.1 INTRODUCTION

The quest for intelligent digital design tools for building proposals over the last five decades has resulted in the current crop of building information modeling (BIM) tools. The greatest potential of BIM lies in enabling a collaborative process coordinated by a 3D model throughout the building lifecycle. BIM's application in the profession is currently limited to the late phases of design and engineering or early phases of construction, even though its use earlier in the design process will have the greater impact not only on costs, but also on innovation and design quality (Eastman et al. 2008). The knowledge explosion and the increase in the complexity of problems that need to be solved to design a contemporary high-performance building make collaborative decision making necessary. Herein lies the potential of BIM to facilitate an environment for the exchange of information between various human and computational agents and thereby enable a collaborative design process in preschematic stages.

More than ever before, university faculty and students are exploring concepts important to the profession through innovative interdisciplinary collaborative research and teaching practices. The case studies included here illustrate their use in schools and are also applicable to professionals.

This chapter begins with a discussion of the role of collaboration for design innovation and how BIM facilitates human computer collaboration. It then describes the importance of the role of people in the BIM process and outlines strategies to set up a social framework that will enable their ability to collaborate and innovate. Further, it presents how BIM-enabled workflows enhance collective decision making and creativity. It concludes by giving some feedback to academia and the profession on what they can learn from each other.

18.2 THE ROLE OF COLLABORATION IN DESIGN

Most of the significant problems we face today are systemic problems that exceed any individual's specialty knowledge or capacity for problem solving. To cope with these problems requires not only "Renaissance scholars," but "Renaissance communities" in which stakeholders coming from different disciplines can collaborate (Fischer 2013). For example, OMA and Morphosis practice design as a collective activity where the solutions emerge out of interactions among multiple stakeholders starting from the preschematic stage of design. Pritzker Prize–winning architect and design director for Morphosis Tom Mayne describes his approach as a complete opposite of Ayn Rand's notion of the heroic architect who enters the room with a genius idea in his head and lays it out to show to others. By contrast, Mayne enters the room with absolutely no preconception; he needs the interactivity, discussion, and pushback provided by group activity to develop the creative act (Mayne 2008).

This recognition of teamwork in creating buildings extends beyond the design team to those involved in their construction. Although not widely adopted, perhaps because of extensive contract obligations, integrated project delivery (IPD), often assisted by BIM, is a change from the traditional client-architect-contractor hierarchy and offers a collaborative approach for the building industry.

Despite this great promise, BIM tools have yet to mature to be able to fluidly support early stages of design. Most representations cannot be uniformly applied in the conceptual, intermediate, and final stages of building design. A mix of BIM and non-BIM tools (including sketching, physical modeling, and 3D CAD sketching) during conceptual stages will remain necessary at least in the foreseeable future. Workflows and people issues are more important for innovation than any single technology. Yet there is little discussion directed toward harnessing BIM's potential to set up a cooperative environment for humans and computers to collaborate for creative problem solving. Beyond using BIM as a communication technology, there should be more investigation of the role of context and personal interactions to foster creativity in collaborative approaches to design (Achten and Beetz 2009).

18.3 SOCIAL FRAMEWORK

One of the prerequisites for nurturing successful collaboration is facilitating a social environment that cultivates empathy toward others' points of view, encourages experimentation, and rewards risk-taking. The inclusion of digital tools as cooperative agents elevates the human creative potential to solve extremely complex problems that are not solvable by computers or humans alone. Work processes should be based not only on what machines can accomplish, but also what humans can accomplish (Sanker 2012). It is necessary to create an environment for successful collaboration, as well as successful technology implementation (Homayouni, Neff, and Dossick 2010).

BIM = (10% tech) + (90% sociology)

Charles Hardy (Deutsch 2011)

Towards this end, it is important to understand the human side, to define and manage roles, and to facilitate a social process though co-location.

18.3.1 The Human Side

A straightforward, transparent, and collaborative process demands a high level of trust among team members. Input from owners, engineers, and tradespeople with knowledge of the project's life cycle context provides a basis to establish a shared goal and define strategic priorities and constraints. All participants should be encouraged to initiate, criticize, and exchange ideas freely regardless of their expertise or status in the organizational hierarchy. When groups evaluate solutions, instead of talking in the abstract, they should explain how something works or does not work relative to goals and constraints. This eliminates uncertainty in the collective decision-making process. An organic process evolves out of divergent and convergent thinking. In the divergent state people contribute many points of view and strategies that help increase understanding of the problem space and help set up a stage for facilitating a discussion to arrive at a common goal. It is important to note that this is facilitated through compromise and not always by consensus (Kvan 2000). The convergent state seeks specificity to refine or answer the questions generated.

Professional and academic settings have overlapping ways of working with this, but one can start by defining and managing the roles of the participants. In the following case study, students were asked to design and build a temporary modular screen system with recycled cardboard to create an acoustic barrier between the stairwell and the critique space in an atrium (Figure 18.1). Thirty-four sophomore architecture and interior design students collaboratively designed and built it over a three-week period. Students were divided into smaller jigsaw groups of experts. A common 3D model built in form•Z early in the design process representing common goals of the project was used as a reference by each of the teams for their own purposes. Since it was a 3D model-based process, the updates were made immediately, so the groups could continue to work concurrently and complete the project ahead of schedule. The dialogue among the students, for example, resulted in eliminating the horizontal ribs saving considerable time, labor, and resources and creating a more elegant form.

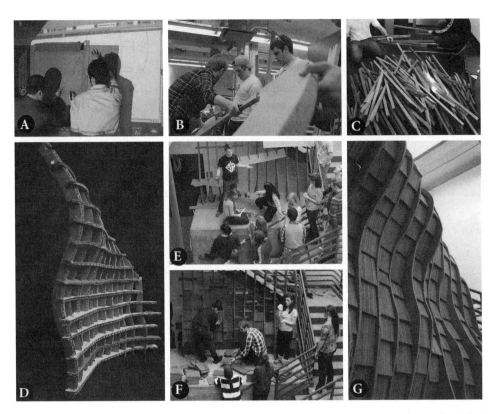

FIGURE 18.1   Collaboration on a studio project (spring 2013). (A) generating templates for fabrication; (B) making components using templates in the shop; (C) recycling waste of construction process to build acoustic tiles; (D) laser-cut scale model made by a separate group; (E, F) assembly group showing their discovery of how acoustic tiles can replace the horizontal ribs to hold the structure in place.

18.3.2 Define and Manage Roles

Managers of the design team should define tasks and assign roles for people by giving them both authority and accountability for completing them. These tasks will have interdependencies and will need appropriate workflows to assemble the results. To accomplish this, it is important to have open communication through regular meetings to provide feedback and quality control and to motivate all involved by spotting any concerns and addressing them immediately.

18.3.2.1 Academic Context

The academic setting is nonhierarchical, with all students starting as equals with no preassigned roles. Once common goals are established, design tasks can be divided and assigned to smaller groups of students to resolve. These groups should be given the authority to research, develop, and share a set of solutions with others. In addition, they are held accountable for successful execution of these tasks in the project implementation. This reciprocal teaching technique is similar to the strategy of putting together a jigsaw puzzle; thus it is called the jigsaw approach (Wang 2007). The division of tasks should align with students' individual media literacy skills, strengths, and areas of interest. It is also important to involve other faculty and experts on campus as consultants or stakeholders by creating course overlaps. Research shows that when participants "work on separate parts of the problem, negotiating occasionally by asking advice from each other" they achieve the most productive results (Maher et al. 1998). Creativity expert Sir Ken Robison once said, "The real role of leadership in education . . . is not, and should not be, 'command and control;' the real role of leadership is 'climate control'" (Robinson 2013).

18.3.2.2 Professional Context

In a traditional design-bid-build model, owners hire architects first, and contractors enter the process once the design is finalized. In the IPD process all stakeholders are involved right from the beginning, which requires a lot of attention and effort upfront. Everyone must bring a collaborative approach to the process and be willing to sign on to common goals. People with the most expertise and experience should take a leadership role in their specific area. The compensation structure should be set up to recognize the value they add to the process. It is the team, the "who" in IPD determines the "how." The "how" can range from big picture decisions to the smaller details (AIACC 2008). Unlike in an academic studio setting, responsibility for completing tasks and balancing interdependencies is easier to manage because risks and rewards are tied to the compensation model.

18.3.3 Co-locating to Facilitate Dialog

Using BIM for information exchange works only for the exchange of explicit knowledge, but not necessarily for tacit knowledge or the reasoning process. Bringing the project team under one roof to facilitate an informal exchange of ideas not only eliminates ambiguity and conflicts but builds common ground and develops more creative solutions. In academic settings, co-location and nearness to other students is usually not an issue. The students are in the same studio space working together day and night. Being together works well for both nondigital and digital collaboration such as building a physical site model or sharing files by passing around memory sticks (Figure 18.2).

In contrast, in a professional setting, team members' roles and leadership correspond to their areas of expertise and experience. Inclusion of experts and specific roles are decided project by project. Typically these experts are geographically separated. Professional settings have mechanisms such as the "Big Room" to facilitate such face-to-face interactions. When fully co-locating entire teams in one place is not possible, it can be accomplished by video conferencing.

This activity should lead to the co-creation of a model that reflects the refined collective understanding. This social process motivates team behavior and ultimately increases the effectiveness of the BIM process (Lamb, Reed, and Khanzode 2009; Neff 2011).

More discussion is needed about harnessing BIM's potential to set up a cooperative environment for humans and computers to collaborate for creative problem solving. Workflows to transfer the essence of the lessons learned through human interactions into a BIM representation need to be explored.

FIGURE 18.2   Design as social activity: students engaged in dialog to figure out what works to meet common goals.

18.4 COMPUTATIONAL WORKFLOWS

Although not a prerequisite for collaborative design, digital tools certainly enhance the process due to their facility for the exchange of (digital) information. Not all designers possess the same digital media skills. No software system can support all construction techniques, materials, and building practices. At least in the near future, a BIM framework will need to also include non-BIM tools (such as form•Z and SketchUp) and analog techniques such as sketches and chipboard models should afford stakeholders a range of media skills for collaboration.

BIM content creation tools are generally too complex to be used for sketching and form generation. Paper and pencil remain dominant tools for such work (Eastman et al. 2008, pp. 166–167), but recording textual and quantitative information is not possible in sketches. However, these visual models can be transferred into a BIM model along with this information tagged. This common model can serve as a reference for various participants in the process to develop parallel lines of thoughts even if they are incompatible for a period of time. Judging when to drop them or resolve the conflicts between them is considered one of the key aspects of creative design, which is well supported by BIM tools (Lawson 2006, pp. 297–298).

BIM representation facilitates developing, sharing, and dialoging multiple parallel models by many separate participants on a scale that has not been possible before. BIM offers valuable tools for collaboration in designing, collaborative prototyping, crowd sourcing, and knowledge capture and sharing in the cloud.

18.4.1 Tools for Designing and Collaborating

The BIM process is rooted in 3D digital modeling that describes and manages the information and relationships between various building components and trades. Emerging analog interfaces to digital (e.g., tablets) and digital interfaces to analog (e.g., 3D printers) allow the stakeholders, regardless of their drawing or visualization abilities, to be linked to this model and dialog in real time. The computer can become a cooperative partner by providing more insights by algorithmically solving well-constrained problems at speeds and scales beyond what is humanly possible. Examples include providing objective input by performing such well-defined tasks as wind, solar, structural simulation, and so on. It could also provide subjective input by generating highly complex design solutions resolving specified constraints via scripting.

In the professional environment, there is a range of tools that facilitate collaboration extending from BIM servers for team collaboration, file sharing online, and video conferencing, to tablet interfaces for design review and presentation (BIM Forum 2011). These require dedicated BIM managers, information technology (IT) staff, and budgets to support automation and smooth operations. In the academic context, achieving this level of automation is neither possible nor always necessary.

18.4.2 Collaborative Prototyping

The creative process is a continuous dialog between positing and testing to exercise critical judgment. Prototypes speed up the process of innovation because it is only when designers put their ideas out into the world that they really start to understand their strengths and weaknesses. The faster that is done, the faster ideas can evolve (Brown 2009). Analog and digital prototypes can be derived from 3D models. Choosing

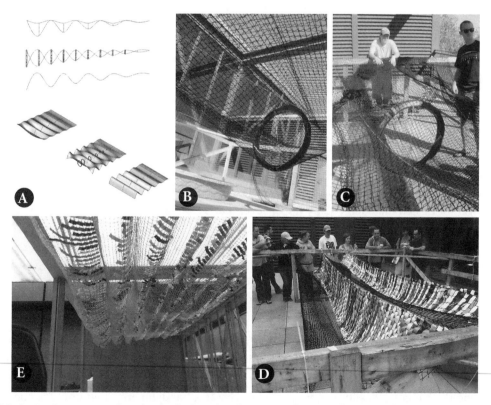

FIGURE 18.3 **During NetPostive shade design development phase (Fall 2012). This group of students used collaborative prototyping to optimize the shape and technique of fabricating the net. (A) Low-fidelity prototypes: Rhino 3D and Grasshopper scripting generated surfaces; (B, C, D) High-fidelity prototypes: full-scale models to study net's structural behavior and to decide how to shape the net and hold the woven banner strips in place; (E) Scale model to study spatial implications.**

the right fidelity (level of detail, scale, and time investment) for the project's current needs is essential to the success of the project and the value of the prototype. Low-fidelity prototypes (anything that is easily and rapidly created such as sketches, chipboard models, and low-resolution digital models) let designers delve more deeply with lower costs. High-fidelity prototypes are slower to create but are useful to understand details. The information learned from each of these prototype studies feeds back into the 3D model.

18.4.3 Crowdsourcing

Crowdsourcing is an overarching term that denotes a number of ways to use the Web as a means to enlist a large number of individuals to perform a particular task (Gerth, Burnap, and Papalambros 2012). Crowdsourcing fits well within the BIM collaborative framework by dividing tasks and involving a large number of people from simply providing an opinion or contributing material to solving a problem. For example, architects could use crowdsourcing at the very earliest stages of design to determine what the community might want included on a public project. The AEC industry currently exploits this potential for content creation (e.g., Google Warehouse) through open-source apps, for outsourcing well-defined tasks (e.g., documentation, fabrication), and post-occupancy evaluation of building performance. In the near future, the wisdom of crowds can be used to tackle the big data created by BIM and convert it into information and knowledge. Further, this will lead to computational tools and processes that harness the cognitive capacity of nonexperts to innovate for creative problem solving. For example, Wiki-house (www.wikihouse.cc) is an open source construction set that allows anyone to design, download, and "print" CNC-milled houses that can be assembled with minimal formal skill or training. Sketch Chair (www.sketchchair.cc) is an open-source software tool that allows anyone to easily design and build a digitally fabricated piece of furniture.

An example of such exploration is NetPositive shade (Figures 18.3 and 18.4). With the aim to minimize solar heat gain and glare on the adjoining freshmen studio spaces, a temporary lightweight shade made with up-cycled used banners and hockey nets was installed on the southern deck. The principal collaboration for design included twenty upper-level undergraduate students, university policy makers, administrators, and experts, including two professional architects, one structural engineer, four physical facilities crew members, and ten faculty members. A 3D model built in Revit provided a reference for the extensive studies that were undertaken to develop a shade surface that not just effectively blocks the sun, but works with wind and snow loads. Additionally, physical prototype studies were conducted to determine crowd-sourced material assemblies, and fabrication strategies that take advantage of human skill to weave. Information from the lessons learned in these studies was tagged to the respective components of a 3D model built in Revit. Subsequently, this 3D model was queried to determine the quantities of unique strips and their location on the net, which was passed on to Excel. This helped manage the procurement of adequate quantities of used banners to cover the required surface area to shade, cutting and grouping the banner strips into appropriate lengths, team assignments, and tracking completion of tasks. The installation was executed in 16 hours with the cooperative participation of 132 freshmen and sophomores, each contributing 2–4 hours of their time based their interest and availability. The emergent outcome of this collaboration represents an overall process gain by achieving much more than any

FIGURE 18.4 Distinct groups working on distinct but interconnected tasks during NetPositive installation. (A) Weaving on a scaffold specifically designed to achieve parametrically generated form; (B) cutting and sorting strips to specific lengths; (C) sorting precut strips into bags; (D & E) groups of upper level students supervise first- and second-year students.

individual could within the allotted time. Upper-level students working with younger students created peer-to-peer learning opportunities. The resulting color and patterns of the banner strips weaves gave the shade a beautiful organic quality.

18.4.4 Knowledge Capture and Sharing in the Cloud

All firms typically reuse existing designs or strategies that work. Unfortunately, these are often proprietary. However, it is important to share knowledge gained in BIM/IPD processes when possible. Digital representations make this process a natural extension without much additional work. Reflections about student design processes and lessons learned from successes and productive failures are important tools for capturing the knowledge gain. These can be collected, organized, and disseminated online

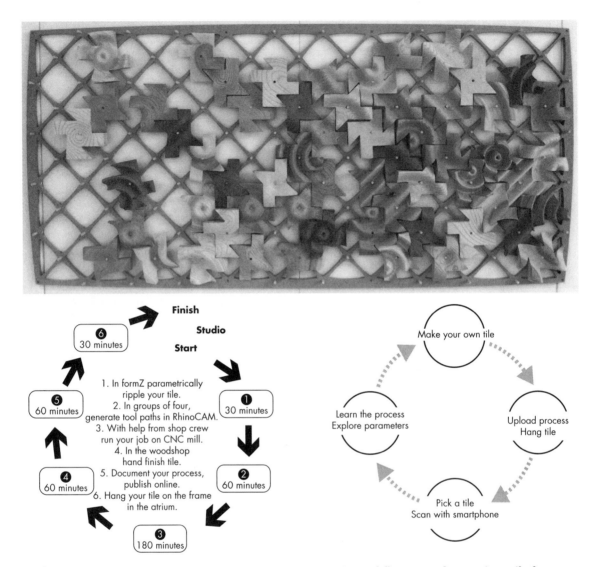

FIGURE 18.5 Ripples sculpture, spring 2011 (top); parametric workflow to make a unique tile from a given 2D shape (bottom left); how knowledge about the manufacturing process is accessed by subsequent students with smart phones (bottom right).

and embedded in the built artifacts as a record of the decision making process. This information can be useful to guide the future operations or modifications to buildings. Another advantage is that the collected data on actual performance can be meshed with the predicted information used by the BIM model developed for design and construction, leading to the acquisition of evidence-based knowledge that can shape future practices.

Figure 18.5 shows a collaborative parametric process to generate a wall sculpture by over seventy students in second-year studio. This was organized as a joint project between studio, graphics, and the department shop. Each student generated a unique tile following a defined 3D model-based parametric workflow and then documented the parameters used and lessons learned in the process. A QR code etched on the back of the tile makes this data accessible to anyone with a smart phone. Some students' individual choice of drill bits and the tool path option to skip one or more passes created interesting and unpredictable striations. This inspired others to experiment and achieve organic qualities that were not originally foreseen. Curious passersby were encouraged to interact with the pieces and shift the tiles around like puzzle pieces. These tiles became shareable artifacts that facilitated knowledge exchange and social interaction, bringing about an emergent process that Fisher (2001) refers to as "social creativity."

18.5 CONCLUSION

There are important lessons that both academia and the profession can learn from each other's practices about the value BIM adds to facilitate collaboration for innovation.

18.5.1 Feedback to Academia

The NCARB 2013 report identifies greater collaboration and improved communication skills, as well as hands-on experiences for increased undertaking of construction materials and assembly as the key priorities for architectural education (Nutt 2013). This indicates that the traditional notion of the individual author of buildings is outmoded and can no longer be a pedagogical goal in accredited schools of architecture. Moreover, it means that graduates of accredited programs will enter the profession with very different expectations about what the work of a firm can and should be. The design studio is an opportunity not only to teach architecture students skills and practical knowledge but also to expose them to cutting-edge professional attitudes and values (Austerlitz and Sachs 2006). This is particularly true in the early years of design education.

The projects illustrated confirm that the BIM process can and should be introduced as a strategy for collaborative design at the foundational stages of design education as part of the general education, not just as an elective course or as a professional practice or "comprehensive" studio. Technology and professional knowledge ages quickly, and students should be exposed to the dynamics of collaborative design early.

18.5.2 Feedback to the Profession

Although the building professions already generally employ BIM in the document automation and construction phases of design, more often than not, BIM is seen as a technology for greater productivity and efficiency (by eliminating waste from construction practices), rather than as a revolutionary approach to design and construction. The greatest potential of BIM is its ability to facilitate collaborative processes through a coordinated 3D model during schematic and even preschematic design where innovative practices can have the greatest impact on the project outcomes. As in the academy, the profession should not keep its best practices and lessons learned as proprietary knowledge, but should openly share them for the greater good and the solution of our most difficult problems.

ACKNOWLEDGMENTS

I would like to acknowledge and thank my faculty colleagues, shop crew, university physical facilities staff, and especially all the students involved for their contribution to the projects illustrated in this chapter.

DISCUSSION QUESTIONS

1. What are some of the advantages of using non-BIM tools such as form•Z, Rhino, and SketchUp for conceptual design? Assess their benefits and shortcomings and how you can develop a workflow to take advantage them in a collaborative BIM process.
2. What are the advantages of co-location in a collaborative design process? How can it be accomplished?
3. How does prototyping during conceptual design help innovation? What are some of the ways in which prototypes help overcome the shortcomings of BIM tools?
4. What is crowdsourcing, and how can architects structure BIM processes to take advantage of it?
5. How are conceptual design processes different in IPD compared to conventional Design-Bid-Build?

REFERENCES

Achten H. H. and J. Beetz 2009. "What Happened to Collaborative Design? In G. Cagdas and C. Gulen (eds.), *Computation: The New Realm of Architectural Design*, pp. 357–365.

AIACC 2008. "Experiences in Collaboration: On the Path to IPD." Available at American Institute of Architects, www.aia.org/aiaucmp/groups/aia/documents/pdf/aiab079766.pdf. Accessed August 28, 2013.

American Institute of Architects, California Council. 2008. "Experiences in Collaboration: On the Path to IPD," retrieved August 28, 2013, from American Institute of Architects: www.aia.org/aiaucmp/groups/aia/documents/pdf/aiab079766.pdf. Accessed August 28, 2013.

Austerlitz, N. and A. Sachs 2006. "Community Collaboration and Communication in the Design Studio." *Open House International* 31(3).

BIM Forum. 2011. "BIM Tools Matrix," Available at BIM Forum: http://bimforum.org/wp-content/uploads/2011/02/BIM_Tools_Matrix.pdf (accessed August 23, 2013).

Brown, T. 2009. *Change by Design*. New York: HarperCollins.

Deutsch R. 2011. *BIM and Integrated Design*. Hoboken, NJ: John Wiley & Sons.

Eastman Chuck, Paul Teicholz, Rafael Sacks, and Kathleen Liston. 2008. *BIM Handbook*. Hoboken, NJ: John Wiley & Sons.

Fischer, G. 2013. "From Renaissance Scholars to Renaissance Communities: Learning and Education in the 21st Century." International Conference on Collaboration Technologies and Systems, pp. 13–21. San Diego: IEEE.

Gerth, R, A. Burnap, and P. Y. Papalambros. 2012. "Crowdsourcing: A Primer and its Implications for Systems Engineering." *Proceedings of the 2012 Ground Vehicle Systems Engineering and Technology Symposium*, NDIA.

Homayouni, H., G. Neff, and C. Dossick. 2010. "Theoretical Categories of Successful Collaboration and BIM Implementation within the AEC Industry." Construction Research Congress pp. 778–788. Banff, Canada.

Kvan, T. 2000. "Collaborative Design: What Is It?" *Automation in Construction* 9(4): 409–415.

Lamb, E, D. Reed, and A. Khanzode. 2009. "Transcending the BIM Hype: How to Make Sense and Dollars from Building Information Modeling" Available at AECbytes, www.aecbytes.com/viewpoint/2009/issue_48.html, accessed August 28, 2013.

Lawson, B. 2006. *How Designers Think*. Oxford: Architectural Press.

Maher, M. L., A. Cicognani, S. J. Simoff. 1998. "An Experimental Study of Computer Mediated Collaborative Design." *International Journal of Design Computing* 1. Available at http://Pandora.Nla.Gov.Au/Nph -Wb/19990704130000/, http://www.arch.usyd.edu.au/kcdc/journal/vol1/papers/maher/index.html. Accessed August 28, 2013.

Mayne, T. 2008. Thom Mayne Speaks About Collaborative Practice Architecture. (FamousArchitect, interviewer) YouTube (http://youtu.be/yOPJ3aYPw2o).

Neff, D. 2011. "Messy Talk and Clean Technology: Communication, Problem-Solving and Collaboration Using BIM." *Engineering Project Organization Journal* 1(2): 83–93.

Nutt, S. 2013. Education Report. Available at NCARB: www.ncarb.org/en/News-and-Events/News/2013/03-PAedu .aspx (accessed August 30, 2013).

Robinson, K. 2013. "TED Talks Education." Available at PBS.org: www.pbs.org/wnet/ted-talks-education/speaker/ ken-robinson/ (accessed August 30, 2013).

Sanker, S. 2012. "The Rise of Human-Computer Cooperation." Available at TED: www.ted.com/talks/shyam_sankar_ the_rise_of_human_computer_cooperation.html (accessed August 9, 2013).

Wang, L. 2007. "Sociocultural Learning Theories and Information Literacy Teaching Activities in Higher Education." *Reference & User Services Quarterly* 47(2): 149–158.

CHAPTER 19

BIM and Virtual Reconstruction: A Long-Term View of (Re-)Modeling

Bob Martens, TU Vienna
Herbert Peter, Academy of Fine Arts Vienna

19.1 EXECUTIVE SUMMARY

Virtual reconstruction work on destroyed synagogues has been pursued for over fifteen years. The fact that these sacred buildings no longer exist is a pivotal aspect in this undertaking. Within this relatively long time, the recurring use of a building information model (BIM) required the implementation of conventions for story/layer structures to ensure long-term transparency and comprehensibility of the data model structures, even when the original members of the research team are no longer available for an information exchange. These structural conventions have turned out to be helpful for the researchers working with the data and with a view to long-term usability. In the long run, a transparent BIM structure is therefore indispensable. Frequent software updates make data migration an eternally topical issue.

This chapter focuses on the constraints of this exploration and discusses the options of handling BIM models beyond the life cycle of the original building itself, also with a view to continuing changes in the software environments used. The novel contribution of this work lies in its longevity and future usability of BIM data records that reaches beyond the specifics of the topic area of virtual reconstruction of synagogues.

19.2 INTRODUCTION

For more than fifteen years, the virtual reconstruction of synagogues has been dealt with as a research topic. At first, destroyed sacral buildings in the city of Vienna (Austria) were digitally reconstructed (Martens and Peter 2012). More recently the oeuvre of Viennese architects in neighboring countries (Czech Republic, Slovakia, and Hungary) served as the basis for reconstruction. The "New Synagogue" in Brno (Czech Republic), built by Max Fleischer, will serve as the central visual theme in this chapter (Wolf 2012).

The focus is on sacral buildings that were built around 1900 (i.e., more than 100 years ago). Although historical records are usually available in the form of designs submitted for building permits, implementation records are often missing since the planning firms involved have usually ceased to exist. Reference buildings offer a useful option for filling information gaps, as do historical photographs. The appropriate handling of information gaps is a vital aspect in this reconstruction effort (Grellert 2007).

When buildings that no longer exist in reality are virtually reconstructed, the question arises as to how accurate the reconstruction is, given that it is based on fragmented data. After all, the existing information includes a good number of uncertainties and gaps (Affleck and Kvan 2005, Tan and Rahaman 2009). Any reconstruction work is based on well-researched archived material, the quality of which

FIGURE 19.1 The "New Synagogue" in Brno (Max Fleischer, 1905–06). Preserved historical photographs, dilapidation, and representation within the city fabric. Notably, the location displays the critical issue of orientation toward the east.

is a determining factor for the validity of virtual reconstruction. It must be noted that the majority of reconstructions in this project involve synagogues that were erected in the late nineteenth century. It is quite surprising that, despite some information gaps, a wealth of plan material has been preserved in the archives. When archived material has been lost, the three-dimensional representation has to work within stricter limits, and the process is dominated by speculation, based for instance on comparable reference buildings. A great abundance of various section views and other images of the building structure will notably increase the realistic nature of the reconstruction (Figure 19.1). This is also the case whenever photographic material of interiors exists.

The reconstruction work itself can be compared to a virtual building site. The detailed 3D models were reconstructed through the use of historical plan data and photographs. Of high importance, however, was the logic of the model systematics and embedded objects that allow for future preoccupation and maintenance (Martens and Stellingwerff 2005). Furthermore, the extended period of archival storage is to be regarded as a key challenge, and issues of data exchange and software interfaces resolved. BIM was at the core of this.

19.3 BIM AND VIRTUAL RECONSTRUCTION

There were many potential barriers and drawbacks in the context of modeling issues. Of particular concern were the limited choice of software and the inherent differences of modeling a building digitally

FIGURE 19.2 Example of multiple uses: building elements taken (as library parts) from comparable synagogue models.

versus constructing a real building. These considerations had an impact on the project of reconstructing a large number of synagogues.

Dealing with the growing number of models (currently 30, expected to grow to approximately 100 in the future) and a far larger number of model versions corresponding with a certain software release number called for a clear decision.

The first issue that comes to mind is the quasi-monopoly situation of individual software packages. CAD software manufacturers would like to cement lasting user commitment to an individual product, and users often prefer to stay within one company's suite of software. Data exchanges are also often linked to a certain degree of information loss. Interoperability efforts (e.g., Industry Foundation Class, or IFC) have mitigated this phenomenon to a certain extent. Some software developers lure users by integrating well-loved functions from competitor packages in their own CAD environments, thus making it easier to switch products.

The 3D modeling is to be considered as the point of departure and the options for downstream interoperability as a safety net. IFC thus serves as a vendor-neutral archiving format. The long update cycles are an added advantage in this process.

There was an articulated preference for the ArchiCAD software environment based on the local experience and expertise. On top of this, the issue of object-oriented modeling procedures was considered crucial. The parametrized building elements (the "library parts") may be used not only for the ongoing modeling but also in subsequent reconstruction projects. ArchiCAD looks back on more than thirty years of continuous development. Other BIM software applications currently available on the market have only been around for ten years.

Although to date a separate 3D model was set up for every location, the potential of reusing certain model parts and elements across the whole collection of models will require further attention (Figure 19.2).

The processes involved in virtual reconstruction are fundamentally different from traditional construction processes.

There is only a very limited common use of the BIM model by different groups of professions, and the change management approach works differently; adaptations are only made when new insights/information become available (Figures 19.3A–D). In that case referenced objects will, for instance, be adapted or replaced as the case may be.

In the course of reconstructive modeling, there is a particularly high demand for exactitude of details that is focused exclusively on three-dimensional representation and is not limited to a mere aggregation of 2D representations. This approach suggests itself, since the result of a reconstruction is largely known in its entirety already at the start of a reconstruction project.

One may wonder to what extent this activity actually constitutes BIM. The BIM product is more than just "enriched geometry" (Figure 19.4). The added value of BIM is to keep the sets of information as completely as possible. For example the material properties embedded in ArchiCAD should not be lost after any form of data conversion.

It is the structured development of the BIM that makes this possible especially for model extension and post-editing, since the information gap decreases over time as more and more research results

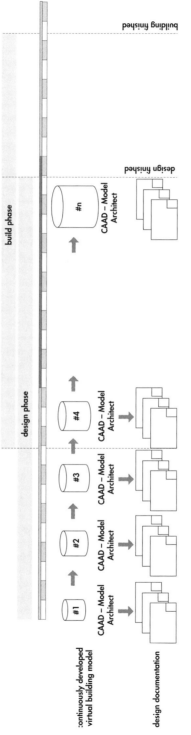

FIGURE 19.3A Traditional process diagram I: Architect's standard timeline throughout the building design phase.

255

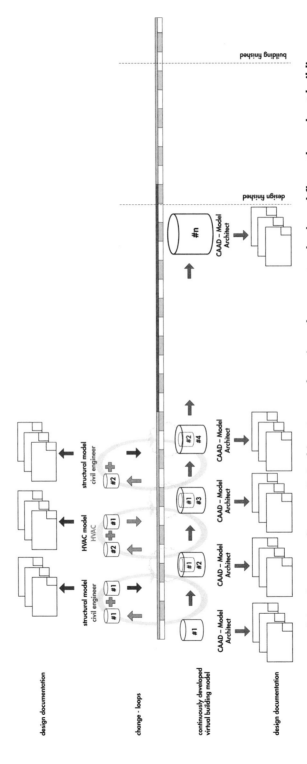

FIGURE 19.3B   Traditional process diagram II: Architect's consultant-interchange—standard workflows throughout building design phase.

256

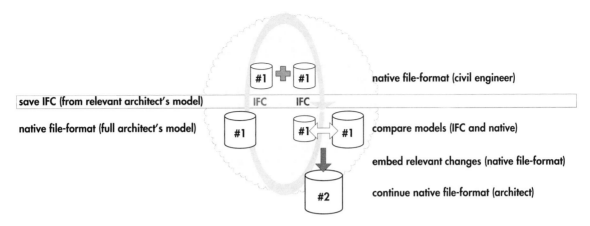

FIGURE 19.3C   Traditional process diagram III: Architect's interchange, critical spot—how to merge building models.

become available. With the growing number of 3D models, the available information base is continually enlarged. In case of "information gaps," access to this growing information base and the new insights it provides may supply useful solutions.

19.4 INFORMATION BASIS: MODEL TREE STRUCTURES

If a 3D model is used only once by a single person for a limited time, what counts is the (visual) result to be obtained in the short term. It is not important whether the structural setup of such a model can be analyzed or understood by third parties. In contrast, this project has already spanned fifteen years, is expected to go longer, and includes researchers who may never meet each other. The framework conditions necessitate the development of standards for the formation of these models that is adhered to by all participants (Martens and Peter 2002a, b). Although BIM is to be "self-explanatory" as a data structure, the projects require compliance with the story and layer structure conventions (comparable to an office standard):

- *Definition of a story structure.* Every building element within a virtual reconstruction needs to be assigned to a story, a level within the building (Figure 19.5). The reconstruction/model can include as many stories as desired and does not have to be identical with the story structure of the original plan documents. Intermediate stories might also be useful; for or example, if a great number of ornaments or ceiling elements are situated above a "one-meter-section." Particularly when several individuals are involved in the project work, the story structure helps figuring out correct positioning of building parts within three-dimensional space.

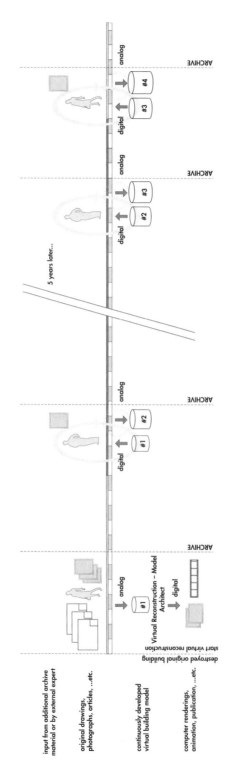

FIGURE 19.3D Virtual process diagram: Workflow and file management through the years.

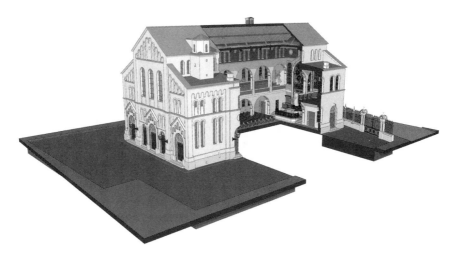

FIGURE 19.4   3D model with a high level of detail: revealed interior space.

First, the original story structure of the building to be reconstructed is entered in the CAD model. Historical plans will, however, often be restricted to "ground floor," "upper floor/gallery," and, perhaps, "attic." This will often be insufficient for the modeling because of the top view approach, which makes it difficult to distinguish between superimposed building elements. This is particularly true of indoor spaces with a wealth of ornamentation, which requires the introduction of additional ArchiCAD stories. The synagogues with a layout similar to three-nave basilicas may serve as a case in point (Figure 19.6). In this case, the projecting central part will be defined as a separate (intermediate) story.

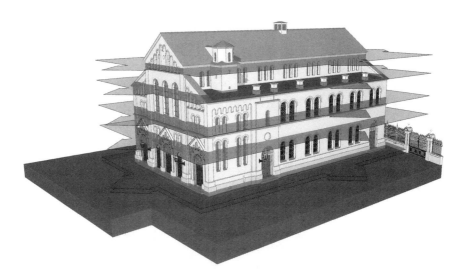

FIGURE 19.5   Story management using the example of the former New Synagogue in Brno (Czech Republic).

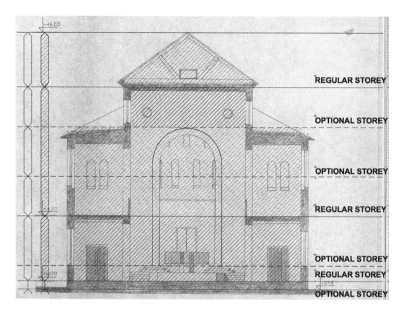

FIGURE 19.6   Story management using the example of a basilica structure.

- *Determining a layer structure*: Next, the number of layers to be associated with the matching building parts needs to be specified (Figure 19.7). The selection of criteria for the allocation of building elements is based on constructional aspects. Building elements of one layer may fall below or exceed the imaginary horizontal boundaries of the story management. On top of this, the naming of a certain layer must be comprehensible.

Possible variants in the building structure, such as annexes or refurbishments, can be added to the ArchiCAD model as so-called layer combinations, which can be made visible or invisible as required (Figure 19.8).

These structural conventions have turned out to be helpful for the operators working with the model data and with a view to long-term usability. It is quite remarkable that a CAD file first created

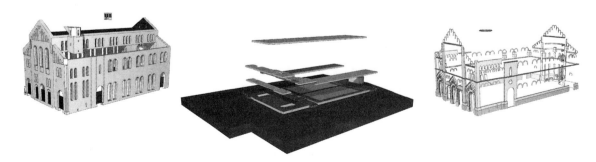

FIGURE 19.7   Sample layer documentation: exterior walls, floors, ornaments.

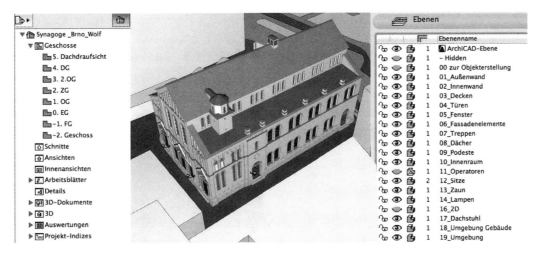

FIGURE 19.8   ArchiCAD model structure with displayed stories and layers.

in the previous millennium can still be read and processed almost in its entirety today. In the long run, a transparent modeling structure is therefore indispensable. Although the process may look trivial, it is time consuming and does not generate immediate benefits. However, in the long term, it has proven to harbor advantages, and it makes sense to archive earlier model versions (including earlier software releases) so that stepping back to earlier states is feasible.

Implemented conventions concerning story and layers into an ArchiCAD model can be made visible in other software applications with the help of the IFC and/or IFCXML data exchange formats.

A few further conventions are required, such as concerning the file name. It is useful to not only specify the ArchiCAD version used, but also the respective date and the synagogue ID. Every building is assigned a unique three-letter ID, which is also used in any relevant file names. This makes it possible to find relevant documents about a certain building very quickly.

The backup conventions are not different from those used for other digital documents, and it is recommended to use several media. The principle is not to delete older model versions but to archive them.

19.5 MODEL PORTING AND DATA EXCHANGE

At the beginning of the very first virtual reconstruction, the ArchiCAD software package had already reached a stable development status. Even so, justifications existed for the need for portability and potential benefits by subjecting "Methuselah files" to an upgrade.

The project period is not limited and immediate and future use over an extended period is a given, even if in the case of individual synagogue models it may take a long time until the existing models are adapted. The requirement of porting to successor software releases should be considered as a safeguard for the research effort undertaken in the past and will ensure data accessibility as such. In the information technology world, changes are omnipresent. One just has to look at developments in the area of storage media in the past twenty years. Rising storage needs led to floppy disks being replaced by Syquest HD cartridges or magnetic-optical media. These became obsolete as soon as the so-called Iomega ZIP-drives were introduced. CDs and DVDs are still in use today, but USB sticks (flash-memory) and external hard disks allow for convenient mobility of far greater data volumes. Archiving digital files is cumbersome and involves many challenges: backup hardware as previously explained, file formats incompatible across different versions of the software, software and operating system incompatibilities, even cabling issues between a computer and peripheral. Model porting and data exchange protocols help alleviate some of the software issues.

19.5.1 Model Porting

In the current stage of the project, in which the first models were created with ArchiCAD release 5.0, all porting steps (i.e., toward subsequent software releases) have been preserved. In practical terms, this means that a new software release was published every twelve to fifiteen months. In some cases the extent of changes to the software was significant. A case in point was the upgrade from v9 to v10, where every GDL (Geometric Description Language) object was assigned a "unique ID," and the object name was no longer used for identification purposes. This meant that some existing GDL objects could no longer be clearly identified. This problem did not affect any modeling that started at a later time, and today the concept of "migration libraries" takes care of this issue.

Even if earlier versions of hardware and software were to be maintained in a growing pool of equipment, this would not only involve a considerable effort but one would also have to expect the support for previous OS versions to be discontinued after a certain time. The license policies might also be amended so that the data formats created under different types of licenses (for example, student versus professional versions) might no longer be compatible. The above notwithstanding, a stable and reliable modeling environment has been available in past decades.

19.5.2 Data Exchange

The main producers of CAD software packages have agreed to use a freely available interoperability format IFC (Industry Foundation Classes), which makes the shared use of building data easier. These developments were instigated by the vendor-independent and nonprofit buildingSMART consortium, which was established in 1994 (formerly known as the International Alliance for Interoperability, or IAI). The certification process ensures that the IFC files generated are of high data quality. IFC is an (open) data exchange format, which does not involve modeling. Existing 3D models are then converted to IFC. Consequently, translation into a different file format disposes of another strategic instrument with a view to long-term archiving.

The IFC-upgrades are scheduled in intervals of every three to five years for major releases, which means data do not have to be exported annually. The vendor-independent platform supports a continuation of virtual reconstruction in different software and hardware environments and thus avoids dead-ends in a project. Despite the benefits of IFC, certain loss of information and change of data still has to be reckoned with (partial loss of material properties, surface colors, etc.).

Before the advent of BIM, "VRML" and "3DS" were the formats of choice. As a "worst-case scenario," "3D DWG" could be used as a storage format purely for geometry data. In all three options, however, the useful story structures and any parametrized "library parts" were lost. They also had a considerable influence on data size. The alternative to story management is to create additional layers, which leads to a rather unmanageable proliferation of layers. For a three-story building this would mean a triplication: "exterior_walls" versus floor01_exterior_walls, floor02_exterior_walls, floor03_exterior_walls, and so on.

The full "intelligence" of the ArchiCAD model cannot be entirely preserved, although it is possible to safeguard the geometry and large parts of the connected semantic information. Even though BIM is based on comprehensive and detailed modeling, this does not mean that all information is automatically embedded in the ArchiCAD file.

For the complex visual representation, the data structure needs to be imported in a render environment, and further processing steps cannot always be transferred back to the "native" ArchiCAD model. It is possible, for instance, to embed information about materials in ArchiCAD beforehand and take it along from there.

In its native ArchiCAD format, the reconstruction model of the Brno synagogue has a file size of about 97 MB. Once the data are exported to an IFC model the size swells up to approximately 256 MB. The increase is mainly due to the fact that each object is stored under a "unique ID." This also applies to absolutely identical objects with different parameters. This is a case where the referenced native GDL macro feature within ArchiCAD models could be used to full benefit in terms of small file size. Given current computer performance levels and the fact that they are subject to continuous improvements, the larger data volumes should not, however, present major problems.

19.6 OUTLOOK: WHERE DO WE GO FROM HERE?

It is unlikely that destroyed synagogues will be rebuilt in the foreseeable future. Apart from the fact that other structures have been erected on these sites, there is not currently the required volume of users. These facts speak in favor of virtual reconstruction.

Advanced parameterization could play an important role in this context. Particularly in synagogue buildings that were designed and built by the same architect at the same time, which do not greatly differ from each other, this approach can support reconstruction with a large degree of authenticity despite a lack of documentation.

In both the profession and long-term research projects future usability of data records needs to be considered. It could also include the establishment of an object repository, harvesting across the models, where recurring and similar building elements can be "reused" beyond the scope of a single 3D model. This predominantly concerns doors, windows, benches, railings, ornaments, and capitals, as well as light fittings.

It was intended that the models be constructed so that there would be a potential of reusing parts and elements across the entire collection of models. Although to date a completely separate 3D model was set up for every building, future planning was instituted for the joint and subsequent use of models and their collection of constituting elements. Nonetheless it is becoming a challenge to locate certain elements in this multitude of models. Some research in the area of automated recognition has, however, been performed already.

19.7 CONCLUSION

This chapter has described the conditions for implementing BIM in the area of virtual reconstruction, focusing specifically on the growing number of 3D models of destroyed synagogues. The research project has been ongoing for a number of years, and the composition of the research team has been subject to change. For this reason, it was necessary to use story and layer conventions. The 3D model may be viewed as a kind of "database environment," where the information can be collected in a structured manner. A typical query might run as follows: "Generate a 3D intersection from the database."

The modeling tools have significantly improved over the past 15 years, leading to fewer workarounds being required in the modeling process to implement complex geometries, which truly makes work a great deal easier.

The modeling conventions developed (to provide a clearly understandable data structure) ensure that the data models can be interpreted correctly and in the way they were conceived over a long period of time, even if they were worked on by temporary users (e.g., students in the context of their diploma thesis).

Although the investment in a CAAD software package always includes a certain financial risk (in terms of insularity), the vendor-neutral and long-lived IFC data format can ensure long-term usability of the data. Moreover, the long IFC update cycles (longer than 12–15 months) provide an additional safeguard for the invested time and money and the information produced.

The above demonstrates that the use of BIM is a necessity given the long project duration in order to ensure accessibility and usability of the data created.

DISCUSSION QUESTIONS

1. Digital projects can sometimes be accomplished alone, but often require a team over a span of time. What does the synagogue reconstruction project suggest about collaboration on building projects in an architecture office?
2. What issues does a researcher have to consider when archiving digital data?

REFERENCES

Affleck, J., and T. Kvan. 2005. "Reinterpreting Virtual Heritage." *CAADRIA 2005 Conference Proceedings*. New Delhi (India), vol. 1, 169–178.

Grellert, M. 2007. *Immaterielle Zeugnisse. Synagogen in Deutschland* [Intangible products. Synagogues in Germany]. Bielefeld: Transcript Verlag.

Martens, B., and H. Peter. 2002a. "Virtual Reconstruction of Synagogues: Systematic Maintenance of Modeling Data," *eCAADe 2002 Conference Proceedings*, Warsaw (Poland), 512–517.

———. 2002b. "Developing Systematics Regarding Virtual Reconstruction of Synagogues." *ACADIA 2002 Conference Proceedings*, Pomona, CA, 349–356.

———. 2012. *The Destroyed Synagogues of Vienna: Virtual City Walks*. Vienna: LIT Verlag.

Martens, B., and M. Stellingwerff. 2005. "Creating Physical Models Using Virtual Reconstructions: Mixed CAM-techniques for a Viennese Synagogue Scale-model," *SiGraDi 2005 Conference Proceedings*, Lima (Peru), 108–113.

Tan, B.-K., and H. Rahaman. 2009. "Virtual Heritage: Reality and Criticism," *CAADFutures Conference Proceedings*, Montreal (Canada), pp. 143–156.

Wolf, K. 2012. "Virtuelle Rekonstruktion der Neuen Synagoge in Brünn" [Virtual Reconstruction of the New Synagogue in Brno]. Vienna University of Technology, Masters thesis.

PART 5

PROFESSIONAL BIM

Managing BIM Projects, Organizations, and Policies: Turning Aspirations into Quantitative Measures of Success

Calvin Kam, Founder, bimSCORE & Director of Industry Programs, Center for Integrated Facility Engineering, Stanford University

20.1 INTRODUCTION

Achieving a positive return on investment in digital practice requires the mastering and integration of management sciences. Adopting technology with the wide range of stakeholders and processes that support the planning, design, construction, and operation of the built environment requires holistic and thoughtful decision making in order to justify business investments, identify potential risks, and ensure measurable improvements in project and business performance. Practitioners and management executives often rely on subjective or anecdotal bases to claim their knowledge, accomplishment, or experiences with building information modeling (BIM) and virtual design and construction (VDC). Most lack an objective and systematic method of evaluating their performance, not answering some of the following important questions when optimizing business decision making, processes, and technologies to support the life cycle of the built environment:

- Is there a way to evaluate the maturity and state of practice of a BIM-enabled project, enterprise, market economy, or country? How can one objectively determine the success or failure of BIM integration at each maturity level?

269

- Is BIM success distributed evenly throughout an organization's teams and projects? If not, where is the best success demonstrated to inform enterprise-wide best practice, and where are the areas requiring attention for improvement?
- Are BIM projects staying on track and improving? If not, what are the areas for concern?
- What metrics can help project managers and clients predict project outcomes? Are there early warning signs of when specific success factors are in jeopardy?
- What are some leading or lagging performance indicators of BIM return on investment (ROI)?
- How complete is a project's BIM Execution Plan (BEP)? Where are the gaps? How can one track the effectiveness of project standards and compliance of guidelines throughout the project?
- What can be learned from VDC implementation in other countries? Which countries enjoy a highly sophisticated ecosystem of BIM-enabled organizations?
- Where are BIM skills perceived as an innovative differentiator, and where will they be entry-level requirements?

If the building industry is to unlock the potential of BIM, it must apply objective, repeatable, and reliable metrics and learn how to extend successful approaches across project portfolios. The methodologies must include reliable evaluation and quantitative measures of performance to help organizations optimize the business decision making, processes, and technologies that are used to support the life cycle of the built environment.

20.2 SCORECARD METHODOLOGY

Scorecard evaluations have become standard methodologies in management sciences to assess performance and identify opportunities for improvement in an objective and quantitative manner. They attempt to decompose management practice and strategy into key measures and core elements of practice. Across industries assessment frameworks like the balanced scorecard or key performance indicators (KPI) have been used to target and track key measures of performance and identify areas where executive intervention is required.

BIM management is not unlike management in other industries and can be broken down into key practices and areas of evaluation. Concepts like the balanced scorecard and KPI can be adopted and applied to BIM implementation, helping organizations to translate their vision to objectives, track their performance, and develop actionable initiatives for improvement. One set of evaluation and performance indicator methods are outlined in this chapter and have been used to evaluate BIM management maturity and performance and align performance with expectations. With the use of these types of metrics, it is predicted that the adoption of BIM can become more predictable, quantifiable, and standardized across projects and an entire enterprise.

bimSCORE evaluations utilize the virtual design and construction (VDC) Scorecard framework and methodology developed by the author at Stanford University's Center for Integrated Facility

Engineering (CIFE) (Kam 2013). Drawing from existing precedents and their own research, CIFE researchers developed a percentile-based scoring system that would be inherently quantifiable and immediately meaningful to architecture/engineering/construction (AEC) professionals. Score percentiles range from Conventional Practice (0%–25%) up to Best Practice (75%–90%) and Innovative Practice (90%–100%), informing the project team how they are performing in relation with the rest of the industry.

The inputs for the scorecard are collected from all project stakeholders with all BIM experience levels via interviews, email, web-survey, and review of project documentation such as the BIM Execution Plan. For example, a high-confidence-level evaluation (79%) involved team members from the architect, general contractor, subcontractors, and client, with over 10 person-hours of interviews, participation in project meetings, and the collection of data for over 50 scorecard measures, which then applied the scorecard weighting to generate ten divisional scores, four area scores, and finally one overall score.

The VDC Scorecard has been proven by over 130 cases across thirteen countries, including evaluations performed as part of bimSCORE professional services and case study or statistical evaluations performed by Stanford CIFE researchers. The knowledge base of evaluations has been used to validate and inform the evaluation measures while demonstrating the scalability and repeatability of the scorecard framework and the value of a global knowledge base of BIM and VDC maturity to benchmark project performance.

The scoring results of these projects are analyzed using statistical approaches in order to establish correlations between practice and outcome as well as to benchmark the current VDC performance in the industry (Figure 20.1). For example, from correlation analyses the number of established BIM objectives (performance goals for adopting BIM) and the percent of stakeholders (architect, GC, owner, subcontractors, engineers, etc.) with documented BIM responsibilities are two of the measures with the highest correlation to the overall score (high performance on these two measures likely means the project is within the range of *Advanced Practice* or above). Further information about the formulation, research, and findings of the VDC Scorecard is available through VDCscorecard.stanford.edu.

FIGURE 20.1 **Distribution of scores by tiers of practice in knowledge base of over 100 unique project evaluations.**

With the scorecard methodology presented here, organizations, project teams, and individuals can objectively and quantitatively benchmark the maturity of their BIM implementations to proven best practices exhibited not only within their organization but throughout industry. Teams and managers can easily identify opportunities for improvement and select the right balance of performance improvements to meet project targets. It is neither necessary nor recommended to push every team to achieve the highest levels of innovative practice in every area. Instead, the goal should be to ensure that current practices are meeting the expectations defined by the organization, whether those expectations are to employ technology in an innovative or typical manner.

20.3 PROJECT EVALUATION

Project evaluations assess current BIM/VDC implementations, benchmark to industry practice, and identify opportunities for improvement in light of project and enterprise-wide objectives. The method supports an executive overview and overall score, allowing executives and project managers to quickly identify areas with opportunity for improvement.

Results are further detailed with four primary areas of evaluation. Example measures in each of the four scorecard areas are given, with possible inputs ordered in ascending scoring value:

1. **Planning**: Addressing objectives, standards, and preparation to meet goals

    Example measure: How have BIM or VDC objectives been formalized among project stakeholders?

    Single stakeholder belief, shared belief among stakeholders, documented by a single stakeholder, documented and shared with multiple stakeholders, documented, shared, and contractually agreed to by multiple stakeholders

2. **Adoption**: The organization and process used in following the plan

    Example measure: During which project phases were model-based analyses applied?

    Predesign, schematic design, design development, construction documentation, construction, close-out, operations, and maintenance

3. **Technology**: The maturity, coverage, and integration of tools used to accomplish projects

    Example measure: What categories of model-use were applied?

    a. Visualization (e.g., 3D renderings, walk-throughs, 4D animation)

    b. Documentation (e.g., quantity takeoff, drawings, 3D laser scan)

    c. Model-based analyses (e.g., energy, thermal comfort, structural analysis)

    d. Integrated analyses (e.g., multidisciplinary coordination, integrated cost and schedule tradeoff)

    e. Automation and optimization (e.g., off-site prefabrication, automated model checking)

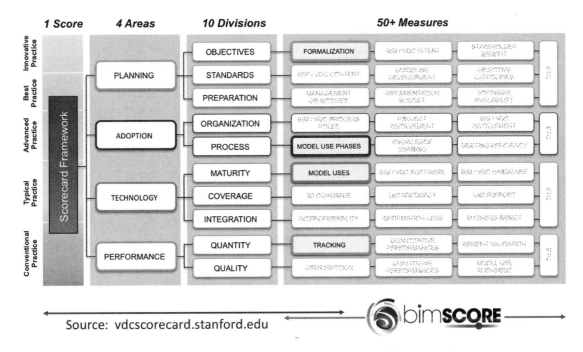

FIGURE 20.2 VDC Scorecard Framework showing example measure (highlighted).

4. **Performance**: The quantitative and qualitative measures of success for outcomes

Example measure: In general, how often are BIM and VDC objectives tracked and/or formally assessed?

Not tracked, once at end of project, yearly, quarterly, monthly, bi-weekly, continuously

Example measures are highlighted in the context of the overall VDC Scorecard Framework consisting of four areas, ten divisions, and 50+ measures (Figure 20.2). Each measure receives a score based on the input selected, and all measure scores within a division are combined via weighted average to produce a division score. These division scores are then combined again via weighted average to produce area scores, which are aggregated again via weighted average to produce an overall score. The exact measures, inputs, scoring, and weights for various measures, divisions, and areas are detailed in the VDC Scorecard research available through VDCscorecard.edu.

Together, the 50+ measures contribute to a detailed score, and more importantly lead to general advice and specific action items for raising practices to higher industry standards of practice. The evaluation results and advice are clearly presented in a dashboard view supporting views at various levels of detail (Figures 20.3 and 20.4).

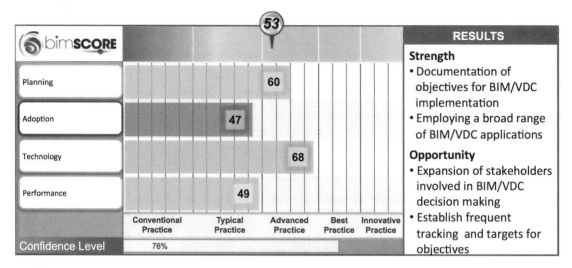

FIGURE 20.3 Dashboard view showing overall score and scores in each area.

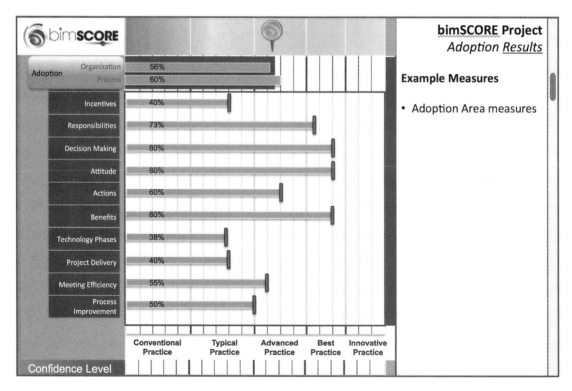

FIGURE 20.4 Detailed view showing scores for individual measures in the Adoption Area.

20.4 CONTINUOUS EVALUATION

Much like healthcare, where a patient undergoes diagnosis, treatment, and post-operation monitoring, evaluation should follow a staged process that is initiated early in the project to identify opportunities for improvement. Advice is provided to correct deficiencies and continuous evaluations are performed to ensure performance is maintained.

Targeting during early design or predesign phases facilitates establishing realistic objectives and targets for BIM and VDC implementation for a project and could be used by owners for the prequalification of contractors and designers to help ensure the necessary level of proficiency and skill sets to achieve expectations for performance outcomes, thus eliminating or filling gaps in an efficient manner. An initial evaluation performed during early design may indicate that established objectives, standards, model uses, and coordination procedures are typical of industry leading practices.

As the project progresses through later design, construction, and operations, evaluations are repeated periodically to track project performance over time, bearing witness to improvements and warning when projects veer off track (Figure 20.5). Express and in-depth evaluations may reveal that the team is not tracking or assessing objectives, or leveraging all of the planned model uses to their full potential. Perhaps the project BIM Execution Plan (BEP) is not being followed, resulting in poor coordination procedures or model progression. These pitfalls typical of BIM and VDC implementation would be reflected in frequent project evaluations, directing the attention of managers, executives, and ground level users to areas of concern. Evaluations can even be performed on a weekly basis, through evaluating weekly coordination procedures or meetings, resulting in actionable advice that can be implemented in a short period.

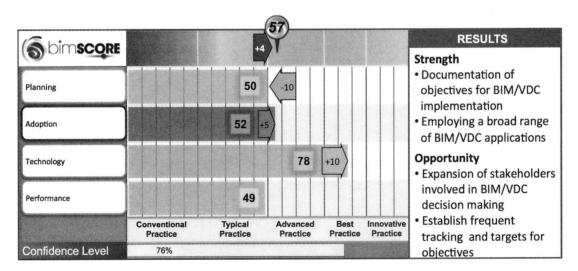

FIGURE 20.5 Dashboard view illustrating how a project score can fluctuate between periodic evaluations.

20.5 PERFORMANCE INDICATORS

To supplement the standard scorecard measures used for industry benchmarking, this application has a menu of performance indicators that focus on success factors of particular interest to owners and other stakeholders. A performance indicator is composed of several metrics, each with an established target and tracking frequency. These metrics combine to provide an overall score computed in comparison with targets to provide an executive-level indicator of performance for critical factors or processes. Performance indicators allow executives and managers to better predict project outcomes, provide early warning when specific success factors are in jeopardy, and formally track performance data for use in establishing targets for future projects.

They are useful in tracking a wide array of vital project success factors associated with BIM and VDC implementation. For example, the adoption of BIM enables model quantity-based scheduling and production rate tracking, as well as more integrated and efficient off-site prefabrication. In adopting these processes and BIM-based prefabrication, a project management team would be interested in tracking the relative difference in cost and production rate between on-site and off-site construction for similar components or the differences in recordable incident rates for on-site and off-site labor. A set of performance indicator metrics can be used to track the benefit of BIM-enabled modularization and

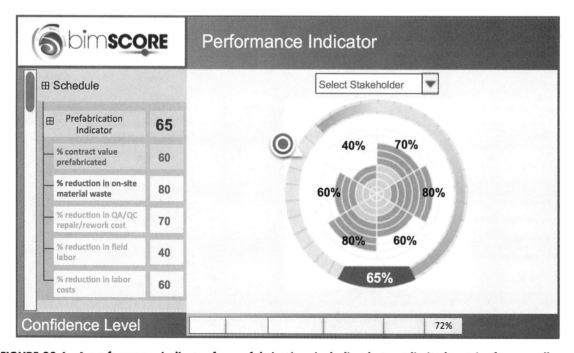

FIGURE 20.6   A performance indicator for prefabrication, including but not limited metrics for overall percentage of contract prefabricated, reduction in on-site waste, reduction in defects, reduction in field labor, and reduction in labor costs.

prefabrication, providing insights into the cost and duration per prefabricated component, reduction in recordable incidents, reduction in defects or punch list items, or reduction in material waste as compared to on-site operations. A specific prefabrication performance indicator would then provide the team with executive-level insights into their overall prefabrication efforts, informing them where best to expand their prefabrication scope, where to deploy additional resources, or where their process can be further optimized (Figure 20.6). Such quantitative tracking and continuous monitoring of performance is often associated with best practice and innovative practice in these evaluations.

20.6 PORTFOLIO EVALUATION

The enterprise-wide dashboard views of BIM performance are of great value to organizations that own and manage project portfolios or those that have the responsibility to design and/or construct large project portfolios across different markets or regions. Best practice knowledge and resulting BIM success is often unevenly distributed within an organization. Knowledge developed "in house" can be especially hard won, often entailing large resource investments to develop practices suited to organizations, project types, and market areas.

For instance, one facility owner had deployed the scoring technique to evaluate several project types discovered commonalities and disconnects between project types and geographic regions (Figure 20.7). The identified disparities were addressed through enterprise-wide action initiated at the corporate level to benefit all future projects. Specific interventions to address commonalities included changes to request for proposal (RFP) language and formalization of a knowledge capture and sharing system; this benefited team members throughout the fabric of the organization.

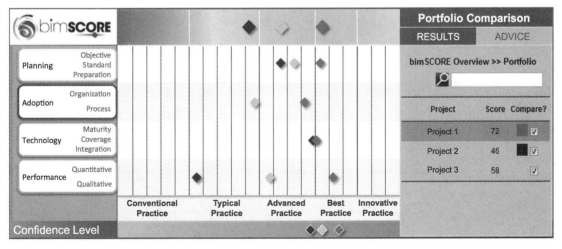

FIGURE 20.7   Using the dashboard view to compare project evaluations by overall score and area score across a particular region, a portfolio, or an entire market.

20.7 COUNTRY-LEVEL BIM EVALUATIONS

International comparisons shed light on the sophistication of BIM implementation and challenges encountered by those regulating or purchasing BIM-enabled services. A comparison of several countries also helps to define the capability development, research and development, procurement, and project delivery of those providing services (Figure 20.8).

In the country-level dashboard view, Singapore clearly leads other nations in planning, largely because its architectural BIM e-submissions program is one of the strongest BIM mandates in the world. It has with well-stated objectives, nationally developed standards and facilitation, and extensive funding to ensure proper preparation and training of the industry. Compliance with the e-submissions roadmap is required in 2013 for all new projects larger than 20,000 square meters, with stronger requirements in 2014 to include engineering BIM and in 2015 to require architectural BIM for all projects larger than 5,000 square meters (BCA 2012).

The United States leads in adoption, with 71 percent of surveyed firms reporting BIM use in 2012 (McGraw-Hill 2012) owing in part to the emergence of new contract models (including such financial performance incentives as shared risks and rewards based on project success factors). These contract models include integrated project delivery (IPD) and integrated forms of agreement (IFOA) in the private sector, progressive national BIM programs led by the public sector such as the General Services Administration (GSA), combined with organizational efforts of the American Institute of Architects (AIA), American Institute of Steel Construction (AISC), and Associated General Contractors of America (AGC), among others. Using such measures of adoption, including BIM involvement and proficiency of project stakeholders, quality of BIM-supported interactions between stakeholders, and presence of appropriate incentives, the United States ranks in the range of innovative practice.

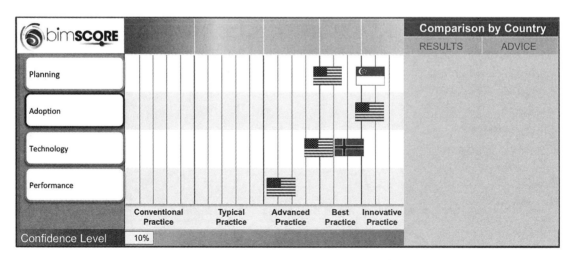

FIGURE 20.8   Using the bimSCORE framework to compare and evaluate countries in their maturity and adoption of BIM and BIM standards.

Technology deployment in the several Nordic countries such as Norway and Finland shows general attainment of best practice status, with BIM used broadly throughout project teams to leverage a wide range and depth of BIM capabilities, from visualization to extremely sophisticated automation and optimization. These countries are strongly supported by national research and development programs that lead initiatives to adopt open standards. They produce sophisticated and powerful applications such as BIM checkers, BIM servers, and program requirement management. Integration of BIM use and data exchange between disciplines is very highly rated in several northern European examples where attention to interoperability and open standards is especially high, resulting in smooth information sharing and quantifiable advantages in time savings, accuracy, and design optimization.

Performance is based on the frequent tracking and assessment of quantitative performance data against numerical targets and of qualitative objectives against established expectations. Even in the United States, most companies lack objectives defined in measurable terms and need to increase the frequency and fidelity of performance measurement to rise to the level of best practice. Organizations that commission and deliver projects often state qualitative goals, such as "deliver BIM as a facility management aid," without articulating quantitative measures of success, such as "lowering average maintenance work order duration by 30 percent." The collection and dissemination of quantitative metrics in the US through organizations like CIFE and *Engineering News-Record* (*ENR*) stand in contrast to markets that rely on notional or subjective assessments of the impact of BIM, which makes the validation of success problematic. For example, an *ENR* article summarizing metrics reported at a CIFE event cited that the adoption BIM and VDC has resulted in 30 percent reduction in cost, 60 percent reduction in overall design duration, and 62 percent reduction in change orders (Kunz and Luth 2012). Even in the United States, however, systematized and rigorous performance measurements based on leading indicators (such as design optimization cycles), rather than lagging indicators (such as number of clashes identified) are rarely seen.

20.8 CONCLUSION

As BIM has passed from the bleeding edge to becoming a qualification prerequisite in many construction markets, the ability to predict and demonstrate performance and justify investments with numerical evaluation of returns is becoming an essential capability for participants in the building industry. Without a systematic method of evaluation, it can be difficult to effectively navigate technology adoption decisions and validate the benefits of adoption, making practitioners susceptible to short-sighted technology investments and advancements.

The building industry should be working towards optimization of the built environment through continuous improvements in business decision making, processes, and technologies. By quantifying BIM and VDC performance assessments and providing actionable advice for improvements, the VDC Scorecard research at Stanford-CIFE and one of its industry implementations through bimSCORE help individual firms, projects, and researchers objectively manage their BIM investments, reducing uncertainty, and focusing human and financial resources on critical tasks. The methodologies must include reliable evaluation and quantitative measures of performance to help organizations optimize the business decision making, processes, and technologies that are used to support the life cycle of the built environment to drive BIM/VDC efficiency across projects, ecosystems, and enterprises.

ACKNOWLEDGMENTS

The author would like to acknowledge the contributions of Martin Fischer, Tony Rinella, Justin Oldfield, Devini Senaratna, and Yan-Ping Wang.

DISCUSSION QUESTIONS

1. What are performance objectives for adopting BIM and supporting processes? What are the criteria for evaluation?
2. How can the performance of and satisfaction with BIM implementation be measured? What are the key categories of evaluation and measures of success?
3. What leading indicators can help project managers and clients predict project outcomes? Are there early warning signs of when specific success factors are in jeopardy?
4. What are some leading or lagging indicators of BIM return on investment (ROI)?

REFERENCES

Building and Construction Authority (BCA). 2012. "Technology Adoption: Building Information Model (BIM) Fund (enhanced)." www.bca.gov.sg/BIM/bimfund.html.

Kam et al. 2013. "The VDC Scorecard," Center for Integrated Facility Engineering (CIFE), Stanford University, http://vdcscorecard.stanford.edu.

Kunz, John, and Greg Luth. 2012. "Wake Up! The Revolution Has Arrived: A Report from CIFE." 2012. *Engineering News Record* (ENR), http://enr.construction.com.

McGraw-Hill SmartMarket Report. 2012. "The Business Value of Building Information Modeling (BIM) in North America: Multi-Year Trend Analysis and User Ratings (2007–2012)." Bedford, MA: McGraw-Hill Construction.

CHAPTER 21

Space: The First (and Final) Frontier of BIM

Stephen R Hagan FAIA, President and CEO, Hagan Technologies LLC

21.1 INTRODUCTION

The premise of this chapter is that spatial BIM has great promise and utility. Spatial BIM simplifies and narrows the focus of what building information modeling (BIM) can potentially do for clients and owners. Yet space as a specific concept in building information modeling technologies remains undeveloped and has had relatively few adopters (Eastman et al. 2008, p. 35). Onuma and Trelligence discussed herein are two. Space is

- Universally considered a core of all projects
- Applicable to upfront strategic planning, facility programming all the way through to construction completion and commissioning, facility management and operations, and portfolio oversight and coordination
- Lightweight in terms of graphical representation
- Able to be embedded or linked to many dimensions of data/information—the "I" in BIM
- Easily generative and dynamic for programming architectural space within projects or programs of projects, by way of algorithms, to visualize scenarios and rapidly develop alternatives

Planning, design, procurement, construction, commissioning, fit-out, occupancy, alterations, and finally demolition and removal of buildings and facilities is an extremely complex process. Inherent in that process is an extraordinary amount of data created, compiled, stored, reused, oft-repeated and inefficiently and ineffectively transmitted stored and processed. Spatial BIM can impose order and provide an anchor spanning across the life cycle of a project and extending from the scale from global to building component.

21.2 HISTORICAL PERSPECTIVES OF SPACE AND THE FACILITY LIFE CYCLE

Space—the entity that is created by architectural components (walls, floor, ceiling, windows, etc.)—is both something experienced (height, length, volume, compression) and something programmed, designed, and constructed. BIM enables both. The "I" in BIM also enables the calculation of architectural space, the categorization of it by occupancy, by space type, by any number of parameters including a "container" of all the contents within the space and all the components that create the space.

Space as a concept didn't enter architectural discourse at all until the nineteenth century; it was really developed as a modern construct. It was first understood and conceived in the context of architecture, according to Sigfried Giedion, with the development of perspective during the Renaissance (Giedion, 1967). Space as a concept for BIM discourse didn't reach its stride and importance until the twenty-first century. Although others (e.g., Onuma) have demonstrated its importance and incorporated it into their work and technologies, it was the U.S. federal government that brought it to full focus. As Yale's Peggy Deamer has noted:

> Modern architects saw space as a polemical, potent shaper of the user. Today, we take space and the programs that shape it for granted, but it does not diminish its essential role in architecture. Indeed, as our government agencies regulating building documentation have witnessed, space is at the core of their concern, and BIM's role in it and in facilities' life cycle is foremost in their programs.[1]

21.3 SPACE, MEASUREMENT, AND BIM

For owners of buildings, space has always been critical and the measurement of that space is a critical to an organization's mission and function (Hensey and Thatcher 2009). Susan M. Hensey FAIA of Little Associates has noted that the standard for measurement of buildings has continued to evolve:

> Space is nothing without definition. BOMA created its first Floor Area Measurement Standard in 1915. IFMA created its first Area Measurement Standard in 1995 and it also continues to evolve. The taxonomy for BOMA and IFMA area definitions were hashed out (almost literally) several years ago through the hard work of a few determined industry leaders to assure Usable

---

[1] Personal communication with the author (email), August 15, 2013.

did not mean two different things! This group's urgency to clarify space definitions was driven by the advent of BIM and the desire to have appropriate measurements available for the BIM users' apples-to-apples analysis.[2]

BIM has the capability of carrying many more attributes and measurements of space and be *computational*. Also, the complexity and continued evolving nature of space measurement standards, along with other standards development that relate to space relate to BIM utility, further reinforces the need for a computational and digital rather than manual and analog (two-dimensional paper-based) approach to space measurement.

21.4 BIM SPATIAL PIONEERS: COAST GUARD AND GSA

The U.S. Coast Guard in 2001 and the U.S. General Services Administration (GSA) in 2003 both conceived BIM as a foundational technology and included spatial BIM as a core strategy. They emphasized how important upstream planning is at the earliest stages of a project.

The U.S. Coast Guard BIM implementation (i.e., "BIM for scenario planning and facility assessment") was thoroughly presented as case study (Eastman et al. 2008, pp. 339–357), where there is a detailed description of goals, methods, and what was accomplished. By making spatial BIM its core technology and then adding data elements to further describe each space, the Coast Guard team was able to create three indices of the agency's portfolio of facilities: Facility Condition Index (FCI), Mission Dependency Index (MDI), and Space Utilization Index (SUI). The Coast Guard's strategy of utilizing space is best illustrated by Figure 21.1. This graphic shows how each space throughout the Coast Guard's nationwide portfolio of facilities was designated with two key attributes (condition and mission criticality) and color-coded (red, yellow, or green). Since the spatial BIM was both a visual and a graphic depiction of space in each building, as well as a database, the spaces that were in bad condition (red) and mission critical (red) could be quickly and easily sorted to the top of priorities. That put the power of information in spatial BIM in the hands of Coast Guard leadership. It is one of the first examples where upper management was able to visualize and recognize the power of BIM in general and spatial BIM in particular for organization prioritization and strategic planning.

Spatial BIM became the first core requirement of GSA's 3D/4D BIM Program starting in 2003 (Yee 2010). Real estate space is at the core mission of GSA, the "nation's landlord," with a portfolio of 330 million GSF (gross square feet) of federal buildings, courthouses, and other building types. At the time, GSA also had an extensive capital construction program. There are over 200 projects in the active pipeline of project delivery and design and construction projects valued at over $12 billion. Ensuring that the space being delivered by capital projects conformed to the originally justified and approved program was critical for two reasons: continued trust and faith by Congress in GSA's ability to deliver what it promised and controlling the scope (i.e., space) and therefore cost of construction being delivered.

---

[2]Personal communication (email) between the author and Susan Hensey, August 8, 2013.

Mission Dependency (MDI)
Linking Facilities to Missions

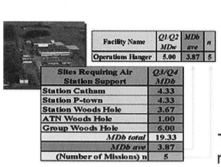

Facility Name	Q1-Q2 MDw	MDb ave	n
Operations Hanger	5.00	3.87	5

Sites Requiring Air Station Support	Q3/Q4 MDb
Station Catham	4.33
Station P-town	4.33
Station Woods Hole	3.67
ATN Woods Hole	1.00
Group Woods Hole	6.00
MDb total	19.33
MDb ave	3.87
(Number of Missions) n	5

Created by Naval Facilities Engineering Service
Center, Port Hueneme CA and co-developed
with the USCG

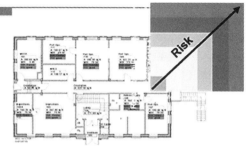

This critical Facility Assessment links facilities to mission from an Operational Risk Management perspective.

MDw	Q1: Interruptability			
	Immediate (24/7)	Hours (min/hrs)	Days (<7days)	Weeks (>7days)
Impossible	4.0	3.6	3.2	2.8
Extremely Difficult	3.4	3.0	2.6	2.2
Difficult	2.8	2.4	2.0	1.6
Possible	2.2	1.8	1.4	1.0

MISSION INTRA-DEPENDENCY SCORE

Q2: Relocatability

MD_W = Mission Dependency Within a Command Entity

FIGURE 21.1   Mission dependency illustrated using spatial BIM (courtesy Onuma).

In a 2003 internal memorandum from the Public Buildings Service (PBS) commissioner, written in response to serious cost overruns on several projects, GSA had the bold foresight to postulate that BIM could be a tool to address the problem (GSA 2006, Yoders 2010). However, in 2003 the BIM industry and underlying technologies were nascent at best. GSA chose to dramatically simplify the requirement for BIM for architects, engineers, and contractors to three conditions:

1. Meet minimum requirement for spatial program BIM. All major projects that receive design funding in financial year 2007 and beyond are required to submit a spatial program BIM prior to final concept presentation for the Public Buildings Service Commissioner approval.

2. Utilize any one of the preapproved BIM authoring tools. The software vendors had participated in developing an interoperable standard for concept level spatial BIM submission to have their BIM authoring tools eligible for this.

3. Understand building information model checking software by developing expertise of how model checking tools such as Solibri can rapidly find missing information and elements and deliver a complete and accurate BIM.

FIGURE 21.2 Initial kick-off meeting of GSA 3D/4D BIM.
(courtesy S. Hagan and GSA BIM Program)

The vast size and breadth of the GSA's portfolio necessitated answering the fundamental question of how to scale BIM to a very large number of complete and ongoing projects. The hallmark of GSA's path-breaking approach (GSA 2007) was to start simply, increase requirements incrementally, and harness the best technologists and minds of the industry by means of government/industry collaboration.

The first technology collaboration meetings began in 2003 (Figure 21.2) and continued for ten years. BIM guides for various processes were developed out of the collaboration over the next decade, but spatial BIM was the first and only mandatory requirement.

A hallmark of the GSA initiative was its focus on interoperability from the outset. The meetings between GSA and technology vendors stressed that GSA wanted to provide the opportunity for multiple

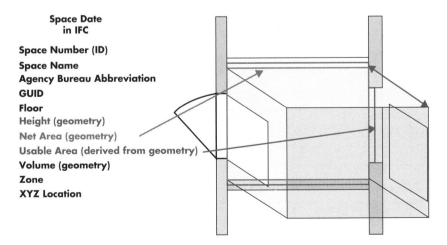

FIGURE 21.3 Spatial data and geometry using IFC as the interoperability standard.

choices for BIM authoring tools as part of its requirement to the architect-engineering (A/E) community. The mechanism GSA implemented was IFC-based spatial concept building information models (Figure 21.3). All of the vendors succeeded in modifying their own proprietary BIM authoring software to export a GSA BIM Guide 02-Spatial Data compliant IFC file. GSA would then check this file utilizing Solibri model checking software to ensure compliance.

The result of this methodology had four positive outcomes:

1. The A/E community was required by contract to create a spatial BIM model.
2. The software to accomplish this was incorporated into commercial software at no additional cost to the A/E, and the BIM authoring software development was at no cost to GSA.
3. By requiring that the spatial model be computational, automated checking tools such as Solibri could be deployed to verify completeness and accuracy. Previous analog and non-BIM processes such as poly-lining a CAD file to manually determine space, which resulted in inefficiencies and inaccuracies, were greatly improved.
4. Similar to the Coast Guard story of putting the computation and visualization power of BIM into the hands of executives, the GSA spatial BIM initiative put the same power into the hands of the A/E, the GSA project manager, and other project stakeholders (Figure 21.4).

BIM Report: Floor Plans by Tenant

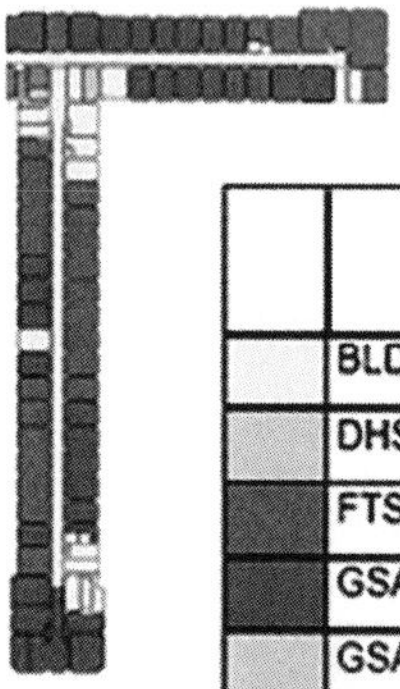

SECOND

Tenant	Usable Areas				
	Office	Store	Building Common	Floor Common	RSF
BLDG	0 sq ft	0 sq ft	2,330 sq ft	14,602 sq ft	0 sq ft
DHS IMIG/CUSTOMS FPS	2,543 sq ft	0 sq ft	0 sq ft	0 sq ft	3,459 sq ft
FTS, NET SVCS FAC	1,939 sq ft	0 sq ft	0 sq ft	0 sq ft	2,637 sq ft
GSA COMPTROLLER	10,536 sq ft	0 sq ft	0 sq ft	0 sq ft	14,329 sq ft
GSA JOINT USE	2,525 sq ft	0 sq ft	0 sq ft	0 sq ft	3,434 sq ft
GSA OCIO	10,843 sq ft	0 sq ft	0 sq ft	0 sq ft	14,747 sq ft
GSA OFF CITIZEN SVCS	1,288 sq ft	0 sq ft	0 sq ft	0 sq ft	1,752 sq ft
GSA OFF GVTWIDE	9,666 sq ft	0 sq ft	0 sq ft	0 sq ft	13,145 sq ft
GSA PBS	12,762 sq ft	0 sq ft	0 sq ft	0 sq ft	17,356 sq ft
GSA VAC UNASSIGN	631 sq ft	0 sq ft	0 sq ft	0 sq ft	859 sq ft

FIGURE 21.4 Visualization and tabular data using spatial BIM; BIM report of floor plans by tenant.
(courtesy GSA BIM Program)

Once GSA demonstrated how BIM was useful in working with data that could be available early in the design process, the next question was how to build on this success. One approach was to move further upstream from "final concepts" (i.e., schematic design) to "early concept" design. Professor Chuck Eastman and his students at the Georgia Institute of Technology researched two aspects of early concept design on how spatial BIM could portray visual and data elements of early concepts and how it could enable further analysis (beyond spatial) of multiple early design concepts, and illustrate the spatial, energy, programmatic, and cost implications of the various alternatives.

A spatial BIM, illustrated by the GSA's Toledo Ohio Courthouse, showed geometrical considerations and considerable analytical data to better inform which of the alternatives should progress to final concept submission (Figures 21.5 and 21.6). The development of further analyses of the early concept BIM models permitted project stakeholders greater participation in the decision-making process.

The true power of spatial BIM to save time and improve project outcomes was illustrated in the extensive case study #10 on GSA's Jacksonville, Michigan, Courthouse (Eastman et al. 2008, pp. 449–465).

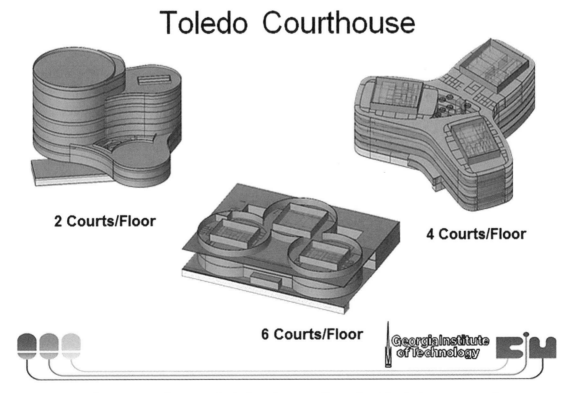

Toledo Courthouse

2 Courts/Floor

4 Courts/Floor

6 Courts/Floor

FIGURE 21.5 **Early concepts of GSA's Toledo Courthouse, all meeting identical programmatic requirements.**
(courtesy GSA BIM Program)

Early Space Program Review for Concept Design Evaluation
Project: U.S. Courthouse of Toledo, OH
(Jun 19, 2008)

# Design parameter	Type	Target Value	2Courts Actual Value	4Courts Actual Value	6Courts Actual Value
1 Number of Building Floors	EA		9	6	4
2 Total building gross area	Area (nsf)		208,755	220,000	224,464
3 Inside parking area	Area (nsf)		21,679	26,729	23,314
4 Total gross minus inside parking area	Area (nsf)		187,076	193,271	201,150
5 Total usable area	Area (usf)		162,237	178,749	182,414
6 Atrium area	Area (nsf)		4,322	8,251	974
7 Building Efficiency (USF/Total gross minus parking area)	Ratio (%)	67%	87%	92%	91%
8 Number of Courtrooms	EA		11	12	9
9 Number of Special Proceedings/Appeals Courtrooms	EA		Not found	Not found	Not found
10 Number of Chambers	EA		11	11	7
11 Number of Inside Parking Spaces	EA		47	58	51
12 Number of Elevator Spaces on the 1st Floor	EA		7	6	9
13 Elevator Ratio (Total Gross Area / Number of Elevator Spaces)	Area (nsf)	25,000	29,822	36,667	24,940
14 Floor to Floor Height for Courtroom	Height (ft)	20	22.0, 8.0, 15.0	22	22
15 Maximum Ceiling Height of Courtroom	Height (ft)	16	9.0, 16.0	9.0, 16.0	10
16 Floor to Floor Height for Sp. Proceedings/Appeals Courtroom	Height (ft)		Not found	Not found	Not found
17 Maximum Ceiling Height for Sp. Proceedings/Appeals Courtroom	Height (ft)	18	Not found	Not found	Not found
18 Floor to Floor Height for Office Space	Height (ft)	14	15.0, 22.0	15.0, 22.0	22.0, 15.0
19 Maximum Ceiling Height of Judges Chamber	Height (ft)	10	10	10	10
20 Total Gross Area to Building Skin Area	Ratio (%)	45-55%	58%	71%	85%
21 Main Entrance's floor level (Ground Level)			Not found (Level 1)	Level 1	Level 1
22 USMS Administrative Office's floor level		2nd or upper	Level 1	Level 2	Ground floor
23 Gross Area of Prisoner Circulation and Holding Cell Area	Area (nsf)		8,069	5,750	9,438

FIGURE 21.6   Analytical BIM data from early concepts for GSA's Toledo Courthouse.
(courtesy GSA BIM Program)

21.5 PROJECT SPATIAL BIM: CONNECTING PROGRAM TO DESIGN, CONSTRUCTION, AND FACILITY MANAGEMENT

The Coast Guard and GSA examples illustrated the power and potential of the strategic and early design implementations of spatial BIM (Teicholz 2013). What about the follow-through to the full project life cycle? Larry Ciscon, PhD, president and founder of Trelligence Inc., describes this BIM-enabled process that is incorporated into their Affinity product as follows:

> From a process point of view, early in the design process the emphasis is much more on rooms and room contents and less around walls, so your tools should let you work at that level. Later it becomes much more detailed, so walls and wall components are more important. One is not a replacement for the other. Realistically the only way to keep the overall data model complete is to maintain both models throughout the process and keep them synced with each other. The key is to never throw away any information![1]

---

[1] Personal communication with the author (email) August 8, 2013.

Ciscon further described the technical requirements of the software systems needed to achieve this, including data about staffing planes, room data, adjacency requirements, and furniture needs that is linked to a spatial model. An enhanced BIM could be used for this.

21.6 GEOSPATIAL, CAMPUS-WIDE, AND SERVICES-ORIENTED SPATIAL BIM

In November 2007, Kimon Onuma conducted his first BIMStorm in Boston (Onuma 2012). Onuma was pioneering demonstrating how new technologies such as web services and geospatial could be used for worldwide crowd-sourced planning and design, and even emergency responses (Figure 21.7).

Navigating a portfolio of buildings or projects, either at a global, city-wide, or a corporate or university campus-wide scale has become easier, more intuitive, and increasingly integrated utilizing geospatial technologies (Onuma 2007, Onuma 2010). Onuma's work on the California Community College facilities encompassed an inventory of 5,000 buildings (71 million sf) and brought separate space utilization and geographic information systems together into a cloud computing BIM platform and won a 2011 CETI Award from FIATECH. As John Young of ESRI has stated, "The interest in geospatial

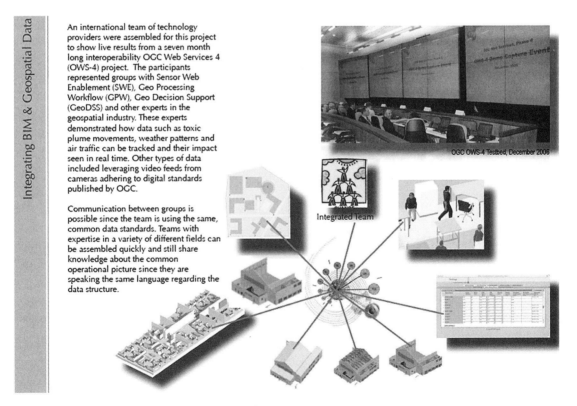

FIGURE 21.7 Integrating BIM and geospatial data in AIA TAP 2007.
(courtesy AIA TAP, OGC, and Onuma)

especially for campus planning and development is skyrocketing." For universities and other campus developments, the focus has been both on asset planning and navigating indoor spaces (Cheuvront 2012, Przybyla 2010, Richardson 2012, Wallis 2012).

21.7 STANDARDIZING SPATIAL BIM: IFMA-BOMA, BISDM, CITYGML, AND INDOOR NAVIGATION

The advent of BIM has prompted new developments in industry standards related to spatial BIM. IFMA BOMA space measurement initiatives were mentioned earlier. The geospatial industry has recently awakened to the value of integrating space and the interior of buildings with the outer geographic reference data. BISDM (the Building Information Spatial Data Model) has gained traction as a reference standard (Penobscot Bay Media 2007a, 2007b). The Open Geospatial Consortium (OGC) has taken a leadership role in establishing a new standard for indoor navigation entitled IndoorGML (OGC 2012). As OGC's George Percivall writes

> We spend most of our lives indoors, yet the GPS services that serve us so well outdoors are blind when they can't see the sky. Fortunately, the indoor/outdoor location gap is closing. Leaps in indoor positioning accuracy provided by a large number of competing technologies, along with the already booming availability of indoor maps, point to a new frontier of indoor location based services.[2]

OGC president and CEO Mark Reichardt adds

> CityGML supports urban 3D models, linking of objects in the model to one or more other internal or web references etc. IndoorGML adds the capability to more accurately define the indoor spaces and to relate indoor location rendering technologies to that space—to support high definition indoor navigation etc.[3]

21.8 CONCLUSION

The decade of growth in both technology and adoption from 2003 to 2013 may well be dwarfed by new technologies coming online and their impact on professional practice and industry perspective. There will undoubtedly be future development in all aspects of BIM, including spatial data. Improvements specifically related to spatial BIM might be further enhanced with the following critical steps:

---

[2]www.opengeospatial.org/taxonomy/term/327.
[3]Personal communication with the author (email) August 30, 2013.

- Levels of development and levels of detail for spatial BIM (Figure 21.8)
- Spatial BIM being defined as the database key to a BIM app and ecosystem world
- A strategic roadmap for BIM based on spatial data
- Expanding the scale of BIM from buildings and portfolios of buildings to urban design and regional urban neighborhoods and districts
- More thorough understanding of the importance of spatial BIM by all stakeholders, not just owners
- Other instances of spatial BIM being implemented, for example, acoustics, the integration between the building elements and the spatial elements, where characteristics of one directly affect the other. A classic illustration of that is Arup's work on the Sydney Opera House (Arup 2007).

Spatial BIM is a compelling and potentially dramatic improvement for the benefit of the entire facility life cycle and a myriad of building types and works across the scale from global to room contents. It remains a frontier yet to be fully explored and its potential to be fully realized.

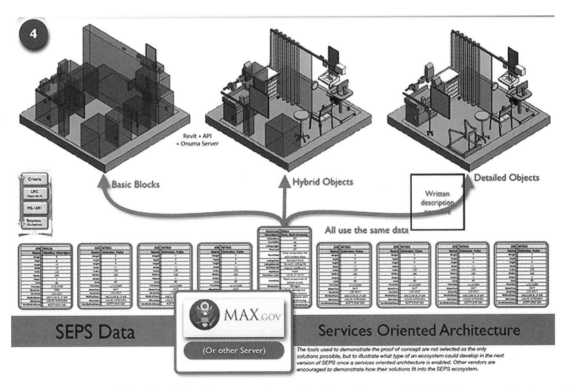

FIGURE 21.8 **Levels of detail and development of spatial BIM, as illustrated in DoD Space and Equipment Planning (SEPS) Strategic Plan.**
(courtesy Onuma)

DISCUSSION QUESTIONS

1. What is the role of the GSA? How has it responded to the increasing use of BIM?
2. Explain the significance of how BIM was used by the U.S. Coast Guard for spatial strategic planning.
3. What is "spatial BIM," and how does it relate to the broader concepts of BIM?
4. What are data elements that can be attributed to spaces in BIM, and how might they be used in the facility life cycle?
5. Explain CityGML and IndoorGML and how they are related to BIM.

REFERENCES

Arup, Ove. 2007. "The Sydney Opera House: Modeling the Opera Theater." American Institute of Architects (AIA) Technology in Architectural Practice (TAP) BIM Awards, Washington, DC. Jury's Choice Award, www.aia.org/aiaucmp/groups/aia/documents/pdf/aiab081587.pdf.

Cheuvront, Aaron. 2012. "The Best of Both Worlds: CAD and GIS at the University of Washington." *ESRI News for Facilities*, Redlands, CA, Winter.

East, E. William. 2013. "Construction Operations Building Information Exchange (COBie)." *Whole Building Design Guide*, a program of the National Institute of Building Sciences (NIBS), Washington, DC. Available at www.wbdg.org/resources/cobie.php.

Eastman, Chuck, Paul Teicholz, Rafael Sacks, and Kathleen Liston. 2008. *BIM Handbook: A Guide to Building Information Modeling for Owners, Managers, Designers, Engineers, and Contractors*. Hoboken, NJ: John Wiley & Sons.

Giedion, Sigfried. 1967. *Space, Time and Architecture*. Cambridge, MA: Harvard University Press (first published 1941), pp. 30–31.

GSA. 2006. 02–GSA BIM Guide for Spatial Program Validation Version 0.90. 2006. Washington, DC: U.S. General Services Administration.

———. 2007. "2006 Pilot Project Successes: Building Information Modeling." AIA TAP BIM Awards, Washington, DC. 2007 Jury's Choice Award, www.aia.org/aiaucmp/groups/aia/documents/pdf/aiab081586.pdf.

Hensey, Susan Meridith, and Meredith Thatcher. 2009. "The 'How-To' of IFMA Area Measurement." IFMA white paper no. WP09 (October). Available at http://spaceneedsanalysis.com/wp-content/uploads/pdf/article-how-to-area-measure.pdf, Thatcher Workplace Consulting, Kanata, ON.

Onuma, Kimon. 2007. "Integrating BIM and Geo-Spatial Data." AIA TAP BIM Awards, Washington, DC, www.aia.org/aiaucmp/groups/aia/documents/pdf/aiab081585.pdf.

———. 2010. "Location, Location, Location: BIM, BIM, BIM." *Journal of Building Information Modeling* (Fall). Available at www.wbdg.org/pdfs/jbim_fall10.pdf, accessed September 1, 2013.

———. 2012. "BIMStorm: Fusion+CCC+Onuma," Pasadena, CA: www.onuma.com/FUSION/, accessed September 1, 2013.

Open Geospatial Consortium. 2012. "The OGC Forms the IndoorGML Indoor Locations Standards Working Group." OGC, January 20.

Penobscot Bay Media, 2007a. "Interior Space Database Diagram." Camden, Maine.

———. 2007b. "GIS Data Model for Interior Space." Camden, Maine, February 21. http://www10.sharecg.com/nbc/articles/1/615460/Penobscot-Bay-Media-Collaborates-With-ESRI-Publish-Open-Data-Model-Managing-Facility-Assets-Operations.

Przybyla, John. 2010. "The Next Frontier for BIM: Interoperability with GIS." *Journal of Building Information Modeling* (Fall): 14–18.

Richardson, Karen. 2012. "A 3D GIS Solution for Campus Master Planning." In *GIS in Education: Across Campuses, Inside Facilities*. Redlands, CA: ESRI, pp. 10–12.

Teicholz, Paul (ed.). 2013. *BIM for Facility Managers*. Hoboken, NJ: John Wiley & Sons.

Yee, Peggy, C. Matta, C. Kam, S. Hagan, and O. Valdimarsson. 2010. "The GSA BIM Story." Available at www.fsr.is/lisalib/getfile.aspx?itemid=6995.

Yoders, Jeff. 2010. "Bringing BIM to Public Buildings." Building Design + Construction, (August 11). Available at www.bdcnetwork.com/bringing-bim-public-buildings, accessed September 1, 2013.

Young, John. 2010. "Convergence Yields Smarter Facilities: Practice Applications for Building Planners and Operators." *Journal of Building Information Modeling* (Fall): 23–25.

CHAPTER 22

Translating Designs for Construction + Operations: The Future of BIM in a World of Material and Energy Scarcity

Franca Trubiano PhD, OAQ, Int. Assoc. AIA, University of Pennsylvania

22.1 BUILDINGS, INFORMATION, AND MODELING

22.1.1 The Promise

This chapter investigates the role that architectural data and its modeling can play in reconciling the long-standing divides that exist between design, construction, and operations; that is, between a building's initial conceptualization, its subsequent materialization, and its post-construction maintenance. Architectural modeling is at the very center of a comprehensive practice that maximizes the value proposition of building information modeling (BIM) for the benefits of life-cycle assessments and energy accountability.

Architects communicate design intent during the initial phases of a project as well as offer clear directives for the material detailing of their designs when completing the requisite construction documents. Far more exciting, however, is the prospect that documents produced during the design and construction phases of a project can also be employed for ensuring the long-term stewardship of a building and its inhabitants. With this goal in mind, this chapter maintains that building information modeling affords the building industry an important opportunity for expanding the range, comprehensiveness, and critical dimension of how buildings are conceived, fabricated, simulated, and monitored. Not only is it capable of altering the architect's relationship with construction, it is equally adept at transforming the profession's engagement with architectural design and building operations. It does so by enabling the production of construction documents that enrich the conceptual activities attendant to initial design phases all the while facilitating our awareness of how buildings and their occupants perform.

By the very nature of their structure and organizational framework, architectural documents produced using BIM significantly advance the design process by resituating the architect's imagination within the realm of materials, building assemblies, production methods, and fabrication, encouraging designers to recognize the value that the manipulation of matter has on architectural outcomes. Moreover, the use of BIM in bringing an architectural project to completion inspires the development of process protocols aimed at the long-term monitoring of how buildings consume embodied and operational energy. With the goal of simulating ever more precise energy performance profiles of buildings yet to be built, a range of specialized software has been developed that maximizes BIM's capacity for interoperability.

BIM renders visible that which is difficult to see with our eyes and complicated to measure with our bodies, including the full range of transformations that occur in the material and energy profiles of a building over time. The vast data-scape that underpins the use of BIM in designing, constructing, and operating buildings offers the architectural profession a path to invention by expanding designers' capacities for form finding, visualization, and representation and by productively challenging the outdated modes of engineering, construction, and building operations. Said otherwise, BIM's multiparty and multisector platform has the capacity to transform the way in which we conceive, build, and analyze the work of architecture.

Traditional design and documentation processes remain incapable of accounting for the material and energy use encumbered by a particular project. Line work without data is inarticulate as to BTUs, R-values, coefficients of expansion, or levels of acidification. By contrast, building information models not only have the capacity to store large amounts of data about the physical building yet to be built, they also support a vast network of queries about how it may perform in future time. Hence, the question this chapter addresses is, how does the integration of BIM capabilities contribute to the development of an expanded definition of design practice, both within and beyond architecture, in a way that privileges questions of material and energy accountability?

22.1.2 The Critique

Surely, information systems have fundamentally redefined the architect/ builder relationship, if not that between architect and client. Whether foreseeable or desirable, much of contemporary design is at present conditioned by quickly mutating networks of information with the building industry predicated on the rapid exchange, accumulation, and verification of analytics amongst an increasing number of specialized consultants, all of whom are charged with assuring the highest levels of building performance (Eastman et al. 2011, Deutsch 2011). For many, the unchecked and uncritical deployment of building information modeling heralds a world of hyperbolic metrics, deterministic controls, and nothing short of the contamination of design. Building models can be burdened by excessive material descriptions including quantities, weight, dimensions, structural resistances, costs, embodied energy, product manufacturer, country of origin, and even first available shipping date, if desired. For its detractors, BIM remains a highly prescriptive mode of representation whose organization and methods significantly reduce the qualitative practice of architecture, regimenting the design process, and undermining the architectural imagination's predilection for spatial invention. Insufficiently adept at form finding and requiring a surfeit of material and building technology information at the conceptual stage of a project, BIM is poorly suited to the demands of architectural design.

These and similar criticisms represent significant barriers to the uptake of licensed BIM products amongst architectural, engineering, and construction (AEC) firms. In Western Europe (UK, France, and Germany), barely a third of AEC professionals currently use BIM in their practices and of those who have not adopted BIM, as much as 25 percent are uninterested in considering its introduction within established work flows (McGraw Hill Smart Report 2010). In Western Europe, architects who have not yet adopted BIM are the least likely of professionals to consider its advantages. In the United States, the numbers are somewhat more optimistic. The percentage of AEC companies using BIM has increased significantly since 2007, from 28 to 71 percent in five years. And for the first time, a greater number of building contractors are using BIM than architects (McGraw Hill Smart Report 2012).

And yet, notwithstanding such evidence of growth in the adoption of BIM platforms across all sectors of the AEC industry, a number of significant questions remain, foremost among which is how this wholesale transformation in the way in which architects communicate their design intentions has altered the very nature of design.

22.2 THE CHANGING CHARACTER OF ARCHITECTURAL REPRESENTATIONS

Why architects continue to use drawing conventions first developed and adopted more than 2000 years ago—even in the face of ample evidence of their limited scope and value for buildings designed, constructed, and operating in the twenty-first century—remains unclear. Should not the particular exigencies of our highly technological world inform the invention of alternative modes of depiction that capture more successfully the full spectrum of questions important to contemporary practice? The qualitative and quantitative imperatives of high-performance buildings, whether implicitly or explicitly championed by both private and public clients, surely summon the appearance of representational modes far different than those employed to date. Why, therefore, are architects still reluctant to alter the representational language of their practice, given the vast transformations engendered by BIM, digital fabrication, and advanced modeling software?

Regretfully, an excess of perspectival imagery still permeates the highly mediatized promotion of professional practice. Rarely are the glossy phantasmagoric depictions of contemporary works of architecture communicative of anything other than the most superficial of intents and affects. In addition, the ubiquitous triad of plan/section/elevation used by architects to communicate qualities of space, materials, and details poorly captures or conveys many of the recent technological advances that have taken place in the fields of design and construction. Albeit well suited to descriptions of preliminary design intent, these highly abstract projections are incapable of capturing the far more complex material transformations that organize the construction and operation of a high-performance building. Why, therefore, do they continue to populate and organize the core of drawing sets used on building sites across the world?

Truth be told, there is nothing universal or trans-historical about the use of plans, sections, and elevations. Historically, architects have always adapted their methods of representation to suit the ends of building. And in the face of vast transformations in the nature of building technology, a review of our descriptive methods is required anew. In Book 1 of Marcus Vitruvius Pollio's first-century A.D. treatise *de Architecture*, no mention was made of this particular triad of drawings (Vitruvius 1960). Rather, in discussing architectural ideas with his patron Caesar Augustus, Vitruvius wrote of the use of the *ichnographia*, the *orthographia*, and the *scaenographia*. While the first two drawing types are commensurate with plans and elevations, the third drawing type is in no way equivalent to our building section. Rather, in the term *scaenographia* Vitruvius had described an early form of perspectival drawing more akin to the foreshortened paintings that once adorned the patrician home of Romans and the seaside villas of Pompeians.

In fact, prior to the publication in 1615 of *L'Idea dell'Architettura Universale* ("The Idea of Universal Architecture") by Vincenzo Scamozzi, whole building sections were rarely used as design tools in the architect's repertoire (Scamozzi 1615). When Sebastiano Serlio in 1545 set out to teach architects how to draw in his book, *On Geometry—On Perspective*, there was scant discussion of the building section; included instead were instructions for drawing perspectival theatrical backdrops (Serlio 1551). For Scamozzi, however, coded in the cut of a building was the vision of an artifact metaphorically, if not literally, dissected and exposed to view and light. And to make the point, in an accompanying illustration Scamozzi used directional line work to indicate the penetration of light within the deep interior of a centralized building. Possibly for the first time in the history of architectural representations, the interior void space of a building was represented as contiguous with its exterior via the medium of light (Figure 22.1).

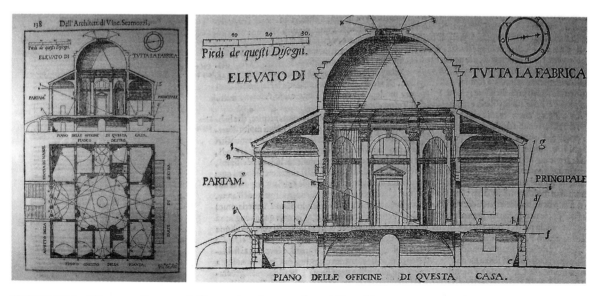

FIGURE 22.1   Vincenzo Scamozzi, illustration from *L'Idea dell'Architettura Universale* (1615).
(Gift of G. Holmes Perkins, Anne and Jerome Fisher Fine Arts Library, University of Pennsylvania)

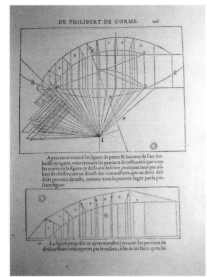

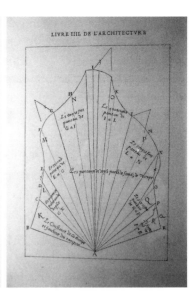

FIGURE 22.2   Philibert de l'Orme, illustrations from *Le Premier Tome de l' architecture.*
(Anne and Jerome Fisher Fine Arts Library, University of Pennsylvania)

The invention of a new form of architectural representation was equally the result of the particular genius of sixteenth-century French stonemason and architect Philibert de l'Orme, who devised a form of orthographic projection for instructing masons in highly complex stereotomic stone cutting techniques (de l'Orme 1567). Using enigmatic 2D line work, de l'Orme codified the fully spatial and material practices of the stonecutter and setter called on to erect complex nonorthogonal vaults, otherwise impossible to conceive solely in the mind's eye. These highly sophisticated drawings, evidence of which he included in his 1567 treatise *Le Premier Tome de l' architecture*, sought to reconcile the gap between design projection and construction technique for nonorthogonal masses. Fascinated with shapes as complex as those contained in the "trumpet," de L'Orme explicated in geometric traces a degree of building complexity whose constructional methods remain difficult to decipher. Sadly, the ability to interpret the codes contained within his highly abstract line drawings has been, for the most part, lost to modern masons and architects. However, what de l'Orme sought to create was a method of representation, which could simultaneously communicate geometric, material, and constructional techniques for some of the most complex shapes ever imagined (Figure 22.2).

22.3 FACILITATING THE TRANSLATION FROM DESIGN TO CONSTRUCTION—WITH MATTER

Inventing representational means is far from a thing of the past. Facilitating the translation from architectural idea to built artifact remains of keen interest to contemporary architects. When operating in a

global building industry defined by an ever-increasing number of material suppliers and product manufacturers, materials invented and developed in commercial labs, as well as fragmented and deskilled
labor markets, identifying methods of representation that more systemically communicate the integration of these and other disparate forces is paramount. BIM is uniquely qualified to address these issues,
subtending a range of computation technologies for the production of architectural representations—
whether models, drawings, or data sets—that

- Enable the communication of design ideas via the modeling of construction details
- Privilege the detailed description of a building's material technologies alongside its geometry
- Function as a searchable, downloadable, and transferable repository of verifiable data
- Export building element information to collateral computational interfaces to facilitate coordina-
  tion with structural, mechanical, electrical, and plumbing engineers
- Facilitate life-cycle assessments and carbon accounting
- Encourage environmental design simulations, for light and energy

Never mere drawing lines, building elements in a BIM model are defined by a set of data points that
characterize each element as well as its parametric relationship to other elements in the model. BIM
occasions an inversion of the typical design process, encouraging material investigations alongside those
of form and the collection of data simultaneous with the development of appearances. Moreover, its
protocols promote a reversal in the field of representation by rejecting visual abstraction as a necessary
precondition for the production of construction documents. For decades, the character of drawings used
in the process of building has increased in complexity, rendering them difficult to decipher and navigate by anyone other than an expert in the process. Many subcontractors turn away from these highly
abstract drawings, and in so doing, render them useless in the process for which they were intended.
A desire to alter this condition of practice is the premise that guides the two examples discussed here
below in which BIM innovations have contributed to transformative practices of great interest for architectural representation.

To begin with, a significant challenge to the present culture of construction drawings is clearly evident in the structure and content of a series of high-quality graphic publications produced by the UK
design team of Newtechnic, led by architects Andrew and Yasmin Watts (Watts 2013). For the first
time, collected in four separate but related publications dedicated to advancing the idea of synthesis in
design and construction practices, is an entirely new vision for communicating the value of architectural
building details. In *Modern Construction Handbook* (3rd ed.), *Modern Construction Envelopes*, *Modern
Construction Facades*, and *Modern Construction Roofs*, Andrew Watts has produced a body of work
predicated on the explication of detailed case studies of signature buildings and their assemblies as a
vehicle to knowledge. In so doing, this set of publications precipitates an expansion in the assumed function of detailed architectural wall sections—the most ubiquitous of drawing types invented by architects
during the twentieth century. Beyond its capacity to communicate highly abstracted material instructions for the building of assemblies and composite building elements, the detailed section is transformed

into a highly communicative form of representation that valorizes the role of construction based data in design decisions. Watts has customized his models to produce an array of cut-away views both rendered and not, that describe all aspects of the assembly in question. And given their ability to depict the textural and material qualities of building elements as diverse as masonry, steel, aluminum, glass, fabrics, and polymers, Watts's highly virtualized building models register significant gains for the design centered visualization of construction related information (Figure 22.3 and Figure 22.4).

Hence, in having favored the sectional perspective, Watts has combined in one image spatial, material and data based information. In the cut of the section and in the projected extension of the building element, viewers are introduced to the spatial definition of the building component as well as to its measured material characteristics. And in capitalizing on the overtly representational capacity of building element modeling, Watts has formulated an operational bridge across the often difficult-to-navigate divide between design and construction. So too should the entire array of BIM modeling tools be used in the production of architectural construction drawings.

Another example of an expanded practice terrain supportive of BIM tools is clearly evident, this time in the delivery of design information for the purposes of fabrication, in the herculean effort to complete the Sagrada Familia, the large-scale ecclesiastical project initiated by Catalan architect Antonio Gaudi at the end of the nineteenth century and still under construction today in Barcelona. For the past three decades and under the intellectual leadership of New Zealand architect Mark Burry, a vast network of highly mediated parametric models have been generated and their data translated for the digital fabrication of complex building masses made of solid masonry stone and concrete (Burry 2010). Constructing the highly complex geometric forms associated with this project would have been inconceivable without the range of BIM interfaces developed by Burry and his team. Gaudi's artisanal hand plaster modeling techniques, developed more than a hundred years ago, required substantial computational interpretation in light of the complex mathematics they subtended. According to Burry, the presence in Gaudi's formal language of paraboloids, hyperboloids, and hyperbolic paraboloids necessitated an architecture of "real absence and virtual presence" in which coordinated BIM exchanges are customized to translate complex geometrical information directly to fabrication. As conceptualized by Burry in *The New Mathematics of Architecture*, "real absence" describes the mathematical modeling that generates material profiles as a function of Boolean deletions, while "virtual presence" denotes the designer and builder's ability to precut in digital space the host of profiles destined for physical construction. The use of five- and seven-axis digitally controlled stonecutting technology minimizes waste, produces highly customized masses, and translates geometry into matter (Figure 22.5).

Thus, among the millions of bits of data and the intricate array of ruled surfaces that subtend the vastly customized BIM protocols of the Sagrada Familia, reside the structure and organization of a collaborative platform that translates its mathematics of form into scripts for material fabrication. The graphic, mathematical, computational, and machine-based practices devised by Burry and his team not only facilitate the translation from design to construction but, more effectively, contribute to an expanded definition of design itself. As such, this project remains a stellar example of the advanced use of BIM for reducing, if not eliminating, the gap that persists between conceptualization and fabrication. Chapter 26 by Mark Burry elaborates further on this project.

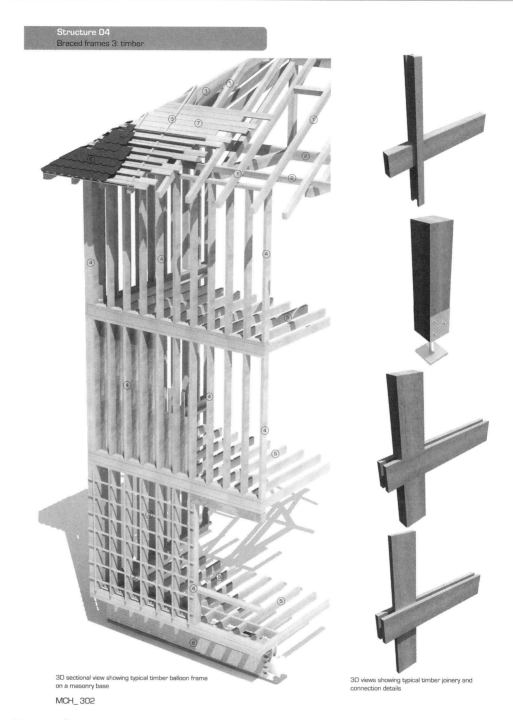

Structure 04
Braced frames 3: timber

3D sectional view showing typical timber balloon frame
on a masonry base

MCH_ 302

3D views showing typical timber joinery and
connection details

FIGURE 22.3   Andrew Watts

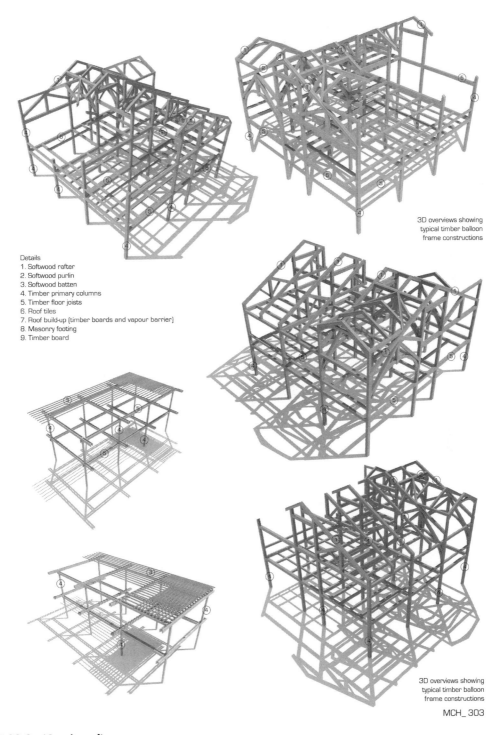

3D overviews showing
typical timber balloon
frame constructions

Details
1. Softwood rafter
2. Softwood purlin
3. Softwood batten
4. Timber primary columns
5. Timber floor joists
6. Roof tiles
7. Roof build-up (timber boards and vapour barrier)
8. Masonry footing
9. Timber board

3D overviews showing
typical timber balloon
frame constructions

MCH_303

FIGURE 22.3   (Continued)

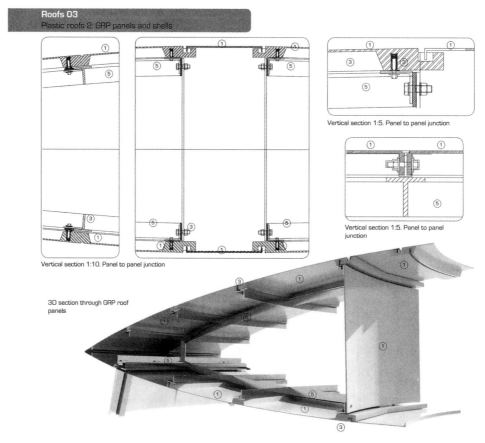

Roofs 03
Plastic roofs 2: GRP panels and shells

Vertical section 1:10. Panel to panel junction

Vertical section 1:5. Panel to panel junction

Vertical section 1:5. Panel to panel junction

3D section through GRP roof panels

MCH_ 270

System design

While glass reinforced polyester (GRP) rooflights, discussed in the previous section on rooflights, are made as panels which are joined to form translucent rooflights, opaque GRP panels can be made as monolithic, self-supporting shells, usually made from panel segments which are brought to site and bolted together. The segment sizes of GRP shells are made in sizes which are suitable for transportation by road, usually set upright on a trailer. The shells can then be lifted by crane into place as a completed assembly, which makes them quite different from roof structures in other materials.

The example shown is of a small shell for a rooflight. The shell consists of a set of segmented panels which are bolted together to form a roof shell of approximately 7.0 metres diameter, supported by an additional frame. Panels are made in a mould, usually from a single segmented panel type to form a complete rooflight. Moulds are usually made from plywood to create the shape and are then finished in GRP to create the negative shape of the panel being formed. GRP panels are fabricated by first applying a release agent to the mould to allow the finished panel to be removed easily, then thermosetting polyester resins are applied to the face of the mould with flexible fibreglass mat

being laid into the resin, usually with rollers. The process of fabricating GRP panels is very labour intensive, but requires no expensive equipment, making panel production a craft-based technique rather than an industrial process. When the panels are released from the mould they are trimmed along their edges and ground smooth where necessary. An alternative method is to apply a mixture of resin and glass fibre particles as a spray directly into the mould. The mixture is applied to a thickness of 3mm to 5mm depending on the panel size required.

In the example shown, GRP panels are supported by a light metal frame beneath. The frame comprises steel or aluminium T-sections which are welded together to form a structure that supports the complete outer skin. The frame has curved members that radiate from the centre at the top to the edge and from the centre at the lowest point of the structure, back to the perimeter. The radiating 'spokes' of the wheel are held in place by T-sections that, in plan, form concentric circles. This 'bicycle wheel' form is supported near its perimeter by a metal ring beam that is set immediately above the glazing beneath the GRP roof. The ring beam is supported by posts that are fixed to the roof deck beneath.

FIGURE 22.4   Andrew Watts

(Copyright AMBRA publisher, taken from Andrew Watt, *Modern Construction Handbook*, 3rd Edition, ISBN 578-3-99043-454-3. AMBRA/V.)

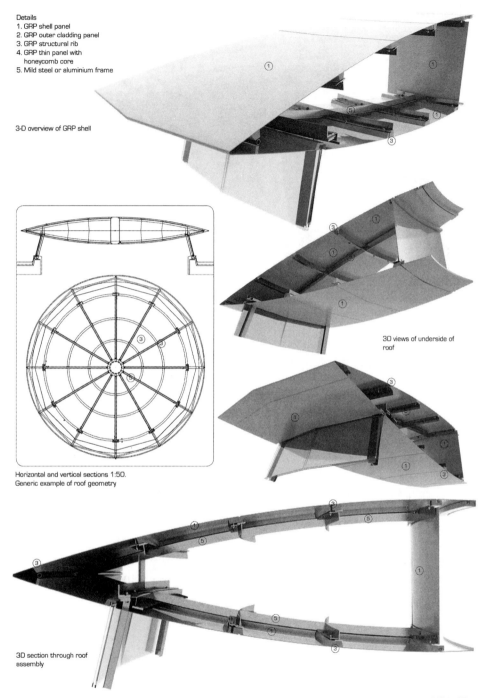

Details
1. GRP shell panel
2. GRP outer cladding panel
3. GRP structural rib
4. GRP thin panel with
   honeycomb core
5. Mild steel or aluminium frame

3-D overview of GRP shell

Horizontal and vertical sections 1:50.
Generic example of roof geometry

3D views of underside of
roof

3D section through roof
assembly

MCH_ 271

FIGURE 22.4   (Continued)

FIGURE 22.5 Sagrada Familia
(Photos by the author, 2012.)

The extent to which eliminating this gap remains an important goal for architectural design is best captured in Adrian Forty's book *Words and Buildings*, wherein Forty reminds his reader that "design" as a practice liberated from material constraints is a fairly modern invention, the result, in fact, of a transformation in the very definition of "design" during the nineteenth and twentieth centuries (Forty 2000). So ubiquitous is the term's use today that we scarcely remember its history. Having originated in the sixteenth-century Italian word *disegno*, it referred to both the drawing produced by the architect to convey the measurable limits of an intended project and the project idea rendered manifest in proportional *lineamente*. Prior to the eighteenth century, however, a project's design was always commensurate with the building's order and organizational logic, that is, with its intended structure. As Forty (2000) writes:

> "[D]esign/structure" was an accepted and well understood trope in the eighteenth century, as a way of describing two aspects of a single activity—architecture. This convention continued throughout the nineteenth century, but in the early twentieth century this distinction, hitherto belonging only in speech and thought, was to become manifested as two discrete activities. (p. 137)

And as noted by Forty, changes in architectural education furthered the divide between design and structure when the currency of professional apprenticeships was supplanted by the growing vogue for attending university in the pursuit of architectural knowledge. In universities, architectural education was understood as an intellectual pursuit exclusively centered in the academy, and:

> [W]ith the separation of education from practice, "design," rather than being a convenient way of conceptualizing a particular feature of architecture, came to be seen as a pure and self-sufficient activity within itself. Education made a real division that had existed previously only in discourse. (p. 138)

While much remains that is true in this portrayal of contemporary design as conceptually divorced from the building's structure, there are many as yet untapped opportunities for resynthesizing design to construction. Surely, if design continues to be "a mental activity disengaged from the world" and an "end in itself," it will poorly accommodate material and operational definitions of architecture. Given, however, the current exigencies of material and energy scarcities, the proliferation of ever more complex fabrication technologies, and the persistent labor disparities that exist in the world, only the most material interpretations of design will succeed when called upon to address the pressing challenges faced by the building industry today.

That this is precisely what BIM provides the design process is of keen interest to this chapter, particularly as manifest in the innovative work of a team of researchers at KieranTimberlake. For more than a decade this U.S.-based architectural firm has been at the forefront of practice-based research with projects as diverse as Smart Wrap™ (2003), Cellophane House™ (2008), and the publication of *Refabricating Architecture: How Manufacturing Methodologies Are Poised to Transform Building Construction* (2003). In 2012, the KieranTimberlake Research Group, consisting of architects, environmental scientists, and software engineers, created Tally, an app for Revit (the most commonly used BIM software program in the United States), to assess in real time the environmental life-cycle costs of our material choices. Designed, with support from Autodesk Sustainability Solutions, and intended for use by architects, engineers, and constructors committed to rigorous and detailed accounting of the environmental impacts of buildings, the tool adopts a cradle-to-grave framework for assessing the ecological value of a design (Figure 22.6).

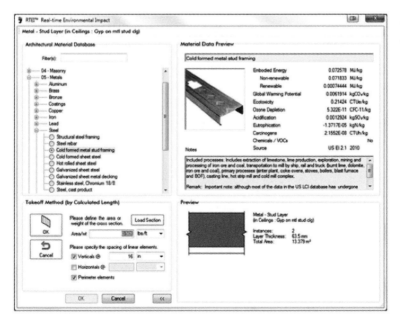

FIGURE 22.6   Screen shot from the Tally Interface.
(© KieranTimberlake)

Certainly, there is no shortage of informed and robust tools in this space. Whether familiar with the Athena EcoCalculator or the Building for Environmental and Economic Sustainability Tool (BEES), building professionals throughout the industry have adopted the tenets of life cycle assessment (LCA), recognizing the inevitability of accounting for material and energy excesses incurred during the material production, design, and construction phase of a project (Konig et al. 2010). To date, however, few if any software tools have the computational capacity to be used directly in the design process. The EcoCalculator, for example, is a spreadsheet-based program requiring the external input of all material quantities in order for the software to run an assessment. And similar tools are equally cumbersome to deploy, particularly at the beginning of a project when what is sought are quick assessments with the power of altering design outcomes.

Addressing this need is the objective of the Tally application developed by the Research Group at KieranTimberlake. Tally was conceived to enrich the user's workflow by facilitating the measurement of a project's embodied energy count in real time. By querying directly the vast data sets that naturally result when modeling in Revit, the application computes the environmental impact of materials and building assemblies by running computational scripts attendant to widely accepted assessment categories including carbon dioxide emissions, ozone depletion, and water acidification.

Following its beta testing in various professional and educational environments in order to ensure workability, debugging, and user satisfaction, Tally is scheduled for commercial launch in 2014. Will it become the much-needed resource that champions the value of material accountability within design practices? Surely, time will tell, but when design is practiced in a collaboratively in a manner that engages all AEC professionals in an accounting of the project's material definition, the value added potential of BIM attains its maximum potential.

BIM protocols can, in fact, be charged with reconciling the all-too-familiar divide between a project's conceptualization and its material becoming. In its data-rich potential, in its representational verisimilitude, and in the virtualized body of the building, reside opportunities for increasing our knowledge of materials and methods as well as for challenging accepted notions of design and construction. For only in this way can that which is invisible in the act of building be reconciled once more with that which is material, constructed, and structural within a "single activity—architecture" (Forty 2000).

22.4 FACILITATING THE TRANSLATION FROM DESIGN TO OPERATIONS—WITH ENERGY

Similar to the way in which a material's environmental impact is increasingly central to architectural practice, BIM protocols can also facilitate awareness of energy-related topics of importance to design professionals. The ease with which we can now model, simulate, and measure the energy profile of high-performance buildings is, in part, due to the highly interoperable structure of BIM. While engineers and building scientists have used sophisticated building simulation programs for decades, only recently have architects begun to engage the field of environmental simulations. Required was a significant shift of performance-based BIM software from analysis to design.

In the early days of energy simulation programs, whose development was actively sponsored by the U.S. Department of Energy, most available programs adopted spreadsheet-based interfaces whose manipulation required skills more akin to a computer programmer than a designer. Sophisticated programs such as eQuest and EnergyPlus ran in code and were for the most part rarely, if ever, used by architects. With the advent of ever more sophisticated modeling capabilities, many energy modeling programs have now achieved greater market uptake by deploying easier to use graphic interfaces.

In the space of "whole building energy analysis," DesignBuilder, which was first introduced in 2003, continues to run complex EnergyPlus calculations for assessing a full range of building and system outcomes. Users create simplified geometric models alongside robust data sets that describe the building's materials and engineering systems. The program imports weather data, simulates internal temperatures and humidity levels, calculates heat transmission through materials, and models natural ventilation, as well as predicts heating and cooling loads, with results conveyed in a myriad of ways, including by fuel type or timetable (yearly, monthly, hourly, etc.). For many architectural engineering professionals, it remains the program of choice when conducting whole building energy analysis. However, after more than a decade of commercial use, rarely is the program of interest to design architects. The reasons for this are many, including its inability to accurately and efficiently model buildings with significant geometric complexity.

More recently, OpenStudio launched by the National Renewable Energy Laboratory and the U.S. Department of Energy continues to advance the use of software tools for whole building energy analysis. It runs EnergyPlus for energy calculations and Radiance for lighting based calculations; it has a Plug In for SketchUp alongside a Parametric Anaylsis Tool. Building Design Advisor (BDA) was first developed by Lawrence Berkeley National Laboratories in the mid-1990s, and offers an object-based graphic interface for modeling the energy consumption of buildings. Its "Schematic Graphic Editor" is the drawing application that supports the visual modeling of all rooms, doors, and windows that define a building's layout. And while it supports a daylight computation module and one for electrical lighting, it too has a limited capacity for modeling complex geometric figures. Similarly, the MIT Design Advisor is an early-phase whole-building energy modeling tool, distributed by its creators for the simulation of heating, cooling, and lighting loads by nonprofessionals. It integrates basic information on geometry, room dimensions, roof materials, and window materials in calculating primary energy loads (reported either annually or monthly). And while it is far easier to use than the programs described here above, it offers the greatest constraints in being limited to the modeling of smaller, non – multistory buildings.

Autodesk's Green Building Studio, deployed in conjunction with Revit, promotes whole building energy modeling in a way that tries to maximize BIM's capacity for interoperability. It is both a cloud-based and stand-alone program that computes the energy consumption profile of a BIM model produced in Revit. It uses the DOE-2 engine to simulate not only energy consumption but also water and carbon emissions. It has built-in weather data and is capable of evaluating energy values against LEED or Energy Star accreditation scores. Most critical for assuring uptake by the AEC industry is its vastly expanded capacity for modeling complex building forms. By exporting design files using the gbXML format exchange, even the most detailed and articulate of models can in theory be evaluated. Whether produced using building elements or conceptual masses, a Revit building information model can be exported for detailed analysis. Once results are received and analyzed, the program encourages users to define a range of design alternates for bettering the model's energy performance, and in so doing furthers the users' control of the project's design.

In fact, the running of energy simulations has been successfully reappropriated by designers and climate engineers intent on expanding the range of design questions made possible by the software. At present, all of the most advanced digital surface modeling software, including Rhino, Grasshopper, Vasari, DIVA For Rhino, and Ladybug, are used to model and analyze optimal responsive solutions for solving the riddle of energy and lighting simulations. In a manner far more computationally sophisticated than ever before, designers are scripting a full range of spatial responses, including the use of genetic algorithms, in the quest for high-performance buildings (Trubiano, Roudsari, and Ozkan 2013). And while energy auditors, modelers, and simulators contribute levels of specialized knowledge previously unavailable to design, a new breed of digital designers are now raising energy-related questions of programmatic and formal importance. The most innovative of this group successfully offer a range of billable services rarely considered important prior to the twenty-first century. The work of Transsolar, Atelier 10, Front, ARUP Associates, Buro Happold, and Werner Sobek Engineers is exemplary in this regard.

Hence, contrary to previous decades, wherein building performance was a specialized science that developed data-specific responses to questions of building technology, today's use of energy simulations by the design community has resulted in a culture of productive approximations. Rather than seeking data-based results for its own sake, energy modeling by designers seeks to compare spatial and material options for the sake of design. For only in this way can BIM-centered energy simulations facilitate the translation of architecture from design to operations. Moreover, whether any of the digital interfaces described here will enjoy significant uptake remains to be seen; yet the ability to foresee a time when design and environmental analysis occur across a consistent modeling platform is important. And that the same set of interfaces can accomplish the long-term monitoring of a building's operational energy, is all the more desirable. For in so doing, the full circle between design, construction, and operations will be closed by the use of a singular integrated framework for architectural representations.

22.5 CONCLUSION

That a building information model produced during the design and construction phase of a project can also be used for ensuring the long-term stewardship of a building and its inhabitants is truly a thrilling prospect. Building information modeling affords the building industry and the design community an important opportunity for expanding the range, comprehensiveness, and critical dimension of how buildings are conceived, fabricated, and simulated. While capable of altering the architect's relationship with construction, BIM is equally adept at transforming the profession's engagement with architectural modeling, material life-cycle assessments, digital fabrication, energy simulations, and building operations. It enables the production of construction documents that enrich and embolden the conceptual activities attendant to design, all the while facilitating designers' awareness of high-performance buildings. For these and other reasons, this chapter promotes the future of building information modeling in the translation of designs for construction + operation, particularly for buildings destined for a world of material and energy scarcity.

DISCUSSION QUESTIONS

1. How can BIM alter the nature of architectural representation in a way that is of particular use for twenty-first-century building practices?
2. How can BIM contribute to an expanded knowledge of architectural materials and operational energy?
3. In what way can BIM contribute to reconciling the gap between design and construction practices by valorizing the role of matter?
4. In what way can BIM contribute to reconciling the gap between design and building operations by valorizing the lessons of building energy?

REFERENCES

Burry, Jane, and Mark Burry. 2010. *The New Mathematics of Architecture*. London: Thames & Hudson, pp. 34–39.

De l'Orme, Philibert. 1567. *L'Œuvre de Philibert de L'Orme comprenant Le premier tome de L'architecture et Les nouvelles inventions pour bien bastir et à petitz frais*. Paris, Libraries-imprimeries réunies, 1894.

Deutsch, Randy. 2011. *BIM and Integrated Design, Strategies for Architectural Practice*. Hoboken, NJ: John Wiley & Sons.

Eastman, Chuck, Paul Teicholz, Raphael Sacks, and Kathleen Liston. 2011. *BIM Handbook: A Guide to Building Information Modeling for Owners, Managers, Designers, Engineers and Contractors* (2d ed.). Hoboken, NJ: John Wiley & Sons.

Forty, Adrian. 2000. *Words and Buildings: A Vocabulary of Modern Architecture*. New York: Thames & Hudson, p. 137.

Konig, Holger, Niklaus Kohler, Johannes Kreissig, and Thomas Lutzkendorf. 2010. *A Life Cycle Approach to Buildings, Principles, Calculations, Design Tools*. DETAIL Green Building, Institut fur Internationale Architekten–Dokumentation.

McGraw Hill Construction, SmartMarket Report. 2010. *The Business Value of BIM in Europe*, pp. 7–10.

McGraw Hill Construction, SmartMarket Report. 2012. *The Business Value of BIM in North America, Multi-Year Trend Analysis and User Ratings (2007–2012)*, pp. 4–10.

McGraw Hill Construction, www.construction.com/about-us/press/new-research-by-MHC-shows-dramatic-increase-in-use-of-BIM-in-North-America.asp, accessed September 20, 2013.

Scamozzi, Vincenzo. 1615. *L'Idea dell'Architettura Universale*, Venetiis, expensis auctoris.

Serlio, Sebastiano. 1551. Tutte l'opere d'architettura. New York: Dover Publications, 1982 (English ed.).

Trubiano, F., S. M. Roudsari, and A. Ozkan. 2013. "Building Simulation and Evolutionary Optimization in the Conceptual Design of a High-Performance Office Building." Proceedings of IBPSA/BS 2013: 13th Conference of International Building Performance Simulation Association, Chambéry, France, August 26–28.

Vitruvius, Marcus Pollio. 1960. *De Architettura*, Courier Dover Publications. Originally published in the first century A.D.

Watts, Andrew. 2013. *Modern Construction Handbook* (3rd ed.). Boston: Springer.

CHAPTER 23

Marx, BIM, and Contemporary Labor

Peggy Deamer, Yale University

23.1 BIM AND WORK

The real fascination of BIM is not its optimization of production, but its reconceptualization of architectural work. Architecture's professional status is shrinking as it limits its exposure to risk; its contractual divorce from building and construction pits architect against both builder and owner. Principles struggle to get heard or paid by their clients; staff work well over 40 hours a week for minimal monetary reward, virtually no security, and little knowledge of or control over their contribution to the larger design (or social) enterprise. Architectural work as we have experienced it for the last 60 years must change.

The introduction of BIM and integrated project delivery (IPD) into the workplace can, should, and will change this. They have stimulated not just a rethinking of architecture's place in the labor market but an awareness of our industry as a domain of labor.

While large architectural/engineering offices attend to management and human resources, the majority of architectural offices in the United States think only of the immediate needs of per-project staffing. If there is any thought given to how an architectural worker can move up in a firm, share in its rewards, pass knowledge on from one project to another, be trained in new techniques, or weigh in on what and why projects are taken on, it is rarely codified or shared. While the cost of procuring and managing labor takes up nearly 50 percent of the architectural office budget, we rarely discuss its implications (Tombesi et al. 2007). But this is beginning to change as the need for the information coordination that comes with BIM expands. The use of BIM, if deployed as more than a rendering tool, makes it virtually impossible to conduct business as (unmanaged) usual.

In order to evaluate how BIM management was actually managed, between July and August 2013, I interviewed by phone 15 BIM managers in large and small offices, in design-focused firms and firms specializing in technically complex "finished buildings," in firms dragged to BIM by the owners, and in others pulling their clients and contractors to it. While almost none of those interviewed wanted to be called BIM managers (they are instead "directors of integrated design," "digital design coordinators," "digital design vision group heads," "Revit leaders," "building smart managers," or "design application managers") they all, for convenience sake, will be called here "BIM managers," which covers a wide range of differing responsibilities. I asked about their educational and employment background; about their placement in the organization; about their methods for training staff; about the respect they garnered in the office; about their personal/personnel skills; about the advantages or not brought by BIM for their firm; and about their relationship to design decisions.

Yes, the BIM manager's task is first and foremost to create an organizational framework, establish and update the BIM Execution Plan, schedule and chair meetings between team members for model consistency, back up and restore data, and maintain model security (Lareau and Nowicki 2010). But beyond this, the manner in which "BIM management" is itself managed is equally important and less obvious.

23.2 BIM MANAGERS: WHAT THEY ARE DOING

The striking interviews revealed that the work of the BIM manager contrasts greatly with that of BIM itself: where BIM makes work efficient, quantifiable, and predictable, the manager's work is subjective, ad-hoc, and open-ended. Where BIM is valued for its informational transparency, the BIM manager is valued for his/her empathetic subtlety. Where BIM makes decision making linear, the BIM manager's own decisions are multi-aspirational. The reason for this might be obvious—the BIM-manager is dealing with people, BIM with a building—but the specific issues that the BIM manager faces in bringing together people and building illuminates the real picture about the nature of BIM work, not just BIM technology. And the BIM managers present a complex, unsettled, and encouraging picture, one equal to the idiosyncrasies of architecture itself. Three major issues confront the BIM manager regarding design versus technology, networked tasks, and political/organizational change.

23.2.1 Design versus Technology

The first set of issues faced by the BIM manager resides in the inherent tension between design and technological, conflicting logics that BIM is not the first platform to introduce but which it exacerbates to an extreme. The aesthetic, illogical, nonlinear process of design simply doesn't conform to a technology that is meant to streamline and quantify decision making. Likewise, design wants a coherent formal concept, whereas BIM a data-rich plethora of information. The BIM manager, in order to function in this, must acknowledge sympathies for both while not expecting a seamless synthesis.

This tension is indicated by the backgrounds of the BIM managers interviewed. All the managers except one are architects trained in design but whose concern for design was accompanied by another interest—technology, process, or quantifiability—that drew them to BIM and a technical career trajectory. After this, however, 75 percent wanted to and did return to architecture and design. For example, one began as a sculptor, then trained as and taught architecture, introducing BIM into the curriculum, and then became a façade consultant, his interest in materials and fabrication leading him to BIM. But wanting to return to the full design of a building, he moved to a high-design architectural office. Another loved the design complexity of his thesis at architecture school, but wondered how design decisions could be made more quantifiable. Finding that in BIM and having developed that expertise as a BIM consultant, he rerouted to a boutique design office that produces highly craft architecture. Another, working in an architecture office, was entranced with the improvement in process brought on by CAD and then BIM, and made standardization his expertise, but changed offices when he felt stuck in an information technology (IT) role and divorced from the actual projects. In each case, the manager was bringing BIM into his or her specific offices via a first, pilot project.

This then raises the issue of BIM managements' most effective location: architecture or IT, embedded within a team or outside and separate. Each choice symbolizes design versus technical identity. In both small and medium-size offices, there was general agreement on the importance of being in a project, not just an expert "drop-in," the implicit idea being that the BIM manager is most effective if embedded in the design decisions. In the large offices, the departmentalization is more complex and varied. About 50 percent of the BIM managers had started in IT but had been moved to architecture, primarily so they could be working in project teams. The other 50 percent valued their ability to set standards not related to specific projects.

The largest multicity firms that not only separated architecture from IT but research and development (R&D) from in-house training don't escape the tension of in-house versus out-of-house work, coordinating both innovation and implementation R&D people while also overseeing BIM trainers in the regional offices. And while these managers worked in firms that were not "design" oriented, they still saw their work as supporting an architectural, not merely technical vision. A subset of this question was whether BIM work, as IT work, should be budgeted under overhead or under the billable, project-specific hours. The two managers I spoke to whose work was billed as overhead felt strongly that this was a mistake, since it was more expendable and encouraged a lack of team accountability.

If all the BIM managers agreed that their work was to support architectural quality, they varied on how or where BIM supported this. In certain offices, small and large, this meant not using BIM in schematics or design development so that the traditional design process (sketches, etc.) could remain undisturbed. Others felt strongly that the design advantage of BIM was missed if it was not used at the start, since BIM invites/expects upfront detail knowledge that offers a broader palette of design thinking.

The good news, in other words, is that BIM managers have architecture backgrounds that shape the context of the technological drive; the interesting news is that this background sits in provocative, if undigested, organizational contexts.

23.2.2 Networked Tasks

The second set of issues confronting the BIM managers stems from the particular collaborative and networked character of BIM work. Much has been made of BIM's support of collaboration, and indeed, the ability of engineers, fabricators, environmentalists, and so on to collaborate early in the project is important, complex, and significant; BIM managers, we know, need to be good communicators and organizers.

But the specifics of collaboration in the architectural office also require the BIM manager to reconfigure knowledge and skills. When the design work is three-dimensional, not two-dimensional; when the work is informational and not visual; and when construction knowledge is necessary for all participating in the virtual model, the task assignments must adjust. In one of the major distinctions between CAD and BIM work, inexperienced staff must be brought up to some level of expertise quickly. As one manager noted, the distinction between architect and draftsperson disappears. As another put it, the collaborative, 3D nature of the model made it "a constantly moving monster" requiring different jobs to control it. If Bonnneau wisely suggests thinking of job descriptions in four categories—project administrator, modeler, annotator, and detailer (Bonneau 2012)—it is the BIM manager's job to identify and enact this.

Likewise, the task of building the BIM model is chained, not individual work, and the chain is only as strong as the weakest link. Production problems are not helped by throwing more people/drafters at the task. The linked nature of this structure contradicts the compartmentalization of most architectural offices, and BIM managers must determine how best to deal with linked rather than pyramidal organizations. As one manager said, the training can only go as fast as the slowest person, and, as a consultant, he had to be very patient and listen hard. As another put it, the team working on the BIM model needs to be small and tightly knit, and her role was to facilitate team "ownership" and continuity, not selfish pride. Another insisted that the reason a single BIM manager didn't work at their firm was that such siloed expertise was inappropriate to communication that needed to happen at many different levels and in many different directions.

Coordination, in other words, is not merely handled by standards, charts, and critical paths, but by appreciation of the emerging entities and evolving chains of command.

23.2.3 Political/Organizational Change

The skill set needed to support this rhizomatic work structure is made more complicated by the political context in which it is embedded, and this leads to the third set of skills required by BIM managers. The firm leaders are generally of an older generation, primarily design oriented, and more experienced in construction; a younger generation, digitally evolved more than formally savvy, are the IT innovators. The nurturing of the bottom-up, of those working "on the ground," is essential, but today's BIM manager must operate in the politically difficult position of empowering the younger tech-savvy staff while not threatening the principals or those having moved up in the firm pre-BIM. One manager said that you not only can't count on top-down directives for this, but you constantly need to move people "on the ground" around so they don't plateau. Others indicated that when a project is scaling up, you have to be sensitive to and not demand much of the "CAD folks" who see BIM only as a 3D model. Another indicated that staffing needs have definitely changed, but the formula for this is not obvious, since it depends on the final product. With IPD, the model is more significant and BIM-skilled people are necessary; if not, the team can absorb less-trained people to do things that can't erase information. Staffing is delicately handled, indirectly manipulated.

On the other hand, because staffing is not generally a BIM manager's call, buy-in from the top is essential. The leadership role of the BIM manager is only as real as the power structure allows it to be.

Without this authority, the BIM manager cannot do the training, make productive staffing and critical-path changes, nor purchase the needed equipment. This can be hard to come by when the design partner doesn't want to or can't change his or her own working method. It is exhilarating when it is there. Two of the larger offices with seemingly the most advanced uses of BIM were those where principals required the change from CAD to BIM to happen in one day, no questions asked.

In general, beyond the specific organizational changes to work brought on by BIM, institutional and disciplinary change is just hard, and the BIM manager needs special skills. Many said that they needed to adjust the delivery of their protocols depending on who they were addressing: the principal, the project architect, the new staff member. In arguing for change, managers must identify the nature of that person's resistances: adherence to known procedures or lack of desire to collaborate, say, in the case of principals; personal ambition to please the boss and not the BIM manager on the part of the project architect; peer pressure to "design" and not merely learn software on the part of a staff member. Likewise, the protocols, while standardized in outcome, were not achievable by all in the same way. Like a sports trainer who knows that all individuals learn differently, the BIM manager must adjust training techniques. Ultimately, for all the standardization, the BIM manager essentially gives the team access to what is possible without knowing or controlling the outcome. The one BIM manager who left the technical realm of façade design to work in a high-design architecture office did so partly because, in the new office, the lack of fixed BIM protocols made the job feel organic; it had the adventure of a startup. And many managers mentioned the fact that now, more than ever, job retention is essential, and for this it was as important to make sure that those they worked with were happy as it was to make them productive. (As an aside, it is interesting to note that *all* the BIM managers loved their jobs even as many said they had "a love-hate" relationship to BIM itself. Many were shocked at their own quick rise in their firms, becoming leaders at a very young age.)

23.3 THE ENACTMENT OF ENLIGHTENED MANAGEMENT THEORY

The above description of the precarious and uncodified nature of BIM management work is meant to describe not its fallibility but rather its creativity. The story is not about BIM as an efficient tool that misperforms because of human error. The manager operates not as a technician in control of organizational rules but as a "craftsman," a practitioner of the art of management. As we move toward a future of more pervasive BIM use, the goal should not just be the streamlining of work but its staying light on its feet, ready for change. The one BIM manager who was not an architect but trained as the structural engineer—the oldest person interviewed and the only woman—objected to my suggestion that BIM would soon become pervasive and managing change would soon be irrelevant. She pointed out that it took 20 years to adapt to CAD; 7 to adapt to BIM; the next thing will come quickly and with its own timetable of new demands.

This observation and the general desire for production flexibility draws on the optimistic if not utopian management strategies of organization theorists in the 1950s and 1960s, many of them immigrants from Europe who saw the full promise of American corporate exceptionalism. Moving beyond the early twentieth-century infatuation with division-of-labor Taylorism, these thinkers—Kurt Lewin, Donald Schon, and Peter Drucker primary among them—encourage enlightened management.

When confronting change, they suggest that one should evaluate the fluidity and complexity of the social context. While we might think that the most direct way to produce change is to increase the driving forces, in fact the most effective approach is to lessen the resisting forces. Don't conserve old hierarchies when given new tools; celebrate complexity. Listen to the wisdom of the system. Indeed, don't just manage change, encourage it. As Kurt Lewin said, "If you want to truly understand something, try to change it."

When setting management protocols, encourage knowledge that is activity-embedded, not abstract or academic. "Problem set" rather than "problem solve." Decentralize to be responsive. Defy disciplines and expand time horizons. Balance a variety of needs and goals and don't adhere to one value.

When contemplating future production, move from mass-production to mass-customization. Move from a made-in-house mindset to learning with various entities. Penetrate local markets. Avoid expanding into areas to be avoided. Produce fewer products. Prepare for "planned abandonment" and don't cling to yesterday's successes. Serve the customer, the reason for the firm's existence. Recognize that the real business of business is grasping that the essential question is not how to do things right but how to find the right thing to do.

When dealing with the worker, stay humble and be a learner. Remember that the manager's job is to prepare and free people to perform. Remember that the most intelligent and flexible in the system is the human being. Create conditions in which the individual is committed to an action because it is intrinsically satisfying, not because it provides external rewards.

It is here that Karl Marx provides background: the well-being of the worker was the heart of his socialism. His goal was to excise capitalist-induced alienation: alienation of the worker from other workers by competition for jobs; alienation of the worker from his products by the division of labor; and the alienation of worker from self by the false drives toward consumption. While *Das Capital* seems antithetical to American management, the goal for both is the same: the creative, supported, cooperative, satisfied, and productive worker. It is the same goal as the successful BIM manager.

The future work that this points to is laid out by Peter Drucker in his *Post-Capitalist Society* (Drucker 1993). Describing the emergence of a new type of worker within late twentieth-century "capitalism," he points out that in the eighteenth century, knowledge was applied to tools; in the nineteenth and early twentieth century, knowledge was applied to productivity (Taylorization), or knowledge applied to human work. Today, it is being applied to knowledge itself. As a result, a new breed of "knowledge workers" is appearing, workers who are different than previous eras because of their high level of education. These workers, Drucker says, own the means of production, that is, knowledge itself.

More than this, because the skills held by these workers—research, product design, fabrication, marketing, advertising, customer consulting, financing, contracting—allow technical insights to be linked to marketing strategy and financial acumen, the traditional distinction between goods and services breaks down. The traditional factors of production—land, labor, and capital—have become restraints rather than drivers. Indeed, no class, he points out, has risen or fallen as quickly as the blue-collar worker.

23.4 CONCLUSION: POST-CAPITALIST ARCHITECTURE

This gives us a framework for imagining the future work of architecture. Our skills, with the aid of BIM and IPD, can easily be understood as "research, product design, fabrication, marketing, advertising, customer consulting, financing, contracting" if we reconceive our mission. We should no longer assume that our work is delivering a building but rather delivering built environmental intelligence. Consistent with this, we should no longer leave the maintenance of the building to others, but embrace this as proof that our work is the ongoing stewardship of the things we put on this earth. We should no longer ignore the status of the laborers—architectural or constructional, white-collar or blue-collar, domestic of foreign—who produce our buildings. We should embrace the power given to us by BIM not merely to find the right way to do things, but find the right thing to do.

At this transitional moment in the profession, when design responsibility and financial savvy are shared among various players, the constitution of a new model for architectural practice is entirely up for grabs. Now is the time to think expansively about what we want this new practice to look like and how its organization might be linked to larger social, political, and economic formations. As new players in the management game—since we have avoided even seeing ourselves in the labor/management schema—architects are free to move directly toward an imagined ideal.

DISCUSSION QUESTIONS

1. Explain the role of the BIM manager in the office. What characteristics are needed to fulfill these responsibilities?
2. How are BIM with IPD changing the relationship of the team in architecture offices compared with CAD and design-bid-build?
3. How can existing examples of BIM management be models for future, better architectural office management?
4. Are there other qualities besides efficiency and cost savings that can be promoted by BIM?

REFERENCES

Bonneau, Kirstyn. 2012. "Need to Know Basis: Managing Varying Levels of BIM Proficiency on a Project Team." In *Practical BIM 2012: Management, Implementation, Coordination, and Evaluation*. Proceedings of the Sixth Annual Practical BIM 2012 Symposium (July 2012), USC School of Architecture, pp.147–152.

Drucker, Peter. 1993. *Post-Capitalist Society*. New York: HarperCollins.

Lareau, Lance, and Richard Nowicki. 2010. "Developing BIM Standards." Fourth Annual USC Symposium on Building Information Modeling + Analytics (August 4), USC School of Architecture.

Tombesi, Paolo, Blair Gardiner, and Tony Mussen, eds. 2007. *Take 5: Looking Ahead: Defining the Terms of a Sustainable Architectural Profession*. Canberra: Royal Australian Institute of Architects.

PART 6

BIM SPECULATION

Beyond BIM: Next-Generation Building Information Modeling to Support Form, Function, and Use of Buildings

Yehuda E. Kalay, Technion University
Davide Schaumann, Technion University
Seung Wan Hong, Technion University
Davide Simeone, Sapienza University

24.1 RATIONALE

Predicting and evaluating the expected performance of buildings that have yet to be constructed is of cardinal importance for architects and their clients. But because of their size and cost of their construction, buildings are the kind of product that does not lend itself to prototyping. A building is a one-of-a-kind artifact, a prototype of itself. If the designer makes a mistake, and that mistake is not recognized before the building has been constructed, it can only be corrected at great cost or not at all. To overcome this problem, architects have been using building models and a host of simulations to help them represent, predict, and evaluate the product of their design before it is realized.

The importance of architectural models has been recognized for more than 2,500 years. First came physical scale models, which were often crude and imprecise approximations of the actual building. They were limited to informing designers and their clients of the gross shape of the building, and some of its unique features. But they could not provide cost estimations or energy calculations, and most importantly, they were unable to predict the spatial experience the intended environment would provide to its users.

The invention of scale drawings and perspective rendering in the fifteenth century, as means for design conception, representation, and communication, allowed architects to conceive and represent buildings on paper before they were committed to timber and stone. They could thus contemplate alternative design solutions, involve more people in the decision-making process, and evaluate the desirability of potential outcomes. But these drawings suffered from excessive abstraction, providing a spatial experience of space akin to the one that musical notations provide of the actual music they represent: coded information, interpretable only by well-trained professionals.

The advent of computer-aided design (CAD) in the 1960s allowed architects to further evolve the representational means at their disposal, mostly in terms of photo-realism and control over detail. The emergence of BIM (building information modeling), at the end of the twentieth century, added much needed nongraphical data to the formerly mostly geometric representation.

At the same time, in certain engineering disciplines, such as electrical and mechanical engineering, digital representation tools have evolved much further than they did in architecture. Electrical engineers, for example, can place millions of transistors on a chip of silicon, simulate their actions, evaluate their performance, and fabricate them all without leaving their workstations. Aerospace engineers "flew" Boeing's 777 plane for over 500 hours before the first sheet metal was cut, thereby discovering and eliminating errors, optimizing parts, and reducing the airplane's certification time considerably. All of this led to significant cost and time savings, and winning its designers the 1995 Computerworld Smithsonian Award for the first airplane to be 100 percent digitally designed and preassembled on computer (Snyder et al. 1998).

This did not happen in the building industry. As Brian Lawson put it succinctly some 15 years ago: "The best test of most design is to wait and see how well it works in practice" (Lawson 1997).

His observation is still valid. Although architects and their clients now have at their disposal tools that can help them predict and evaluate many building performance characteristics like cost, energy consumption, and structural adequacy, they have no means to help them tell how well the proposed building will perform from a user's point of view before it has been constructed and occupied.

The importance of making buildings perform well not only structurally and aesthetically but also functionally has been acknowledged ever since Vitruvius (Morgan 1960) coined his famous three predicates: *firmitas, utilitas, venustas* (solidity, usefulness, beauty). Many have argued that, more than anything else, a building's success depends on how well it serves the needs of its uses:

> The architect has something in common with the gardener. Everyone can grasp the fact that the gardener's success depends on whether or not the plants he selects for the garden thrive there. No matter how beautiful his conception of a garden may be, it will, nevertheless, be a failure if it is not the right environment for the plants, if they cannot flourish in it (Rasmussen 1964, p. 12).

Rasmussen's metaphor puts the *users* at the center of the building design process and stipulates that a building that does not meet their needs cannot be considered a successful product of the design process.

With the exponential increase in computing power and the availability of new simulation systems, analyses of human-environment interactions have begun to be introduced into building performance evaluations. They are gradually overcoming the shortcomings derived from the heretofore domination of normative approaches (Koutamanis and Mitossi 1996). Yet, at present, their real contribution is limited to the representation of specific occurrences and/or specific aspects of human behavior (e.g., fire egress, pedestrian movement, crowd simulation). More extensive and comprehensive simulation models of human spatial behavior in built environments, able to predict not just future users' movements but also the effects of the environment on their activities and conceptions, are still missing.

24.2 THE SHORTCOMINGS OF BIM

This shortcoming should be attributed to the inadequacy of current building modeling tools, rather than to lack of knowledge concerning human environmental behavior. Contrary to the prevailing hype, BIM models provide a poor, inadequate representation of buildings: they represent only the physical and material characteristics of buildings. But buildings, unlike other products, cannot be understood independently of their context, of their intended use, and of their intended users. It matters, for example, whether the building is used as an office, as a school, as a dwelling, as a place of worship, or as a hospital. A building cannot be understood just from looking at drawings and models. Rather, it should also include the purpose and function of the building, and the social, cultural, and economic profile of the people who will use it. It is not the same "product" if the building is used by children or by the elderly, in North America or in India. In other words, a building cannot be understood without knowing how, and by whom, it will be used.

Unlike a building, the functionality of a cell phone, for example, is independent of its users. It does not matter if the user is old or young, male or female, Christian, Jewish, Muslim, or Hindu, and whether it is used in North America, Europe, or Asia. Obviously, some users may be more proficient at using the phone than others, but the nature and character of the phone itself do not depend on the level of their skillfulness. Therefore, it is possible to evaluate the quality of a cell phone independently of who will use it, and where it is used, which explains why consumer-oriented websites that compare and rate products like cell phones are so popular.

There are no websites that compare and rate buildings; their quality can only be assessed individually. To understand and to be able to evaluate the quality of the building as a product, one must consider, in addition to its form, also its context, its specific function, and how it is used. More formally, to fully understand a building, and to be able to evaluate its performance, the information that describes it must include

1. The form and materials from which it will be made.
2. The function it is intended to serve.
3. How and by whom it will be being used.

Considering, for example, a simple object like a door. Modern building modeling systems can only represent its form: its shape, the materials it is made of, its color, cost, manufacturer, and so on.

They have no capacity to represent the second and the third aspects: its function and use. Therefore, the objects depicted in Figure 24.1 would be considered a door even though they obviously do not function as such.

Extending the representational model to include form, function, and use will provide two main advantages:

1. It will help the different participants in a design process to better understand each other's design proposals, or at least not to misunderstand each other's intentions.
2. It will help to evaluate the design more thoroughly and more completely, because the evaluation can go beyond the form aspects of an object, and discern its ability to perform the task it is intended for.

Such a comprehensive representation will even be able to automate some aspects of the design process and its evaluation. Objects may be able to automatically and autonomously trigger self-evaluations of the kind that will exclude the doors depicted in Figure 24.1 from being considered doors.

FIGURE 24.1   A door that is not a door.
(Gate, 2013; wood and steel, 200x90x90, designer Ron Gilad, image courtesy of Tel Aviv Museum of Modern Art)

The same technology can be used to represent building components and objects that are inherently dynamic: a door can swing open or shut, it can be locked or unlocked (which would make a big difference in the case of fire emergency), elevators can move up/down and their schedule of operation can be compared to the load generated by the building's users. Even the people who will inhabit the proposed building can be represented as autonomous entities, simulating the building in use, once it has been occupied. This is in contrast to how people are often depicted in architecture renderings or animations as stationary manikins that provide mostly scale and visual decoration to current building models or animations choreographed by the designer herself to promote the design rather than to discover its shortcomings.

A modeling system that comprises *form*, *function*, and *use* will thus be a step forward, compared to the current state-of-the-art of building information models, which ignore these important aspects of a building.

24.3 FORM, FUNCTION, USE

To more formally define the three main components of the proposed model, the following discussion elucidates the nature of *form*, *function*, and *use*, and the relationships among them.

24.3.1 Form

Form is concerned with questions of size, shape, and relative position of objects, as well as with their properties (material, color, weight, etc.). It describes the physical characteristics of a building and its parts, and answers such questions as "What does it look like, and what is it made of?"

Form plays an important role in architectural design, representing architectural elements such as walls, windows, columns, floors, and so on, and the spatial/topological links between them. Nonphysical objects can also have form, such as rooms, courtyards, and other spaces, each composed of objects that are linked with others, topologically. Each architectural object is composed of such forms, linked with other forms. BIMs are a systematic digital representation of forms, and the topological information that connects them.

24.3.2 Function

Function is a set of conceptual attributes that add meaning (semantics) to the object's form characteristics. It can answer such questions as "What does it mean? What do we call it? What can be done with it?"

Function is independent of form, as many different forms can have the same function. Conversely, the same form can have different functions. In fact, function, or meaning, can only be established from the three-way relationship between the object (stimulus), its referent (consequent), and the conscious observer, as explained by the American philosopher Morris Cohen (1944):

> [A]nything acquires meaning if it is connected with or indicates, or refers to something beyond itself, so that its full nature points to and is revealed in that connection (p. 47).

That is, function is both referential and inferential; objects and concepts acquire meaning by association with other objects and/or concepts, after this reference has been established by an observer. This definition explains why the same object may hold different meanings with different observers; the referential nature of its meaning permits different observers to associate the object with different referents, while the inferential nature of its meaning allows them to interpret the reference differently. The potential for different interpretations grows if the dynamic nature of the inference process is factored in. The same observer may associate the same object with different referents under different circumstances and to interpret the reference differently at different times.

The reference may be direct, as in "this is a door," which indicates that the referring object ("this") is an instance of a class of objects known to have doorlike functions, such as allowing controlled passage of people-sized objects between adjacent spaces. A consequence of this reference may be the inference that, in case of an emergency, "this door" will afford egress—an inference that may prove to be false if the door has been locked, thereby invalidating its referent's premise of allowing passage. On the other hand, the objects depicted in Figure 24.1 should be associated with the referent "work of art" rather than "door," even if their form information is consistent with that of door-like objects.

Building information models do not explicitly represent function. Instead, they rely on the assumption that the professionals who use them all share a common understanding and therefore will interpret the meaning of the represented objects in a similar way. The reliance on shared cultural, educational, and experiential backgrounds is risky, because it involves assumptions that are themselves rarely communicated and are not always shared by different people (especially by professionals who have been educated to understand their world in discipline-specific ways). This concept of representing explicitly the functional relationships between objects has been elegantly captured by modern spreadsheet software, where the formulae that link one data item to another are explicitly represented and are therefore subject to analysis and verification in and of themselves.

24.3.3 Use

Use is a property that adds time-based, sociocultural information to the represented object. It answers such questions as "Who uses it, and how is it used?"

Use is both a quality of an object, or an environment, and of the individual or group of people who activate it. It is the set of qualities that depends on the object itself, but can only be expressed by a person who employs it. It is a social/cultural quality, based on the interaction between people and the object.

The notion of use has been central to twentieth-century philosophy, especially in the works of Husserl, Heidegger, Merleau-Ponty, Dreyfus, and Noë, as demonstrated most aptly by Martin Heidegger's two most basic neologisms, "present-at-hand" and "ready-to-hand," which he used to describe various attitudes towards things in the world (Heidegger, trans. 1962; Dreyfus 1995, p. 162).

Building information models have ignored use so far. For example, elevators are represented statically, by a symbol or a geometric model that is stationary. The capacity of the elevator to move people up and down tall buildings must be inferred from its implied function (being an elevator). But there is no information that can tell the observer whether the elevator is operational or out of service or whether

Table 24.1 Classification of form, function, and use

Classification	Form	Function	Use
Questions	"What does it look like?" "What is it made of?"	"What is it?" "What does it mean?"	"Who uses it?" "How is it used?"
Examples	Geometry Topology Material	Ontology Semantics	Time Performance Use
Dependency	Point of view	Context Relation to other entities Social agreement	User's intentions

its schedule is adequate to the needs of the users. Such information is not included in the model itself. Rather, it must be gleaned from external knowledge, one that is the province of observers and depends on their experiences.

24.4 DEPENDENCIES

Form, function, and use are not independent of each other: they are influenced by, and influence, one another (Figure 24.2). Clearly, function and use are influenced by the form of the object; function influences use, and vice versa. Even form, which is seemingly a given, can change if time-based use, and different functions, are introduced, as they are in real life (i.e., the building is remodeled to accommodate changing needs).

24.4.1 Form versus Function

Whether one does or does not agree with Louis Sullivan's famed proclamation that "form follows function" (Sullivan 1896), it is clear that form and function have much to do with each other: a hammer takes its form from its function, and a knife works better if it has a specific form.

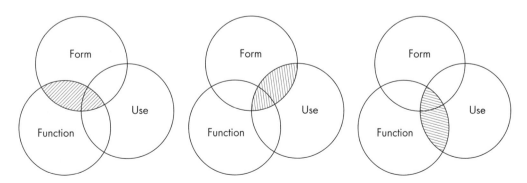

FIGURE 24.2 Form versus function, form versus use, function versus use.

24.4.2 Form versus Use

An object's shape and size expresses its affordance, thus informs its use, as was discussed earlier. That does not mean that the object cannot be used differently, but when it does, it may perform less optimally than if used as designed (Gibson 1979, Norman 1999).

24.4.3 Function versus Use

Objects are used not only according to their form, but also according to the function, or meaning, associated with them. Hence the "door" in Figure 24.1 works perfectly well as an object of art, even if its form is that of a door because the function of the door has been changed; it took on the semantics of an object of art, qualified to be exhibited in a museum.

24.5 OBJECTIVES

To explore the efficacy of form-function-use as a building information modeling system, a more capable building representation is needed, one that can support simulation of buildings in use rather than only their built shell. Such simulation can be used to evaluate the fit between the building and its intended functions and users, under normal and under emergency conditions. The significance of this approach lies in the centrality of the model as it applies to the design of buildings. Since each building is a one-of-a-kind artifact, there is no other place to improve its design other than at the design phase, before it has been committed to stone, steel, and glass. Errors that can be corrected at the design phase can save large sums of money during construction, and—more important—during the building's life. A better building product will lead to better utilization by its users, thus potentially improving or even saving their lives. In an era when the irrevocable impact of the built environment on the cost, quality, and perhaps even possibility of life on earth has been recognized, the need to make every effort to improve the tools used by building designers is self-evident.

Rather than improving just one facet of the design of buildings, as BIM has done, the proposed approach aims to engage the design process at a more holistic level, by improving the modeling of the information that is used by designers and users of buildings.

24.6 METHODOLOGY

The main methodological challenge in achieving the stated objectives is the judicious allocation and location of the three main information types: the combination of form, function, and use. It is not additive, nor is there a specific best construct to accommodate all three data types. Two direct approaches to making objects intelligent have been tried and failed: the "strong" artificial intelligence (AI) of making the system as a whole knowledgeable about all that goes on in a building, and the object-oriented approach of embedding intelligence within individual objects themselves.

The AI approach has proved to be impractical, for the same reasons other heavy AI approaches failed. There is much going on in a building, requiring the representation of too much knowledge, exceeding the capacity of current computational systems even when they are divorced from form-intensive applications such as modeling buildings (Kalay and Irazabal 1995).

The second approach attempted to endow each object with intelligence. That too proved too cumbersome, and insensitive to the shifting needs of the users. In effect, it was not able to respond to the different referential needs, as discussed above (Kalay, Carrara, and Novembri 1994).

A third approach is to use a connected, distributed network of intelligent objects. The data that are used to represent function and use can be disaggregated and located within different constructs (objects), linked to each other in a kind of social network. For example, rather than making the door object exclusively responsible for knowing all there is to know about doors (such as its form, its function as a barrier to movement, as well as its use), this information can be disaggregated and distributed. The door has basic knowledge of its form and its function. This information is partially augmented by knowledge residing in the objects representing the users, who know how to reach and open a door, step forward or backward when swinging it open (depending on which side they approach the door), even knowing when to knock before attempting to open the door. This last piece of knowledge is derived by the user-object from both social/behavioral attributes associated with the user, as well as data associated with the room protected by the door. The room, which is itself an object, thus has knowledge about the activity that goes on inside it, whether it is a private activity, such as a meeting, or whether the activity in the room is accessible to the user. That information, in turn, is linked to the user's profile (a data set). The room thus knows whether the user knocking at the door is allowed to participate in the activity (Lee 2006, Kalay and Lee 2009).

24.7 IMPLEMENTATION

Current building modeling systems, such as Autodesk's Revit, Graphisoft's ArchiCAD, and Bentley's MicroStation, are data-rich and are appropriate for the purpose of representing complex entities such as building. However, their very richness makes them inadequate for representing dynamically changing use scenarios. Thus, they can represent the form of buildings, but not how they are used. Video game engines, on the other hand, such as Garage Game's Torque and Dassault Systèmes' 3DVIA Virtools, are designed for the representation of people in action, allowing fast rendering at the expense of data richness. They can represent dynamic activities and embedded intelligence, but are not suitable for representing complex buildings. Neither BIMs nor game engines can represent the function or meaning of buildings; that information depends on references to other entities, or classes, and are context and observer dependent. The representation of meaning is the province of ontology modeling systems such as Protégé, a free, Java-based open source ontology editor and knowledge-based framework. The project described here uses a combination of BIM, ontology modeling, and game engines to derive a composite system, which can represent all three components of the proposed model (Figure 24.3).

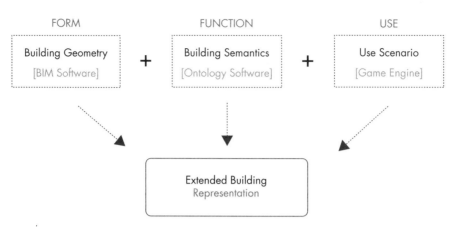

FIGURE 24.3 Schematic diagram of the system.

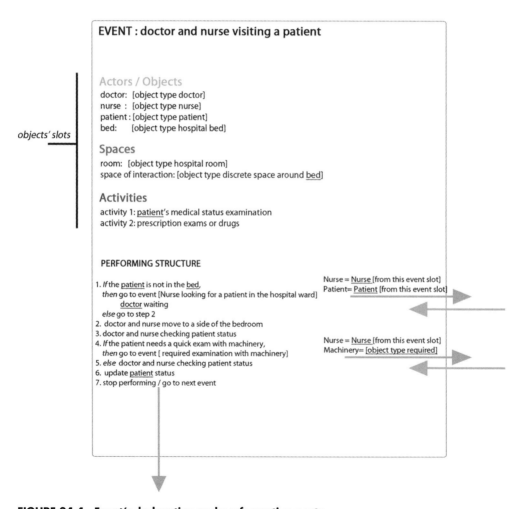

FIGURE 24.4 Event's declarative and performative parts.

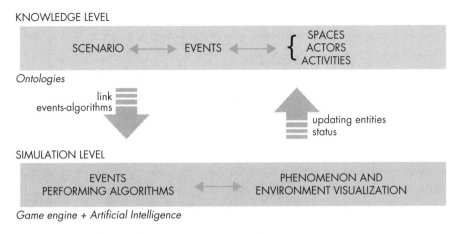

FIGURE 24.5   The simulation conceptual model.

The entities used to encode information about use scenarios are called *events* (Yan and Kalay 2005, Simeone and Kalay 2012). Events comprise two distinct parts: a declarative part and a performative part. In the event's declarative part is defined as all the entities involved (actors, spaces, building components) and the typology of structuring activities. Each entity is made explicit in a specific, named slot (with an associated facet identifying the type of object requested) and with a selection of its properties affected by or related to performing the event.

In the performative part, the event-performing process is represented by means of a sequence of rules involving the entities specified in the declarative part. Performing these rules checks for the initial necessary condition for the event, controls the actions of each single entity involved to reliably represent the dynamics of its action, updates their properties to show how the event affects the model, and evaluates their status in order to take next decisions (Figure 24.4).

The combined entity thus includes both object-oriented information (typically found in BIM programs) and semantic information (typically found in ontological modeling systems). The combination of object data and rules accommodates the function part of the proposed model. Moreover, by linking event entities into a network, the combined attributes allow each object to inform other objects of its abilities and affordances. For example, a door is able to inform other objects, such as a human user represented as an avatar, of its state of usability—whether it is locked, openable, even blocked. Consequently, a user-object can choose its actions in an informed manner using the built-in scripts to make use of the environmental data.

The third component, simulation, is provided by the game engine. The database formed by the events structure communicates with the visualization/action component to activate the event entities in a manner similar to agent-based systems. Each state of database is transformed into other possible states by processing the rules in the simulation part of the system. The simulation, in turn, causes changes in the state of the data, which are communicated back to the database, causing activation of other rules, and so on (Figure 24.5). Together they accommodate all three parts of the model: form, function, and use.

24.8 CONCLUSION

A comprehensive building model should include form, function, and use information. By simulating the building in-use, such a model will allow designers and their clients to make more informed decisions about the product they are designing and its potential impacts on the people who will use it. The designers will be able to predict the performance of the building from a user-centered point of view, something they can only imagine today.

By combining BIM, game engines, and ontology modeling systems, a composite system can be developed that can represent all three components of the proposed model. In order to combine form, function, and use information in a single building model, a new distributed data placement and management approach is required, enabling the parts to behave as a whole without overtaxing the system.

ACKNOWLEDGMENTS

The model is currently being developed under grants from the European Research Center, No. 340753; and the Israel Science Foundation, No. 1161/11.

An abstracted version of this paper was published in *Architecture in Formation: On the Nature of Information in Digital Architecture*, edited by Pablo Lorenzo-Eiroa and Aaron Sprecher (Routledge, pp. 120–123).

DISCUSSION QUESTIONS

1. Can users be modeled?
2. How can data about building use processes be collected to be encoded in the system?
3. How can differences in culture, which influence users' behavior and their use of buildings, be accounted for and encoded in the system?
4. In what ways will modeling a building's form–function–use in a BIM environment influence the design process and practice?

REFERENCES

Cohen, Morris R. 1944. *A Preface to Logic*. New York: Henry Holt & Co.

Dreyfus, Hubert. 1995. *Being-in-the-World*. Cambridge, MA: MIT Press.

Gibson, James J. 1979. "The Theory of Affordances." *Perceiving, Acting, and Knowing*, Robert Shaw and John Bransford (eds.). Hillsdale, NJ: Lawrence Erlbaum Associates, pp. 127–143.

Heidegger, Martin. 1962. *Being and Time*. John MacQuarrie and Edward Robinson, trans. New York: Harper & Row.

Kalay, Yehuda E., Gianfranco Carrara, and Gabriele Novembri. 1994. "Knowledge-based Computational Support for Architectural Design." *Automation in Construction* 3(2–3): 157–175.

Kalay, Yehuda E., and Clara Irazabal. 1995. "Virtual Users (VUsers): Auto-Animated Human-forms for Representation and Evaluation of Behavior in Designed Environments," internal report. Department of Architecture, UC Berkeley.

Kalay, Yehuda E., and Yungil Lee. 2009. "Auto-Animated Humanforms for Simulation, Evaluation, and Population of Virtual Environments." Report to the Korean Culture & Content Agency (in Korean).

Koutamanis, Alexander, and Vicky Mitossi. 1996. "Simulation for Analysis: Requirements from Architectural Design." *Proceedings 6th EFA*, European Full-scale Modeling Association Conference, Vienna, pp. 96–101.

Lee, Jaewook. 2006. "Designing Intelligent Virtual Environments with a Multi-Agent System." PhD dissertation, UC Berkeley.

Norman, Donald A. 1999. "Affordance, Conventions, and Design." *Interactions*, ACM 6(3): 38–43.

Rasmussen, Steen Eiler. 1964. *Experiencing Architecture*, 2d ed. Cambridge, MA: MIT Press.

Simeone, Davide, and Yehuda E. Kalay. 2012. "An Event-Based Model to Simulate Human Behaviour in Built Environments," H. Achten and Dana Matejovska, eds. *Proceedings of eCAADe*, Prague.

Snyder, Charles R., Charles A. Snyder, and Chetan S. Sankar. 1998. "Use of Information Technologies in the Process of Building the 777." *Journal of Information Technology Management* 9(3): 31–42.

Sullivan, Louis. 1896. "The Tall Office Building Artistically Considered." *Lippincott's Monthly*, Philadelphia.

Vitruvius, Pollio. 1960. *The Ten Books on Architecture*. Morris Hicky Morgan, trans. New York: Dover Publications.

Yan, Wei, and Yehuda E. Kalay. 2005. "Simulating Human Behavior in Built Environments." *CAAD Futures*, Vienna.

CHAPTER 25

Engines of Information: Big Data from Small Buildings

Chandler Ahrens, Washington University in St. Louis
Aaron Sprecher, McGill University

25.1 INTRODUCTION

The influence of information technology on the field of architecture can be found in the rapid adoption of information-centric models from the earliest design stage through the operations of the building. Today, buildings produce a vast array of data that can be collected and mined to uncover patterns of behavior that translate into useful information and can be recorded and managed through the computational model of the building. The current utilization of the information model is both for predictive simulation in the design stage and operational analysis after the building is occupied. In the design stage, there is a vast amount of knowledge contributing to an array of decisions, from traditional sources of transdisciplinary collaboration and increasingly from nontraditional sources such as the sciences, information technologies, and mathematics through the common computational platform of the building information model (BIM). The current form of BIM focuses more on the end result rather than embedding the knowledge exchanged during the design process. The increasing computational capacity allows for this knowledge to be embedded into the model to promote informed decisions about how future adjustments to the building will affect its performance measured against the context of the original design intentions. The information model simultaneously discusses the form, its formation, and the information that brought the building to life.

25.2 DATA TO INFORMATION

Continually advancing computer speed along with increasing storage capacity of information has enabled vast quantities of data produced daily on the order of 2.5 quintillion bytes.[1] With so much data generated, the current discourse involves harnessing the data and filtering it to become useful information known as "big data." Giants in the field of technology such as Google, Facebook, and IBM have research teams racing to find better ways of mining massive amounts of data for their use or providing public access to it. The method of data mining will influence the potential for particular useful information to be uncovered. Therefore, if a company wants to use big data for targeted advertising, then the way they write the algorithms to comb through the data will focus toward that end result. With such large datasets, there are endless patterns that can be uncovered, which points to the critical role the algorithm plays to filter and identify recognizable patterns. This is where providing access to the data to companies, researchers, and individuals becomes interesting to encourage open source sharing of mining methods. For Google, this is part of their company's core value; they state that their "mission is to organize the world's information and make it universally accessible and useful."[2] Even the United States government provides data for public use on its website.[3] Providing access to "big data" is part of a larger quest to make an information panopticon even though it has the potential to be misleading (Bergstein 2013).[4] With such large datasets, the focus should not be the quantity of data, but the context of the data in order to create a platform for pattern recognition to be measured against while reducing unwanted noise (Lorentz 2013).[5] The context provides an informed filter to transform data into useful information.

The project Evolutive Means (at Pratt Institute, Brooklyn, NY, 2010) exemplifies the process of gathering data, mining it, filtering out noise, and generating useful information to organize and form an exhibition for ACADIA 2010. A text-based dataset was gathered from all of the papers and projects submitted and then mined for word frequency. The mined data was filtered by ignoring words that were out of the context of the exhibition such as prepositions. The resulting keywords were the useful information that became the context of the overall ACADIA community to measure the selected project against. An algorithm was developed that auto-located the projects in gallery space relative to the overall keywords (Figure 25.1). Various attributes from the mined data were translated into three-dimensional forms that created individual display spaces for the projects (Figure 25.2). Data mined from a large dataset uncovered patterns that became useful information that ultimately translated into

---

[1] IBM website: http://www01.ibm.com/software/data/bigdata/ (accessed June 2013).

[2] Google company website: www.google.com/about/company/.

[3] United States government website for free data: www.data.gov.

[4] Bergstein describes the current obsession with big data as technological hubris that naively overvalues data with the potential to conclude misguided knowledge.

[5] Lorentz discusses the challenge of identifying noise within large datasets that should be disregarded because it can produce misleading results. The context that the data was generated within is a valuable way to measure the data to determine if it is useful or noise.

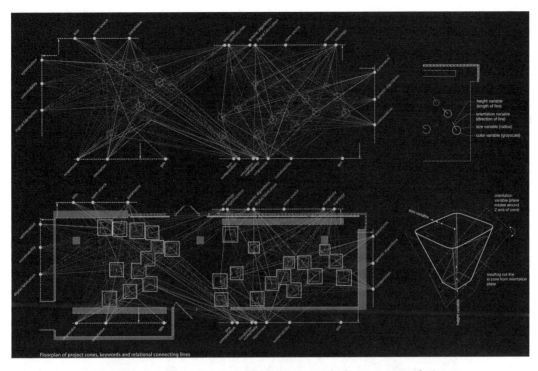

FIGURE 25.1 Auto-location of projects relative to keyword placement, Evolutive Means, ACADIA 2010. Brooklyn, NY. Design team: Chandler Ahrens, John Carpenter, Axel Schmitzberger, and Michael W. Su.

(www.o-s-a.com)

FIGURE 25.2 Spatialization of data attributes, Evolutive Means, ACADIA 2010.

(Photography by Open Source Architecture, www.o-s-a.com)

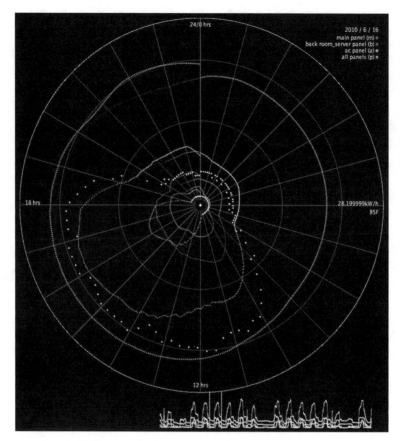

FIGURE 25.3   Energy performance data visualization from Morphosis Architects' office by John Carpenter.

knowledge about how the projects in the exhibition related to the overall ACADIA community (Ahrens and Carpenter 2010).[6]

25.3 LOOKING THROUGH THE LENS OF DATA

The presence of big data provides an opportunity to overlay multiple forms of information to alter occupants' perception of the built environment. In particular, buildings are engines that produce large amounts of data that can be filtered to uncover patterns that transform data into useful information (Figure 25.3), creating an abstract language to read the building. The manner in which the data is

[6]More extensive description of the project and the process of translating data to information into knowledge can be found in the article.

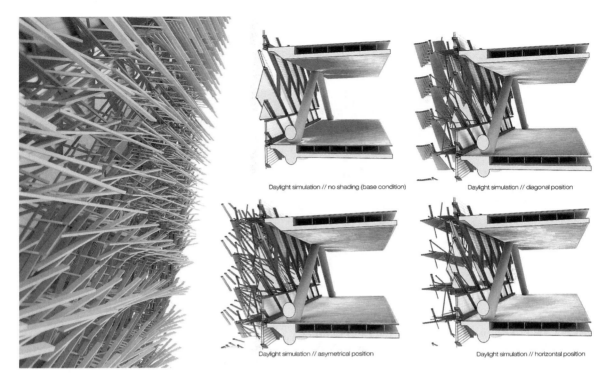

Daylight simulation // no shading (base condition)

Daylight simulation // diagonal position

Daylight simulation // asymetrical position

Daylight simulation // horizontal position

FIGURE 25.4 Prototypical façade system designed by Open Source Architecture that adapts the location of the louvers to maximize daylight penetration while minimizing solar heat gain.

(www.o-s-a.com)

processed at the scale of a building affects the possible patterns uncovered. The building is the context to read the data against, but what comprises the building's context will determine how the data is evaluated and ultimately made useful. The focus on data itself as an instigator in the design process ahead of drawings and the 3D model (Eastman et al. 2011) reinforces the context in which the data operates.[7] Thus if the light and thermal quality of an interior environment is the context, then solar intensity data becomes useful information to determine the form and organization of a façade system to regulate the performance in terms of daylight penetration and shading from solar heat gain (Figure 25.4). For the project Floss (2013), a prototypical façade system, the design process uses data measured against a specific context to produce a dynamic condition while simultaneously adjusting the perception of the built environment from a static view to a dynamic understanding of climatic, programmatic, and energy variables in flux.

---

[7] The advancements in CAD design tools have shifted the focus from drawings and 3D models to the data itself (Eastman et al. p. 15). The authors also discuss how describes a dynamic process of people actively creating and embedding useful information. The current types of information embedded in a model include geometry, time, cost, and performance. Embedded information concerning geometry includes X, Y, Z coordinates, manufacturer's details, and collision detection. Time includes constructability and sequencing, while cost includes quantity take-offs and unit pricing among others.

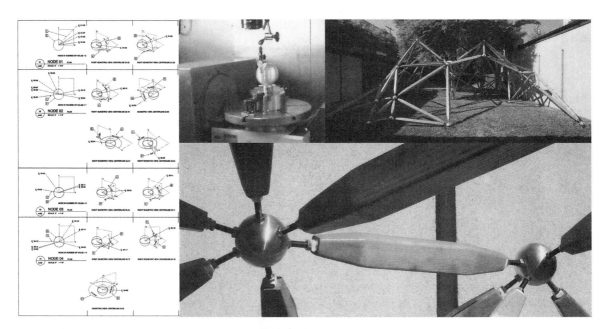

FIGURE 25.5   Geometries where data creates geometry that is transformed into material objects through digital CNC manufacturing for the Hylomophic Project by Open Source Architecture, MAK Center for Art and Architecture, West Hollywood, California 2006.
(Photography by Joshua White, www.o-s-a.com)

25.4 BUILDING AN INFORMATION MODEL

Of the types of information currently embedded in a building information model, performance becomes particularly interesting due to the dynamic nature of environmental variables (daylight, thermal, and energy usage) or material efficiencies (Eastman et al. 2011). In the search for material efficiencies, the Hylomorphic Project (at the MAK Center, West Hollywood, 2006) utilizes structural performance data integrated in a form-finding algorithm to simultaneously generate the geometry and structural calculations for a canopy. Wood member cross sections, member lengths, and the spherical joints were generated from the data and were transformed into material objects through digital CNC manufacturing based on the data as a design instigator (Figure 25.5). The algorithm used for the Hylomorphic Project promotes multidisciplinary collaboration through a common computational platform that optimizes the structural and spatial performance through a predictive method.

The utilization of the information model for performance can be parsed into two areas: predictive and operational. A predictive condition may explore the potential relationship of objects using parametric design tools to examine geometry, time, and cost. A predictive condition can also create simulations of behaviors over time to examine performance. The project Parasolar (Tel Aviv 2008) utilizes simulations of solar conditions to predict the behavior of an installation to create microclimates to combat the

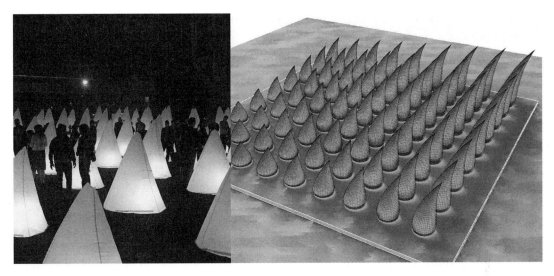

FIGURE 25.6 **Predictive radiation simulation for ParaSolar by Open Source Architecture, Tel Aviv, Israel, 2008.**

(www.o-s-a.com)

harsh sun in Tel Aviv (Figure 25.6). While predictive simulations explore potential in the design process, the operational use of BIM can uncover patterns of use in the finished building. Collection of the operational data can occur through sensors, energy usage readings, and post-occupancy studies such as those conducted by Berkeley National Laboratories. The resulting data can be compared to simulations in the design process or more likely used to tune building systems for maintenance. A common regard for the BIM model is as a "leave-behind" or artifact for operations and maintenance of a building.

25.5 THE PRESENT FUTURE

The current trajectory for the future of BIM seems slated to continue both predictive and operational analysis, but with greater accuracy, pattern recognition, and the potential for feedback loops. The collection and processing of data produced during operations will be used to evaluate real-world performance compared to the predictive performance based computer simulations. Clearly there is real value in understanding how accurate the predictions are for future design projects and beginning to amass knowledge of what aspects are closer to empirical evaluation. There is a difference between zero tolerance mathematical protocols of a digital model and the required tolerance of the physical building. As an example using the Hylomorphic Project mentioned earlier, the algorithm evolves the design through an iterative process measuring structural capacity, material thickness, and inhabitable spaces according to a fitness function until an optimized design is achieved. The digital model was optimized to have zero moment at all of the joints, but when the model was given the safety factor by the structural engineer, two additional members were added to alleviate moment in the structure.

The disconnection between the tolerances of digital versus physical has produced a myth of accuracy. With current predictive analysis software, how accurate is the simulation? It is important to understand the current situation relative to developments in the near future. All too often data is offered as proof of performance, which endangers information superseding our knowledge of building systems (Addington 2009). Computational systems currently do not have the capacity to model accurately according to the laws of real-world physics, but rather create simulations of isolated conditions using rules of physics. In particular with heat flow and fluid dynamics the simulations are not replicable in buildings because the conditions are far too complex. Simulation should be used not as objective fact, but rather as more enlightened information on the performance of a system, which still needs to be translated into knowledge. The design decisions made using the knowledge gained from simulations is the important information to be embedded within a model; therefore, the knowledge from performance analysis can create a feedback loop for the next generation of design.

As humanity approaches the singularity in the near future where computational power surpasses that of biological brains (Kurzweil 2005), the ability to model real-world conditions will be achievable, but for now there are limitations to simulations with limited variables.[8] The advances in accuracy will further the value of simulations measured against evaluation of the built edifice to create feedback loops in the design of the next generation of buildings. For existing buildings, the information model will be a living model in the sense that it will update as new information is generated during the operation and life of the building. Sensors embedded in equipment will provide real-time data to the information model to process and evaluate while alterations to the building will be recorded to adjust the operation performance.

In general, the current thoughts on the future of BIM focus on constructability and operations, but what about decisions made in the design process that forms the building? The context of the data collected for the BIM model comes into question again, since "however objective data may be, interpretation is subjective, and so is our choice about which data to record in the first place. While it might seem obvious that data, no matter how big, cannot perfectly represent life in all its complexity, information technology produces so much information that it is easy to forget just how much is missing" (Bergstein 2013).

25.6 IM: DROP THE (B)

Information modeling (IM) expands the type of information embedded within the digital model because it is not just about the building (B) as an artifact, but also the process that brought the building to life—form, formation, information. The design process is an engine of information since each building is custom designed to specific parameters unique to its context, program, and performance. The specificity of each building requires specialized knowledge to negotiate the range of conditions. The inclusion of the design process expands the discourse on the type and value of information included in the IM.

---

[8] Ray Kurzweil (2005) discusses the singularity as the point in time when the speed of computing, according to Moore's law of exponential acceleration in computing, will surpass the human brain's capacity.

The transdisciplinary collaboration that occurs in the design process of any building is quite complex, yet there is typically no record, except for the final resulting building. Transdisciplinary collaboration operates efficiently using an iterative design process that creates feedback loops to advance the design. Many informed decisions occur that shape each iteration according to complex measurement criteria from multiple disciplines similar to a fitness function in an evolutionary algorithm. Tracing the decisions is a form of recording and embedding the knowledge in the form of information into the IM.

Many disciplines come together to design a building, and each person has a specialty that makes him the expert and more knowledgeable than the others about their field. The collaborative design process evolves as each decision is negotiated between many experts, yet the decisions are only recorded in the final built form without recording the reasons behind them. Through this condition, much of the knowledge in the design process is abandoned, and the owner and building manager are left with the physical building without the context of the design intention. The information model is an artifact along with the physical building itself, yet has the ability to store vast amounts of information from both the design process and the information that the building will generate during its life. In the project Slrsrf (in Culver City, 2013), the formation of the roof according to optimized solar conditions became the impetus for the overall form of the building and affected the subsequent design decisions (Figure 25.7). Without the knowledge of the context of the formation process, future owners, architects, or contractors will not know how to make changes without decreasing the intended performance of the building.

As the design field opens up the realm of possible design methodologies through the common platform of computation, the ability to include nontraditional expertise into the design process is increasing, which expands the inclusion of transdisciplinarity. The expanded field of collaborators increases the

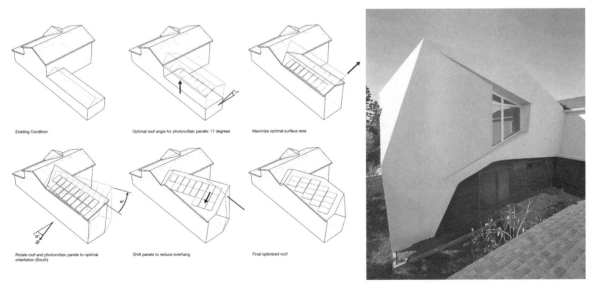

FIGURE 25.7 Conceptual formation diagram according to solar optimization for the project Slrsrf, Culver City, California, 2013 by Open Source Architecture.
(Photography by fotoworks, Benny Chan)

FIGURE 25.8   n-Natures installation was a collaboration between Dr. Edward Mosteig (mathematician), Paul Kalnitz (computer scientist), Open Source Architecture, and J. Bonn & Associates, located at the Rhode Island School of Design, Providence, Rhode Island, 2009.
(Photography by Kevin Deabler, www.o-s-a.com)

amount and type of information generated by and potentially recorded in the IM. Some of the disciplinary typologies involved in more experimental projects might include computer scientists, computational artists, information technologists, mathematicians, biologists, and the natural sciences, among many others. The exchange of information, ideas, and knowledge from the expanded field of collaborators transforms the design studio into a quasi-scientific laboratory (Sprecher 2012). The computational platform of the information model is the tissue that promotes the exchange of information that may not be science, but increasingly resembles scientific procedures.

Such a transdisciplinary exchange of information through the information model can be found in the project n-Natures (at RISD, Providence, RI, 2009), which was developed between a mathematician, computer scientist, and architects. The information model contains the mathematical function, color codification script, and fabrication details (Mosteig 2010) where all of the decisions are recorded in the coding of the digital model (Figure 25.8).[9] The future of information modeling will be able to record multiple formats, sources, and types of information, revealing the complex decisions from the design process in an expanded field of transdisciplinarity through the operations of the physical object.

---

[9]The information model consists of the mathematical function developed in Mosteig (2010). Mathematica software was translated into Rhino and adjusted with Rhino scripting. Even though the model goes through the translation, it remains code-based and therefore the design decisions are written into the code for future evaluation and analysis.

25.7 INFORMATION TO KNOWLEDGE

Information modeling, not just the information model, is a process and human endeavor (Eastman et al. 2011) that promotes transdisciplinarity on a collective computational platform. The information generated both in the design process and by the building operation gains value when it is transformed from data measured against a specified context. The context provides a consistent datum since the information model can be a living entity that adjusts to changing conditions over the life of the building. Inevitable future adjustments to the building can be weighed against the context of the design intentions similar to a fitness function in an algorithm, providing predictive analysis and simulations to optimize the performance of the future alterations. Embedding the specific context into the information modeling process transforms the information into embedded design knowledge.

25.8 CONCLUSION

Information modeling, not just the information model, is a process and human endeavor that promotes transdisciplinarity on a collective computational platform. The information generated both in the design process and by the building operation gains value when it is transformed from data measured against a specified context. The context provides a consistent datum since the information model can be a living entity that adjusts to changing conditions over the life of the building. Inevitable future adjustments to the building can be weighed against the context of the design intentions similar to a fitness function in an algorithm, providing predictive analysis and simulations to optimize the performance of the future alterations. Embedding the specific context into the information modeling process transforms the information into embedded design knowledge supplementing and surpassing the current scope of building information modeling.

DISCUSSION QUESTIONS

1. With the current form of BIM focused so strongly toward construction, operations, and maintenance, what is the value for architects considering the goal of enhancing the quality of the design concept other than budgetary and scheduling, which are construction related?
2. With the capacity of the BIM model to hold valuable information increasing with advances in software and hardware, what is missing from the design process that would be useful to be included in the final model?
3. If operational performance analysis is useful to determine essential features of the operations of a building, what is the value of using predictive performance analysis in the design process to determine performance goals?
4. Almost all architectural projects require multiple disciplines to collaborate. How does information modeling encourage transdisciplinarity through the common computational platform of the digital model?

REFERENCES

Addington, Michelle. 2009. "Sustainable Situationism." *LOG* 17 (Fall): 77–81.

Ahrens, Chandler, and John Carpenter. 2010. "in:Formation on Curatorial Design." In *ACADIA2010 LIFE in:Formation*, exhibition catalogue, Chandler Ahrens, Axel Schmitzberger, and Michael Wen-Sen Su.

Bergstein, Brian. 2013. "The Problem with Our Data Obsession." *MIT Technology Review* (February 20).

Eastman, Chuck, Paul Teicholz, Rafael Sacks, and Kathleen Liston. 2011. *BIM Handbook. A Guide to Building Information Modeling for Owners, Managers, Designers, Engineers and Contractors* (2d ed.). Hoboken, NJ: John Wiley & Sons.

Kurzweil, Ray. 2005. *The Singularity Is Near: When Humans Transcend Biology*. New York: Viking/Penguin Group.

Lorentz, Alissa. 2013. "With Big Data, Context Is a Big Issue." *Wired* online (April 23) (available at www.wired.com/insights/2013/04/with-big-data-context-is-a-big-issue/).

Mosteig, Edward. 2010. "The Shape of Collaboration: Mathematics, Architecture and the Arts." *MAA Focus*, 30(1): 24–25.

Sprecher, Aaron. 2012. "Informantionism: Information as Architectural Performance." In Yasha J. Grobman and Eran Neuman (eds.), *Performalism: Form and Performance in Digital Architecture*. London and New York: Routledge.

CHAPTER 26

BIM and MetaBIM: Design Narrative and Modeling Building Information

Mark Burry, RMIT University

26.1 BACKGROUND TO A SERIES OF DILEMMAS

Authoritatively stating what designers do and how they do it is a contested space for all those who seek a single tidy definition. Tidy definitions are very handy for everyone grappling with the finer points of BIM, not so much for the information modelers but for those who create the tools for those who model building information and for those who describe their use as BIM experts. The toolmakers endeavor to anticipate how their BIM tools will be used by designers. Software engineers may have rather little idea of how individuals design, what their design process is, or how they might use the BIM tools created for them, but programmers have to have a very clear idea (obviously) of how their software will be used collectively as a "tool." They also have to consider how their tools will work with others.

Accepted standards for object definitions, such as industry foundation classes (IFC), developed to allow easy transfers between different software as one strategy to secure greater interoperability between different (information) modeling environments. Evolving standard protocols that either seek to be ambitiously the industry standard or more modestly devised as the office *lingua franca* are less easy for the toolmaker to be able to anticipate if they have not actually created them, and it is no doubt a matter of extreme frustration when they have to deal with criticism from users about alleged software deficiencies when, from the toolmakers' perspective, the software is being abused.

At the individual designer level, beyond the methodologies that defined as well as straight-jacketed Modernist practice for two generations, the current acceptance of a pluralist architectural language (style even) is complemented by a distinct lack of orthodoxy in the way designers approach their task. In working from an initial idea toward achieving the outcome as artifact, most designers do not want to be constrained by peculiar digital strictures that limit their software's deployability, nor by office protocols overly predicated on its ideal rather than unconventional use. And how do the software tools developed for "everyone" deal with singular design solutions?

This chapter outlines a case study where nearly every aspect of the design is unique. It is a large auditorium space "floating" 70 meters above the center crossing of Gaudí's Sagrada Família Basilica in Barcelona, the *Sala Creuer* ("crossing room") shown in plan and section in Figure 26.1.

From a BIM case study viewpoint, this case study thwarts the needs of the typical tidy success story for the building information modeling sector. Nevertheless, this account aims to be helpful within the BIM cause and is offered with two objectives in mind. First, it honors those designers grappling with BIM from the standpoint of being sympathetic to the objectives of BIM, but frustrated by its obvious limitations in highly creative contexts. Second, the chapter honors those BIM software developers who truly want to understand the designer and develop the necessary flexibility to work *with* them rather than seek to rehabilitate designers towards a standard but nevertheless highly restrictive design methodology. For the first group, the highly creative designer, this account contributes a "safety in

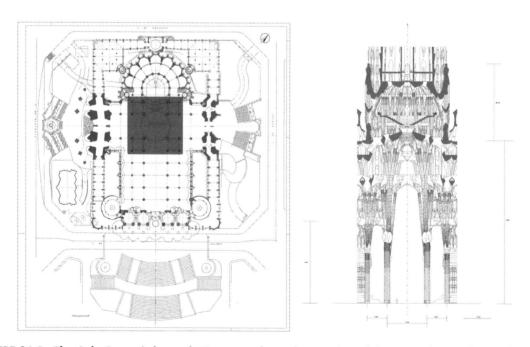

FIGURE 26.1   The *Sala Creuer* is located 70 meters above the crossing of the Sagrada Família Basilica (left). Cross section of the Sagrada Família Basilica as built showing the auditorium conceived as a floating bowl allowing light from four sides to illuminate it and the vaults over the main space below (right).
(Drawings by Xavier Moreno, Sagrada Família Basilica)

numbers" angle, one of "you are not alone" in worrying about the current limitations of BIM in servicing the entire gamut of your innovative zeal. For the second group, the brief outline provided of the process leading to the soon to be completed *Sala Creuer* details some of the gauntlets thrown down by a creative team frustrated by the tools currently available to ideate, conceptualize, represent, and ultimately document an unfamiliar architectural space, and how those gauntlets were picked up using processes more familiar to vehicle and aeronautical designers than architects.

26.2 A CASE IN POINT: THE SAGRADA FAMÍLIA BASILICA *SALA CREUER*

This chapter draws on my (at the time of writing) 34-year association with the continuation of the Sagrada Família Basilica as researcher and architect. For the first two decades I worked as an apprentice helping unravel the mysteries of Gaudí's design for the building through detailed study of the restored 1:25 and 1:10 scale models that had been destroyed during the 1936–39 Spanish Civil War, a decade after the year that he had died. Most of the main areas of the building had been modeled by Gaudí in three iterations of design development and reveal their constituent geometries sufficiently well to inform the builders who construct this *magnum opus*. Pope Benedict XVI consecrated the Basilica's interior on November 7, 2010.

For the last 15 years I have been working with colleagues on the areas of the building that derive from less certain material, including the narthex of the Passion Façade, which has been based on a photograph of a drawing by Gaudí, a unique albeit highly elaborate depiction of his intentions, and the *Sala Creuer* based solely on a cross section.

26.2.1 *Sala Creuer* Documentation

The *Sala Creuer* is based on even less auspicious material than the fine-grained photographic plate of the single detailed drawing/painting of the Passion Façade narthex. In this case the only evidence is a longitudinal section of the basilica, highly detailed in every area except the *Sala Creuer* itself, which he simply left hatched-out: close to zero modeled building information (Figure 26.2). In Gaudí's section (surviving as a published engraving), despite the high level of detail in the interior elevations exposed by the cut through the main body of the basilica, his intentions for the space within the towers above the ceiling vaults 60 meters above floor level are not immediately apparent. Clearly it is a considerable volume, but there is no actual evidence of how significant the space was to be from Gaudí's viewpoint. We are therefore obliged to extrapolate from the high level of thinking and ingenuity that he deployed for the four towers of the Nativity Façade and transept completed around the time of his death in 1926. It seems logical to assume that he would have made something more of the space beyond considering it to be merely the service space that visitors pass through on their way up to the cross, 174 meters from the ground. With Gaudí no detail is casual, regardless of a relatively lowly status within a sophisticated functional hierarchy.

FIGURE 26.2   Reproduction of Gaudí's longitudinal section through the Sagrada Família Basilica. The original drawing is lost but it was published in 1928, two years after Gaudí's death. The *Sala Creuer* is within the hatched-out space. The section offers no definitive clue to the degree of elaboration Gaudí intended for this space forming the base of the principal tower for the basilica.
(Copied from Ràfols, 1928, published two years after Gaudí's death)

26.2.2 Project Phases

There are 20 principal towers to the Sagrada Família Basilica; the *Sala Creuer* is the base of the highest tower dedicated to Jesus Christ. Work began in earnest in 2005.

As with all the other projects on site, there are four distinct phases:

1. Predesign and schematic design (Phase 1)
2. Design (Phase 2)
3. Documentation (Phase 3)
4. Construction (Phase 4)

In the case of the *Sala Creuer*, atypically, not even Gaudí had attempted the predesign, as the section shows. Decisions were made early on, including considering creating an auditorium in the space above the vaults below. This needed to be done in such a way that light would nevertheless penetrate below the raked circular seating area, spilling through the magnificent ceiling vaults above which the auditorium might be made to float, the spatial crescendo of the basilica itself.

It is at this point that the "design as narrative" takes over from any other consideration of design such as "design as representation" or "design as strategy." This narrative emphasis approach characterizes the Phase 2 design arena. Consider the difference between Phases 1 and 2: pre-design versus design. The critical considerations are provided in a grossly simplified (but accurately) abbreviated list of questions; the responses are also included.

Phase 1: Schematic Design

1. Primary purpose? To be an agglomeration point for everyone ascending to the top of the building, the central tower dedicated to Jesus Christ, not a place for religious observance.
2. Primary challenge? To link all the routes from the ground floor of the building through this central elevated space to a single route to the top through the core of the tower below.
3. Role in an emergency evacuation? To be a critical node in what has to be an unequivocally clear evacuation strategy in the case of an emergency; all decisions will need to be framed around this non-negotiable performance requirement.

Figure 26.3 shows the early mappings of the schematic design, and the collaborative decision-making process is captured in Figure 26.4.

FIGURE 26.3   State-of-play in 2005. 3D schema for the various elements that comprise the *Sala Creuer*, principally the auditorium. At this early stage it was envisaged that the auditorium would span the entire void.
(Schematic model by Frederic Fargas, Sagrada Família Basilica)

FIGURE 26.4   The design at the Sagrada Família Basilica is not a linear process; rather, the whole team is involved from the sketch design. The principal decision-making environment is the model makers' workshop where traditional and digital media are combined without embarrassment.
(Photo by Mark Burry)

Phase 2: Design (Some Key Examples)

1. Relationship between the raked auditorium and the external walls? Keep them separate to allow the maximum amount of light to pass underneath the auditorium for the vaults below.

2. Access? Should be at two levels with four upper-level connections to each of the four flanking Evangelists' towers and lower from the two Evangelists' towers via a suspended glass walkway to the *vomitoria* on either side (Figure 26.5).

3. How to arrange a series of twelve windows around the perimeter that meld with the four flanking towers between which they span? Introduce curved (in plan) windows for the first time on the project.

4. How to connect the central tower to the twelve windows that surround the *Sala Creuer*? Provide an undulating vault between the two.

5. How to ensure that all surfaces are doubly ruled but not fail to benefit from not being able to use simple offsets and trims? Use optimization tools within the BIM software environment.

Figures 26.6, 26.7, and 26.8 show the development of the scheme design into a more robust proposal.

Answering the question, "What did Gaudí intend to do with the space above the crossing?" becomes the basis of a design narrative. In Phase 1 it is a functionally driven set of answers developing into a fresh

FIGURE 26.5 Floor plan of the *Sala Creuer* showing its access at two levels to the four Evangelist towers that flank the central tower (left); reflected ceiling plan of the *Sala Creuer* (right).

(Drawings by Xavier Moreno, Sagrada Família Basilica)

FIGURE 26.6 Three versions for the project were ultimately considered, with the favored version taking the *Sala Creuer* space out to all four Evangelist towers. All three were rapid prototyped at a scale of 1:200.

(Photo and parametric model by Mark Burry; 3D print by Sagrada Família Basilica Taller de Modelistes)

FIGURE 26.7   Exterior view of 1:200 schematic model (left); interior section of the 1:200 schematic model (middle); detail of the schematic model of the *Sala Creuer* interior (right).
(Photo and parametric model by Mark Burry; 3D print by Sagrada Família Basilica Taller de Modelistes)

set of questions in the Phase 2 design characterized as "but how will we achieve this?" If developing this narrative into a successfully completed built work is contingent on choices of approach to building information modeling, which it is, in our project discussions this aspect is hardly a feature of any crucial interaction with colleagues and fellow professionals (see Figure 26.4). BIM is always running to catch up with the desires of the design team, not vice versa. Rather than the design narrative being

FIGURE 26.8   Rendered view of the *Sala Creuer* auditorium (left); *Vomitorium* exit from auditorium floor (right).
(Parametric model by Mark Burry, with contributions from Barnaby Bennett and Michael Wilson; rendered by Jim Loder)

tailored to any limitations of the software used, the opposite happens: the software is modified when parametric variation opportunities allow, or if there is no orthodox within which we can be creative, we find workarounds. Routinely these astound the software producers every time the innovative workflow is revealed to them and has surprised them with the degree of unconventional exploitation (Figure 26.9). This was the case in the early adaptation of aeronautical and vehicle parametric design software such as Computervision's CADDS5 in 1992.

26.3 CREATIVE DIGITAL WORKFLOW AS BIM

An unexpurgated account of how we have produced highly precise building information through a shared model beyond the contemporary BIM capability would be rather tedious. Instead, essential pointers are offered here to stimulate a more adventurous development of BIM by thinking beyond it: *metaBIM*.

Not atypically, a project with this degree of spatial complexity demands that new and therefore unique approaches to its information modeling be conjured up during the actual design process (Phase 2) and not entirely during schematic design (Phase 1), as would otherwise seem logical. It could be argued that the need for such processes ought only to be identified as part of the schematic design well

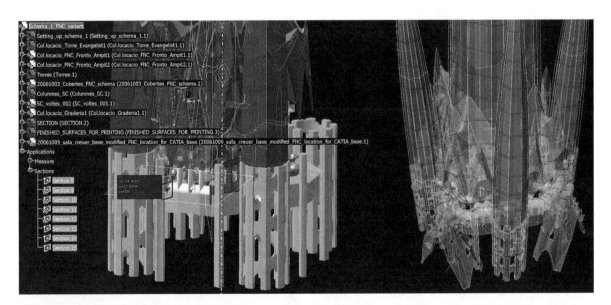

FIGURE 26.9   First go at a shared 3D model, in this case CATIA. The model is an assembly of individual parts that affords the opportunity for a fully parametric (flexible) model (left). A fully composed spatial design for the *Sala Creuer* as a Rhino model, which acts as the schema that narrates the design decision making as the project proceeds (right).

(Parametric model by Mark Burry, with contributions from Barnaby Bennett and Michael Wilson)

before major design decisions are made, but this luxury has consistently proved to be elusive to us. One example of such "late thinking" strategies for information modeling was how to optimize the roof vaults comprised of two hyperbolic paraboloids which, as a sandwich of inside and outside surfaces they define a solid in the space between them. To maintain their geometrical integrity, whereby both surfaces benefit from being doubly ruled surfaces, one surface cannot simply be offset from the other maintaining a required even thickness even though such evenness is demanded (for weight and strength). With highly sophisticated modeling environments such as CATIA, both surfaces can be made to conform to these non-negotiable geometrical constraints computationally constrained to a minimum and maximum thickness through optimization calculations within in the software design environment. This is an opportunity sought on presentation of the problem. It is not unlikely to be foreseen at the schematic design stage when, in this case, this particular geometrical conundrum was not yet envisaged.

Our difficulty is that such dilemmas and their resolution seem only to arise in the doing (designing). More thinking about the "doing" before the actual doing can be organized during schematic design, of course, but this is often at the expense of subsequent creative thinking opportunistically enriching the design, which has otherwise been restrained by a set of preordained BIM protocols. An engineer, for example, might regard such nodules of design computation as needing to be tackled at the outset rather than later within the fray. Generally, architectural designers would rather not be shoehorned so early in the process and certainly do not appreciate any efforts to get the BIM tail to wag the design dog. If designers and software engineers join in a shared narrative approach, typified as *metaBIM*, their respective interests will mutually advance more quickly. The shared goal is excellence, and Gaudí's challenges at the Sagrada Família Basilica have been an excellent challenge for all in this regard.

Figures 26.10 through 26.17 form a visual essay where readers will be able to imagine the highly sophisticated digital workflow from schematic design to design to design documentation, and then construction with millimeter precision. The cross current, rather than the idealized flow, is the nexus of this narrative. In terms of the challenges faced in completing Gaudí's Sagrada Família Basilica we are still in

FIGURE 26.10 The formwork for the *Sala Creuer* auditorium seen from the crane (left); platform used to marshal the precast and cut stone elements (right).

FIGURE 26.11 *Vomitorium.*

FIGURE 26.12 Permanent formwork with robot cut stone for exterior (LHS) and artificial stone on the interior (left); window nearing completion (middle); top of central window seen from the interior (right).

FIGURE 26.13 Looking down toward the nave roof construction (left); column capitals joining the perimeter of the ceiling vaults within (right).

FIGURE 26.14 Undercroft of the auditorium.

FIGURE 26.15 Exterior view of completing the vaults. Note the reinforcement exactly follows the straight-line rulings of the constituent hyperboloid of revolution geometries (left). Each rebar is drawn in 3D in Rhino (right).

the very early days of the development of BIM with the conclusion that BIM aiding design process thinking is more the current goal than looking for BIM to be a total software environment, as their producers would often have us believe.

26.4 WATCH THIS SPACE . . .

In our team based at RMIT University (SIAL), we prefer to work with high-end aeronautical software and have especially enjoyed the facility in which parts of the building are assembled as one model, with relational databases gluing all the significant amounts of information together. We have experienced

FIGURE 26.16 Looking down at the removable interior formwork. Once the reinforcement is in place, preassembled stonework is lowered in place prior to concrete being poured within (left). Exterior of the *Sala Creuer* nearing completion (middle). A hint of the intended light effects as the space nears completion (right).

FIGURE 26.17 View from Passion Façade looking up to the *Sala Creuer* construction from ground level.

relatively little difficulty exporting and importing highly complex geometries between rival software, and at no point in our experience has interoperability been an issue in this regard. At the time of writing we have moved from the schematic design of the Glory Façade that we completed in October 2013 to the design itself. This will be undertaken as seven discrete components worked on by seven separate teams. In terms of complexity it will be akin to linking geometrically seven *Sala Creuers* together complete with all the necessary co-dependency. In my view it is the *metaBIM* that has been and remains our principal challenge: getting our story right, that is, ensuring we have a narrative we can all read from designer to maker, and one within which our software developers and programmers can equally participate.

ACKNOWLEDGMENTS

I acknowledge the Sagrada Família Basilica Foundation, which generously invites university-based research teams such as ours to collaborate in the challenges Gaudí has bequeathed his successors. The Australian Research Council provided my Federation Fellowship that has afforded the overall research context. The project described here is obviously the work of many.

DISCUSSION QUESTIONS

1. Explain what is meant by the term *metaBIM*.
2. What benefits could be accrued by designers talking with software developers?
3. What changes would it take to the current state of building information model to have BIM be truly part of a creative digital workflow?

Glossary

These terms were specifically chosen by the chapter authors as important for understanding of their key concepts.

adaptive components: A set of tools in Autodesk Revit that allows for design elements to adjust automatically to different orientations and scales upon placement in a model.

AECO: Industries relating to architecture, engineering, construction, and building operations.

AGC BIMForum: The BIMForum's mission is to facilitate and accelerate the adoption of building information modeling (BIM) in the AEC industry (www.bimforum.org).

American Institute of Architects (AIA): The AIA is a professional organization for architects in the United States (www.aia.org). One of its Knowledge Communities (KC) is Technology in Architectural Practice (TAP) that sponsors annual BIM awards. (http://network.aia.org/technologyinarchitecturalpractice/home/).

analytical model: A representation created for simulation purposes.

application programming interface (API): A vendor-software mechanism for accessing data in a proprietary file format from user-written software. It specifies the access interface to a computer application in order to expend the functionality of the application through computer programming. The API's software structure allows for programmers to use functions of specific software programs or to create interoperability among different pieces of software.

architectural ontology: A glossary of concepts by which buildings and other architectural works may be described, including both the physical objects and the relationships among the objects.

asset planning: Activities and processes related to managing an organization's infrastructure and other assets to deliver an agreed standard of service.

big data: Extremely large amount of data produced daily by computers or anything with a processor.

BIM analytics: Building information modeling used to supply the 3D geometry and data as a representation for simulation and performance-based design studies.

BIM ecosystem: A network of interacting products, processes, and people (including companies and other stakeholders) that collectively determine the development and evolution of BIM related products and services (based on Moore's 1993 definition of business ecosystem).

BIM manager: A staff member who is entrusted with establishing BIM protocols and BIM training in an office and often is the office's expect on BIM software, hardware, and implementation. Also referred to as BIM coordinator.

BIM, building information model: A digital representation of a physical entity, whether existing in the physical world or intended to exist in the future; an integrated, structured database, informed by the building industry, and consisting of 3D parametric objects. It is a systemic innovation in the AECO sector that impacts all aspects of the industry, beyond just the development and adoption of a specific technology. The resultant data structure is capable of being shared among all the actors of the process and at any of the steps involved in the lifecycle of the building from design to demolition.

BIM, constructability: A building information model usually created by the construction team for explaining how to construct the building.

BIM, design: A building information model usually created by the architecture team for explaining design intent and producing documentation.

BIM, federated: A design ecosystem in which software from different vendors is used on a single project in a "separate but equal" fashion.

BIM, gap: Interoperability issues between different building information models. For example, the architect's design BIM is usually not the same as the contractor's constructability BIM. The gap between them leads to refining or redoing of the BIM.

BIM, Open: "Open BIM is a universal approach to the collaborative design, realization and operation of buildings based on open standards and workflows. Open BIM is an initiative of buildingSMART and several leading software vendors using the open buildingSMART Data Model." (http://www.graphisoft.com/archicad/open_bim/open_bim_program/#faq06)

building energy modeling (BEM): An aspect of building performance simulation (BPS) and BIM analytics representing energy performance within a building.

building integrated photovoltaics (BIPV): Photovoltaic materials integrated into whole building design and construction.

Building Owners and Managers Association International (BOMA): A network of professionals involved in building ownership, management, development, and leasing (www.boma.org).

building performance simulation (BPS): Key abstractions representing functions of particular building elements.

capital project delivery: Phases necessary for the completion of projects in the capital investment sector.

CityGML: A common information model and XML-based encoding for the representation, storage, and exchange of virtual 3D city and landscape models and is an official Open Geo-spatial Consortium (OGC) standard. It also plays an important role in bridging urban information models with building information models to improve interoperability among information systems used in the design, construction, ownership, and operation of buildings and capital projects (www.citygml.org).

collaborative design: A design practice shaped by multiple participants, human and computational agents, actively contributing and critiquing to accomplish something together that cannot be accomplished by any individual or computational participant by themselves.

collaborative platform and BIM decision framework: A systematic approach to facilitate BIM adoption and guide decision making on implementation within a multidisciplinary project team. The key activities and decisions involve critical assessment of BIM readiness of key stakeholders through mapping product (technological), process (cultural, operational, and organizational), and people (organizational, cultural, and skill) dependencies; effective BIM project scoping and work process roadmap definition, and informed selection and application of appropriate BIM technologies.

collective decision-making: A compromise made among a group to select the best solution that best meets the defined project goals.

collective intelligence: The use of social interaction, typically through the Internet, to collaboratively share information improving the logic of a design.

component: An individual element of construction, such as a beam, a sheet of drywall, or a bolt or piece of trim.

computational fluid dynamics (CFD): The computational simulation of energy flowing through matter.

computer aided drafting or design (CAD): A software program for creating 2D representations, for example, architecture plans, sections, and elevations. The term is use in other fields such as engineering. CAD sometimes refers to a 3D modeling program.

conceptual energy modeling: Energy modeling completed during the intuitive and creative early design phase of a project.

constraint modeling: A method of representing a design by defining conditions and ranges of values that must be satisfied.

Construction Operations Building Information Exchange (COBie): A relational format for the publication and use of building information to support the operation, maintenance, and management of facility assets. A COBie model contains no geometry and represents a subset of the building model.

Construction Owners Association of America (COAA): COAA supports project owners' success in the design and construction of buildings and facilities through education, information, and developing relationships within the industry (www.coaa.org).

craft model of design: The ability of a single person to design and construct a solution to a problem.

crossing: The center of a traditional Christian church or cathedral where the transepts (the lateral arms to the plan) intersect or "cross" the main body of the building (the nave).

crowdsourcing: Denotes a number of ways to use the Web as a means to enlist a large number of individuals to perform a particular task.

database management system (DBMS): A collection of computer-based applications that control the creation, application, and maintenance of the database of an organization and its end users.

design cognition: Cognitive processes, primitives, and strategies used in the design process.

design delivery process: All formal phases of generating a design and converting it into a real object.

design drivers: The rules, regulating lines, or other logic that dictates the composition of an architectural design.

design ecosystem: The collection of software used by an architect to conduct design.

design expertise: A type of knowledge developed and used by designers through the process of solving a specific design problem.

digital design decision support tool (DDDST): A computer program capable of analysis of buildings.

digital fabrication: The production of custom components using computer numerically controlled (CNC) manufacturing equipment.

direct manipulation: In the field of human-computer interaction, the name for the interface style utilizing "click and drag" type graphical editing.

DMLSS-FM: The DMLSS-FM tool is used to track and maintain facilities supporting the Department of Defense (DoD) Military Health System's (MHS) mission execution of delivery of health, dental, veterinary and related research (http://facilities.health.mil/home/dmlss-fm).

document management systems (DMS): A collaboration platform developed specifically for managing documents shared by multiple parties in a project.

drawing exchange format (DXF): An Autodesk file format for drawing data, usually clear-text.

energy use intensity (EUI): A performance indicator widely used to determine energy performance of buildings and other facilities.

events: Computational entities that represent the activities that are performed by users of a built environment. They structure information about the expected preconditions and outcomes of the activities, the actors involved, and the place where they are performed.

evolutionary algorithm: An iterative process, typically computationally driven, that seeks to improve a condition where each new iteration is an improvement compared to the previous one until an optimized condition has been determined to have been reached. Each iteration is measured according to a fitness function, and only desired traits are reintroduced to subsequent iterations.

evolutionary computing: A process through which an algorithm searches the range of potential outcomes seeking a desired result.

extensible markup language (XML): A general-purpose clear text data-encoding standard from the W3C.

facility condition index (FCI): Used in facilities management to provide a benchmark to compare the relative condition of a group of facilities. The FCI is primarily used to support asset management initiatives of federal, state, and local government facilities organizations. This would also include universities, housing and transportation authorities, and primary and secondary school systems.

feedback loop: An iterative process where valuable information uncovered or knowledge gathered during each iteration is reintroduced to subsequent iterations until a resolution is reached. For example, the architect might go back and forth between building information modeling software and energy simulation software until the design reaches specified performance metrics.

fitness function: A quantifiable process that measures a condition against a set of rules for an ideal or desired condition.

form: Describes the physical properties of an entity, including its size, shape, position in space, and the materials it is made of. It can answer such questions as "what does it look like, and what is it made of?" *See* **function**.

function: Indicates the semantic properties of an entity. It adds meaning to the entity, in relation to a specific context. It can answer such questions as "what does it mean, what do we call it, and what can we do with it?" *See* **form**.

General Services Administration (GSA): A unit of the federal government in charge of standards for all federal facilities, including sustainable design, construction services, and project management. The GSA manages federal property, including operating and maintaining buildings, supplies and transportation acquisition, and communications management (www.gsa.gov).

genetic algorithm: A computational search method that mimics the process of natural selection.

geographic information systems (GIS): GIS is a technological field that incorporates geographical features with tabular data in order to map, analyze, and assess real world problems (giscloud.com 2012).

geometric description language (GDL): A parametric programming language similar to BASIC and based on ArchiCAD. It describes 3D objects and 2D symbols, which are saved as "library parts" with a particularly compact size. Embedded scripts describe the 3D geometry, 2D symbols, and the properties of a construction element. Geometrical structures can be generated via logical links.

geospatial: Relating to or denoting data that is associated with a particular location. Geospatial analysis is an approach to applying statistical analysis and other informational techniques to data that has a geographical or geospatial aspect.

graphical user interface (GUI): A computer user interface that allows users to interactively input or access data through graphical controls such as forms and menus.

green rating system: Methods of certifying and scoring environmental stewardship of a project. Different rating systems have been developed under the auspices of different organizations, for example, LEED, Green Globes, or BREEAM. Ratings systems can be fine-tuned for different types of projects.

host relationship: A relationship among two objects such that one is attached or connected to the host object and transformations of the host affect the hosted object.

IFC-based spatial concept building information models: The initial requirement by the U.S. General Services Administration in their BIM Guide Series 02 for architects and engineers to provide a final concept (i.e., schematic design) level BIM in the IFC interoperable format as part of their contract deliverables.

IGES: A type of common file format that allows different software to share 2D and 3D information.

indoor navigation: The ability to map interior spaces in buildings and structures, similar to outdoor navigation through highways, roads, streets, and neighborhoods.

IndoorGML: A graphic markup language and emerging OGC standard for indoor navigation applications. IndoorGML covers a wide spectrum of application areas such as indoor location-based services, indoor Web map services, indoor emergency control, guiding services for visually handicapped persons in indoor space, and indoor robotics.

industry foundation classes (IFC): An open object-oriented data format developed in an independent consortium (formerly IAI, now buildingSmart) with the objective of providing efficient vendor-neutral CAD data exchange between planners with a minimum of data losses. It is used to describe building models and enable data exchange between different proprietary software applications.

information modeling (IM): An endeavor that privileges information as the generator of a design process.

input data file (IDF): A file format used to run simulations in EnergyPlus.

integrated analysis: Analysis functions performed directly on a parametric 3D model in the same application environment. Example types of analysis include area take-offs, shadow analysis, solar radiation studies, daylighting, whole building energy calculations, and structural and cost analysis.

International Energy Agency (IEA): An organization that works to ensure reliable, affordable, and clean energy for its 28 member countries (www.iea.org).

International Facility Management Association (IFMA): IFMA, founded in 1980, is the world's largest and most widely recognized international association for facility management professionals (www.ifma.org).

intuitive skills: Skills that operate through intuition and heuristic constructs of the mind.

levels of development (LOD): "The Level of Development (LOD) describes the minimum dimensional, spatial, quantitative, qualitative, and other data included in a Model Element to support the Authorized Uses associated with such LOD." Definition from the American Institute of Architecture (AIA), 2013, "Guide, instructions, and commentary to the 2013 AIA digital practice documents."

material constraints: The use of a material's characteristic as a method for linking parametric data to an overall form.

mental models: Abstract constructs that explicitly show mental entities and their relationships.

meta-BIM: The narrative or story that ties all the building information together as something beyond a simple set of facts.

mission dependency index (MDI): An operational risk metric for assessing the criticality of facilities and describing their relative importance based on the owner's mission (i.e., strategic plan) for its entire portfolio of facilities (http://www.assetinsights.net/Glossary/G_Mission_Dependency_Index.html).

non-uniform rational B-spline (NURBS): A mathematical model for generating and representing curves and surfaces.

object-oriented physical modeling (OOPM): A programming paradigm that uses objects as data structures to design computer-based applications. In an object-oriented building model, building elements are represented as objects that can contain both geometric and nongeometric information. It is used for modeling large-scale physical systems of multiple domains.

ontology: A shared specification of an abstract, simplified view of a world that is represented for a purpose—formally, it is a description of concepts and their relationships within a domain. Ontologies are designed to facilitate knowledge sharing and reuse.

operational performance analysis: Determining the essential features of the operations of a building that can be used to measure the effectiveness of the intended performance.

optimization software: Software that is used to create an analysis and then further refine specific building design elements seeking the best available option.

parametric BIM SIM: An integrated parametric modeling, BIM, and simulation process.

parametric design: The linking of data to geometry using computational modeling, and a method to model a system by defining system parameters and their relationships.

parametric modeling: A form of computational modeling in which the object itself contains information regarding its behavior and the intended interactions with other objects in the model. The model is capable of maintaining these as the model is manipulated.

parametrization: A process that defines variables within the script in order to enable the use of individual subsets of geometries with different values as regards certain attributes (dimensions, color of materials, selectable options, etc.). In this way, one single "library part" can, for instance, be used to generate a great number of different geometry variants.

Pareto-optimal: An outcome that cannot be further improved without making particular aspects of it worse. For a given problem there may be multiple pareto-optimal solutions, each one a little bit worse and a little bit better than the others. Compare with **satisficing**.

performance metrics: A performance metric is a measure of the overall performance of a building; it is typically a combination of a measurable quantity (minimum lux on the desktop, say) and a qualitative measure (number of hours per year the minimum lux is provided by daylight, without exceeding some defined glare criterion).

performative design: The use of building performance and metrics as guiding principles in architectural design.

predictive performance analysis: Creating simulations of essential features or conditions, typically for buildings that have not yet been realized.

problem solving: A view of design cognition that assumes that solutions to given problems are developed with explicit goal directed methods.

quality assurance: A process of systematically testing and thus ensuring the quality of a process; in building performance simulation a process for ensuring the model represents reality and therefore the simulated performance is believable.

reasoning mechanism: Independent, disciplinary specific analysis software that is able to parse the component network and perform analysis.

reconceptualization of work: The analysis of the labor used to perform a task in order to redirect its outcomes and effects.

regulating line: A line in a design that establishes the fundamental geometric symmetry and alignment of the composition.

Sala Creuer: The auditorium space situated above the Sagrada Família Basilica's crossing vaults.

satisficing: A decision-making strategy that aims to satisfy and suffice rather than seek the optimal. Often used because an optimal choice either does not exist or is too costly to identify. Compare with **Pareto-optimal**.

scripting language: A small computer program written in a dynamic high-level general-purpose language, such as Perl, Python, or Javascript. These often exist inside of modeling programs to allow for quick customization.

sensitivity analysis: The study of how sensitive an outcome is to changes in parameters. This is typically analyzed by slightly varying the parameters to an equation and measuring the difference in outcome. Often used in energy analysis to determine what component or parameter is having the most effect on energy consumption.

Space and Equipment Planning System (SEPS): A health system planning tool jointly developed by the DoD and VA for use in developing detailed space plans and associated equipment requirements (http://facilities.health.mil/home/SEPS).

space utilization index (SUI): A method for comparing actual to allowable space. Actual space measurements are made during a space utilization assessment. Allowable space is based on the commandant space standards, which define approved space allowances on the basis of personnel and other factors. The SUI is calculated by dividing actual square feet by allowable square feet (www.nap.edu/openbook.php?record_id=11226&page=44).

space: The entity created by architectural components (walls, floor, ceiling, windows, etc.).

spatial BIM: A building information model that has as its primary focus space instead of building elements.

spatial topology: In the context of the architecture domain, spatial topology refers to the relationships that can exist among the various spatial components of a building. For example, two spaces that share a physical separating element are adjacent and two spaces that share an opening are connected. Spatial topology has its origin in the mathematical field of topology that studies the properties of a shape under different transformations.

standard measurement of buildings: BOMA created its first floor area measurement standard in 1915. IFMA created its first area measurement standard in 1995. Its original intent was for the planning, space management, and internal chargeback of space. The current standards were reviewed and supported by ANSI and ASTM for conformity and integrity. This lengthy process allows both BOMA and IFMA future standards to speak a common language and communicate with confidence.

STEP: Generally refers to a clear text file adhering to the ISO 10303 standard for describing 3D product information.

tacit knowledge: Knowledge that is not explicit to the holder of that knowledge.

transdisciplinary: A process where different disciplines collaborate on a problem or project where the distinct territory of each is blurred. Current forms tend to communicate via a common computational platform, further blurring the distinctions of each discipline.

urban energy modeling: Modeling energy flows in and around buildings ranging from individual buildings to neighborhood scale.

use: A property that adds time-based, sociocultural information to the represented object. It answers such questions as "Who uses it, and how is it used?"

virtual design and construction (VDC): Use of multi-disciplinary performance models of design-construction projects, including the product (i.e., facilities), work processes, and organization of the AECO team in order to support business objectives.

virtual reconstruction: A process for the true-to-nature replication of buildings or construction sites that no longer exist with the help of historical plans and photographs or other depictions. The method also serves to visualize planned buildings that were never erected. The objective is not physically to build the reconstructed edifices but to visualize the building within its urban context.

visual programming language (VPL): A programming language that uses graphic elements to create a program. Examples of these used in conjunction with architecture design software include Grasshopper and Dynamo.

Web services: A Web service is a method of communication between two electronic devices over the World Wide Web. It is a software function provided at a network address over the Web or the cloud; it is a service that is "always on" as in the concept of utility computing.

World Wide Web Consortium (W3C): The governing body for the Web.

Author Biographies

CHANDLER AHRENS, RA, is an assistant professor at Washington University in St. Louis as well as a co-founder of Open Source Architecture (OSA), which is an international research and design architectural practice. He holds an MArch from the University of California Los Angeles and a BArch from Savannah College of Art and Design. He has worked for several large international architectural firms, including nine years as a senior project designer at Morphosis Architects. His work with Open Source Architecture has been extensively published internationally and is part of the collection at the Fonds Regional de Architecture (FRAC) in Orleans, France. He was a co-curator of the Gen(h)ome Project (MAK Center, Los Angeles 2006) and co-exhibition chair of ACADIA2010. He has lectured at various academic institutions, including University of California Los Angeles (UCLA), University of Southern California (USC), Cal-Poly Pomona, University of Tel Aviv, Rhode Island School of Design (RISD), and the Technologico de Monterrey in Mexico.

ÖMER AKIN, PhD, AIA has been a professor of architecture at Carnegie Mellon University, Pittsburgh, Pennsylvania, since 1978. He is a well-published researcher with several hundred reviewed publications. Books include *Representation and Architecture* (1982), *Psychology of Architectural Design* (1989), *Generative CAD Systems* (2005), *A Cartesian Approach to Design Rationality* (2006), and *Embedded Commissioning of Building Systems* (2012). His research interests include design cognition, generative CAD, case-based instruction, ethical decision making, and building commissioning. He has served as the Head of the School of Architecture and the director of the graduate programs.

NINA BAIRD is a researcher, educator, and consultant at the Center for Building Performance & Diagnostics, School of Architecture, Carnegie Mellon University, Pittsburgh. Her doctoral research focuses on the sustainability of district geothermal heat pump (GHP) systems. She is an author/editor for the National Ground Water Association's *Hydrogeologic Guidelines for Large Scale Ground Source Heat Pump Systems* (in draft). Baird also authored the "Geothermal Conditioning" chapter in the Springer *Encyclopedia of Sustainability Science and Technology* (2012) and recently completed field assessment of a direct exchange CO_2-based GHP system. Baird teaches graduate courses at Carnegie Mellon in zero energy housing, sustainable renovation, and global building rating systems and is funded by DOE to evaluate ARRA-funded weatherization of multifamily affordable housing. With colleagues at CMU, the International District Energy Association, GLHN, and NRG Energy, she is working on community energy planning and district system assessment. Prior to coming to CMU, Baird was Vice President at ATL International in Germantown, Maryland, directing environmental health projects in contracts with federal agencies OSHA, EPA, and DOE.

CHRIS BEORKREM is an Associate Professor in the School of Architecture at the University of North Carolina at Charlotte. He currently serves as a coordinator for the Digital Arts Center (darts.uncc.edu) in the College of Arts + Architecture. He received his BArch from Iowa State University and his Masters of Science in Advanced Architectural Design from Columbia University. He teaches studios and workshops in digital design and fabrication in the School of Architecture. His research has focused on the pursuit of digitally augmented construction processes driven by materials constraints and systems. He published *Material Strategies in Digital Fabrication* (Routledge Press, 2012), which looks at intelligent digital fabrication methods in a post-Great-Recession design world. The book discusses methods designers have employed over the last decade that advocate for more responsible uses of technology.

PHILLIP G. BERNSTEIN is a Vice President at Autodesk, a leading provider of digital design, engineering, and entertainment software, where he leads Strategic Industry Relations and is responsible for setting the company's future vision and strategy for technology as well as cultivating and sustaining the firm's relationships with strategic industry leaders and associations. An experienced architect, Phil was formerly with Pelli Clarke Pelli Architects, where he managed many of the firm's most complex commissions. Phil teaches Professional Practice at the Yale School of Architecture, where he received his both his BA and his MArch. He is co-editor of *Building (In) The Future: Recasting Labor in Architecture* (2010) and *BIM In Academia* (2011). He is a Senior Fellow of the Design Futures Council and former Chair of the AIA National Contract Documents Committee.

TAJIN BISWAS, LEED AP, Assoc. AIA is currently a PhD candidate in Architecture Engineering and Construction Management (AECM) at Carnegie Mellon University, Pittsburgh. Her research focuses on supporting building information requirement for sustainable design assessment by examining current green building rating systems and building information models. As a research assistant at Carnegie Mellon University, she has worked on projects with Autodesk developing a sustainable BIM, CERL-ERDC using COBie for LEED, and NSF-funded project-developing LEEDXML for a project life-cycle support system. With a background in architecture, sustainability, and computation, she has contributed to developing graduate courses over three years and has been a teaching assistant to parametric modeling with BIM and graduate instructor for special topics in AECM. Tajin received her MArch from Pratt Institute, New York and graduated from Bangladesh University of Engineering and Technology with a BArch.

MARK BURRY has published internationally on three main themes: the life and work of the architect Antoni Gaudí in Barcelona, putting theory into practice with regard to challenging architecture, and transdisciplinary design education and practice. He has published widely on broader issues of design, construction, and the use of computers in design theory and practice. He is the founding director of RMIT University's Design Research Institute (DRI—2008). The Institute brings over 100 university design researchers together with their industry, government, and community partners in order to access and stimulate a broad spectrum of design thinking. Since 1979 Burry has been a key member of the Sagrada Família Basilica design team based on site in Barcelona. For over three decades, he has been helping untangle the mysteries of Gaudí's compositional strategies for his greatest work, especially those strategies coming from his later years, the implications of which are only now becoming fully apparent as they are resolved for building purposes. In the last decade he has led the design and detailing of the Passion Façade rose window and the narthex above the porch and the auditorium space sitting above the crossing where the six principal towers intersect with the body of the basilica (the *Sala Creuer*).

MARK CLAYTON, PHD has been involved in computing methods in architecture as a designer and as an educator since the early 1980s. He earned a BArch from Virginia Tech, an MArch from UCLA, and a PhD in Civil and Environmental Engineering from Stanford University. He has contributed research in climate responsive design, building information modeling (BIM), design methods, and design education. Clayton has been a member of the faculty at Texas A&M University since 1995, where he has served as Executive Associate Dean, Interim Department Head, and Associate Director of both the CRS Center and the Center for Housing and Urban Development. He has also been a member of the Steering Committee of the Association for Computer Aided Design in Architecture (ACADIA) and served that organization as President and Vice President.

DANIEL DAVIS, PHD is a Senior Design Technology Specialist at CASE. Daniel recently completed a PhD at RMIT University entitled *Modelled on Software Engineering: Flexible Parametric Models in the Practice of Architecture*. He has taught computational design internationally, both in architecture and fashion design. His writing can be found in *AD*, *IJAC*, and *CAADFutures*, as well as on his blog, danieldavis.com.

PEGGY DEAMER, PHD is Assistant Dean and Professor of Architecture at Yale University. She is a principal in the firm of Deamer, Architects. She received a BArch from the Cooper Union and a PhD from Princeton University. She is the editor of *Architecture and Capitalism: 1845 to the Present* (Routledge), *The Millennium House* (Monacelli Press), and co-editor of *Building in the Future: Recasting Architectural Labor* (MIT Press), and *BIM in Academia* (Yale School of Architecture) with Phil Bernstein. Recent articles include "The Changing Nature of Architectural Work," in *Design Practices Now* (the Harvard Design magazine, vol. 2, no. 33) "Detail Deliberation," in *Building (in) the Future: Recasting Labor in Architecture*; "Practicing Practice," in *Perspecta 44*; and "Design and Contemporary Practice" in *Architecture from the Outside* (Dana Cuff and John Wriedt, eds.).

MICHAEL DONN, PHD is a building scientist at Victoria University School of Architecture (VUWSoA), teaching building performance to building science and design students. He has taught collaborative digital modeling and daylight simulation, animation as moving image and aural representations of buildings, and design of healthy, sustainable workplaces. His 30-year-plus research career includes four International Energy Agency (IEA) research collaborations; the first on passive solar design resulted in New Zealand Design Guides and sparked an interest in quality assurance in building performance simulation. His first involvement with BIM in the early 1980s was supervising a graduate student who proposed a "common building model" for interoperability. Two of the IEA projects focused on daylight, resulting in publications on digital simulation of daylight and a CIE publication on daylight program validation. In the most recent IEA collaboration, he has co-led a research subtask focused on solution sets for Net Zero Energy Buildings (NetZEBs).

CHARLES EASTMAN received his BArch and MArch degrees from the University of California, Berkeley. He has held faculty joint appointments in Architecture and Computing throughout his career, first at Carnegie-Mellon, then UCLA, and is currently at Georgia Institute of Technology. He directs the Digital Building laboratory, an industry supported AEC research consortium. He is the author of 5 books and over 80 referreed papers on computing, CAD, parametric modeling, design databases, interoperability, BIM, and design cognition. He is co-author of the *BIM Handbook*, which has been translated into four languages.

GLENN GOLDMAN, FAIA, IIDA is a registered architect in Massachusetts, New Jersey, and New York; a licensed professional planner in New Jersey; and is holder of NCARB certification. A Fellow in the American Institute of Architects, he is a Professor of Architecture and the Founding Director of the School of Art + Design at the New Jersey Institute of Technology (NJIT). Working with digital media and three-dimensional modeling since 1985, he was an early pioneer in the use of computational technology and graphics investigating applications in the products and processes of architectural design. Goldman has been cited twice for innovation in education by the American Institute of Architects Education Honors program, was named one of the top innovators in the use of technology in higher education by *Campus Technology* magazine in 2005, and was a co-recipient of a *Progressive Architecture* Citation in Applied Research for his developmental work with digital media. He has published numerous articles about architecture, graphics, and computation; and is the author of *Architectural Graphics: Traditional and Digital Communication* (1997). He was designated as a Master Teacher at NJIT in 2010. Goldman received a BA from Columbia and MArch from Harvard.

NING GU, PhD has made significant research contributions in architectural and design computing, including topics such as virtual environments, generative design systems, computational design analysis, computer-supported collaborative design, and BIM. The research outcomes have been documented in over 130 peer-reviewed publications. He has been a reviewer and guest editor for various international journals including *Design Studies*; *Automation in Construction*; *ITCon* and others, and he has been a reviewer and chair for a wide range of international conferences in the field. He was a visiting scholar at MIT, Columbia University, and Technische Universiteit Eindhoven. Gu's career highlights include receiving an Australian Research Council Discovery Project Grant to develop computational design analysis of twentieth-century canonical buildings and being the Research Leader of a Cooperative Research Centre for Construction Innovation (CRC-CI) project to examine the use of BIM as collaboration platforms for the architecture, engineering, and construction industry.

STEPHEN HAGAN, FAIA is recognized as an industry expert on technology and innovation, real estate, and the construction marketplace. In August 2012, Stephen retired from the federal government after 37 years and is now consulting about BIM, innovation, and online technologies as President and CEO of Hagan Technologies LLC. Hagan was a founding member of the U.S. General Services Administration (GSA) 3D-4D Building Information Model (BIM) team and was also program and project management lead for the GSA Public Buildings Service (PBS) Project Information Portal (PIP). The American Institute of Architects (AIA) Technology in Architectural Practice (TAP) BIM awards program, which Stephen founded in 2003, will celebrate its tenth year in 2014. The BIM awards include partnerships with COAA, IFMA, and the AGC BIM Forum. In 2012–13, Hagan Technologies partnered with Onuma Inc. on development of a Strategic Plan and 5-Year Road Map for the Space and Equipment Planning System (SEPS) and the worldwide facility management system (DMLSS-FM) for the Department of Defense (DoD) and Veterans Administration (VA).

ANTON HARFMANN is a licensed architect and builder with considerable engineering background who teaches BIM, construction, and structures courses in the School of Architecture and Interior Design at the University of Cincinnati. He led the effort to develop and implement a cross-college Architectural Engineering program at the University of Cincinnati and was the lead faculty member for the University's participation in the 2007 Solar Decathlon competition. He has taught net-zero design studios on several occasions since and lectures frequently on energy strategies. His research interests include net-zero architectural design as well as Building Information Modeling (BIM) at the component level, and he has published many papers on this approach since the early 1990s.

TIMOTHY HEMSATH, AIA, LEED AP is currently Associate Professor in the College of Architecture at the University of Nebraska-Lincoln. He has over 10 years of combined industry and educational experience in the design, construction, and research in energy efficiency and sustainable design. Recently, he was awarded an AIA UpJohn Fellowship in 2013 to research energy efficiency in residential design. He was the architect for the ZNETH and ZNETH II energy efficient prototypes working with the College of Engineering. He has served as the principle investigator for a Nebraska Research Initiative–funded project to build research capacity surrounding zero-net energy research at the University of Nebraska.

SEUNG WAN HONG, PhD is Lady Davis Postdoctoral Fellow and adjunct faculty at the Faculty of Architecture and Town Planning at the Technion—Israel Institute of Technology. He holds a BEArch and MSc in Architecture from the University of Ulsan, South Korea; MArch from the University of Michigan, Ann Arbor; and PhD in Architecture from the University of California, Berkeley, with a designated emphasis in new media. His research field covers computational creativity, online multiuser virtual environments to support creative collaboration and design studio education, building information modeling and design process, and human behavior simulation to support architectural design evaluation and communication.

MATT JEZYK is Senior Product Line Manager for AEC Conceptual Design Products at Autodesk. He has been in the architecture and engineering industry for 17 years and has spent the past 13 years developing Autodesk Revit and various other design tools. As one of the original architects hired by Revit Technology Corporation, Jezyk helped build what are now called Revit Architecture and Revit Structure. He is experienced in building both parametric and geometric modeling tools on the Revit platform. Recently he has focused on emerging markets and technology and has developed a suite of new technologies. His development teams have created multiple new applications: Autodesk Vasari, a popular Autodesk Labs project now in public beta, and Autodesk FormIt, the first architectural form modeler on the iPad. Jezyk and his group also contribute code to the open-source Dynamo Visual Programming tool for Revit and Vasari.

BRIAN R. JOHNSON is an Associate Professor of Architecture at the University of Washington, where he has been on the faculty since 1980. He teaches courses in digital media and design computing. He is also Director of the Design Machine Group [DMG], a collaborative interdisciplinary research group based in the Department of Architecture and home to the department's Master of Science in Architecture, Program in Design Computing, in which students explore and create new opportunities for computing in architecture. His own research interests include online collaboration, representation and design, human-computer interaction and tools to enhance communication between humans as well as between computers and humans, and design computing pedagogy. He received the ACADIA "Award of Excellence in Research" in 2002 and the ACADIA "Society Award" in 2010.

HENRY JOHNSTONE, PE holds a Master of Science in Aerospace and Mechanical Engineering from the University of Arizona. He is currently Director of Mechanical Engineering at GLHN Architects and Engineers in Tucson, Arizona, a multi-discipline firm specializing in planning and design of campus and urban scale infrastructure including roads, sewers, parks, light rail, institutional buildings, and central energy utilities. His 25-year experience at GLHN includes analysis, design, and implementation of heating, cooling, and combined heat and power systems at universities in Arizona, Arkansas, Alaska, Illinois, and New Mexico; Medical Center Campuses operated by Department of Veterans Affairs across the United States; and a downtown district energy system in Tucson, Arizona. He is currently working with the International District Energy Association, under a DOE grant, to develop a district energy screening tool for use in initial evaluation and planning for community energy concepts.

YEHUDA KALAY, PhD is Dean of the Faculty of Architecture and Town Planning at the Technion—Israel Institute of Technology, and holder of the Henry and Merilyn Taub Academic Chair. Prior to assuming the deanship at the Technion, for 18 years he was professor of Architecture at the University of California, Berkeley, where he co-founded and directed the Berkeley Center for New Media. Prior to his tenure at Berkeley, for 10 years Professor Kalay taught in the Department of Architecture at the State University of New York at Buffalo. Professor Kalay holds BArch and MSc degrees in Architecture from the Technion, and PhD from Carnegie Mellon University, Pittsburgh. He is a founding member and past president of *ACADIA* (Association for Computer Aided Design in Architecture) and former co-editor-in-chief of *Automation in Construction*, an international refereed journal (Elsevier, UK). He is a licensed architect in the State of Israel.

CALVIN KAM, PhD, AIA, PE, LEED AP is the founder of bimSCORE (USA, Singapore, and Hong Kong), the "GPS Navigator" for any enterprise or project team charting a course for construction innovation. He is also the Director of Industry Programs and a Consulting Associate Professor at Stanford University's Center for Integrated Facility Engineering (CIFE), where he specializes in strategic innovation such as building information modeling (BIM) and virtual design and construction (VDC). He is the Senior Program Expert and a co-founder of the National 3D-4D-BIM Program with the GSA Public Buildings Service and is an appointed international BIM expert for the Singapore government's Building Construction Authority. China National BIM Union has appointed Kam as the only international Honorary Director, and he is also co-principal investigator with Disney Research China. He is on the Board Knowledge Committee of the American Institute of Architects (national), where he also serves as the co-chairman of AIA Center for Integrated Practice and the past Chairman of AIA-TAP Knowledge Community.

KAREN KENSEK, LEED AP BD+C, Assoc. AIA teaches in the field of performance-based design in architecture. She received her SB at Massachusetts Institute of Technology and MArch, University of California, Berkeley. She currently teaches at the University of Southern California, School of Architecture. Her research work includes BIM + sustainability, BIM Analytics (BIM + simulation), virtual reconstruction of ancient places, the role of ambiguity in reconstructions, solar envelopes, and digital design. Previously she taught computer seminars and assisted with computer-aided design studios at the University of California, Berkeley, where she was the recipient of numerous grants. She is past president of ACADIA. She has hosted seven building information modeling (BIM) symposia at USC (2007–2013) with subthemes on education; sustainable design; construction and fabrication; analytical modeling and evidenced-based design; BIM management, implementation, coordination, and evaluation; and the future of BIM both from academic and professional viewpoints. She has been invited to speak at the AIA Annual Conference several times and has, with the USC School of Architecture, received the Autodesk Revit BIM Experience Award in 2008 and an Honorable Mention from the AIA TAP Group in Building Information Model in 2010. Along with Douglas Noble, she has been designated the recipient of the 2014 ACSA Creative Achievement Award.

RAMESH KRISHNAMURTI, PhD is a Professor of Computational Design in the School of Architecture at Carnegie Mellon University and the Director of its Graduate Program. He has taught in Canada, United Kingdom, and Taiwan. His research focuses on the formal, semantic, generative, and algorithmic issues in computational design. His research has a multidisciplinary flavor and includes shape and spatial grammars, spatial algorithms, computer simulation, graphic environments, interactivity and user interfaces, integration of graphical and natural languages, war games, analyses of design styles, geometric and parametric modeling, knowledge-based design systems, sensor-based modeling and recognition, building information modeling, and "green" cCAD. He has a BE (Honors) in electrical engineering from the University of Madras, BA in computer science from the University of Canberra, and MSc and PhD in systems design from the University of Waterloo. His research has been funded by the Science and Engineering Research Council (UK), DARPA, Japan Research Institute, National Science Foundation, Autodesk, U.S. Army Corps CERL-ERDC.

KHEE POH LAM, PhD, RIBA is a Professor at the Center for Building Performance & Diagnostics, School of Architecture, Carnegie Mellon University, Pittsburgh. Lam is an educator, researcher, architect, and consultant who specializes in life-cycle building information modeling and computational design support for total building performance analysis and building diagnostics. He has completed many major funded research projects and is currently Carnegie Mellon's Project Director in the DOE Energy Efficient Buildings Hub. He is an Editorial Board member for the *Journal of Building Performance Simulation* (Taylor and Francis, UK), and *Building Simulation: An International Journal* (Springer and Tsinghua University Press). Lam is a member of the Energy Foundation Board of Directors and works with their China Sustainable Energy Program. He is also a Board member of the Global Buildings Performance Network (GBPN), an international network of affiliated organizations, the ClimateWorks Network. He is a building performance consultant for several major award-winning projects in the private and public sectors in Singapore, China, and the United States.

He is currently Visiting Professor at Tsinghua University, China, and the School of Architecture, Chinese University of Hong Kong.

KERRY LONDON, PhD is Professor of Construction Management at RMIT University, Melbourne. She is Director of the Centre for Integrated Project Solutions. She was the first female Australian Chair of Construction Management. London was invited by the Federal Minister to be a member of the Built Environment Industry Innovation Council and was also on the National Working Party for Building Information Modeling Implementation. She is Joint Coordinator for BIM Legal and Regulatory Issues for CIB the International Council for Research and Innovation in Building and Construction. London researches innovation adoption through actor-network analyses and action research methods. She has written two research books on supply chains and has more than 140 peer reviewed publications. Her PhD students have won numerous awards. She has led more than $1M in competitive nationally funded research projects. She is currently co-authoring a book *Building Information Modeling and Management: Legal, Procurement and Regulatory Risks*.

BOB MARTENS studied architecture and urban planning in Eindhoven (The Netherlands) and Vienna (Austria). In 1994, he habilitated at the TU Vienna in the specialized subject "Spatial Simulation and Space Design". He publishes and gives lectures on the design of space and on questions of spatial simulation. He has been associate university professor at the TU Vienna since 1997. He has also worked extensively with Herbert Peter: an ArchiCAD-Reference book (Springer, 2002 and 2004), co-operation on virtual reconstructions since 1999 and supervision of master thesis work related to virtual reconstruction, and publication of a research outcomes in a city guide (Mandelbaum Verlag, 2009, and LIT-Verlag 2012), and involvement in a European research platform (www.synagogen.info).

NATHAN MILLER is Associate Partner and Director of Architecture & Engineering Solutions at CASE, where he is responsible for leading the efforts on architectural technology strategy, project information management, and computational design implementation. Prior to joining CASE, Nathan held the position of Associate Architectural Designer and Lead Computational Designer at NBBJ. There he focused on the development and implementation of computational design systems for generative design, production efficiency, and building performance. Miller earned his MArch from the University of Nebraska-Lincoln and has been a frequent contributor of lectures, articles, and white papers for venues such as ACADIA, the ASCA, TEX-FAB, Facades+, and the USC BIM Symposium.

DOUGLAS NOBLE, FAIA, PhD is currently Chair of the Ph.D. program in Architecture and Discipline Head for Building Science at the University of Southern California where he also teaches in the design studio. He hosts the FACADE TECTONICS conferences in Los Angeles each year and is the editor of the *FACADE TECTONICS Journal*. He is a licensed architect and the former president of the Association for Computer-Aided Design In Architecture (ACADIA). He is the co-editor/author (with Karen Kensek) of *Mission - Method - Madness: Computer-Supported Design in Architecture* and *Software for Architects: The Guide to Computer Applications for the Architecture Profession*. Noble obtained his Bachelor of Architecture from Cal Poly Pomona, and his M.ARCH and Ph.D. degrees from the University of California at Berkeley. A special project of his is *NotLY: Not Licensed Yet. NotLY* seeks to help young people in architecture successfully transition from the university to the profession. The primary focus is on organizing architecture licensing study sessions and programs. Along with Karen Kensek, he received the 2014 ACSA Creative Achievement Award for the work done with *NotLY*.

PASI PAASIALA received an MS in Mechanical Engineering from Tampere University of Technology, Finland. He worked as a researcher at the university in the Laboratory of Intelligent Hydraulics and Automation, where worked on developing Simu, software used to simulate fluid power systems. Later he moved to the Laboratory of Mechanical Engineering, developing knowledge-based systems for design automation. In 1997 he moved to Design Power Europe as a software developer. In 1999 he joined Solibri as one of the founding partners and has had the CTO post from the beginning. At Solibri Pasi he has been a key player in developing the Solibri Model Checker. He has also acted as Solibri's representative in Building Smart's Implementers' Support Group. He is one of the authors of BIM Collaboration Format (BCF), a standard to communicate issues between BIM software.

MURALI PARANANDI has been an Associate Professor of Architecture at Miami University since 1996. He received his MArch and a graduate degree in CAAD from Ohio State University in 1994. His research and teaching focus on discovering effective ways to engage emerging digital media for design. He has presented papers at several national and international conferences, and his articles have appeared in architectural journals and magazines. He published a book in 2007, *Digital Pedagogies*, with more than 25 articles by leading practitioners and educators from around the world on diverse approaches to enhance design with digital media. His research work received funding from the National Science Foundation, the Ohio Board of Regents, Miami University, and others. His students from Miami University have won several design awards at national and international forums both for design quality and for the use of digital media in design.

HERBERT PETER studied architecture at the TU Vienna, Austria. During his studies he worked in various architects' offices in Vienna. He taught at the TU Graz (1995–96) and, since 1997, has been teaching at the Academy of Fine Arts in Vienna. Since 2003 he has been working in the field of architecture and related services in a partnership entitled iT4eXperts/artuum architecture. He has also worked extensively with Bob Martens: on the *ArchiCAD* reference book (Springer, 2002 and 2004), co-operation on virtual reconstructions since 1999 and supervision of master thesis work related to virtual reconstruction, and publication of research outcomes in a city guide (Mandelbaum Verlag, 2009, and LIT-Verlag, 2012), and involvement in a European research platform (www.synagogen.info).

SHALINI RAMESH is a second-year PhD student at Carnegie Mellon University, Pittsburgh, in the Building Performance and Diagnostics program. She received her BArch from India and Master of Landscape Architecture from Virginia Polytechnic and State University (Virginia Tech). Her research focuses on urban energy modeling, studying the effects of urban heat islands with the application of building information modeling (BIM) and geographical information systems (GIS). Presently, she is developing an interactive web-based platform to communicate building simulation results on an urban scale using Autodesk Revit. In the past, she has worked on the DOE Energy Efficient Buildings (EEB) Hub project to create the energy model for

Building 661. Her research on urban energy information modeling was presented at the EnTool Symposium in Germany in June 2013. She is part of the Steinbrenner Institute at CMU and received a Steinbrenner Fellowship for the academic year 2012–13.

PAOLA SANGUINETTI, PHD received a BArch from the University of Kansas, an MS in Advanced Architectural Design from Columbia University, and a PhD at Georgia Institute of Technology. Sanguinetti's research focuses on important aspects of design computation and design verification, including building information modeling and energy simulation. Her dissertation topic developed a framework for analysis of uncertainty and risk in building performance assessments for façade retrofits. She is currently an Associate Professor in the Architecture Department at the School of Architecture, Design and Planning at the University of Kansas. Her courses promote student investigation of sustainable strategies in architecture.

DAVIDE SCHAUMANN is an architect and PhD candidate at the Faculty of Architecture and Town Planning at the Technion—Israel Institute of Technology. He holds BA and MSc degrees in Architecture from the Politecnico di Milano, Italy, and has worked for emerging architectural firms in Italy, Spain, and Israel. His research topics involve human behavior simulation in built environments to support design evaluation, knowledge representation, and management within the design process, and the design and evaluation of social places in virtual environments.

HUGO SHEWARD is a professional architect with three degrees in architecture. He is currently an instructor at the University of Missouri Department of Architectural Studies, and a design computation PhD candidate at Georgia Institute of Technology. Sheward is particularly interested in the development of design performance evaluation tools for early stages of design. Sheward's research has concentrated on the development of building information modeling technologies. He has worked in the development of design tools and software specification for the United States General Services Administration and for the implementation of BIM tools for the purpose of laboratory design. His current work focuses in the development of automation of ventilation systems performance estimation for early stages of laboratory design.

DAVIDE SIMEONE is a building engineer and PhD candidate at Sapienza University of Rome. He holds an MSc in Architectural Engineering from Sapienza. During his PhD Program, he has been Visiting Scholar at the University of California, Berkeley (2013) and Visiting Researcher at the Technion—Israel Institute of Technology (2011–12). His current research focuses on developing models to simulate human behavior in built environments, representation of users' activities in BIM models, and knowledge management for collaborative design. He is currently involved in several research projects in Italy, the United States, and Israel.

VISHAL SINGH, PHD is currently an Assistant Professor of Computer Integrated Construction (BIM) in the Department of Civil and Structural Engineering at Aalto University, Finland. He received his PhD from the University of Sydney, Australia, where he was an Endeavour Scholar and worked in the area of design computing and design science. Singh's research approaches BIM and computer-integrated design and construction as a socio-technical system, focusing on the interaction among products, processes, and the people. His research builds on the prior research in design computing and cognition, drawing upon theories and models from related areas such as agent-based simulations, computer aided design, computer-supported collaborative work, construction management, design management, and design methodology.

AARON SPRECHER, RA, MRAIC has been Assistant Professor at the School of Architecture in the McGill University Faculty of Engineering since 2008. In parallel, he is co-founder and partner of Open Source Architecture, a collaborative research group that brings together international researchers in the fields of design, engineering, media research, history, and theory. He studied at Bezalel Academy of Art and Design in Israel and at UCLA. His research and design work focuses on the synergy between information technologies, computational languages, and digital fabrication systems, examining the way in which technology informs and generates innovative approaches to design processes. Sprecher is co-curator and co-editor of the exhibition and catalogue *The Gen(H)ome Project* (MAK Center, Los Angeles, 2006) and exhibition designer of *Performalism* (Tel Aviv Museum of Art, Israel, 2008). He recently co-edited the book *Architecture in Formation—On the Nature of Information in Digital Architecture* (London: Routledge/Taylor and Francis, 2013). He is a recipient of multiple grants including the prestigious Canada Foundation for Innovation and is a member of both the Board of Directors of the Society for Arts and Technology (SAT, Montreal) and the Royal Architectural Institute of Canada.

VARVARA TOULKERIDOU is currently pursuing a PhD in Computational Design from Carnegie Mellon University, Pittsburgh. She has received an MSc in Design and Computation from Massachusetts Institute of Technology and a Diploma in Architecture from Aristotle University of Thessaloniki, Greece. She has contributed to the School of Architecture at CMU for several years as a teaching assistant for courses on parametric modeling, scripting, and descriptive geometry. Her recent research at CMU, funded by the CERL-ERDC, has focused on developing prototypes for deriving spatial topology graphs from IFC models and facilitating queries on spatial relationships. She has interned for Autodesk, developing visual programming and scripting tools for the Revit API group. Prior to coming to the US, Varvara has practiced as a licensed architect in Thessaloniki.

FRANCA TRUBIANO, PhD, OAQ, Int. Assoc. AIA is an assistant professor at the University of Pennsylvania and a registered architect with research areas in construction technology, materials, tectonic theories, integrated design, architectural ecologies, and high performance buildings. She is editor of the recently published *Design and Construction of High Performance Homes: Building Envelopes, Renewable Energies and Integrated Practice* (Routledge Press, 2012), which features 18 essays on high performance in design, architectural innovations in building envelopes, energy-free architectural design principles, advances in building-integrated photovoltaics, engineering strategies for net zero, and a review of integrated design in residential construction. Her work is also published in *Architecture and Energy* (Braham and Willis, eds., Routledge Press, 2013) and in the forthcoming *Architecture and Uncertainty* (Benjamin Flowers, ed., Ashgate Press, 2014). Trubiano is a principal investigator with the Energy Efficient Building Hub, a U.S. Department of Energy–sponsored project where her funded research develops integrated design roadmaps for members of the AEC industry in pursuit of advanced energy retrofits. Since 2011, she has been an elected Member of the Board and Treasurer/Secretary of the Building Technology Educators Society (BTES), and since 2013 an invited Member of the Editorial Board of the *Journal of Architectural Education*.

WEI YAN, PhD is an Associate Professor of Architecture at Texas A&M University. His research and teaching area is Computational Methods in Architecture. His recent research has been funded by NSF, NEH, DOE, ASHRAE, and Autodesk. He received a best paper prize in the International Conference of Design Computing and Cognition in 2006. He is a 2013 American Institute of Architects (AIA) Latrobe Prize Finalist. He holds degrees from Tianjin University, China (BE in Architecture and ME in Building Science), Swiss Federal Institute of Technology (ETH) Zurich (Postgraduate Cert. in CAAD), and the University of California, Berkeley (MS in Computer Science and PhD in Architecture).

ANDRZEJ ZARZYCKI is an architect and educator who employs building information and generative tools as a common platform and focus for both studio and nonstudio courses. He is an Associate Professor at the New Jersey Institute of Technology (NJIT) with duties in both Architecture and Digital Design. His research focuses on validation methodologies of generative designs through building performance analysis and simulation tools. Zarzycki presently teaches courses in building systems, interactive technologies, and simulation-based form-finding as well as architectural and digital design studios. His prior teaching experience includes computational design at Rhode Island School of Design (RISD) Interior Architecture Department. Zarzycki has been published repeatedly in journals and proceedings and is recipient of multiple professional awards in the field of architectural representation. His work is widely exhibited and published in national and international magazines and he is a co-winner of SHIFTboston design competition 2009 and co-founder of TUTS (the-tuts.org). Zarzycki earned his MArch from the Technical University of Gdansk, Poland, and MSc in Architecture Studies from the Massachusetts Institute of Technology, Cambridge.

Index